THE TALKIES

ARTICLES AND ILLUSTRATIONS FROM
A GREAT FAN MAGAZINE 1928-1940

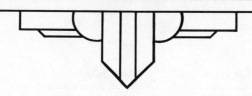

Selection, Text and Arrangement by

RICHARD GRIFFITH

Foreword by

LAWRENCE J. QUIRK

Dover Publications, Inc., New York

Published in Canada by General Publishing Company, Ltd., 30 Lesmill Road, Don Mills, Toronto, Ontario.
Published in the United Kingdom by Constable and Company, Ltd., 10 Orange Street, London WC 2.

THE TALKIES is a new work first published by Dover Publications in 1971 and is an anthology of selected articles and illustrations from PHOTOPLAY Magazine which appeared between 1928 and 1940. The selection, text and arrangement of this material are exclusively by Richard Griffith, Lawrence J. Quirk and the editorial staff of Dover Publications, who are not connected in any way with the current publishers of PHOTOPLAY Magazine.

The Publisher would like to thank the Louisville Free Public Library for making available copies of some of the material reprinted in this edition.

International Standard Book Number: 0-486-22762-6
Library of Congress Catalog Card Number: 75-154347

Manufactured in the United States of America
Dover Publications, Inc.
180 Varick Street
New York, N.Y. 10014

JAMES R. QUIRK

An Appreciation by Lawrence J. Quirk

PHOTOPLAY Magazine celebrates its sixtieth anniversary in 1971. This anthology is one of several books that will commemorate that anniversary, including my biography of my uncle, James R. Quirk, the magazine's founder and its editor-publisher-owner in its great and golden days. This present volume covers the interesting transitional period 1928–1940.

The magazine has had a checkered, colorful—and tragic—history. For roughly the first twenty years of its existence, PHOTOPLAY boasted authentic class and quality, and under James R. Quirk's aegis was a positive and constructive force in the motion picture industry as well as a profound and widespread influence on the movie-going public.

But after the forcefully dynamic and shrewdly tasteful James R. Quirk's death in 1932, the magazine started on a downhill course. After it fell into the hands and control of Bernarr Macfadden in 1934, the shift to commercialism and expedient sales gimmicks accelerated. After 1941, when the magazine was reduced from 25 cents to ten cents a copy and combined with a garish rival, MOVIE MIRROR, under the title PHOTOPLAY-MOVIE MIRROR, the deadly process of metamorphosing a one-time silk purse into a latter-day sow's ear continued unabated. By 1963, I was noting, in my VARIETY article, "Fan Mags: The Pros and Cons" (January 9, 1963), that "the decline of PHOTOPLAY from the greatness it knew under James R. Quirk is one of the saddest facts in magazine history, and numerous film commentators have remarked on it."

The world of the 1970's, in which so many once-cherished standards have declined, finds PHOTOPLAY numbered among the many current fan magazines which specialize in screamy coverlines, teaser-titles and come-on blurbs.

It wasn't always like this. Once, difficult as it may be to believe, PHOTOPLAY knew a "splendor in the grass, glory in the flower," and the Photoplay Gold Medal Awards, which James R. Quirk had proudly instituted in 1920, were the most prestigious and coveted in the industry, invariably going to productions of genuine merit.

Bosley Crowther, the distinguished former critic of the New York TIMES, once commiserated with me on the earlier PHOTOPLAY that my uncle had built to an eminence now lost forever. "It is gone," he said, "like so much else in American life that was good and solid, and it will never return." And he added, "But we have our memories, don't we?" Mr. Crowther told me that he had relied heavily on the files of the PHOTOPLAY of the 1920's in researching his splendidly authoritative books on Metro-Goldwyn-Mayer and Louis B. Mayer.

Other film historians and writers, men like Lewis Jacobs, Kevin Brownlow, Edward Wagenknecht, William K. Everson, Terry Ramsaye and Ezra Goodman, have cited the PHOTOPLAY of the Quirk era for its vitality, its sterling forthrightness and independence, its countless editorial and literary excellences.

Even the controversial and hard-hitting Irving Shulman, of *Harlow* and *Valentino* fame, in his recent book *"Jackie!" The Exploitation of a First Lady,* in which he excoriated the current fan magazines in the bluntest terms for their tastelessness and low journalistic standards, drew a dramatic comparison between the past and present PHOTOPLAY, and had nothing but praise for James R. Quirk, whose positive editorial concepts he contrasted dramatically with the negative policies operating in today's fan magazines. This was all the more significant in view of Shulman's noted (and/or notorious) penchant for *not* pulling his punches about film journalists past and present. Yet James Quirk wins even Shulman's all-out admiration.

Benjamin Hampton, in his history of the movies to the early 1930's, gave credit to James R. Quirk and the PHOTOPLAY files for aid in researching and illustrating the manuscript, which was published in 1931 and has recently been reissued by Dover under the title, *History of the American Film Industry.*

Lewis Jacobs, the respected film historian, wrote in his 1939 book, *Rise of the American Film:* "The effort toward artistic quality in motion pictures was further quickened by the critical comments of a fan magazine of the day, PHOTOPLAY. Under the editorship of James R. Quirk . . . it encouraged and praised genuine artistry in films." Mr. Jacobs then goes on to cite a typical Quirk editorial of 1918, which reads in part: "Will you think of your art as a business or your business as an art? Will you say, 'Make this picture because it will sell?' or 'Make this picture because it deserves to sell?' "

Terry Ramsaye was commissioned by James R. Quirk to write a history of the movies, highly admired to this day and noted for its accuracy and scholarship, which ran in PHOTOPLAY for 36 installments (1922–1925) and later appeared in book form (1926) as *A Million And One Nights.* It has proven a reliable original source book for many later film historians.

In my 1955 article on my uncle, "Quirk of Photoplay," in FILMS IN REVIEW, I quoted Terry Ramsaye thus:

> It was of a piece with Jim's outlook on the industry to believe that a sincere telling of its whole story, shorn of myth and the clutter of falsehood which was deeply coloring all its traditions, would be a contribution to that industry. There is tribute to Jim's professional integrity in the fact that he was willing to wait through almost two years of research before a chapter went into type, and that he most generously supported a continuously widening field of inquiry, here and abroad, for three years. About the time I sent him Chapter 18, going into the second year, I was fishing a delectable pool in the Canadian wilds where Lake Nipigon starts down the wilderness stairs to Lake Superior. A courier du bois, a glum Cree Indian, paddled forty miles up river from the railway to deliver me a telegram from New York: "What year in your story will we get to Mary Pickford? Jim." It was his encouragement and enthusiasm, too, which helped me pile on more research and do the whole job over again and write *A Million and One Nights.*

The star editor is no more. George Horace Lorimer, Harold Ross, Ray Long, George Jean Nathan, H. L. Mencken, Robert Munsey, S. S. McClure, Frank Crowninshield, James R. Quirk —none today compare with these.

Adela Rogers St. Johns, one of James R. Quirk's first protégés and one of the great literary orna-

ments of the Quirk-operated PHOTOPLAY, once told me, "Under Jimmy, PHOTOPLAY was essentially a one-man operation, and without that one man, it couldn't do much." She has described him, in her recent autobiography, *The Honeycomb,* as

> A fanatically fastidious and dramatically *comme il faut* editor—a vital stimulant in [Hollywood's] growth, a witty and often sternly critical voice, again almost prophetically. Most important to me as a writer was his eagle eye and good taste for . . . anecdotes. His never-tell-it-if-you-can-show-it is an editorial demand I'd met before though not as definitely, but you could no more fool Jim Quirk with a press release or get by with a small fake than you could fool [Walter] Howey [famed Chicago newspaper editor].

Another fiery independent, silent film star Pola Negri, who like Shulman doesn't pull punches when she does a book (or does anything else), warmly praised James Quirk, in her recent *Memoirs of a Star,* as a journalist of unimpeachable integrity who advised her wisely on her public relations and who defended her in PHOTOPLAY against salacious and tasteless stories put out by irresponsible sources about her life with Rudolph Valentino, to whom Miss Negri was engaged at the time of his death. Miss Negri also referred to James Quirk as the one journalist who enjoyed the close friendship and complete trust of Valentino.

In my two-part series, "Jimmy Quirk—Hollywood's Father Confessor," published in 1966, I told of how my uncle had arranged Valentino's funeral and chosen the casket. To save the film idol's body from the wear and tear, and possible desecration, implicit in a public wake and funeral, he had substituted a wax dummy for the body, and called in an artist who was skilled at creating perfect likenesses. "The man did his job well," I wrote. "*Rudy Le Bien Aimé* lay in peace in a cool, dark vault downstairs and Jimmy's wax figure did the 'star honors' and took the brutal punishment for Valentino upstairs." "Rudy treasured Jim's friendship more than that of any other man," Adela St. Johns told me decades later. "How glad he would have been to know that Jimmy was looking after things."

In that 1966 series, I quoted Adela St. Johns thus:

> During Jim's 1919 visit to Hollywood (he went faithfully every year) while we were riding from Universal City to downtown Los Angeles, he and I talked about how Hollywood had become the trade name for the movie capital, when in reality the studios were scattered all over the area, at Santa Barbara, Culver City, Burbank, Universal City, the San Fer-

nando Valley. Even Universal City seemed awfully far out from the center of town.

Jim told me, "It's a pretty small area at that, when you consider what the population is going to be. They will assemble here together a lot of young people who are attractive enough, strong enough, emotional enough, so that the world will want to see them and be willing to pay money to do it."

Mrs. St. Johns adds that his eyes grew solemn and meditative as he continued: "And if they have any real talent, the most emotionally sensitive, too. Put them all together here and give them more fame and money than a gold rush and there *must* be fireworks."

Mrs. St. Johns added that James R. Quirk was the first person she ever heard use the term "gold rush" to describe those fabulous early days in Hollywood. She adds that he was also the first to see the need for older hands and minds to steady and guide these incredibly beautiful and gifted young personalities.

"Everybody consulted Jimmy—literally," Mrs. St. Johns told me, "Mayer, Zukor, the Schencks, DeMille—all the top producers and directors. Jimmy promoted many reforms and germinated many ideas that other people took the credit for. He worked so quietly behind the scenes that few realized what a many-faceted genius he was."

The famed director Marshall Neilan once told me that my uncle was "the best public relations man the industry ever had, but he took no nonsense from Hollywood and refused to be pushed around."

During a 1949 interview, Will Hays told me that James R. Quirk had been of invaluable assistance in protecting the industry's public image during the hectic Twenties. Mr. Hays went on:

> He was an independent force, full of Celtic idealism, and he truckled to no one, no matter how important, but he was always on the side of the true, the good and the beautiful, and his instincts were deeply affirmative and unfailingly courageous.
>
> Jim Quirk loved the film medium and wanted to see it put its best foot forward. He worked with me to clean up the abuses in the film world that were uncovered by such tragic events as Wallace Reid's death from complications brought about by drug addiction in 1923; the scandal that destroyed Fatty Arbuckle's career in 1921 after he was involved in the death of a young girl at a wild party in San Francisco; the murder of director William Desmond Taylor in 1922, a murder in which screen stars Mabel Normand and Mary Miles Minter found themselves innocently involved.

. . . He tried to protect Hollywood and raise its sights, not exploit the weaknesses of its personalities as did other journalists. He did not batten off Hollywood's troubles for mercenary gain at the newsstands, as did some of his colleagues. Rather he offered it an independent-spirited but honorably encouraging medium in PHOTOPLAY. Along with me, he could be firm in dealing with recalcitrant elements in Hollywood, and the power of his typewriter was greatly feared, for he could be coldly chastising when chastisement was needed, but to the public he tried to present a fair, balanced—and basically compassionate—picture of Hollywood's problems during its growing pains in the 1920's.

The legend of James R. Quirk has inspired many later-generation film historians and writers in addition to myself, for instance the young Englishman Kevin Brownlow, who in his recent (and highly praised) study of the silent film, *The Parade's Gone By,* wrote:

> Throughout the book I have quoted frequently from [the pre-1932] PHOTOPLAY. Fan magazines are not noted for their accuracy or wit, but PHOTOPLAY had nothing in common with its present-day counterparts. It was a forthright, hard-hitting, well-balanced and highly entertaining publication, and it was a gold mine of information about the making of pictures. [Quirk] gave it a sort of clinical accuracy which none of the other magazines shared.

Another of my contemporaries, the talented and scholarly William K. Everson, in his book, *The Western,* called the Quirk-operated PHOTOPLAY "the most influential and intelligent of the fan magazines of the Twenties. It was respected by Hollywood and not merely used by it; its articles and editorials were excellent, its reviews discerning, and its 'fan padding' at a minimum."

Magazine executive Daniel Henderson, a shrewd observer of his distinguished contemporaries of the 1920's, once told me:

> James Quirk's liberal mind, broad knowledge and dynamic spirit made him the most distinguished editor to apply his talents to the motion picture field. Instead of publishing just a fan magazine, he brought out a general magazine focussed on a motion picture audience and exercised an independent judgment heedless of advertising interests which made his word and work highly respected.

Mr. Henderson agreed with others that in those boom years of the 1920's, so important to the motion picture industry's growth, James R. Quirk brought movies—and movie people—a new self-respect. He was hailing the film as an art, and a potentially great and international one, at a time when others were calling it a mere entertainment medium and writer Jim Tully was sarcastically dubbing James Quirk "the Mencken of the Morons."

Elsewhere in this anthology, a detailed account of James R. Quirk's pioneering activities with PHOTOPLAY is given—and a pioneer he was, in the finest, truest sense of the word. He made many stars. Fredric March told me many years later how much James Quirk's boosting had meant to him in the early, formative years of his career. In my 1968 book, *The Films of Joan Crawford* (which I dedicated to James R. Quirk's memory, referring to the PHOTOPLAY of his era as "proud and beautiful"), I quoted a 1927 review of her work in *The Taxi Dancer* in which James Quirk said, "Joan Crawford rides high over the inferior material. Here is a girl of singular beauty and promise. And she certainly has IT." He then added the fatherly admonition: "Just now she is very much in need of good direction." This review had come at a time when practically no one but James Quirk sensed the potential of a girl who was later to be one of Hollywood's top stars. His shrewd showcasing of Miss Crawford in PHOTOPLAY in the middle and late 1920's had much to do with her eventual success, as she once told me, adding, "Your uncle Jim was one of the greatest talents ever, was always kind and helpful to me, and had great authority and dignity." He was first in the cheering section when Miss Crawford married Douglas Fairbanks, Jr. in 1929. Fairbanks' father, Douglas Fairbanks, Sr., was then married to *grande dame* Mary Pickford, the pioneer film star, and together they presided over fabulous Pickfair, where many greats from all walks of life were entertained. "Joan will make it at Pickfair," my uncle told skeptical friends. "She may have come up the hard way but she has intrinsic class."

According to director Marshall Neilan, "both Mary Pickford and Charles Chaplin were profoundly influenced by Jim's ideas and advice. It was Jim who advised Pickford to cut off her curls and take more 'grown-up' roles. And had Jim Quirk lived, Chaplin would not have gone through his long period of exile and bad publicity in the 1940's and 1950's."

In my 1955 FILMS IN REVIEW article on my uncle, I wrote of the Quirk-Chaplin friendship:

Indeed [James R. Quirk] saw Chaplin for what he was—an idealist with the artist's touch of naiveté, brilliant, simple and profound when transposing his inner vision through the art of which he was master,

ill-advised and inept when attempting to couple that inner vision with social or political theories.

Ed Sullivan told me in 1960:

Jimmy Quirk was a prime example of the old-fashioned, tremendously competent journalist. He had a great instinct for stories, knew everybody worth knowing, and had more than a bit of genius as an editor. He was the kind of guy that young writers could always go to for wise advice, and to whom older writers could always go for the tonic of an approving or encouraging word when things got too tough.

Walter Winchell told me that my uncle had given him many a scoop. "He was wonderful to me when I was starting," he said. "He was most generous with news-tips and advice, and he was so *positive* in his emanations—a 'builder-upper,' not a 'tearer-downer.' " Then Winchell added, "But God help anyone who really crossed him, or tried to hurt the movie industry!"

According to Adela St. Johns, my uncle's "Cal York" column, the name of which he had derived from California (that is, Los Angeles) and New York, the two important news sources, was the original inspiration and model for Winchell's later-famous column. Winchell never forgot my uncle's kindnesses, nor did Louis Sobol and Sidney Skolsky. All three gave me "plugs" in their columns in later years, thus proving they were no fair-weather friends of the Quirk family.

My uncle inspired and nurtured a prodigious array of later-famous writers. Some of the most prominent folk connected with the film medium and the worlds of journalism, criticism and literature were either associated with him, worked for him or were his protégés originally. He gave Louella O. Parsons a helping hand in 1918 when she badly needed work and kept her busy writing for him until she found the columning spot that took her on to major success. He continually boosted Hedda Hopper during her floundering period as an actress in the Twenties and early Thirties, and was one of the first to encourage her journalistic ambitions. "If you can write with the same breezy insouciance with which you talk, you'll go places," he told her. "And you know Hollywood." By 1938 Miss Hopper had taken his advice and begun a columning career that rivaled that of Louella Parsons. On a visit to Hollywood in 1964 I talked with Miss Hopper about my uncle. She herself had only about a year and a half to live, but at 74 she was still sprightly. "Life wasn't easy in the old days," she told me. "I was knocking around Hollywood, agenting, doing odd jobs, acting—sometimes. Your uncle had a unique gift for imparting his positivism to others. I was one of the lucky recipients. He made you believe you could do *anything*, if you wanted to badly enough."

Miss Parsons' daughter, Harriet, who started on PHOTOPLAY in 1929 as a staff writer and later became a well-known film producer, told me in 1952: "James Quirk taught me all I knew." Margaret Ettinger, who before her death in 1967 was an eminently successful public relations counselor, did a three-year staff apprenticeship with James Quirk. Famed public relations man Steve Hannagan also learned at Quirk's side. According to Adela St. Johns, Robert E. Sherwood, soon to be one of America's finest playwrights, credited James Quirk with inspiring him to write his excellent film criticism of the 1920's in LIFE and other publications. Burns Mantle, an ornament to Broadway dramatic criticism in his day, marveled when he went to work for PHOTOPLAY as a film reviewer in 1920 because my uncle, always quick to spot genuine originals, had told him he could write about pictures just as they struck him, and without kowtowing, slanting, tampering or catering to any interests, advertising or otherwise.

One writer told me:

> Your uncle would have had no truck with the polls by which so many latter-day magazines are edited. He published what he himself liked, and because he himself had humor and vitality, his magazine was humorous and vital. Jimmy Quirk loved PHOTOPLAY. PHOTOPLAY was his child, and because the child was loved, it behaved well. Under him it had confidence and personality. It was a reflection of the master, essentially a one-man operation like all creative magazines should be.

His shrewd showcasing in PHOTOPLAY from 1926 on did much to build the reputation of Greta Garbo with the American public. My uncle was one of the first to recognize The Sphinx's singular talent. He always enjoyed testifying, though, that the legend of her shyness was true. According to one story, he had her to a party in his New York apartment, and she spent the entire time hiding in the bathroom!

He also favored what he called a "reverse technique" in publicity gimmicks concocted for his own amusement as well as for PHOTOPLAY's circulation, which by 1926 had boomed fantastically. Around 1929, in an effort to drum up a fresh wave of interest in Miss Garbo, whose career (a year before her triumph in *Anna Christie*) seemed to be threatened by the talkies, he suggested in PHOTOPLAY that the real reason Miss Garbo remained so glamorously silent was that in actuality she had simply nothing to say! Hundreds of thousands of mightily incensed Garbo fans sprang to their goddess's defense, and PHOTOPLAY's office was inundated with outraged and denunciatory letters—which was exactly what my uncle had wanted. A new wave of interest in Miss Garbo resulted—as well as a circulation boost for PHOTOPLAY. "If a magazine doesn't make its readers mad, it has no vitality," was one of James Quirk's favorite apothegms.

James Quirk's good friends H. L. Mencken and George Jean Nathan wrote for PHOTOPLAY, as did Rupert Hughes, Channing Pollock and F. Scott Fitzgerald. Like his contemporary Frank Crowninshield of VANITY FAIR, James Quirk was truly an editorial giant and the PHOTOPLAY of the pre-1932 years glowed with his genius. But VANITY FAIR was to know a better fate; it died completely in 1936 with its quality essentially unimpaired, and with Crowninshield guiding it to the bitter, but mercifully clean-cut, end. PHOTOPLAY, however, was to suffer a painful and gradual diminution and adulteration of its standards from the time of James Quirk's death, until by 1940 it had lost all vestiges of its founder's unique imprint.

This 1929–1939 anthology, therefore, has its own built-in fascination, since it sets forth graphically the transitional period that followed James Quirk's death. The first four years of the anthology covers the last of the Quirk period (1929–1932). From 1932 to 1935 the attempts of my uncle's right-hand woman Kathryn Dougherty to salvage PHOTOPLAY's quality and maintain it in the Quirk image can be discerned. From 1935 on, the efforts of still another Quirk protégé, Ruth Waterbury, to retain the essential flavor and standards of the departed Master can be tellingly observed. But there is no imitating an original beyond a point; all becomes repetitious and perfunctory and stylized; gimmicks supersede genuine inspiration; mechanical parrotings and sterile echoings fail to compensate for the lost outpourings of a genius's instincts. Moreover, both Miss Dougherty and Miss Waterbury were dealing with a Macfadden regime that was obsessed with sales. By 1941 the magazine had subsided into a complete mediocrity from which it was never to emerge.

Many people have asked me what my uncle

would probably have thought about the Jacqueline Kennedy cover-and-coverline hysteria that has made the current fan magazines the laughing-stock of the country. In reply I can only quote from a 1965 piece of mine on the matter:

> If anyone had ever suggested to [James R. Quirk] in 1927 that he run Charles A. Lindbergh on fan mag covers just because Lindy was young and handsome and had just flown the Atlantic, or if anyone had ever suggested that same year that he go trotting afield for Queen Marie of Rumania as a fan mag cover subject just because Her Majesty, quite a glamor girl albeit a superannuated one, had visited the U. S. that year with mucho fanfare, he would have told them to jump in the lake. Or he would have suggested a straitjacket and a nice quiet rest in the country.

The wonderful, courageous, always loyal and affirmative Kathryn Dougherty, who was my guide and mentor in the film industry at the beginning of my career, knew the saddest three years of her life during that 1932–1935 period immediately after my uncle's death when she tried so valiantly to save the unsavable. The details of her travail are set forth elsewhere in this anthology. Once she told me:

> In the very first days of PHOTOPLAY, in 1914–1915, when there were many difficulties, organizational as well as financial, your uncle's Irish blue eyes would snap and sparkle whenever he sensed my doubts. "Look here," he would say, "This job is pretty nearly as new to me as it is to you, but you're Irish and I'm Irish. Together we will fight this thing through." Your uncle had a constant note of buoyancy, and confidence, and high-hearted courage, that spirit that all is well with life if we but have the courage to face it unafraid. Life to Mr. Quirk was not a grim thing to be taken with a long face, but rather with a laugh. One of his favorite stories was that of a man who, falling off a skyscraper, in his downward passage remarked, "I have just passed the sixteenth story. Everything is safe so far." When your uncle had overcome some unusual difficulty he would say, "Well, Kay Dee, we have just passed the sixteenth story and we are safe so far!"

Is there hope for the fan magazines of the future?

As I wrote in VARIETY as far back as January 9, 1963 (and it applies now as it did then):

> Since adult readers have now, it seems, permanently turned to other publications for their entertainment news, criticisms and personality profiles, and since the fan magazines still engage their young readers heavily, what, then, should be their function

if they are to grope their way to some sensible medium between healthy circulations and editorial self-respect?

The thought I offered was that the fan magazines

> can point a good moral for immature minds, sugar-coating it to order. They can subtly uphold right values for courtship, marriage and later family life. And if you add to a basically moral content (and by "moral content" I don't mean preachy, antiseptic, puritanical Pollyannaism) the values of literacy, taste, originality and liveliness (all geared, and stirred-in for teenage palates)—and above all, truth and common sense—then fan mag editors might feel a greater sense of fulfillment and creativity than they have for thirty years now.

When PHOTOPLAY was James R. Quirk's and all was right with the world, he had his offices on the top floor of 221 West 57th Street in New York, a tall gray sandstone building next door to the Lincoln Art movie theatre. The Photoplay Publishing Company, as it was then known, occupied the two top floors. My uncle had a paneled, tastefully furnished office at the back, where he could look out over the great expanses of Central Park.

Sometimes through the years, when bleakly discouraged over the problems that have arisen and the compromises that have been exacted in my efforts to retain his standards and his ideals, I have taken the elevator up to the top floor of old "221" to pause a moment in the corridor leading to James R. Quirk's old office, while a wondering young receptionist gave me a "what-is-your-business-here?" look. At times like these, I ruminate with a combination of sorrow and anger on the PHOTOPLAY in whose stock my family lost the controlling interest in long-gone 1934 . . . that PHOTOPLAY so proud, so beautiful, so magical— now lost to all of us, never to return. I think then of the words of James R. Quirk's old friend, movie trade publisher Martin Quigley: "Your uncle always kept the faith, and looked for the best." That is what those of us he influenced so greatly, and in whose hearts he will always live, have sincerely tried to do, and I hope that somewhere, somehow, James R. Quirk knows that.

> Though nothing will bring back the hour
> Of splendor in the grass, glory in the flower,
> We will grieve not; rather find
> Strength in what remains behind.

New York, N. Y.
May 1971

CONTENTS

LIVING AND WORKING IN MOVIELAND

Hollywood

On the Set

Behind the Camera

THE FANS AND THEIR MAGAZINE 169

PICTURES AND TRENDS 201

The Talkies, the Depression and "Decency" 201

History and Literature, Musicals, Screwball Comedy 223

INTRODUCTION*

Round about 1910, the little movie companies then burgeoning in astonishing numbers on the Eastern littoral around New York dreamed up a new source of revenue for themselves. They began admitting visitors to their "studios" at ten cents a head. Go to the Vitagraph plant in Flatbush, Brooklyn, and you could join a long line of such visitors which slowly shuffled past five, six, seven, even ten active "sets," cheek by jowl. Each set was like a little stage, with the open end presented to the line of onlookers. On one, comedians pounded one another on the head, while on the next a diva ran the gamut of kinematographic emotion, to an obbligato of the bawling and hammering of carpenters erecting still another set nearby. The sets were not jammed next to each other in this way for the convenience of the visitors; cramped quarters, and the mass production of one-reelers week in and week out, made crowding a necessity. Nor were the tourists ordinary rubberneckers. They were "fans." The word had come in around the turn of the century, chiefly in connection with baseball, but it soon spread to every other form of sport and popular entertainment. The movie fans were the most virulent specimens of the breed so far known, and the opening up of the studios shot them up to seventh heaven. It was something like being taken back to the locker room to hear the coach outline strategy.

Growing complexity of production,[1] and the removal of most of the movie companies to California, put an end to the studio tours in the course of the ensuing five years. But the feverish interest in any and every aspect of movie-making which they revealed had signaled an opportunity to sharp-eyed men in the new movie business. These original studio visitors had been mostly "locals" with a few out-of-towners; how many millions more of them might there be out there in the dark who yearned to get close to the movies—as close as humanly possible, or even closer? In 1911, the Motion Picture Patents Company, octopus of the early industry, financed the publication of MOTION PICTURE MAGAZINE. This was the first movie fan magazine, still on the newsstands 59 years later. Among its instant and numerous competitors, one called PHOTOPLAY started inauspiciously indeed. Put out as a sort of theatre program in Chicago, it fell into the debt of the W. F. Hall Printing Company, which took it over in 1914 and decided to cast about, in 1914, for an editor who could metamorphose it into a magazine worthy of the name, one that could keep pace with the rising movie industry.

The job of salvage was entrusted to James R. Quirk. Their choice proved to be a wise one.

Quirk, who was thirty years old in 1914, had already amassed an impressive record in newspaper and magazine journalism. The child of Irish-American parents, Martin and Mary Quirk, who had risen to a degree of prosperity and prominence in their Boston-Irish milieu, he was born in Boston, Massachusetts on September 4, 1884. A product of Harvard and Boston University Law School, he had gone to work for a Boston newspaper while still a student, and after several years as a reporter with THE BOSTON ADVERTISER, his vital personality and promising talents were noted by a family friend, none other than John F. Fitzgerald, famed Boston mayor and father-in-law of Joseph P. Kennedy. This grandfather of a future president of the United States had embarked temporarily on a journalistic venture. As publisher of a Boston political newspaper he hired young James Quirk, then twenty-one, as his top aide and editorial overseer.

---

*[From this point, the new text in this book is by Richard Griffith. This section, however ("Introduction"), contains much material by Lawrence J. Quirk, particularly the details on, and evaluation of, the early PHOTOPLAY and the careers of James R. Quirk and Kathryn Dougherty. THE PUBLISHER.]

[1] Complexity in itself is no insuperable obstacle to a fixed interest in the fast buck, as the recent revival of studio tours by Universal attests.

This led, in time, to an offer from the Washington TIMES, where Quirk rose shortly from news reporter to city editor—taking time out, in 1908, to marry a minister's daughter, Elizabeth North, mother of his daughters Frances and Jean, and his only son Robert, who died in infancy in 1922.

In 1909, word of Quirk's editorial feats having spread cross-country, he was invited by a Chicago publisher to take over the then-ailing POPULAR MECHANICS. Within three years he had put the magazine permanently in the black and had won himself, at 28, a reputation as a "magazine doctor." Determined to go into business for himself, thus achieving the independence that his individualistic and strong-minded nature required (and, incidentally, putting himself into a position to reap what he conceived to be the just rewards of his endeavors) Quirk left POPULAR MECHANICS to open an advertising agency. He missed the challenges of the magazine field, however, and the PHOTOPLAY offer proved irresistible.

From the beginning, PHOTOPLAY under James R. Quirk was pretty much of a one-man show, depending for its sustenance and growth on the brains, creativity and drive of Quirk, who had more than enough to spare in all three departments. Quirk was eventually to purchase control of PHOTO-PLAY, after which he formed the Photoplay Publishing Company, James R. Quirk, Publisher, Editor and Sole Autocrat. It stayed that way until his death. Quirk surrounded himself with people who were personally loyal to him, most notably Kathryn Dougherty, widely known in the industry as "Kay Dee," who started with PHOTOPLAY as an office clerk and rose to become Secretary-Treasurer of the corporation.

The field Quirk entered and transformed was originally a very humble and unpretentious one. The people whose nickels and dimes were making the movies rich lived on the next-to-the-lowest level of American life, and what they knew of the rest of that life they mostly got from seeing films. The primitive, pre-Quirk movie publications had not attempted to supplement what these people learned from the screen but merely to duplicate it. They consisted almost entirely of "fictionizations" of current films—little stories and serials, barely literate though excruciatingly genteel.

Quirk swiftly changed the pattern. In all logic, he decided, people were interested primarily in the pictures, not their stories, and he instituted the first important film review department to be offered anywhere, "The Shadow Stage"—a title he valued so much that it was always subtitled in the magazine "Reg. U. S. Patent Office." He had meanwhile hired a talented Broadway press-agent and reviewer, Julian Johnson, who also served the busy Quirk for a time as editor (the ubiquitous and fantastically energetic Quirk was drumming up advertising, handling circulation, distribution, public relations, writing, interviewing, visiting Hollywood, *and* serving as editor-in-chief). Quirk himself wrote many of the reviews, and continued to do so until the end of his life—a Quirk review being easily recognized by its inimitable style and flavor—and its unerring appraisals of films' merits or demerits —appraisals which caused Adela Rogers St. Johns, one of his earliest protégés, to label James R. Quirk "the first great film critic."

Quirk's reviews, along with those of his employees Julian Johnson and (later) Burns Mantle, highlighted, in those early years, the swift progress in narrative film technique which made the 1914–1920 period an exciting one in which to watch the screen. That they were not enough to satisfy his public, Quirk was instinctively aware. Under him, fiction serials derived from films quickly dwindled, to be supplanted in the magazine by the serial story of movie life in Hollywood. By 1919 Julian Johnson had left PHOTOPLAY to seek his fortunes in the Hollywood studios, winding up (until his retirement, 1955) as story editor of 20th Century-Fox.

Stars, all knew by then, were the focus of public interest in the movies, and the stars—who they were, where they came from, what they were "like" —became the predominant subject of Quirk's PHOTOPLAY, with all the other movie magazines, which had by then sprung up, following in its train.

For the stars were a major symbol of that upswing in social mobility which accompanied the Great War of the Teens and the Great Boom of the Twenties. By 1920, the total movie audience had come to encompass most of the middle class as well as the whole of blue-collardom. But the eagerest moviegoers—the fans—clustered around the median between top proletariat and bottom bourgeoisie. Little qualified for success as they thought of success, they lived on dreams of luck, and these the movies fed, off-screen as well as on. *Per aspera ad astra* was their unconscious motto. Stage "artists" some of the stars might be, but an ever-increasing number of them were unknown lads and girls whom blind chance had thrust in front of a camera. While general audiences might dream moonily over the fairy-tale adventures of Norma Talmadge and Rudolph Valentino on the silver sheet, the fans had a closer, more tangible dream centered around the career adventures of these lucky few off it. By the mid-Twenties, PHOTO-PLAY had instituted a department called "As We Go to Press: Last Minute News from East and West," which featured such items as: "Olga Baklanova has been signed under a five-year contract with Paramount. It is said that Miss Baklanova will be groomed for Pola Negri's position on the Paramount program. . . . Rod La Rocque's option calling for a raise from $3,500 to $5,000 (per week) was not exercised by Pathe. . . . Eva von Berne is here. Her name was Eva von Plentzner and she is the daughter of an Austrian army colonel. Irving Thalberg saw her picture in a Viennese magazine and signed her during his recent trip abroad. . . . Finding no producer ready to sign him up at his figure, $3,500 a week, Rod La Rocque has gone ahead with his plans to leave the picture business. . . . Pauline Starke leaving M-G-M to free lance . . . ."

Why was the "signing" of the daughter of an Austrian army colonel stop-press news? What was an "option," what "free-lancing"? How did you "groom" one star to take another's place on a "program"? Such terminology, such reporting, would have been Greek to the innocent moviegoers of fifteen years earlier, but the fans of 1928 knew the vocabulary by heart and could parse for its dread portent even such a euphemism as "has gone ahead with his plans to leave the picture business." The studio contract system and the contracts themselves, right down to the "acts of God" and "morality clauses" in the fine print, were of greater interest than the plots of current pictures. As well as its glory, they had the pathology of stardom at their fingertips. They knew what "slipping" and "has-been" meant, and scorned or suffered with the victim as their allegiances took them. And those allegiances, those fevered loyalties, delicious though they were, caused them plenty of heartburn. If Clara Bow was suddenly the greatest, who was the less thereby? T. S. Eliot said of literature that each new masterpiece subtly alters the order and balance obtaining between the old ones, and this proved true also of the stars, those ephemeral masterworks. To be a dyed-in-the-wool movie fan in those great days was to live twixt hope and fear, "busily seek-ing in continual change."

Engrossed in the game of measuring stellar magnitudes, the fans often tried to throw their own weight in the scale. Even when they liked his latest picture, Ramon Novarro's fans invariably wrote in to insist that it was his worst, hoping thus to spur his studio to greater efforts in his behalf. Before she had ever made a picture, Anita Page found herself the startled recipient of five hundred letters a week; the fans simply wanted to welcome a well-publicized newcomer to the stellar tourney. The more obsessed of these votaries formed fan clubs, designed among other things to convince their idol's employers that he had greater and more puissant legions than the box office said he did, and the furtherance of fan club activities became a life work for more than one lonely soul. Some of these, in pride of office, were capable of losing sight of their original objectives. Irene Dunne was once so tactless as to inform her fan club that she could no longer give it financial support. The indignant madam president sought solace and counsel from a fan editor of the period. The star had said that she couldn't afford any more to pay the costs of the mimeographed news letter the club sent out to all its members each and every week. Where did Miss Dunne think she got off? That was gratitude for you. And after all they'd done for her! The president intimated that she was considering transferring loyal devotion *en masse* to Ann Harding. Or did he, she asked the editor, think that Ginger Rogers or Dorothy Lamour, being newcomers, might be more "grateful?" "I told her," the editor said, "to let her heart be her guide."

For fans like these, and they numbered about five million Americans, the drama of Hollywood had supplanted the drama of the screen in their affections, had become the real center of their thoughts and the object of their monthly quest for movie information. Of course reviews were still important. Even the most maniacal fans could not spend all their time simply reading about their favorites. They had to see the new films as well, in order to talk about them and to keep track of the rise and fall of careers—to check up on how Pauline Starke was making out since she "left" M-G-M to free-lance. But by the time PHOTOPLAY really hit its stride, information about the film world was as important as criticism. "As We Go to Press" was a mere pendant to the voluminous column appearing under the rubric "Cal York's

Good News." Cal York had no existence; his name was an abbreviation of California and New York, the two principal sources of studio news. He was, of course, Mr. Quirk, plus his entire staff, plus all those Hollywood contacts, friends, and hangers-on who could be induced to contribute items in the hope of winning PHOTOPLAY's good will, or in that of stirring up a little trouble for somebody deemed deserving of a good whack or two.

Yet, in the fullness of time, Cal York came to have a sort of life of his own. His subject matter was equally divided between production and career news, with a running fire of anecdote and comment on the status of important marriages, love affairs and divorces, in prospect, in fact or in liquidation. His style was slangy, egalitarian—and ruthless. Short of libel, he was no respecter of persons, though the studious fan could often discern Quirk's preferences and prejudices as through a glass darkly. But in general, if you had it coming to you, you got it; too bad, pal, but things are rough all over; and what else is new? He seemed a fatalistic Solomon, giving judgment after execution. His genial forthrightness and at times painful honesty had a clout because it dealt with the charmed circle of the great stars and other major figures in the closed circle of fabled Hollywood—a clout unmatched today, no matter how boldface the name-dropping.

Aside from its specialized departments, the remainder of PHOTOPLAY as Quirk elaborated it came to consist of an expansion of Cal York—criticism and comment in a variety of formats. The first of these, started by Quirk in earliest days, was the star interview, inclined to be worshipful and for that reason to obey the law of diminishing returns as far as reader interest was concerned. Later Quirk invented the, so help me, symposium. Writers who had never heard of Plato were assigned to secure the views of a number of stars on any topic which was thought to be hot. Hot topics were innocuous indeed to begin with, resembling in form and substance the "write-ups" in high school yearbooks: what's your favorite flower, your favorite color, your ideal man? But later "symposia" tended to zero in on such subjects as "How Twelve Stars Make Love." Beyond these two forms there came to exist a third one, without a fan magazine label but which might be called the embryonic, or stillborn, think-piece. A horde of soothsayers, from psychiatrists to astrologers, were hired to discuss such topics as "Love Pictures—The Doctor Tells

Us Why We React To Them" or "Which Movie Star Dominates You?" (this turned out to depend on which zodiacal sign you were born under). But whatever its nominal subject, the fan magazine article was immutably founded on current Hollywood gossip: who had just done what?—said what? —been caught with the goods, or with his pants down?

But Quirk could get incendiary on his own editorial page, and no one from Louis B. Mayer on down was spared if Quirk thought spanks—or even solar-plexus belts—were warranted. That a movie magazine should have had an editorial page at all may come as a shock, but Quirk's widely read editorial column, first titled "Speaking of Pictures" and later "Close-Ups and Long-Shots," soon made him highly respected and greatly feared, and the rival movie magazines which had followed his lead from the beginning had to try to imitate it. None acquired a comparable influence.

Bibulous, garrulous, gregarious, Quirk went everywhere, accompanied by his second wife, the beautiful silent star May Allison, whom he had married in 1926 after a divorce from his first wife. He counted his friends on all levels of the movies, and since he was himself a pioneer and, before the 1929 crash, a millionaire several times over, he hobnobbed with the top figures on equal terms.

The industry's attitude toward the fan magazines had from the start, nonetheless, been ambivalent. The movie moguls craved above all things a respectability which was not willingly vouchsafed them, and the symbol of respectability was respectful treatment in the press, also not easily forthcoming. But when Adolph Zukor looked for editorial recognition in the New York TIMES for some contribution to the national weal, and didn't get it, his myrmidons could console him by drawing his attention to Mr. Quirk's encouraging words in the latest issue of PHOTOPLAY. The fact that the sturdily independent and at times stingingly chastising Lord of PHOTOPLAY might give him a solid whack in the following issue did not essentially minimize a Zukor's gratitude for gracious words printed.

Quirk laid about with broom, broom-handle, and occasionally stiletto, and Mayer, Laemmle, the Schencks, you-name-him, felt the hot breath of his disapproval. He could chastise Mary Pickford for her aloofness from publicity, Pola Negri for her tasteless pursuit of it, or Charlie Chaplin for his obdurate refusal to become an American citizen. But the magnates knew that, when the chips were down, PHOTOPLAY could be counted on if the movies had to present a united front to the rest of the world. Quirk was hell on censorship, even when attacking it meant attacking the churches, his own church included.

PHOTOPLAY continued a one-man show as always, but Quirk couldn't write it all (though some of his enemies, usually in their cups, enjoyed insisting that he did). Many famous literary names were snared for PHOTOPLAY, usually because they admired and respected James Quirk and his editorial aims. And whatever the "names" may have thought they thought about a subject, no more than the rest of us could they resist the movies' magnetic pull. Among the early contributors were David Belasco, O. O. McIntyre, Channing Pollock and Kenneth Macgowan. To his eternal credit, Quirk inspired Terry Ramsaye, one of his earliest protégés, to write for PHOTOPLAY a lengthy serial in 36 installments (1922–1925), "The Romantic History of the Motion Picture," which in book form (1926) became the classic history *A Million And One Nights*. Robert E. Sherwood, Willard Huntington Wright ("S. S. Van Dine") and Sally Benson also served their terms on PHOTOPLAY, as well as H. L. Mencken, George Jean Nathan (good friends of Quirk's), Scott Fitzgerald, Theodore Dreiser and Sherwood Anderson. Mencken's regard for Quirk's talents and judgment was so high that he drafted the Lord of PHOTOPLAY to write for his AMERICAN MERCURY.

PHOTOPLAY continued to evolve splendidly as an independent spokesman for the movie audience as well as the movie-makers. In 1920 Quirk instituted the highly coveted Photoplay Gold Medal Awards which were *the* industry prizes until the Oscar awards, especially after Quirk's death, gradually eclipsed them. Quirk also developed an impressive stable of top writers, including Katherine Albert Eunson, Leonard Hall, Herbert Howe, Kirtley Baskette, Ruth Waterbury, Ruth Biery, Marquis Busby, Harriet Parsons and Adele Whiteley Fletcher. Quirk's brightest star was the amazing Adela Rogers St. Johns, daughter of famed criminal lawyer Earl Rogers, and who was "discovered" by Quirk in 1918 when she was a newspaper reporter. Under Quirk's tutelage she developed into a first-class writer. Later he introduced her to his close friend Ray Long, famed editor of COSMOPOLITAN, thus catapulting her into a major career on national magazines. She went on to write novels, short stories, screenplays and books.

Out of these variegated elements, James R. Quirk created PHOTOPLAY. No question of its success; in circulation and advertising it consistently outstripped its rivals, who certified its commanding position by careful imitation of all its components. Quirk proudly called his magazine "The National Guide to Motion Pictures." He contended, and with ample justification, that its readership consisted of "the whole family." Reviews which highly recommended current films were apt to end: "Leave the dishes in the sink." They also meticulously warned mother and dad of anything in even the best films which might conceivably be thought offensive, or unsuitable for children. PHOTOPLAY, like its creator, was not a stuffed-shirt magazine; it was not averse to using slang and sly innuendo, but it was inherently tasteful, and drew the line on anything vulgar or cheap. By the end of the Twenties, PHOTOPLAY had become truly a national institution.

Then the magazine field in general felt the velocity of an ill wind. The Depression hit the magazines considerably before it struck the movies themselves. Circulations dropped, advertising shrank. In 1930 appeared NEW MOVIES, a glossy newcomer to the field, joining MODERN SCREEN, MOTION PICTURE and other publications which had developed in the wake of PHOTOPLAY. NEW MOVIES was distributed through a chain store and sold for only a dime. A price war followed; most of the magazines dropped their prices from twenty-five cents to fifteen, to ten, some even to a nickel. PHOTOPLAY, despite the gloom of unemployment and economic collapse, determined under Quirk to ride out the storm, maintained its price at a quarter and continued to offer more for the money. And so things remained until, in August 1932, Quirk died of a heart attack induced by pneumonia, during his annual visit to Hollywood.

His death was a great shock to the industry. An influential and trenchant voice had been stilled, and the void was notable. Louella Parsons and other journalists wondered in print what PHOTOPLAY's fate would be, it having been so closely the reflection of James R. Quirk's intellect and personality.

Kathryn Dougherty, who had been at his side since 1914, succeeded Quirk as editor and publisher. The controlling stock in the magazine remained in the hands of Quirk's heirs, his first wife and his two daughters, as per his last will and testament. The second Mrs. Quirk had abandoned her acting career in 1927 and, encouraged by her husband, had taken up writing. For a time she joined PHOTOPLAY as a feature writer, but remarried a year and a half after Quirk's death and retired altogether from the Hollywood–New York scene.

Miss Dougherty, who had been molded by Quirk, had no other ambition than to continue his style and maintain his values. She succeeded remarkably well in adhering to the high Quirk standards for the next two years, considering that her previous post had been as Secretary-Treasurer of the Photoplay Publishing Company. Then, through no fault of Miss Dougherty's, a series of catastrophes struck. Quirk had once told her, "Don't let them stampede you," and with the courage of the hardy Chicago Irishwoman that she was, Miss Dougherty fought to stem the "stampede." But events proved too much for her. Robert M. Eastman of the W. F. Hall Printing Company, known affectionately as "Uncle Bob," had been Quirk's and Miss Dougherty's solid standby from the beginning. Soon he also died. The removal of this sterling source of support brought an added breach in the walls of Miss Dougherty's citadel.

Miss Dougherty, who had more than her share of spunk, managed to last through 1933 and most of 1934, but economic and other problems continually assailed her. A series of complicated stock negotiations and "inside" maneuverings resulted eventually in the sale of PHOTOPLAY to Bernarr Macfadden, who up to this time had won his chief fame (or notoriety) for "physical culture" propaganda and his TRUE STORY and by-then-defunct NEW YORK GRAPHIC. Neither of these publications had, to put it gently, any pretensions whatsoever to class or culture, and Miss Dougherty, who had found herself checkmated by events through no fault of her own, went into a terminal one-year editor-publisher contract with Macfadden Publications with a heavy heart and negative forebodings. She later said that she felt that during that year (October 1934 to October 1935) all that Quirk and she had worked to build was slowly being eroded away. When she took her departure late in 1935, it was the grim conclusion of a great era.

The influence of James R. Quirk was to linger on, however, in one form or another, until 1940, as one after another of his protégés attempted valiantly to imitate and further the standards that had made PHOTOPLAY great—and this under a new publisher who was more concerned with sales than

with quality.

Macfadden, anxious to achieve new sales records, proceeded to try a series of editors, including notably Ray Long, a close James Quirk crony who had made so great a success of the old COSMOPOLITAN for Hearst, but the winner in this experimental competition turned out to be another Quirk pupil, a vintage movie magazine writer, Ruth Waterbury.

Miss Waterbury had been a "chatter-chippie," as fan magazine writers were known, since she had come to James Quirk's attention with a scoop on Rudolph Valentino in the early Twenties. Macfadden made the resources of his organization available to her, but she found herself confronted with the same problems which had unnerved her predecessors. She decided that the answer to those problems was more of the same—more news, more fashions and above all more "glamour," a slightly shopworn value since it was done to death in the early Thirties, but, for want of a successor, still the yardstick by which stars, the stellar life and the publications which dramatized them were judged. PHOTOPLAY, she determined, would continue its upward course as a "class" magazine in the tradition of James R. Quirk—without, of course, losing a single one of the humblest of its readers. Macfadden went along to some extent with Miss Waterbury's ideas, though the net result of their alliance was to be an ever more pronounced slanting of the editorial matter to exclusively feminine audiences and the floodlighting of fashions and cosmetics.

It became, however, a case of too many cooks-behind-the-scenes muddying the broth, and PHOTOPLAY, deprived sadly of the authority and strong individual voice of Quirk, floundered in a morass of gimmicks, some successful, some not. Miss Waterbury, to her credit, did the best she could to keep the Quirk ghost alive, but unlike her departed hero, she was not the owner and final authority but rather a mere employee.

The experimentations continued without let-up, as the magazine went through one restless, disconcerting format shift after another. In 1937 PHOTOPLAY was enlarged to the size and format of VOGUE and HARPER'S BAZAAR and given a fresh new layout. Though color reproduction was still rudimentary, color was used as much as possible. PHOTOPLAY, this time thanks to somebody's brainstorm that for once proved felicitous, was redubbed "The Aristocrat of Motion Picture Magazines." A growing crowd of "name" writers, seduced by higher rates than any film magazine had offered before, joined the regulars for "special" contributions.

The Hollywood of the late Thirties which was presented in this setting was not the land of Cockaigne of earlier days, nor the factory town portrayed by its detractors, but a sort of world pleasure resort where, by some coincidence, films were made. The stars were still its dominant inhabitants, but they too were sort of different— glamorous still, yes indeed, and romantic, more than ever before, but above all things successful —insistently, remorselessly successful.

Success was no longer measured month in and month out by options dropped or taken up; the new stars seemed to be above all that, and the dropouts were mentioned less and less. The star careerists were now shown as big-shot men and women of affairs, who had above all things "contacts," adventuring as they constantly did in the great world of business, finance, art and fashion. The day of café society had dawned, and though its natural habitat was New York, PHOTOPLAY transferred it bodily to Hollywood.

The stars were shown mingling in a marathon party with Elsa Maxwell, the Countess Dorothy di Frasso, Cobina Wright, Sr. and Jr., Jock and Liz Whitney, Joseph P. Kennedy, Leopold Stokowski and a host of well-known playboys and playgirls who were said suddenly to prefer Hollywood over their usual haunts "because it was such fun."

What the 1937–1940 PHOTOPLAY was offering was a sort of prototype of today's international jet set —photographed by the prototypes of the *paparazzi*, innumerable young cameramen spawned by the rise of pictorial journalism. It was, in fact, the new popularity of LIFE, LOOK and PIC which, inevitably hurting all the fan magazines, had motivated PHOTOPLAY's transmogrification. Among the non-cinematic "celebs" who now dotted PHOTOPLAY's pages was, more and more frequently, its publisher, Bernarr Macfadden. In her quest for success, Miss Waterbury left no stone unturned. Using a ploy long familiar to the studios, Miss Waterbury saw to it that on his increasingly frequent visits to the Coast, the ageing medicine-ball man met all the new cuties and went to all the best parties and was photographed at them. Revamping PHOTOPLAY cost money.

At the center of this glittering web was, of course, Miss Waterbury herself, and sometimes it seemed she was its *stella assoluta*. She was not alone in self-dramatization. Her rivals among the female fan editors, a numerous breed, were also much given to it. "The lady editors," said Norbert Lusk, "portrayed themselves as glamour-girl intimates and confidants of the stars, but this harmless deception was exposed by the photographs they published on the editorial page as infallibly as their signatures in facsimile, which grew masterfully larger." Miss Waterbury far outstripped the others; she seemed to be in every third photograph in the magazine, and she was fond of telling cute stories about herself. The realism of one of these perhaps gave the game away. Leaving for Hollywood at Grand Central, she was accompanied to the 20th Century Limited by a brace of photographers assigned to record the event for PHOTOPLAY. Her impressed Pullman porter was later disappointed to learn that she was not, after all, a star. "Not that you look it, lady," he added.

Autointoxication was possibly the inevitable fate of an editor who had to sell everybody, including herself, on the belief that PHOTOPLAY could maintain itself as a class magazine while catering to the masses. But kid herself though she did, the formula Miss Waterbury tried to apply was out of phase. It didn't make a great deal of sense to pay a distinguished critic like Gilbert Seldes a large sum of money to write a piece about the stars' wacky investments, especially when the facts had to be supplied to a not-very-interested Mr. Seldes by PHOTOPLAY's regular staff. Situated between the picture magazines on the one hand and the fashion journals on the other, PHOTOPLAY circa 1940 was an anomaly. In spite of all the window-dressing, it was still very obviously a fan magazine geared to a primarily feminine audience, and suspicion was rife that it was not finding its way to the best coffee tables, or anyway not enough of them. Circulation rose through the Thirties from 600,000 to more than a million, a remarkable achievement for those days. But the "right" advertising did not follow it. Under the Waterbury regime, PHOTOPLAY's ads consisted largely of bust-developers, cures for acne, and—a dead giveaway—courses in self-improvement, from stenography-at-home to lessons in simple English grammar.

Late in the Thirties, market research revealed that the magazine's average reader was, not the smart suburbanite of Miss Waterbury's dreams, nor some royal nonesuch on page 200, but rather a 26-year-old housewife married to a Detroit assembly line worker. What had actually happened became clearer and clearer; the fans were getting a free ride. At the same bargain rate, they were buying a classy-looking magazine which in spite of its looks attracted no new class of reader. World War II priorities provided an excuse for ending the experiment. Ruth Waterbury withdrew in favor of Ernest V. Heyn and Fred R. Sammis, and contented herself with a writing career that has flourished right up to the present. Her day as a "glamour editor" was, however, conclusively over. The Messrs. Heyn and Sammis, acting on orders from above, began the process of liquidation and forever dimmed the grandeur of Photoplay by merging it with a cheap competitor, Movie Mirror. The combined magazine, selling for ten cents with cheapened paper and a reduced, cheapjack, catch-all format, was really Movie Mirror disguised as Photoplay from the issue of January 1941 on. On it pushed into the Forties in down-to-earth pursuit of the immediate interests of the time—patriotism, military service and keep-the-home-fires-burning. The image of the glamour girl was displaced by that of Rosie the Riveter. If any reader ever looked back to the days of Miss Waterbury and her café society *élégantes,* it was as to a condemned playground.

Today, the fan field has greatly diminished. As many magazines are published as ever, including some of the old-timers—Motion Picture, Silver Screen, Screenland and Photoplay itself—but the market for them has shrunk to the female teen-ager. She and almost nobody else; the magazines are still standard equipment at the beautician's, but they are read there in a sort of trance, if you can call it reading at all.

As for their contents, glamour and beauty as ideals to be striven for have gone with the wind, along with cleanliness. What readers want is vicarious experience, which has to be elemental and preferably should be connected with wealth and power, excitement and mobility. It hardly matters whose wealthy and exciting and powerful mobility; Elizabeth Taylor, though far too old for reader-identification, is nevertheless a prime star of the contemporary magazines because of the continuous explosions in her life off the screen. Her principal rivals, besides the intergalactic Mia Farrow, are Jacqueline Onassis and Ethel Kennedy, who have never appeared in a movie at all! What has happened to the old conception of stardom is well illustrated in a fairly recent issue

of Photoplay. At the end of a story about Barbara Parkins, the editor appends the admonition: "See Barbara Parkins in *The Kremlin Letter,* 20th Century-Fox." The clear implication is that the reader may never have seen Barbara Parkins on the screen before, or perhaps never heard of her before; she has read the story for its intrinsic interest, not because she adores Miss Parkins. The same identifying label is added to virtually every interview in the magazine, including Burt Lancaster's and Natalie Wood's—though Ruth Waterbury's (yes, *Ruth Waterbury's*) account of the death of Robert Taylor has the grace to conclude with the simple finality of "The End."

Because of their tight market, the contemporary fan mags have to be produced as economically as possible. The days of the star-editor and the star-chatter-chippie are long gone; the magazines still feature ageing veterans of the gossip wars like Sidney Skolsky, and occasionally the semi-retired Miss Waterbury, but the bulk of the material is produced almost anonymously. According to Pauline Kael, the magazines make a practice of employing recent high school graduates and drop-outs, girls—and boys—so bemused at the chance to write about their far-off dream world that they will work for peanuts. The stuff sounds like it. Presumably it satisfies, at least for a split-second. But the writer can testify from long professional experience that when today's teen-agers stumble across a batch of the ancestral fan magazines in cellar or attic, they spend more than a split-second on them. They sit down on the floor with them and pore over them for long hours.

Do they marvel at the relative innocence of the old Photoplays compared with that current self-proclaimed sophistication which is actually a sort of soiled ignorance? The generation-gap prevents one from answering. But—again from personal experience—it can be said that when their mothers are confronted with the old magazines, they too pore, and they also shed a tear, furtive or otherwise. Are these the same tears that *their* mothers (and grandmothers) shed over a faded daguerreotype, a pressed flower in a book? Not exactly. The pressed flowers and the daguerreotypes were mementoes "embalmed and treasured up on purpose" to be cherished till the end of life. The Photoplays of the Thirties were items packaged for sale and bought for use and then discarded—put away, along with other childish things. Their practical use was, fundamentally, self-improvement.

Per aspera ad astra. By emulation of the stars, we would make ourselves better—help ourselves to grow up. And here, perhaps, the *hypocrite lecteur* should be warned that he reads on at his peril. The old Photoplays are a lot of fun to mull over today, for young and old. They have other effects as well. They measure that vast acceleration of events, that continual mutation of feeling and purpose, which is the leading characteristic of the century. They say, "But everything turned out so differently!" As Siegfried Kracauer wrote of the old films themselves, "What was once our life is now stored away, and we have gone on unknowing."

PHOTOPLAY

November, 1928

Close-Ups *and* Long-Shots

By James R. Quirk

PHOTOPLAY readers were singularly calm in face of the news that Mary Pickford had bobbed her curls. In fact, some fans were cruel enough to say that, five years ago, the event would have been news, but today Mary's bob is of no more interest than Jackie Coogan's long pants. It's an odd sidelight on movie popularity, gleaned from PHOTOPLAY's letters, that the dead Valentino is of more interest than the living Mary.

Poor Mary is facing a new public that no longer believes in "America's Sweetheart," a public that thinks the very word "sweetheart" is a little ga-ga. For years Mary, as a human being, has been withdrawing from the public. In trying to remain a legend, she has sacrificed her human appeal.

IDOL worship is no more. There are no longer any gods and goddesses on the screen; just human beings of varying degrees of interest. PHOTOPLAY's circulation is increasing because this magazine is not trying to create gods and goddesses; it is concerned with the men and women of the screen and their pictures.

Clara Bow and Greta Garbo are not saints in the eyes of the public, nor are they trying to pass themselves off as criterions of manners and morals. They are popular because they are interesting and because their names carry the guarantee of pictures worth seeing.

John Gilbert and Emil Jannings can draw huge audiences in any theater in this country or in Europe. There are no wings sprouting on Gilbert. But he can act. Jannings is no sample of moral and physical perfection. But he is a great artist and, as such, he spreads more glory on the movies than if he were received socially in every court in Europe.

TO go back to the tragic case of Mary Pickford: Mary is thinking of making "Coquette," which is the story of an unmarried girl who is going to have a baby and who kills herself.

Bland Johaneson, the really intelligent motion picture critic of the *New York Mirror*, says that if Mary makes the picture one of three things will happen: 1, the girl will be really married; 2, it will be a dual rôle film with an angelic twin sister; 3, the story will be so completely changed that there will be nothing left but the title.

But none of these makeshifts will do. Mary must make, not only an adult picture, but a picture with artistic sincerity. It must be more than a good picture; it must be a great one. Mary's name means just exactly fifty per cent less than it did five years ago.

STARS, COMEDIANS,
CHILD STARS, "SUPPORT"

The Nineteen Thirties saw the maturation of the Hollywood star system. The Teens were a period of wild parturition, when producers, to nail down the services of the sudden new favorites, all but gave them the studios. The Twenties saw the development of systematic nurture—"discovery," "grooming" and the five-year contract with options, options available to the producers themselves but never to their bejeweled wage-slaves. The Thirties introduced the seven-year contract, bespeaking a studio determination to winnow the new entries and back heavily only the most likely winners. It is from then that we date stellar longevity. Some of the Thirties stars are still around. Thanks to TV, all are still part of our consciousness.

In his editorial on the facing page, James R. Quirk used the case of Mary Pickford to signalize a *Götterdämmerung*. On balance he was right. In the realistic Thirties, the idols of the screen declined to, or grew up to, the estate of mortal men and women—still the darlings of the gods, but no longer gods and goddesses themselves. The sole exception was Greta Garbo. Her unique status only proves the rule, but what an exception she was.

"One God—one Garbo!" exclaimed the wife of a Kansas City druggist to PHOTOPLAY's letter department, and no one called sacrilege. This preposterous *cri du coeur* somehow did express an almost universal feeling. Miss Garbo's account of herself on the screen, and her blank refusal to give any account of herself whatever off it, made a perfect mix for a wised-up fan public whose illusions had been shattered time and again, but who still longed for illusion. "Garbo is the scale by which we measure our stars," wrote another fan, and the lesson was not lost on the imitative and competitive studios. Universal trotted out Tala Birell, RKO Gwili Andre, and Sam Goldwyn Anna Sten as ersatz Garbos, and Marlene Dietrich's slight resemblance to Miss Garbo almost blotted out her own individuality in the early stages of her career. Established favorites like Joan Crawford and Norma Shearer felt the gravitational pull, and unwisely altered their make-up and general appearance in tribute to the universal idol, while the advent of newcomers prompted fan editors to set up mock-combats in the form of articles on "Garbo vs. Dietrich," "Garbo vs. Hepburn," and even "Garbo vs. Helen Hayes"—though no editor went so far in unrealism as to propose "Garbo vs. Mae West." The paradox was that Miss Garbo, while refraining altogether from participation in movie publicity, nevertheless dominated it in this specialized field. From the beginning of the period covered in this book, January 1929, until her departure for Sweden in mid-1932 for a year's holiday, virtually every issue of PHOTOPLAY featured an article about or a portrait of Greta Garbo, to say nothing of endless lineage in the gossip column.

As the Thirties wore on, as Miss Garbo's pictures grew fewer and her trips to Sweden longer and more frequent, Garbomania gradually subsided. But its subject remained the unofficial queen of the Hollywood she so frigidly ignored. To movie journalists of all kinds, but especially to those of the fan stripe, Garbo was an itch they couldn't scratch. They *had* to crack the Garbo pose of mystery and silence, even when the lengthening record made it clear that it wasn't a pose at all. Besides, she had a bad influence on other stars, who were moved by her successful example to demand private lives of their own. What would become of movie publicity if this evil were allowed to spread? Worse still, Miss Garbo's instant excommunication of those of her friends, servants and business associates who talked about her threatened the very foundations of the Hollywood spy system on which film journalism depended. She held the fan press in an ambivalent vise: they couldn't get a story, and they couldn't stop writing about her even when there was nothing to write.

The contradiction kept the Garbo legend alive throughout the Thirties, even when her box office draw waned.

Among male stars of the Thirties, only Clark Gable held a position comparable to Garbo's, so far ahead of the field as to have no real competition. His rise was so abrupt—from bit parts to stardom in six months—that the fan writers were caught off balance. They could at first discover little about Gable, and that little was highly questionable as fan fodder. In the first flush of his new success he married, but pictures of the lucky lady were withheld from publication as long as possible at the behest of his studio, M-G-M. When at last they appeared, as they had to, the public discovered by ocular evidence that the bride was a lady of no particular attractions, unconcealably older than her husband. She was also known to be wealthy, and to have helped him in his days of obscurity. It looked as if Gable's marriage to her, after he finally made it big professionally, was some kind of a payoff. Research now revealed that he had married twice before, each time to a vintage lady who was in position to further his career. Further prying brought out the fact that he had been leading man in stock to two ageing ladies of the stage, Pauline Frederick and Alice Brady, reputedly on the basis of services rendered after each night's final curtain. It began to look to the reporters who dug all this up as if What-A-Man-Gable (so dubbed by PHOTOPLAY) had got where he was primarily as a stud, if not an outright gigolo.

Feast or famine is the lot of the fan press; from Garbo's history they could get no story at all, from Gable's far too juicy a story to print. But fan hunger for facts about their new man would not be denied, and gradually the facts were let out in the magazines, in discreet doses. Pieced together under the spotlight, their implications were unmistakable. And yet, no lightnings crashed about Clark Gable's head. Everybody liked—not admired or worshipped, but *liked*—him on the screen so much that they couldn't care less how he got there. When Gable fell for Carole Lombard; when his old wife refused to be put away; when the situation lasted through three agonizing, publicity-filled years, public sympathy was all with Clark and Carole. That was in part Rhea Gable's doing; she had clung too long and bargained too hard to keep the sympathy of even the most straitlaced. The eventual marriage of Lombard and Gable seemed so "right" to the fans as to erase all memory

of the latter's climb to the top over the bodies of willing women.

No other stars of the Thirties posed such "policy" problems to fan editors as these two front runners. The suicide of Jean Harlow's husband, Lee Tracy's scatological affront to the Mexican soldiery during the making of *Viva Villa,* John Barrymore's appalling descent into alcoholism, all these took place behind a semi-transparent curtain; references to them were of the now-you-see-it, now-you-don't variety. By this time editors and writers could fairly assume that readers knew the facts of these enormities through the newspapers, and that they themselves could confine comment to a tut-tutting footnote. The fan magazine problem was not the suppression of scandal, it was how to make bricks with a minimum of straw. Scandal aside, it was hard to come to grips with any of the facts of Hollywood without making powerful enemies somewhere in the studio labyrinth. There were, to be sure, "safe" topics. The state of Joan Crawford's soul as she clawed her way to the top through a tangle of work and love was good for a story twice a year. Nor was it altogether "dangerous" to imply that Norma Shearer's position as First Lady of Hollywood was in some part due to her marriage to M-G-M's gifted overlord, Irving Thalberg. But there were limits to how far one could go with such as Mr. Thalberg. Of an article detailing Gloria Swanson's decline, the editor who published it said later: "Like most fan magazine stories, this one failed to hit the nail on the head. It refrained from telling exactly why Miss Swanson had made no picture for her most recent studio, and why no other apparently wanted her." The nail which would have had to be hit on the head here was the fact that Miss Swanson, under contract to M-G-M, flouted Irving Thalberg's professional advice, whereupon he sent her to Coventry, as did everybody in Hollywood who revered his judgment, which was all but everybody. To attack a producer of Thalberg's standing was simply out —so the article trailed off into nothingness, as did most stories which dealt with studio politics.

There were, in fact, few safe formulas. PHOTO-PLAY duly chronicled, slightly behind the event, the changing fashions in feminine stars, from the "glamour and sophistication" of the period of Garbo's greatest influence through the "naturalness and humanness" of the Helen Hayes era to the "wacky" heroine exemplified by Carole Lombard and Jean Arthur, with analogous sidelights on the development of the male stellar stereotype during the Thirties. The one formula which was always sure-fire with fans, and which therefore had to be staple with the magazine was Romance, meaning two stars who were sleeping together, or planning to. With due discretion, this tricky implication could always be "handled"—though the fighting Flynns and the battling Bogarts were a godsend to fan writers because their "romantic" fireworks were legitimatized by marriage. The *sine qua non* of this routine was that at least one of the players involved had to be a star, and both had to be young enough to make their liaison exciting. That left out, among others, comedians, male and female. He Who Gets Slapped could be funny or pathetic, but not the central figure in a fan magazine drama-let of triumphant, or even thwarted, offscreen love. The same liability of course held good for child stars. Shirley Temple's supreme popularity forced the editors to try to find a way to give her space in Photoplay, but beyond Adela Rogers St. Johns' inspiration, "Shirley Wants the Quintuplets for Christmas," there was little they could come up with. Supporting players were hardest of all to deal with. There was evidence in Photoplay's correspondence that many of them commanded the abiding interest of fans, and Marie Dressler and Will Rogers were among the most-beloved figures the screen has ever created. But the fan press didn't know what to do with them, except to print frequent portraits and very occasional stories confined for the most part to the back of the issue. In part this was because the steady careers of character actors lacked the drama of meteoric rise and fall which went with stardom. In greater part it derived from the magazines' imprisonment in formulas of their own devising. Their hierarchy of values exactly reflected those of screen credits: "Starring"—"featuring"—"supported by"—"with."

Garbo-Maniacs

One of Them Screams to the High Heavens Garbo Can Do No Wrong—The Slightest Criticism in PHOTOPLAY and the Post-office Works Overtime

By LEONARD HALL

HOLLYWOOD puts its hand where its heart should be and swears that its Heaven is full of film stars.

Billboards scream it—press agents toot it on their E-flat cornets and boom it on their big bass drums. Electric lights spatter stellar names across the night, and starry voices squawk out upon the evening air.

But I am in the trenches, and I wink a roguish eye. I know better. There are only a few great stars left in the skies of filmland, and of the whole kit there is one outstander—Greta Garbo, Scandinavia's gift to the world. Explorers, scientists and practitioners of other arts are dim figures when set against this astonishing woman with the pale face and yellow hair.

There are those who say that the star system is on its death-bed and rattling its last. In any event, it is a safe generalization to say that the smartest, craftiest talking pictures that have so far squeaked into the public fancy have been the product of what we used to call "all-star casts," or of troupes with no stars at all. In other words, pictures are bigger than the stars.

AND out in Los Angeles a funny thing happened. In the heart of the sound-maddened movie world, an old-time silent picture came slinking across a screen. When the smoke had cleared away and the casualties had been counted, the head men found that the picture had broken all existing records for the theater, sound or silent.

And need I add that the star of the voiceless opera was Greta Garbo, the Stockholm storm?

True, there are plenty of so-called stars shining their little hour. But there is only one queen, aloof and majestic on a lonely mountain top, who can do no wrong. That's La Belle Garbo, the woman who makes honest, home-loving American burghers look dubiously at their faithful, lawful wives.

It didn't use to be so.

In the noble days every star was fought for by her own group of maddened maniacs. To hint that Mary Pickford wasn't all she should be was to court a kick in the face. He who suggested that Fairbanks had his flaws was in jeopardy of a stinging left jab to the jaw. The Gishes, Pearl White, Jack Kerrigan, Wally Reid, Valentino—all were swallowed hook, line and wiggling worm by their bands of devotees, who made the nights hideous with brawls over the merits of their favorites.

Those maudlin days are long gone. They ended with the era of debunking, which hit motion pictures at the same time it struck the other lively arts.

Mary Pickford has been under fire for some years for various alleged professional misdemeanors, and no critic has been hanged or shot at. Fans and critics have been announcing the end of her long reign for years. Even now she is everlastingly sniped at from various quarters, as she sits on the lonely throne her husband erected for her at Pickfair.

Formerly she was the adored idol of millions—now she is courted by stray nobility touring Hollywood to look at the animals.

Fairbanks is in no better case. Nor is Clara Bow, Joan Crawford, Dick Barthelmess, Billie Dove, Jack Gilbert or any other of the newer crop of stars. Let them speak out of turn, and around their ears rattles a barrage of epistolary criticism—not from enemies, but from their own gang of fair-weather fans.

The modern kings and queens can do plenty wrong. Their thrones are built of raspberry jello. One false squirm, and away they go!

Queen Garbo in the plain old coat and slouch hat that seem to comprise her pet outdoor costume. Right, one of the quaint, unfashionable gowns she wears on the screen. But let us hint that they are in any way odd or out of order and, swish! Off go our editorial heads!

ALL but Garbo! That weird and wonderful woman from the far north never seems to fumble a grounder, no matter how hard hit. She could ride around Hollywood on a howling hyena and leading a stuffed duck, and it would be all right with the Garbo-maniacs. Greta gets away with personal idiosyncrasies that would send other stars' fans shrieking away in droves.

But everything's all right. It's Garbo. And Garbo can do no wrong.

The Greta's position, in this respect, is unique.

Drolly enough, the more writers play truth about Greta, the more bitterly they are attacked and the more fiercely her fans rally round the standard, to fight and die for God, for Sweden and for Garbo.

[PLEASE TURN TO PAGE 270]

GARBO, is strange fascination, unique in filmdom, leaves the screen to smite men and women with equal force. Almost nothing is known about her, but she has millions of devoted followers who take her part against the world, the press and the devil. The slightest criticism, however kindly, stirs a storm of protest. There are a million raging Garbo-Maniacs!

THE Garbo in whom fact and legend meet—the Garbo of the tweed topcoat, the crumpled felt hat, the flat-heeled shoes. And on her face the smile that we too seldom see, lighting up the surrounding territory like a Scandinavian sunrise! She's busy, again, directed by Clarence Brown.

Greta Garbo, real name Greta Gustafsson, was born in Stockholm, Sweden, Sept. 18, 1905. She's 5 feet, 6; weighs 122, has light brown hair, blue eyes

Exploding *the* Garbo Myth

By Katherine Albert

A veteran picture writer and critic expresses her opinion. And now for the fireworks

"LET'S get down to brass tacks about this mystery woman of the screen."

In the files in our office there is one folder marked, "Garbo, Greta." It lies, not at all mysteriously, between "Gallagher, Skeets," and "Garon, Pauline" and it is full to running over with reams and reams of printed copy ranging from a magnificently beautiful piece of lyrical writing in a national magazine (not usually concerned with picture people) to some pretty cheap twaddle in lesser publications. I've just re-read it all and (although I find much of my own stuff there) I'm pretty dog-gone bored.

Do hear me out—then dust off the old family shotgun, prepare the burning oil, excavate the Spanish torture chambers and do with me as you will. I've simply got to say it.

I'm bored with Garbo! And I believe that because I'm a fairly average person with fairly average tastes there must be others like me. I'm not alone in my heresies. At least I find company in Hollywood.

Here are the facts: Great directors and executives of the cinema who once hailed Garbo as the Bernhardt, the Dusé, the Mrs. Siddons of the screen have confided (behind locked doors and in whispers) that Garbo is no great shakes as an actress.

Co-workers of the famous star who once alluded to her deep silences and aloofness as the epitome of mental brilliance now admit (also behind locked doors and also in whispers) that, in reality, Garbo is phlegmatic.

And others say (but very discreetly, mind you) that what has been called her great artistry is no more or less than a facial trick which in some way piques the imagination.

Well, let's analyze the thing and see where we get and what I get (besides a hand grenade hurled through my bedroom window).

HER artistry? Listen! This occurred on the set while Garbo was making "Romance." Do you remember the scene where Garbo, as the great singer, interrupts an amorous moment to listen to an organ grinder on the street below? She throws him some money from her bag.

Gavin Gordon, as her lover, objects and asks her why she made such a gesture. And the Diva shrugs her shoulders and says, in effect, "Why not? We are one—he and I. Do we not both make music?" It was, of course, one of the most charming lines in "Romance" and the complete tip-off on the singer's character, one of those beautiful bits that make a character live.

But Garbo, herself, objected to that line. "It is silly," she said. "It means nothing. I would never say a thing like

Is she a mystery woman or like your next-door neighbor? The writer, who knows her, says there is no mystery about her

that." And only by their coddling her petulance and doing the scene once her way and once the right way was she persuaded to go on. She still thought it a stupid, ridiculous line.

Does such an attitude give you an impression of a finely attuned, sensitive woman, a great artist with a great love of life, a perceptive, rich character? I think not.

Her brilliance? With the exception of her bald statements, "Garbo likes" or "Garbo does not like," I believe I'm safe in saying that Garbo has never expressed an opinion. I remember in the early days when she was first beginning her amazing career and I was in the publicity department I used to go out on the set with what is called a symposium idea. This means that a writer for a magazine or newspaper had requested that I ask the stars for certain of their opinions on various subjects. I grant you that some of these "ideas" were pretty terrible, but others there were that might have promoted a little interesting discussion.

INVARIABLY Garbo said, "Oh, dot's silly. I do not want to be quoted." That was all right and she was, in those days, just beginning to build up that tremendous reputation of mystery. We weren't anxious to have Garbo quoted, either, but I used to say, "Very well, you won't be quoted, but just between ourselves what do you really think about the question?" And Garbo always answered, "Dot's silly."

Her intellectual, lonely life? A very excellent reporter trailed Garbo for one day and recounted her activities. The story was good because it was about Garbo, but stripped to the bare facts, it was the most average twenty-four hours you can imagine. She dined at a little Mexican restaurant (where many stars go and continue to go) with a friend, attended a puppet show with him and the next day went to a party which was also attended by a large portion of Hollywood's foreign colony. But you thought Garbo didn't go out? You thought she didn't like people and parties? Uh-huh. The twenty-four hours with Garbo was as dull and ordinary as twenty-four hours with your next-door neighbor.

NOBODY has ever had such a place in the film firmament. Nobody has ever had such a hold on the imaginations of the people.

Garbo has been publicized as not liking people, not liking parties, not liking to go out, not liking Hollywood. I saw her one evening at one of the most select and brilliant of gatherings. The few people there were the real intellectuals of the colony and not a word of the banal chatter

[PLEASE TURN TO PAGE 271]

"Touch Not Yon Blonde

WHAM! The warfare Katherine Albert started when she wrote the article in a recent issue of PHOTOPLAY called "Exploding the Garbo Myth." Sky rockets, pin wheels, Roman candles, hand grenades, shrapnel shells and poison gas came popping, banging and hissing into PHOTOPLAY's office. Through the rockets' red glare with bombs bursting in air, our neighbors began to wonder if PHOTOPLAY was still there.

The only thing we didn't get was a time bomb, and this was only because no one thought of it. We even heard from insane asylums, old soldiers' homes, maternity wards and orphan asylums.

No story ever printed about a screen personality started as many fireworks as Miss Albert's story that Garbo is tainted with humanity and is not a goddess.

All bulky packages addressed to Katherine Albert were delivered to the Police Bomb Squad to be soaked in water before opening. The editor of another screen magazine received a long article denouncing Miss Albert and proclaiming the divinity of Garbo, with the statement that unless the article was printed in that magazine the writer would publish a magazine of her own.

Miss Albert was denounced in bombastic, flaming epithets that made her cute little pink ears turn a livid purple and crinkle at the edges. She was put in a class with Benedict Arnold, Nero and Judas. Lucrezia Borgia, she discovered, was just an amateur poisoner compared to herself. And all because she had the temerity to suggest that Garbo was less than Divine.

THE fact that she did say many nice things about Garbo didn't save her from abuse.

"Nobody has ever had such a place in the film firmament," wrote Miss Albert. "Nobody has ever had such a hold on the imagination of the people."

And again: "Garbo's a nice girl."

And again: "She's invariably lovely and kind to the new actors and actresses who work with her. She is touched by illness and sadness and expresses herself in flowers and gifts to those who are ill or sad."

But no matter. Miss Albert thought the Garbo legend of mystery was just a myth—and the war was on!

When the smoke of the Garbo vs. Albert battle cleared we discovered numerous letters in praise of "Skippy." How the kids loved it! "The Front Page" caused

a sensation; hats were doffed high to Adolphe Menjou for a grand performance. "Dracula" stirred up much excitement, too much for those with jagged nerves. Complaints galore because the music had been removed from "Fifty Million Frenchmen." There is a decided yearning creeping into the fan mail for more music in the talkies. The pendulum is swinging back.

GEORGE ARLISS' admiring throng thought "The Millionaire" a great picture and they liked to see him playing an American for a change. Evalyn Knapp as his daughter received nothing but bouquets and was nominated as a sure candidate for stardom. Claudette Colbert and Fredric March in "Honor Among Lovers" won the popular vote. Robert Montgomery is dodging brick-bats and picking up bouquets at the same time. Lew Ayres is a boy wonder. Paul Lukas is g-r-r-rand! Better stories are demanded for Charles (ex-Buddy) Rogers. He's still a big favorite.

Insistent cries for more romance in the talkies, less sensationalism, worth while stories with some plot; cut out misleading advertisements.

And always the Garbo Army for the Defense telling us—commanding us—to watch our step and leave the Divine Woman unassailed.

Now for the barrage that landed, some 15,854 strong, on our defenseless heads and left us groggy and hanging on the ropes!

For and Against

GARBO is all soul in an age where soul is forgotten.

BLANCHE DRISCOLL,
Philadelphia, Penna.

I'll never read another story by Katherine Albert as long as I live, unless it is entitled "I Apologize to Garbo."

ELLEN BROWN,
New York City

Garbo is the scale by which we measure our stars. No one has ever reached her standard.

ELIZABETH WALTER,
Baldwinsville, N. Y.

Miss Albert has failed in her attempt to discredit the world's greatest actress.

ROSE LANE,
Medford, Ore.

Weight 98 pounds. Fifteen thousand Garbo-Forever fans pounced on her. She still maintains that Garbo is not divine

a Hair of Head," *etc.*

a. crouch

Once in an age a vibrant, magnetic personality is given to the world—such a personality is Garbo's.

MERLE DELANEY,
Montreal, Can.

I've bought my last copy of PHOTOPLAY.

J. D. SISSON,
New York City

We know our Garbo! She is as we want her to be. Don't try to put us "wise" to her.

NELL LAIZELERE,
Birmingham, Ala.

That our Divine Garbo is brilliant and talented is too obvious a thing to bicker about.

GENE CARTWELL,
Brooklyn, N. Y.

Give up the hopeless task of trying to destroy our illusions about Garbo. No matter what she is, no matter what she does, we'll go right on worshipping her.

A. M. AMBLER,
New York City

Get Katherine Albert off your staff quick! Anyone calling the Great Garbo an "emotional machine" will ruin PHOTOPLAY.

MARY JANET BROWN,
New Orleans, La.

Fifty million people can't be wrong. Katherine Albert's article hasn't convinced me that Garbo's charm is caused by a "facial trick."

MAXINE DIES,
Denver, Col.

The Public—which after all is the greatest boss—judged Garbo and found her NOT lacking.

ROSE ANDERSON,
Flag Center, Kan.

Down with this joy-killing debunker who cannot let us worship our Goddess in peace!

ANNA McLEAN,
Enderlin, N. D.

PHOTOPLAY is the most outstanding screen magazine in the world, but if Katherine Albert writes against Garbo, the Immortal, we shall never read PHOTOPLAY again.

MARY LEE,
Chicago, Ill.

Exploding—that's how I feel after reading Katherine Albert's article on the unsurpassable Garbo. Garbo is the greatest living actress.

A. F. SANDERSON,
Pittsburgh, Penna.

Don't give us any more articles like "Exploding the Garbo Myth." No one wants to know that her idol has clay feet. Leave us our stars untarnished by the glare of unflattering reality.

SARA MIDDLEMAN,
Philadelphia, Penna.

"Garbo is no great shakes as an actress," says Katherine Albert. At that rate "Anna Christie," "Romance" and "Inspiration" must have been optical illusions.

ANNA M. BIENEMAN,
Philadelphia, Penna.

This kind of criticism can hurt no one. When Garbo reads it she'll probably give one of her entrancing smiles and say, "Oh, dot's silly." That's what we think.

HELEN H. ALDRICH,
Evanston, Ill.

If Garbo is "no great shakes as an actress" and her artistry is "merely a facial trick," then, dear me, what in the world is wrong with the few million of us who sit and twiddle our thumbs waiting for the release of her next picture?

HAZEL BRIGGS,
Greenville, Mich.

Best Letters of Month

The $25 Letter

To the movies I owe a debt of gratitude. During my hardest years they offered me respite and escape. When life is pretty thick, money scarce, clothes shabby, just slip into the grateful darkness of a movie theater for a couple of hours. I remember one occasion in particular. After nursing the kids and their father through a siege of flu, cold packs, hot packs, aspirin, orange juice and the rest, I had them at last safely convalescent and slipped out to a show. It was a romance as picturesque as an old tapestry. And did I enjoy it! I walked home in the rain with new energy to tackle my job.

Time has passed. My children are older, life a little easier, but I still go to the movies for the pleasure they give me.

MRS. MARIAN RODGERS,
Portland, Ore.

The $10 Letter

From the beginning of motion pictures to the present time there have been a large number of clergymen who seem to have nothing but destructive criticism for the screen.

They are denouncing something they know nothing about. For an example, on a Sunday evening a few weeks ago, I listened to a minister tell about what a menace the movies were. He wound up his discourse by saying that he and his children had never been in a picture show.

I said to myself, "Brother, if you had gone to see 'The Devil's Holiday' last week, you probably would have had a better text for your sermon this evening."

PEARL ELLINGTON,
Long Beach, Calif.

The $5 Letter

The creed of the box office seems to be to make pictures appear a little off-color or the public will be bored. Many a so-called "bad" picture is in reality a beautiful thing, subtly and delicately handled and not the indecent type one is led to expect from its lurid title. The "badness" of a picture often lies in the way it is advertised.

LAURA BELLE CONNER,
Battle Creek, Mich.

ADRIAN ANSWERS 20 QUESTIONS ON GARBO

A scene from the newest Garbo film, "Anna Karenina." Fredric March is her leading man. This is the twentieth picture the Swedish star has made for M-G-M

A friend of Garbo's for years, Adrian, the designer, now risks her displeasure by discussing the star because he wants to correct the false ideas people have of her

UP to the present time, Adrian, famous Metro-Goldwyn-Mayer designer, has steadfastly refused to give out any interviews or answer any questions pertaining to the glamorous Garbo. It is Hollywood legend that once a person begins using her name promiscuously, Garbo no longer includes him in her small circle of friends.

Adrian has been a loyal friend of many years standing. He has such respect and admiration for Garbo, no one has ever been able to get

The star has never worn lovelier clothes, nor clothes that interested her more, than those Adrian designed for her which you see in "Anna Karenina"

Garbo never dresses her hair in the mode of the moment. She creates her own hair arrangement, and it usually starts a new style. Adrian's problem is to design hats that go with her hair

him to commit himself in any way. Since her first days of silent pictures, Adrian has been dressing her for her rôles. Theirs has been a happy and successful working combination. He knows her better, perhaps, than any other person in Hollywood. Therefore it is obvious that he has very good reasons for talking and has agreed for the first time, to answer these muchly-asked questions.

Q.—Why have you avoided giving out stories on Garbo, when you haven't objected to talking about other stars of similar importance?

A.—Simply because there is nothing I could say about Miss Garbo, that would not infringe upon her own desire for her personal privacy.

Q.—Why are you willing to discuss Garbo now?

A.—So many people have printed ridiculous things about her and have misquoted me very often. I feel that if I can clear up of the fantasy concocted about her, I shall be glad.

Q.—Is Garbo's perpetual fleeing done for effect, or because she really doesn't like people?

A.—It surely isn't done for effect. It's done because she would love the privilege of having her own privacy in spite of being a motion picture star. You know as well as I do that there are certain types of people who like and demand large groups of friends around them. And there are those who live very quietly. Garbo happens to be one of the latter. She hates being stared at and being made a fuss over. Do you think that's extraordinary?

Q.—Does Garbo realize that a movie star is public property?

A.—I think she recognizes that a movie star is considered public property, but I don't think she has accepted that in her own consciousness, and is rebellious. She has often said that she would give anything in the world to have the privilege of the freedom of walking about, shopping, traveling, etc., without being noticed. You   [PLEASE TURN TO PAGE 272]

A "modern" Garbo, a ga[y]
Garbo, that's what they prom
ised us! So "Ninotchka" (he[r]
first film in almost two year[s]
her first comedy in eons) give[s]
us Greta as a serious worke[r]
of the new Russia, swept u[p]
in the lightheartedness [of]
ageless Paris — with Melv[yn]
Douglas ably supporting th[e]
cause of love and laughte[r]

TWO portraits of quite a batch of young ladies. The girl
on the left is a lot like the late lamented Jeanne Eagels,
about the nose and brow, and there's a hint of Phyllis Haver.
The lady on the right is very much Garbo. Both are
Marlene Dietrich, new Paramount player from Germany.
Now if she can act like her features—

Garbo *vs.* Dietrich

By Leonard Hall

Her uncounted thousands of fans have risen as one mighty army and shouted "One Mickey Mouse, one Shakespeare, one Joe Doakes, one Garbo!" Frenzied by the thought that anyone dares, even by act of Providence, to resemble Greta Garbo, they are bombarding this editorial trench with heavy shells filled with short, sharp little words that bite and sting.

IS that thunder, mother, that is shaking the plaster down into my bean soup?

No, my child, it is the guns!

The battle of Greta Garbo and Marlene Dietrich—one of the most ferocious in the history of the screen—is now raging.

And nobody started it!

Heaven knows Garbo didn't. She's been toiling on the sets and retreating to her guarded castle in the Santa Monica hills. As far as we know, the gorgeous Dietrich, to her, is still an unconfirmed rumor.

Dietrich didn't. She's a jolly German girl, even more beautiful than sin, who was lured to this country, trained and groomed, and pushed before the camera. Paramount didn't fire the first gun—on the contrary, it fought for peace by demanding that their Miss Dietrich and Metro's Miss Garbo never be mentioned in the same ten breaths. Metro, of course, merely sat out in Culver City, smiling the smile of the Sphinx.

Yet the battle that no one started screams and thunders across this fair republic.

There is an old and toothless gag to the effect that it takes two sides to make a fight. This is strictly the old hooey, or, in the original Latin, the *phonus bollonus*.

IN the case of any argument, bickering or brannigan in which the name of Greta Garbo appears, only one side is sufficient to make a battle of major proportions. That, of course, is the side of the Garbo-maniacs, to whom the Beautiful Swede is only one hop, skip and jump from downright divinity—and sometimes not even that.

The history of the first skirmishes of the Garbo-Dietrich battle is brief and pointed.

Director Josef Von Sternberg "discovered,"—for the American screen—and brought to this country, a very beautiful German musical comedy and screen actress named Marlene Dietrich. The moment her first pictures appeared in the American press, there was a flurry. She bore a distinct resemblance, from some angles, to the current queen, Greta Garbo. She also resembled, in profile, the late Jeanne Eagles.

The Garbo-maniacs, raving mad in their idolatry, issued from their caves and began growling.

In due time Miss Dietrich's first American-made talkie appeared. "Morocco" was a labor of love and justification on the part of Director

The battle is on! Into the dugouts! A verbal barrage thunders over the charms and talents of Paramount's rising star and the goddess of M-G-M's studio

Von Sternberg. With infinite pains he had trained, rehearsed and projected his German find.

No question about it—Miss Dietrich showed definite Garboesque symptoms, at least in the minds of the Garbo fans. The critics remarked on it. The low growls of the Garbo devotees became shrieks, then roars.

THE beautiful German girl, new to the madnesses of Hollywood, lonely for her husband and little daughter in the Fatherland, just trying to make good for God, for country, for Von Sternberg, and for Marlene, became the focal point of a vocal and epistolary storm that is wrecking bridge games, tea fights, family gatherings and erstwhile happy American homes all over the nation.

A couple of months ago PHOTOPLAY stepped into a hornets' nest.

We printed an informative story about Miss Dietrich. It was entitled "She Threatens Garbo's Throne." It described the Prussian Peacherino, and definitely hinted that a potential rival to the solitary Swede was now on deck—another beauty, bursting with a similar allure, possessing more than a dash of screen mystery, and with a talent both wide and deep.

Bang! Sumter was fired on! The Maine had been sunk! The fatal shot was heard again at Sarajevo! Sheridan was at least thirty miles away! And the author, Katherine Albert, ran for her private cyclone cellar.

The Garbo-maniacs, to whom any mention of an actress in the same wheeze is sheer blasphemy, seized their pens, and clattered their typewriters like so many machine guns.

HEAR some shots from the barrage that has fallen on this trembling editorial dugout in the past month:

From M. L. K., of Detroit, Mich.:

"The woman to compete with Greta Garbo will not be born! Garbo to us is not a woman—she is a goddess. There will be one Garbo. Down with the imitators! *Vive la* Garbo!"

From Miss J. D. W., of Chicago, Ill.:

"Garbo's subjects are legion. If she ever descends from the throne, that throne, like Valentino's, will remain vacant! Long live the queen, Miss Greta Garbo!"

"A Garbo-Maniac," situate in Meridian, Miss., takes her fiery pen in hand:

"This Marlene [PLEASE TURN TO PAGE 271]

And here's the unwitting, or innocent, cause of the great Garbo-Dietrich war now raging—the beautiful Marlene herself. Do you think she looks like Garbo—that she's *trying* to resemble Garbo the Great? True, she's blonde, beautiful, mysterious and alluring. But so are several others. We vote that Marlene Dietrich is Marlene Dietrich, and no copy of anyone!

Is It Goodbye to Each Other as a Studio Team?

UNITED they stand, separated they shall fall! Hollywood is whispering this prediction about Josef Von Sternberg and Marlene Dietrich.

Can it be true that two vivid personalities set up an entity for each other—that one becomes a necessary complement to the other?

Before Von sailed away for his "holiday" in Europe, he told our reporter that he was through with pictures—"sick and tired of the silly stories which had been thrust upon him."

He went on to explain, however, that this did not mean he was through with studios or his own ideas about pictures. Von Sternberg claims his mind was trained along philosophic lines and that fiction is no material out of which to make movies.

He is going to see the world, absorb the feeling of the Orient, live in far-off places where he can shake the studio cobwebs from his mind and come back—sometime perhaps—with ideas which he shall develop. He makes no plans, living entirely on inspirations.

Marlene is his pet prodigy. Wasn't it Von who found her as a struggling nobody in Germany and with his genius eye perceived her possibilities?

Marlene says she realizes that without Von Sternberg's guidance she would no doubt have remained just where she was, in a drab little theater, trying vainly for a place in the sun.

When she left America some time ago, she, too, said she was through. But she wasn't, actually. She returned and when the legal battle with Paramount over breaking her contract was finally adjusted, Marlene went back

to Hollywood, like a dutiful little girl, to complete "Song of Songs" under Rouben Mamoulian's direction.

Will Marlene be content to remain in Hollywood under a strange director's tutelage? And if she does, will *any* director, except Von Sternberg, be able to bring out her ethereal loveliness as this one man has been able to do it?

When Marlene came to Hollywood she had already made "The Blue Angel," in Germany, under Von Sternberg's direction, and it was his camera eye which, little by little, developed the soulful qualities which stamp La Dietrich the orchidaceous lady of filmdom.

And Marlene is grateful. Yet, on the other hand, Von Sternberg's genius may never have impressed us if he had not found such promising material as Dietrich with which to work.

No Mickey Mouse!

*A*NN HARDING is now of and in pictures and prefers to stay. Pathe has placed the "million-dollar voice" under contract — and the million-dollar hair, too. Not to mention the million-dollar eyes!

PROBABLY the most highly praised young actress of the last few months—Barbara Stanwyck, who shot to emotional stardom on the strength of her unforgettably beautiful and moving performance in "Ladies of Leisure." This office is bombarded with letters praising her beauty and acting power. We all expect big things of you, Barbara!

What About Clara Bow?

Will the Immortal Flapper Learn Self-Discipline? Or Is She Fated to Dance Her Way to Oblivion?

By Leonard Hall

A demure little maiden as she looked in her first movie, "Down to the Sea in Ships." Yes — it's Clara Bow, the Flatbush Fury, in 1922

ONE RINGING question is agitating the all-wool, yard-wide, full-blown movie fans these days.

It's this—

What's to become of Clara Bow?

And this is no academic poser, either—set up for discussion over tea tables, coffee cups and soda-water bars. It's a live and lusty matter.

On the answer depends the cinematic fun of a good many thousand young folks, the financial interest of a great company for whom the Brooklyn fire-belle rings the cash register, and the fate of the arch-flapper herself.

Will she, in some mystic manner, acquire self-discipline so that she can whip her wilfulness and lack of judgment?

Or will she go on allowing her emotions to gallop off with good sense, and so bring her company, herself and her admirers sky-hooting into unhappiness and plenty of grief all 'round?

As this is written, Clara's being a good girl. After a headlong chase off the reservation, she's back on the lot with a picture to make. That's the time she's happiest and most tractable, for Clara's a trouper born. She tends strictly to her tatting while the cameras grind. When they stop, it's time to howl murder and leap for the cyclone cellars.

Clara's company and her fans and herself are just getting over a bad headache—and one which started to split skulls just as everything seemed entirely serene.

Consider the scene. The eternal and wearying Richman publicity had died to a murmur. Clara, whose billows had been causing wails and moans, had become slimmer and prettier than ever. A passable voice had suddenly popped out of that creamy throat.

The sun grinned down on Clara and her world. Birds sang, the sky was clear, and staid Paramount executives did gay tap-steps for sheer joy. B. P. Schulberg, one of the biggest and most patient of her bosses, announced with pride that Clara was going to be "The Anna Held of the Talkies."

Then, from the cloudless Heavens, lightning snapped and crackled.

Clara, between pictures, was in Dallas, Tex. Newspapers from Coast to Coast screamed a sad, unhappy tale. Reported settlement of an alienation suit brought by the wife of a young doctor—a story that Hollywood had heard and hushed long before. Denials and re-statements—wires from the West Coast suggesting that Clara come back to camp with buttoned lips. Instead, a hurried trip to New York, and more Harry Richman publicity.

A ferociously unhappy and miserable time for all concerned.

And the unhappiest thing about it all was that it was just another of the sorry chapters that have dotted the life and public career of this flaming, moody, undisciplined little girl who has filled screens, hearts and front pages for eight dizzy, dazing years!

CLARA, at the age of twenty-five, doesn't seem to have learned a thing about governing her life!

Still behaving like a headstrong high school girl with forbidden "dates" and wild "crushes"—still pouting when told to be at home by eleven or taste the hard side of pappy's hairbrush!

Is Clara not only going to be the immortal flapper—but the eternal flapper as well? Will she not soak up the indisputable fact that the didoes and fumadiddles which are cute and cunning at eighteen are only sad and unpleasant aberrations in a woman of twenty-five?

Of course, it is hard to blame Clara, in more ways than one.

She lost her mother when she was a young girl. Tasting fame and money, she galloped away—and there has never been a firm and trusted hand on the reins. [PLEASE TURN TO PAGE 275]

Gene Robert Richee

HOLLYWOOD'S wild, wilful, wistful little redhead—Clara Bow, the Brooklyn Bombshell! The delight of the flappers and the despair of her bosses, who goes from triumph to failure and up again before you can say Gustav Von Seyffertitz. What's going to happen to Clara? Will she profit by her errors, or is she starting down the steep chute to oblivion?

Bredell

IF she isn't First Lady of the Screen, just who is? Ruth Chatterton, poised and lovely as always, as she looks in her latest Paramount picture, "Unfaithful." Ruth has signed a sensational contract with Warners, to take effect when her present agreement expires next fall. Read the why and wherefore across the way

"I Want To Live Happily Ever After"

Says Ruth Chatterton, when asked questions about her new contract

By Ruth Biery

IF you were offered three-quarters of a million dollars for two years' work with the possibility of a million and three-quarters for four years, what would you do?

Oddly enough, Ruth Chatterton took it. And by taking it from one company while she yet had three pictures to make for another, she exploded one of the biggest bombs ever dropped into Hollywood—not excluding those used in "All Quiet on the Western Front" and "Hell's Angels."

Ruth Chatterton's signing with Warner Bros. in *January*, when she is under contract to Paramount until *October*, has been considered unethical by many. I have personally heard at least a dozen people criticize it in language which left nothing to the imagination.

Why all the excitement?

Because there is supposed to be an agreement among motion picture producers that the company employing a star should have first option on her services when present contract arrangements have expired. That is, according to this mythical arrangement, Warner Bros. had no right to negotiate with Ruth Chatterton until Paramount had finished negotiations with her.

Any such agreement must do away with competitive bidding among producers for contract players! It must definitely keep the salary scale for stars *down* rather than letting the box-office determine the figure. We remember the day when Gloria Swanson was offered twenty thousand a week for her services. That was because her box-office value at that time was so great that the company could afford to pay it. Whether the agreement has existed or not, it is true that salaries have gone down since the days of the Swanson offer.

RUTH CHATTERTON'S box-office receipts? Among the greatest of any cinema star. In three years her pictures have grown in popularity until Warner Bros. signed her for three-quarters of a million dollars, flat, for two years' work and took an option on her for the next two years at a million.

"I've had no battle with Paramount," she told me. "I have none now. They have been marvelous to me. They have given me by courtesy what Warner Bros. give me by contract. All except money. I mean, I have sat in on every story conference —helped produce my own pictures.

"I cannot understand all the excitement of this move! They made me an offer. I turned it down. I took an offer of twice as much. Is there anything wrong in that?

"As for the gamble Paramount took on me?—Of course they took a gamble. A tremendous gamble. And I appreciate it, but appreciation does not make me independent. Money does. At the end of two years more I can really live without working.

"It is true that Paramount signed me when they didn't know whether I would be a loss or an asset to them. I had been out here for months hunting work. I was so broke that I had to borrow money from my manager to live. In fact, I would have returned to Broadway and given up the thought of pictures forever if it had not been for his faith in me.

"I told him I must get work soon. My funds were getting lower and lower. Months passed. 'I will have to go back to Broadway while I have enough to get there,' I told my manager. Several plays were offered me in New York.

"'Wait!' he urged. 'It is only a matter of a few months. How much do you need?'

"His belief was encouraging—especially since it was a belief which went so far as to offer me money. I told him I needed $1,500 a month to live as an actress should live in Hollywood. I signed my contract in June, 1928. He had loaned me $7,500. It was *his* belief which made Paramount gamble. I cannot help but feel that my pictures have repaid Paramount. It has hurt more than I like to say that people have said I am ungrateful to those who believed in me."

WHAT is Ruth going to do when her contract is finished?

"I am going to retire. I may produce a play or a picture; direct one, perhaps. But no more acting. Whether my contract lasts the four years or ends with the second, I will have enough to live in comfort the rest of my life. The only luxury I want is complete comfort.

"France. A villa a few miles from Paris. I have a friend who has one. Thirty acres with hunting preserves. A house which he has made modern with bathrooms and furnishings but which still has the old medieval appearance and feeling. And what do you suppose this place cost?—" she laughed. "Including original purchase price, improvements, furnishings— $20,000. That is my idea of luxury. Servants at $25 a month. Time to read and relax and enjoy while you are still young enough to enjoy. Six months in a chateau like this; six months in this country—California. No worries—no responsibilities.

"Four more years of real work. Good pictures. I want to make my last three for Paramount my best to date. I want them to make all the money they can from me. But I am not sorry about any of the other—I appreciate what they did for me. They gave me the opportunity to retire in four years and live *happily ever after*. Which is the dream of us all!"

Those Amazing Bennett Girls

AMAZER Number One. That girl Constance, svelte, sophisticated, charming, and making it pay her $30,000 a week. Earning twenty times what her veteran stage father does, and known to more people in a few years than her dad in his stage lifetime, she is virtually the head of the clan

SISTER JOAN is lovely, beguiling, youthful, a different type than the enchantress beside her, yet a star in her own right, collecting $2,000 a week, and a mother. She pursues her career with the same intensity that moves Constance and seems only to be getting into stride now on her upward climb

Hal Phyfe

HAL PHYFE, famous New York photographer, coaxed Janet Gaynor and Charlie Farrell before a lens on the Fox lot. "Give me that '7th Heaven' look!" he pleaded. "Be *Diane* and *Chico* for Uncle Hal!" They gave all—and isn't the result a stunning picture?

IF she gets the right breaks in stories and direction Tallulah Bankhead will become one of the really outstanding personalities of motion pictures.

Ernest A. Bachrach

"BRING on your leading ladies with all their glamour and sophistication," says Bob Montgomery. "I guess I haven't forgotten the gentle art of scene stealing." So we present for your approval (and how you approve!) the famous Montgomery smile with which Bob has so neatly walked away with many a picture

JOHNNY WEISSMULLER rose to fame on the strength of his handsome physique, and lovely ladies, the world over, have gambled with each other ever since for a permanent mortgage on the brawny, tawny *Tarzan*.   First, 'twas Bobbe Arnst, who held claim, then Lupe Velez, and now who shall it be?

Eugene Robert Richee

THE princess looks unhappy! Even with Mae West's ex-boy
friend trying to get her in a good humor. Maybe the thirty days
are almost up! Or maybe an air of dejected disinterest is a brunette's
way of vamping. Anyhow, Cary Grant is falling. Bet in another minute
Sylvia Sidney will smile. They're teamed in "Thirty Day Princess"

● Would you know him? Not with that beard—well maybe! It is George Arliss, costumed in scarlet fur-trimmed robes for the title rôle in "Cardinal Richelieu." Arliss returned from England where he made "The Iron Duke" to begin work on the Twentieth Century film version of the dramatic character

GRAYBILL

Wally Beery, the well-read man, in the library of his new home.
Wally is still on his personal appearance tour, and back at M-G-M
there's a list of pictures scheduled for him that's about this long!

Norma Shearer can well afford to look regal with all of us clamoring for her more loudly than ever. She wears this knockout negligée in ''A Free Soul,'' which you must see. It's tangerine velvet, girls, with one of those trains that is simply ''tripping''!

Milton Brown

SWEET as a June morning is this first photograph of Norma Shearer, waiting at the garden gate, in a scene from "Smilin' Through." Remember when Jane Cowl created the rôle on the stage, followed by Norma Talmadge's interpretation in the silents? What a change from the neurotic heroine as we see Miss Shearer in "Strange Interlude"!

That so very bright star, "Mr. Deeds" Cooper, goes back to adventuring in his next, "Chinese Gold," with the regal English star, Madeleine Carroll

THE *Camera* SPEAKS

Sincerest form of flattery, as practiced by Sandra Shaw Cooper — accompanying husband Gary to Arizona for location scenes of Samuel Goldwyn's "The Westerner" — is to copy the suède jacket Gary himself wears in the title role

Coburn

Gangster

One thinks of Edward G. Robinson as interested in shooting galleries, not art galleries, but his collection of paintings is famous. He prefers historical rôles but Warner's like him as a big shot, so his next is "The Man Behind"

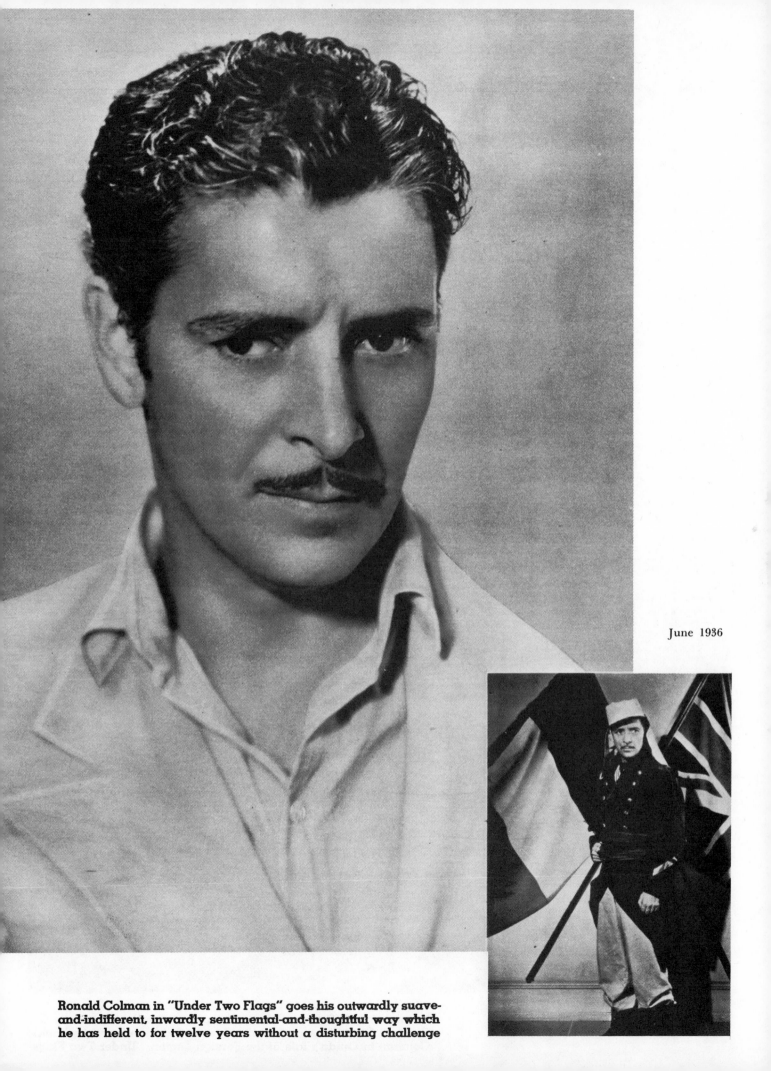

June 1936

Ronald Colman in "Under Two Flags" goes his outwardly suave-and-indifferent, inwardly sentimental-and-thoughtful way which he has held to for twelve years without a disturbing challenge

KORNMAN

Loaned to 20th Century-Fox by Paramount, Parisian Claudette Colbert is right at home as the mischievous Cigarette (opposite Ronald Colman) in Ouida's tale of the Foreign Legion, "Under Two Flags"

Hurrell

IS it necessary to tell you that this handsome, hand-holding pair are Joan Crawford and Doug Fairbanks, Jr.? Both are making remarkable screen progress these days. Maybe it's love!

The Girl with the Haunted Face

By Hale Horton

YOU have seen that haunted face on the billboards, on the screen and in magazines and newspapers. The face of Joan Crawford. You know those too-big, searching eyes, that full mouth which seems to have known suffering, and those gaunt cheeks. Around the studios you'll hear that the Crawford expression is a pose, an attempt to imitate Garbo, a rank affectation. And yet it seems to me that that haunted look could come only from some inherent loneliness or some terrible, futile yearning for a goal beyond reach.

Let us study the woman behind that face—Joan Crawford herself. As this is written she is suffering. She is searching for happiness, but deep down in her heart she believes that she will never find it.

"Happiness to me," she explains, "means peace of mind, which of course is a mental state. And I know that unless I acquire it pretty soon I'll have a severe and protracted nervous breakdown. And yet, on the other hand, if I *should* find a certain peace of mind, it would mean I had come to a point in my life where I no longer cared to develop. In other words I would be standing still, simply existing—for to develop is to live, to stand still is to exist, and to go backwards is death. Obviously, if I arrived at a point in my life where I was standing still, it wouldn't be long until I went backwards . . . . . in the meantime some peculiar force keeps forever pulling me on and on, until I think I shall die unless I find rest."

So Joan is driven on toward tragedy in a wild search for a state of being, which, if she paused for breath, she might find within herself! And the driving force of her life is fear. Haunting, harrowing fear. A fear that develops from a terrible inferiority complex. And Joan knows it.

"I have one of those things all right," she nods. "And I mean it truly. I'm not saying it merely for effect. Perhaps I thought that since I was born without the advantages enjoyed by other girls it would be necessary for me to accomplish something outstanding in order to become their equal. So I determined on a dancing career.

"After the first thrill of achievement, however, I realized that dancing alone was inadequate, that I must look elsewhere if I would taste real happiness, if I would fill that queer, aching void in my soul. I then decided to become an actress. Surely *that* would bring me the respect of the world! But somehow it left me dissatisfied. And since one invariably fears the unknown, I live each day in fear of the future."

Unless curbed, the fierce driving force of the girl, her utter inability to relax, is certain to leave her with a nervous breakdown. Indeed, she fully expects one, although her mania for "development" has left her with no conception of the phrase "over work."

"WHILE making 'Possessed,'" she relates, "I wept each morning on my drive to the studio and I wept all the way back home. And I found it impossible to sleep at nights even though I had a horror of staying awake forever thinking! So I'd lie in bed, contemplating the future. I fear it with all my heart and soul even as I fear the dark.

"I no longer enjoy parties, as I find the inaction and light pleasantries unbearably jarring on my nerves. And when I do attend them, wild thoughts run through my head. On occasion I feel that I must get into my car and speed through the night over some lonely road. Such thoughts fill me with terror and as a result I act on them at once. Naturally people are beginning to think I have gone

a little cuckooo. I'm sorry, but I find a certain consolation in these wild night drives; and especially as my car roars along the road by the ocean, susceptible to my slightest whim, fully under my control, I feel that I'm Lord of All.

"Watching the white foam lash the rocks, I order my car to move faster and faster as though to rush away from the terror of the night even as it hems me in. And during those moments I nearly fool myself into believing that I've succeeded in crushing that restless urge, that I've found peace.

"Sometimes I think that perhaps I'm just going through a period of unrest, and yet sooner or later I always realize that I am not only *not* going through a period of unrest, but that my nature has been the same since the day I was born, that I've always known this fear of the future, this haunting fear which drives me on and on . . ."

And unless Joan realizes that peace is to be found within a person and not necessarily in material achievement, it rather looks as though her life will develop into one mad, futile quest for some Holy Grail that her lips will never touch. Fortunately, through the teachings of a friend, she is beginning to understand the truth.

"When these moods are upon me," she continued, seeming to relax a bit, "I often telephone to a dear friend and beg him to come over. He possesses a great mind and the rare ability to listen. He lets me rave on about my troubles, troubles which to such a man as he must seem pitifully small, and when I calm down he invariably says, 'I understand perfectly. That's quite natural,

Joan Crawford says:

"I was born with such a terrible inferiority complex that I must keep doing things to retain my self-respect. Now I'm a star, and yet that mysterious force keeps urging me on and on.

"Marriage gave me a tolerance and patience that up to then I had never known, but it has not killed that force which drives me on day and night.

"It would be impossible for me to enjoy having my husband place me on a pedestal and worship me. I never could sit home day after day and wait patiently for my husband's return at night.

"Don't think because I have failed to find a certain illusive state of mind, I necessarily want to try another marriage. No one else is to blame. It's all me.

"Perhaps there is a new experience which, when I find and conquer it, will satisfy this longing of mine. In the meantime, I must try to develop.

"Perhaps if I learn to believe in myself I shall lose my fear of the future."

Joan.' He never makes me feel that I'm acting in anything but a normal manner, that I'm doing anything wrong.

"The other day he brought over a book called 'In Tune with the Infinite,' which has helped me through moments of darkest despondency. It's not that I'm necessarily getting religion. It's only that I'm gradually learning to *believe* in things, in life, in people, and most especially in myself. This friend, as well as the book, is making me realize that unless you believe in a thing you can never understand it, and as a result it frightens you. Furthermore he's teaching me to laugh at myself by explaining why it's foolish to take life so hard. Perhaps if I learn to believe in myself utterly and to chuckle at myself when I'm doing something perfectly absurd, I shall lose my fear of the future. Perhaps I'm finding a permanent relief. If so, I shall face life bravely."

And now, do you consider the hungry, haunting look of Joan Crawford's face to be nothing but a superficial mannerism shrewdly acquired for the purpose of increasing her box-office value—or do you feel it reflects the torturing doubt in her soul?

Joan has always known sorrow, but being an intelligent, as well as a courageous woman, she may eventually find happiness.

No one can touch the gorgeous Crawford for consistent glamour. Perhaps it's because Joan continues to grow, mentally, and dramatically. Her newest enthusiasm is music, and when she isn't running her home, playing the title rôle in "The Last of Mrs. Cheyney," or improving her badminton, she is learning operatic rôles

Parties are not the same in Hollywood these days due to the illness of Carole Lombard, unique for her gaiety, charm and wit. Forbidden to go to Alaska for "Spawn of the North," Carole is being good taking a rest cure and gaining weight like mad now

Why Women *Go* Crazy

ON the screen Clark Gable meets every woman with a challenge in his eyes, a mocking grin culminating in a laughing dimple, an aloofness that is not far distant, and a skillful parry for every attempt to throw him off his guard. An adroit opponent in a duel of sex

About Clark Gable

By
James R. Quirk

Clark Gable has some of the qualities that made Valentino the one great idol of the screen. But it is doubtful if he will ever approach the unprecedented heights of Rudy's romantic appeal

CLARK GABLE is the male sensation of the screen today because in every rôle he has played the part of a man who fears neither Jack Dempsey nor Peggy Joyce.

He is a caveman with a club in one hand and a book of poetry in the other.

Here is no tender lover, strumming sweet love songs; no smitten cavalier throwing his mantle over a puddle to save the tender tootsies of his fair one; no ga-ga stripling crying life is o'er lest the sweet object of his tender affections will not permit him to dedicate his life, liberty and fortune to her eternal whimsies.

In one short year he has made most phenomenal and dazzling progress. He may never achieve the heights of romantic idolatry of Valentino, nor the year-in and year-out box office assurance of Chaplin or Fairbanks; but there is no one man on the screen today whose personality so intrigues the feminine audience.

A strange phenomenon of feminine psychology, the almost instantaneous success of this new type of lover. Note that I did not use the word "hero." For Clark Gable's popularity does not rest upon the foundation of noble deeds, tender passion, nor self-sacrifice. As a lover he begins with indifference, demands utter submission, and ends with either complete and uncompromising domination or defeat. And there is no defeat in him save death.

Ace Wilfong, in "Free Soul," was the apex of a series of such characterizations. *Jan* (Norma Shearer), refined and fragile, glories in her infatuation for the man to whose will she must and did yield. The character of the noble self-sacrificing, and honorable lover, played by Leslie Howard, a much more artistic and ver-

It was "The Sheik" that made Valentino the most glamorous personality on the screen. In that picture his wooing of Agnes Ayres was no more gentle than the motion picture love technique that Clark Gable uses with such dazzling success today

satile actor, paled into insignificance in his final victory.

Is it that the ladies and gentlemen of the audience have been fed up with too much super-human nobility, hearts of gold, and all that sort of thing in our motion picture actors?

How often have we watched some nin-com-poop of a fair damsel treat the self-sacrificing and languishing hero like a sap, and make him go through all kinds of hell to come into a close-up with her at the finish, when all the time we wanted to tip him off that she was a selfish, dizzy dame, and not worth the effort?

On the screen Clark Gable meets every woman with a challenge in his eyes, a mocking grin culminating in a laughing dimple, an aloofness that is not far distant, and a skillful parry for every attempt to throw him off his guard. An adroit opponent in a duel of sex.

It is that uncertainty about him, that self-assuredness, that indifference that interests women. He is like a magnet that both attracts and repels. That complex mystery, woman, is baffled

[PLEASE TURN TO PAGE 278]

M·G·M is now known as the House of One Gable, but what a Gable that boy Clark is! Starting in obscure, menace-man parts, he is now Garbo's leading man in the hectic production of "Susan Lenox." He's just promised to love and cherish for the second time

Wide World

HERE, arriving at a Hollywood premiere with her husband, is the lady you all want to see: Mrs. Clark Gable, formerly Mrs. M. Franklin Langham of New York City. She isn't an actress, never has been and doesn't want to be

WHAT'S this—a pinch, and Mae West trying to yarn her way out of it? Well, not quite. They happened to have time out one day while filming "She Done Him Wrong," and Mae just naturally gathered in the coppers who function in the show and started telling them a few good ones. You can judge for yourself whether she got over

MAE WEST makes a glorious, if somewhat buxom, rosebud in all her
floral finery for a burlesque show scene in "It Ain't No Sin."
Not a thorn in sight, and surely Mae couldn't conceal one in that gown.
She is known as "the American Beauty" in her new Paramount picture,
which takes us back to the curves and capers of the Naughty Nineties

"KATIE Takes Sock——"
     "'Break of Hearts' Cold——"
     "Hepburn Opens With That Tired
Feeling——"
     "'Hearts' Is 'No Dice'——"

With such colloquially colorful but pithy
headlines did *Variety*, that shrewd Bible of box-office, record
the popular fate of Katharine Hepburn's last picture, "Break
of Hearts."

No undue mental strain is required to deduce that its reception wasn't so hot.

At the great Music Hall in New York City, where the same
Katie in "Little Women" reaped $110,000 in one week, this
year's big Hepburn picture struggled for half that amount.
In every "key city"—Pittsburgh, Kansas City, Baltimore,
Seattle—all over the nation, to speak in trade terms of the

No actress was ever welcomed to the screen with greater enthusiasm than Katharine Hepburn. And yet, today she is slipping

motion picture business, Hepburn disappointed or Hepburn died.

Still "Break of Hearts," as you know if
you saw it, was a good picture. And Katharine Hepburn's performance in it was one of
the most brilliant of her career.

Why should the admittedly great actress who was the sensation of last year loom as the outstanding floppo of this? Why
should this glorious girl who had them all standing in the
aisles a few months ago with her striking art and her vivid
personality, flash the same thing, the very same thing, on
the screen today and leave the ushers playing solitaire on the
empty seats?

Why should Katie Hepburn, who won more new fervent
fans and worshipping admirers than any actress in a decade,
who leaped out of nowhere to rival Garbo in divine devotion

Is HEPBURN Killing Her Own Career?

The ring-a-round-a-rosy tactics of Katharine may result in another famous case of a star's decline

By KIRTLEY BASKETTE

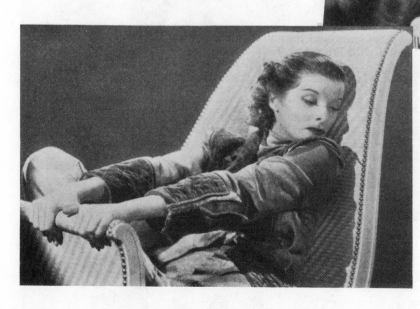

Her film, "Break of Hearts," with Charles Boyer was a good picture. But, somehow, movie-goers didn't bother to go and see it

For a long time Hepburn's worshipping public thought her caprices cute. But now many think she held her one-ring circus too long

with "Morning Glory," prove to be just that, in the lingo of the race tracks—a "morning glory"—burning up the turf at the start and wilting in the backstretch?

Is something killing her career? Or is she killing it herself? Do Hollywood stars commit career suicide?

Do they hang themselves with their own gayly spun webs of eccentricities — acts — attitudes — poses — temperamental displays? Are they killed by the very people who most want to protect them, because those people subconsciously block their paths?

Like Garbo at M-G-M and Dietrich at Paramount, Hepburn is the "prestige" star at RKO. A Hepburn picture rates right at the front of the program. Her pictures carry a *carte blanche* to be best preparation, production, direction and exploitation that that large organization can muster. Every resource of art, money and brains is beneath her to push her up—up. Yet plainly she is slipping. Figures tell few fibs at the box-office.

The public demands little of its idols—movie or otherwise—these days—except sincerity.   [PLEASE TURN TO PAGE 276]

WOULD you take him for a master of laughs? Or a chap who totes stenographers around the office when they call him Buster? Well, the serious visage above is the foundation upon which Charles Laughton builds his powerful studies, comic and otherwise. At the right, is the "home body" side, with Mrs. Laughton. The opposite page tells of his whimsies

Such A Naughty Nero

And he's just as roguish in the studio as he often is on the screen

By Barbara Barry

AN English accent, mind you, on that old tyrant, Nero! It's too funny. The audience, attending the preview of "The Sign of the Cross," howled with laughter. Rolled right out into the aisles, they did. Wailed hysterically on one another's shoulders. Blasé Hollywood simply went wild. And with just cause.

Charles Laughton, our popular English acquisition, has done a refreshingly original job in characterizing the witless emperor, who fiddled on three strings while naughty Rome stewed in its own juice. And how he loved doing it!

You saw him man-handle Tallulah Bankhead, smash up a perfectly good submarine, and drown himself, with blood-curdling sound effects, in "Devil and the Deep." You saw him murder an innocent bystander and lay him among the sweet peas of his own back yard, in "Payment Deferred."

As madly Neronian as ever Nero managed to be—yet using a broad English accent that bowled them over laughing! Isn't that just the turn you might expect, though, from Charles Laughton, shown here as he appeared in "The Sign of the Cross"?

And all the time—even while he sneered and slaughtered—this Laughton chap had a wistful eye on the grinning mask of Comedy. Yearning for a chance to make folks laugh. If murder must be done, he argued, why couldn't it be accomplished by allowing the victims to laugh themselves to death? There you are. A nice clean murder, you know. Splendid! as Charlie himself would put it.

WORKING as desk clerk at the Claridge Hotel, in London, Laughton had an excellent opportunity to study the various types of humanity that passed in review before his discerning eye.

He knew them all. Peered beneath the veneer of civilization and beheld the elemental qualities that made them what they were—plodder, fop, sophisticate.

His tolerant understanding of human nature makes it possible for him to portray the widely diversified rôles he has assumed, so successfully.

For this reason, Charles Laughton need never be "typed," as the casting directors say.

Watching his work on the screen, you are probably convinced that the man himself must be a great deal like his characterizations. Stolid . . . prosaic . . . even a bit sinister. Which is decidedly not the case.

His ability to submerge his own personality so completely, in favor of the character he is portraying, marks him as one of the chosen few. Incomparable. The real McCoy.

The real Laughton is a revelation. In private life, this genial Englishman is a direct contradiction to his screen self. Unselfish, unspoiled, and with a humor as rare as it is subtle, he is a delightful, unforgettable personality.

My own first impression of the man was more or less hysterical.

He sat in the office of Paramount's publicity manager and scattered "still" pictures about the floor with a dead-pan nonchalance that sent the lady p.m. into immediate hysterics.

"*Char*-lee!" she squealed protestingly.

Char-lee's left eyebrow quivered almost imperceptibly. Apparently, he heard nothing. More stills fluttered to the floor and curled about his ankles like a sophomore's socks. His expression was one of gentle dignity and refinement.

"*Char-lee!*" the lady p.m. begged. "Stop that!"

CHARLEE stopped, because there were no more stills to be dropped. Calmly, he inspected the systematic arrangement of publicity paraphernalia on the desk.

His roving eye, with the faintest suggestion of a twinkle, lighted upon a miniature file case.

He pounced. The p.m. pounced. And won by an eyelash.

Char-lee sighed profoundly. A page of studio news caught his attention. Deliberately, he stooped to peruse it.

One paragraph described, in glowing terms, the unselfish magnanimity of one Charles Laughton, who had, voluntarily, arranged with the Powers-that- [PLEASE TURN TO PAGE 275]

Bert Longworth

LIFE is like that; only a few years ago Ruby Keeler stepped out of the Ziegfeld spotlight so hubby Al Jolson might enjoy his own un-shadowed glory. Now that Al has quit pictures, Ruby is having her break. She did so well in "42nd Street," she rated a choice spot with Dick Powell in "Gold Diggers of 1933." Ruby was a Texas Guinan girl

LOOKS like manslaughter—in the "old Spanish custom" manner. The young lady with the sharp knife and an evil glint in her eye is Jean Parker. And the strong-armed gentleman, getting rough in self-defense, is Charles Boyer. A dramatic scene from Fox's "Caravan"

William A. Fraker

THE movies borrowed Grace Moore from grand opera, and now they don't
want to let her go back! It's rumored that Miss Moore may combine the two
arts, making a film version of Bizet's opera, "Carmen." The beautiful young actress
with the golden voice recently scored a hit in Columbia's "One Night of Love"

56   November 1934

Bert Longworth

Latin Glamour

Dolores Del Rio is one star whose glamour does not dim when she's out of her screen setting. A cameraman caught her unawares this time, when she was resting between scenes of "In Caliente." But had she been specially posed for a portrait, Dolores couldn't have looked more alluring

The distaff side wins when Bing goes formal to step out with Dixie

For a guy who hates work, the activities of Bing Crosby, Inc., are many and varied

Bing and Franciska Gaal in "Paris Honeymoon"

CLOSE UP OF
THE
GROANER

Gary, the eldest (next to Bing), is the self-imposed dictator of the twins, Phillip (left) and Dennis (opposite page)

Painted by a master—a picture of that small-town boy, Boo-boo Bing, who steps out of these hilarious pages in startling reality

BY CLAUDE BINYON

The author of this story, one of Holly-wood's most famous dialogue writers, has turned out such hits as "I Met Him in Paris," "Sing, You Sinners" and, now the sequel, "Sing Some More."

YOU can be a writer and like an actor without wanting to write his next picture, and that's the way I was with Bing. A Crosby picture was a thing with singing in it; nobody seemed to care who did what to anybody in the story so long as The Groaner was giving with his throat. That hurt the pride of a lot of writers.

But here Bing was at his Del Mar Race track, ambling about with a bad small-town haircut, wearing those short, flaring sweaters that his wife keeps throwing away, flashing a large button on his chest reading: "Cool Head Main Thing." And there were the solid, human people of the California coast, his friends, talking to him and listening, and none of it about pictures.

The haircut was a thing to see. Bing didn't have enough hair left to lure a flea off a Mexican hairless.

"How did you get it?" I asked him, awed.

The Groaner shrugged. "The barber and I got to talking . . ." he said.

There was another insight when Bing and the postmaster talked it over.

"Things ain't good yet," said the postmaster, concerned. "Second-class mail's fallen way off lately."

"Maybe it's just laziness," said Bing. "I'm getting so I hate to mail a letter myself."

What I'm getting at is that this Bing Crosby wasn't the guy in the pictures. He had character and he looked like a patch quilt—if he got out of the house without his wife seeing him. He was the fellow in every small town who loved life and hated work and would never amount to a darn.

That was more like it. Wesley Ruggles and I talked to Bing about playing that small-town character, bad clothes and all, and Bing was more than ready. Thinking of the character he had inspired, I started writing and forgot Bing. When people asked me what I was writing I told them it was about a smalltown bum. People, meanwhile, were asking Bing. He said I was writing the story of his life.

Once, when we were together, we were confronted by our statements. Bing shrugged. "We're both right," he said. . . .

THAT was the start of the film "Sing, You Sinners," and, when it was previewed, critics said Bing was an actor. He refused to believe it.

Early in the picture he was studying a scene, dubiously. "Look," he said finally, "don't put too much stuff for me in these scenes. I do two kinds of acting—loud and soft."

When Bing learned that Fred MacMurray was to share starring honors with him in the picture, he grinned. "Write plenty of scenes for him," he suggested. "Remember—I live near a golf course."

The Groaner loves big words and has a knack with them. There was the spot in the picture where he was supposed to say simply: "I'm going to Los Angeles."

In rehearsal he flourished and let loose: "Let no foul hurdles besmirch my path, Mother. I'm furbishing my little kit for that excruciating trek to the provocative hamlet of the angels."

His screen mother stared. "Is that in?" she asked.

"I'm sorry," said Bing. "I'm still going to Los Angeles."

Another of his rehearsal pastimes is to sail off on a tangent, playing a scene quite unlike the one in the script. He may start a harmless love scene and wind up as a one-eyed panhandler, begging for five-dollar bills on the streets of Minneapolis.

Actors love to get that heady feeling, and in short order the entire cast may be playing a scene entirely foreign to the one in the picture. Then the director calls for work—and Bing is the only one who knows the lines in the actual scene. Whereupon he stands beside the director and chides the actors for lack of diligence.

By automobile The Groaner goes from point to point in amazingly short time. When questioned, he expounds a method of judging traffic signal changes so accurately that he need never stop. I've ridden with him and he's a liar on all counts.

Those who have seen his broadcasts are first shocked by his weirdly careless style of dress; then charmed by his complete ease of manner. He often has sung of love with gum on his tongue and a pipe clamped between his teeth.

(Continued on page 276)

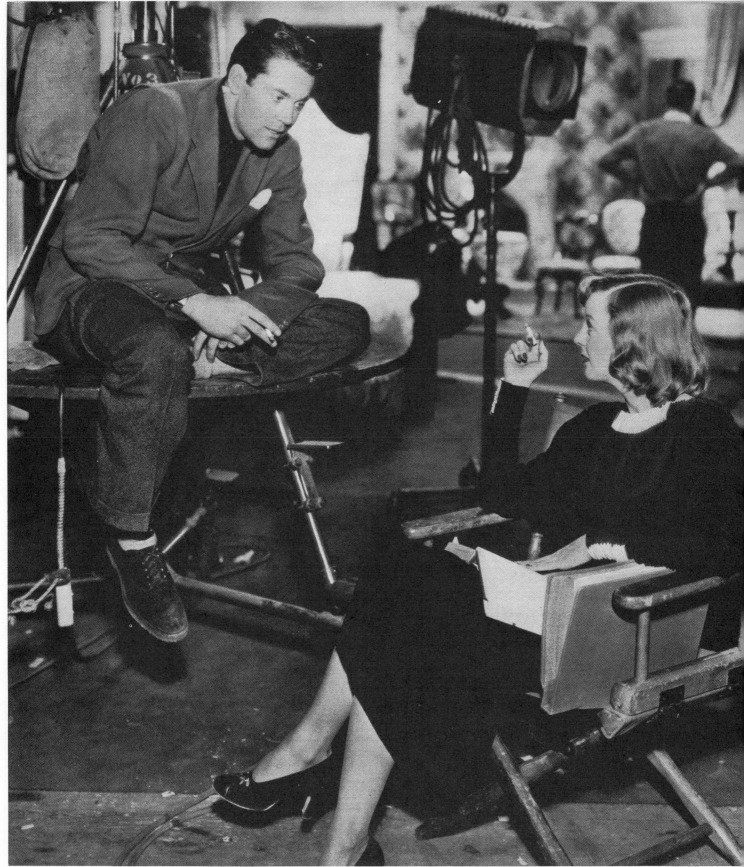

ELLIOTT

MARGARET SULLAVAN recently announced that she was divorced from her second husband, Director William Wyler. When she announced that, she was busy at Paramount making "The Moon's Our Home" with Henry Fonda. On the set he's "Hank" to her; she's "Sullavan" to him. Once upon a time, not so long ago, they acted together on the stage, and lived together off-stage—husband and wife—Mr. and Mrs. Henry Fonda.

Then the giddy wheel of Hollywood drama brought them together again, Margaret, Mrs. William Wyler, wife of one of Hollywood's most distinguished directors, and "Hank" playing the field, with preferences for Shirley Ross, and lately, they say, Jeanette MacDonald.

But in "The Moon's Our Home," "Hank" and "Sullavan" marry again. On the set they chat together constantly between scenes and play checkers. Henry always wins and Margaret always burns. But outside of the checkerboard blues, her fractious Irish disposition seems to be improved by the association. Husband Willy Wyler never has visited the set.

What can "Hank" and "Sullavan" be thinking as they gaze into each other's eyes?

WHAT'S HAPPENED TO

RAINER ?

In this rare interview with the famed

but elusive Award winner, she answers

a question all Hollywood is asking

BY SARA HAMILTON

THEY speak of it in Hollywood as the eclipse of Rainer.

"In heaven's name, what has happened to Rainer?" Hollywood kept repeating between its recessions and retrenchments. "Where is she? What's happened to her? Is it true that she'll never make another picture? Where is she hiding and why?"

After Luise's appearance in "Big City," a picture greeted by the public with a strange mixture of wonder and bewilderment, the little actress suddenly dropped from the limelight. As weeks rolled into months and still nothing was heard of Rainer, who, in her two short years in Hollywood had turned in two of the screen's finest performances, it became almost an accepted fact that little Rainer had been just another luminary that had come and gone.

And then with unexpected suddenness something happened. Rainer appeared out of her obscurity to become again the focus of all eyes in Hollywood. For Rainer was about to make screen history when the Academy Award was given the actress the second time in her short screen life for her performance in "Good Earth," Rainer's rôle in "The Great Ziegfeld" having won her the first award.

"How could an actress that good be neglected and almost forgotten?" Hollywood wondered, and again took up the old question of, "What happened to Rainer?" Why hadn't the studio given the public more of this acclaimed star? Why let her step into forgotten oblivion for almost a year at a time?

IN one of her very rare interviews given a few days after the Academy Banquet, Luise told us exactly what had happened to her. Slender as a reed, her dark eyes glowing with much life within, Luise sat in the dressing room that had once belonged to Jean Harlow and told us this story.

"Three years ago I came into a new life. From my native Vienna I came to America, a new country, a new language and new work. I had never made a motion picture. Never faced a camera. Always I had worked on the stage.

"Exactly as some people choose painting, some writing to give what they have to others, I chose acting as my form of expression. So, after four years on the stage, I came to Holly-wood and went to work. All the little things that came up and seemed so important to the studio I pushed aside as not necessary. Looking over my stills and photographs, giving so much time to publicity and interviews, seemed small things beside my desire to give something really warm and living and understanding to people.

"Gradually I began to see I was but a part of a huge business. So big, the individual became lost in the great mass of machinery. The studio had me under contract and I must work even if there was nothing suitable for me. All this is not their fault, I see that now. They must make pictures and I am here under contract. What is there to do?

"But one day they decide I should be glamorous. 'Oh my god,' I cried, 'don't make me glamorous.' There are so many lovely girls here, so many, I tell them. Please just let me act from the heart and pay no attention to the outward. But after 'Good Earth' they were afraid the public might think I am homely and can play only such rôles.

"So for 'The Emperor's Candlesticks' they wanted me to be glamorous—which is something I can't be. It weighed me down more than the character of O-Lan in 'Good Earth.' I was unhappy. I thought of all the things in my life I want to do. The world is so big—not just here before a camera in Hollywood—but so big a world and people waiting—I began to feel that I must get away from Hollywood, not to become terribly unhappy."

"I felt as if cameramen on the set whispered and looked at me, saying, 'She looks strange to me this morning.' I thought to myself with heavy heart, well, this is my face. I can't help it if I'm not glamorous. What has that got to do with my rôle? And again I begged them not to try to make me glamorous.

"Then they gave me another story. I didn't like it much.

"'No, no, I can't,' I said. 'Please let us do a right one. Not one on just a chance.' But, of course, I did not understand the studio's viewpoint that pictures must be made and often cannot wait for the right story.

"WHEN I saw my great plans going, I knew not where, I lost all perspective. I grew ill. My mental confusion made me ill physically. I would not talk. I could not sleep. I could not eat. I grew thinner and more ill. All life seemed blank despair to me.

"Of course my studio could not understand why I should not go on. 'Is she difficult?' they said, and I wasn't being difficult. I was suffering mentally, physically, spiritually because I felt my whole world had crashed around me.

"No one knows this but I went away to a little town outside of New York, a place my husband found for me, and I stayed there many months. Dark, black months in which all sense of values was gone. I tell you I was in despair.

"Gradually, as I regained some of my lost

(Continued on page 85)

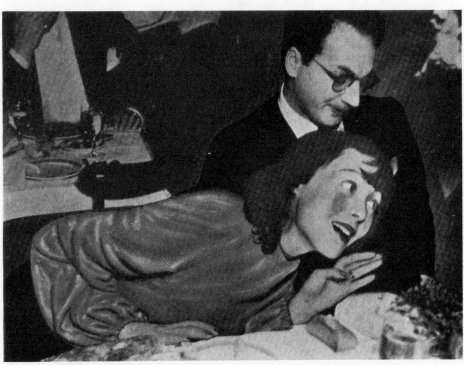

Hollywood wondered about her marriage to Clifford Odets. Luise herself explains it

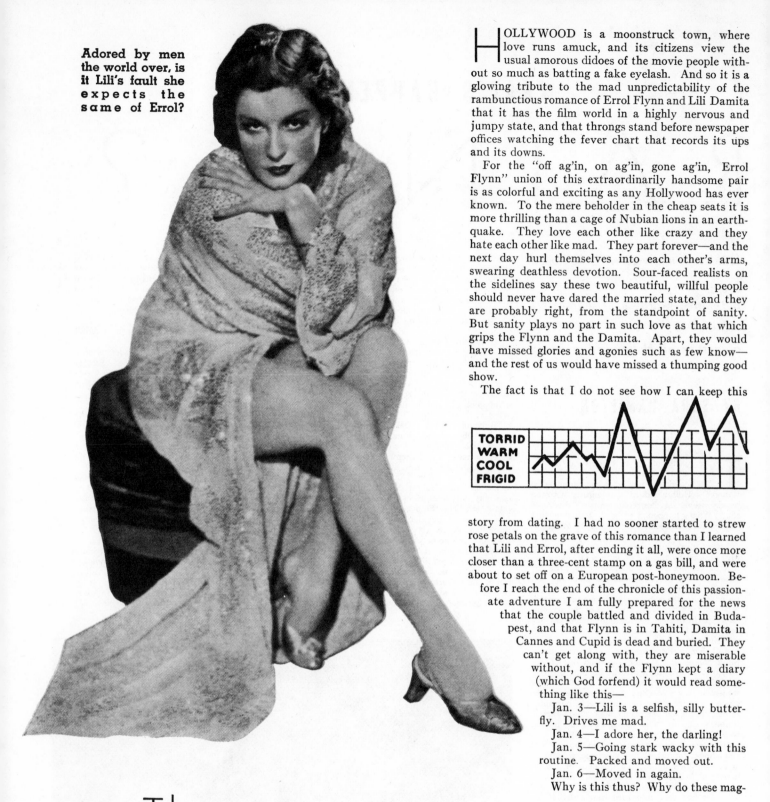

Adored by men the world over, is it Lili's fault she expects the same of Errol?

HOLLYWOOD is a moonstruck town, where love runs amuck, and its citizens view the usual amorous didoes of the movie people without so much as batting a fake eyelash. And so it is a glowing tribute to the mad unpredictability of the rambunctious romance of Errol Flynn and Lili Damita that it has the film world in a highly nervous and jumpy state, and that throngs stand before newspaper offices watching the fever chart that records its ups and its downs.

For the "off ag'in, on ag'in, gone ag'in, Errol Flynn" union of this extraordinarily handsome pair is as colorful and exciting as any Hollywood has ever known. To the mere beholder in the cheap seats it is more thrilling than a cage of Nubian lions in an earthquake. They love each other like crazy and they hate each other like mad. They part forever—and the next day hurl themselves into each other's arms, swearing deathless devotion. Sour-faced realists on the sidelines say these two beautiful, willful people should never have dared the married state, and they are probably right, from the standpoint of sanity. But sanity plays no part in such love as that which grips the Flynn and the Damita. Apart, they would have missed glories and agonies such as few know— and the rest of us would have missed a thumping good show.

The fact is that I do not see how I can keep this

TORRID
WARM
COOL
FRIGID

story from dating. I had no sooner started to strew rose petals on the grave of this romance than I learned that Lili and Errol, after ending it all, were once more closer than a three-cent stamp on a gas bill, and were about to set off on a European post-honeymoon. Before I reach the end of the chronicle of this passionate adventure I am fully prepared for the news that the couple battled and divided in Budapest, and that Flynn is in Tahiti, Damita in Cannes and Cupid is dead and buried. They can't get along with, they are miserable without, and if the Flynn kept a diary (which God forfend) it would read something like this—

Jan. 3—Lili is a selfish, silly butterfly. Drives me mad.

Jan. 4—I adore her, the darling!

Jan. 5—Going stark wacky with this routine. Packed and moved out.

Jan. 6—Moved in again.

Why is this thus? Why do these mag-

The
MADCAP LOVE
of the ERROL FLYNNS

nificent young people hate and worship each other with alternate breaths? Once they are under the microscope it is easy to understand.

Hollywood, ultra-conventional and strictly patterned for all its external goofiness, has never seen precisely the likes of this Flynn boy.

His own master since boyhood, relentlessly following the main chance, in spite of the buffetings of Fate, Errol Flynn is his own man. He is a Hard Guy, a clear-eyed realist and a thorough individualist. The Gene Tunney of the leaping tintypes, he approached the movies as the handsome boxer did the gentle art of mangling noses. It offered big money quickly, and everything indicates that the big boy proposes to get his, make a snoot at the studios, and step into the sort of life dearest to the heart of Errol Flynn. He is a movie career man if there ever was one, and to date he has not made a single professional mistake. His business dealings with Warner Brothers have been both keen and successful, proving once more that personal beauty is no handicap to smartness.

Flynn can write, too, and he will not perform for buttons. The kid has an eye for a pay check with a lot of nice figures on it, and if such is not forthcoming he simply covers the typewriter, picks up his marbles and goes away. Toughened by his boyhood struggles and thoroughly hep to the chicanery of his present profession, Errol Flynn will get what he wants in

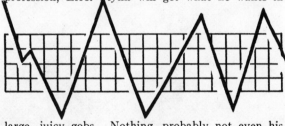

large, juicy gobs. Nothing, probably not even his Damita-madness, will ever stand in his way.

And what of lovely Lili, a heart-demolisher of worldwide reputation?

In the first place, she is one of the most beautiful women I have ever seen, and my professional life has forced me to eye hundreds of them in envy and despair. She had been off the boat but a few days in 1928 when I lunched with her and her mother at a great Fifth Avenue hotel, and so blinding was the beauty of la Lili that I dropped the cutlery, knocked over two illegal cocktails and got Hollandaise sauce in my ears.

All her adult life, men, here and abroad, have been reduced to this sad, gelatinous state by her loveliness. They have trotted about in her wake, yelping wistfully for bones. She has been courted, petted, deferred to and spoiled by a long procession of pop-eyed, incoherent admirers, and they, not she, are to blame if she wants what she wants when she wants it, and then gets it instantly on a silver tray, trimmed with parsley and uncut emeralds!

How in the universe could this professional Dream Girl, secure in the knowledge of her beauty and accustomed to abject adoration from men, hope to cope with the unyielding, realistic individualism of such a Man's Man as the Flynn? She probably never even gave a thought to such insoluble problems. She only knew she wanted him!

Speaking by the book, these two glamorous people should never have come within 10,000 miles of each other. But it is in just such cases that life plays its most comical [PLEASE TURN TO PAGE 282]

They love each other like crazy—they hate each other like mad. The amorous didoes of these two beautiful, willful people have all Hollywood guessing

By LEONARD HALL

If ever a man was not the husband type it's this headstrong young Irishman

Little and luscious, especially in this pose, "Livy" de Havilland is lucky too. Since her debut two years ago she has been consistently in the arms of such idols as Freddie March and Errol Flynn and is now to appear in "A Gentleman After Midnight" with Leslie (Hamlet) Howard. Strangely, one seldom hears of Olivia in an off-screen romance. Is she just smart, or has she a secret sorrow?

Sixteen! The transformation of baby Frances Gumm of Grand Rapids into starlet Judy Garland of Hollywood is complete. But two things have never changed—her desire to sing, which she satisfies in "Babes in Arms"—and her desire to be a doctor, which she satisfies with ambitious plans to build a hospital for children

October 1939

DON, *Alice* AND

The heartwarming story of two men and a woman who have found the secret of Hollywood friendship

BY RUTH WATERBURY

ONE friendship started out of tragedy and the other out of comedy, but added together, they created the riotous Three Musketeers of Hollywood, Power and Faye and Ameche.

There's always talk about there being no friendships in Hollywood, and of how jealous stars are of one another. That's true enough of the time to make this explosive combination the exception that proves the rule.

But Ty, Alice and Don work on the same lot. They play in one another's pictures. They continually sing one another's praises and they go in for horseplay and practical joking between

themselves that gets so rough at times it nearly wrecks the whole Twentieth Century-Fox plant.

Men frequently get together in friendship, but this setup is unique in having a girl mixed up in it. And the fact that two handsome young men think enough of a slim blonde girl to spend hours thinking up new ways to tease her, spells out in letters a mile high what a swell number the Faye is.

This three-cornered friendship (and make no mistake, it is friendship and never was romance) started off on a noble fine note. Tyrone Power, very unknown, definitely unsung, was kicked out of Alice Faye's picture, "Sing, Baby, Sing." Maybe you've heard this before, but it has to be repeated for you to get this unusual relationship going in its proper sequence.

It was Ty's first picture and thus the event was discouraging. At that moment if Alice had acted according to the guide to stardom she would never have spoken to Ty, not because he had done anything wrong, but because it looked as though he were to be that Hollywood thing worse than death, a failure.

Alice, however, barged over at this crucial

moment of artistic disgrace and asked Ty to take her to dinner. She didn't know him then, or he her, but they spent the evening together. They got solemn as owls about everything. Alice gave Ty a great pep talk, and Ty said she was his Inspiration. Alice said he was her Friend. They told each other that each understood. They promised to be friends forever and ever. On such a high, moral, sweetness-and-light plane the Faye-Power friendship rested until Dominic Felix Ameche came along.

Now there is no guy who has been made to seem such a plaster saint in his publicity as Don, and who is, in actual fact, such an impudent devil. Don does go to church every Sunday and he does adore his wife and sons, but those things, and those only, are what he is serious about. Everything else is a laugh to Don, and if you don't laugh with him, he'll soon find a way to make you.

His way of achieving that is dead-pan kidding, right in the middle of any production's most portentous scenes. It's a little difficult to convey to you the nerve tension, the solemnity that ordinarily reigns on sets. I suppose it is

Hollywood calls them the Three Musketeers — Tyrone, Alice and Don—and in their work, and in their play, they've proved they are one for all, and all for one. Don and Alice are together in "Lillian Russell," while Ty is soloing in "Dance with the Devil"

TY

unavoidable. Millions are at stake, moods are the equation on which the whole hinges and the star to keep her moods happy must be pampered. Any star can walk from a scene on any set and without even turning her head, have a chair appear instantly back of her. Hairdressers spring forward wordlessly to run their combs through already perfect locks. Make-up men solicitiously pat cheeks and nose with unnecessary powder. Publicity men flutter and the yes-boys go into their gurglings. The star is either very gracious about it, or pretends she doesn't notice all this fuss, depending upon which type of person she is. Either attitude kills Ameche, and he kills the attitude.

Don and Ty were old friends from their starving Chicago days, and after the "Sing, Baby, Sing" episode Ty had communicated to Don what a regular person Alice was. Don had never met her however until they were cast together in "You Can't Have Everything."

"You Can't Have Everything" was a very important picture to Alice and she was prepared to treat her role with due respect, but the first day Don reported on the set he came equipped with combs, flowers, folding chairs, powder puffs and the firm determination to reduce her to laughter. He was polite as all get out at the introduction but once on the set, every time Alice moved, he popped up to serve her, a mocking gleam in his eyes. He raved over her beauty. He was speechless with adoration when she put over some big scene. The little Faye hadn't grown up on New York's Tenth Avenue and fought her way up through the song-plugging game to movie stardom without knowing a ribbing when she saw it. She knew Don was kidding the socks off her and it made her mad as a snapping turtle. She wasn't actually too happy in those days. She didn't like Hollywood or Hollywood men. She wanted to go back to New York—either that or be a great dramatic actress—and here was this clown, making her want to giggle all the time. She resolved she wouldn't and the more fiercely she resolved that, the more determined Don grew that she would.

THE spoofing feud went on for two whole weeks of production or up until Don enlisted Ty's aid in it. That brought results on the evening of the day Alice had been presented with a new dressing room.

The rooms the boys were dressing in at that time weren't exactly hovels but still there was nothing about them to do them proud. Alice's new dressing room, however, was a Class A, super deluxe special and she didn't hesitate to let them know about it. In fact, she invited them to call and observe her splendor and that was what led to her downfall. For those two pranksters looked at the room's miles of white satin, covering chairs and dressing table and hangings. They saw exquisite Victorian lamps with their big pink shades. They saw the neat closets for Alice's gowns, closets concealed behind mirrors that reached from floor to ceiling. They observed all that and they just waited for Alice to be called away.

The call to return to the set finally came and away tripped innocent Alice. When she returned she saw what their loving hands had done. They'd wrecked the joint, that's all. The lamps were overturned. The bows were off the satin. Her gowns lay in limp attitudes over everything. Her mirrors were scrawled with grease paint. One whole mirror just said "Hello, dear." Alice surveyed that desolation and if those two boys had been anywhere around she would probably have wrung their necks. But they carefully weren't around and then the more Alice looked, the more she realized how big she had taken all this luxury, and how silly that was, and when she thought of that, she began to laugh. Laugh and think about revenge. A simple call to the decoration department in the studio would do away with most of the damage, but she had to do the revenging herself.

She rushed over to Don's dressing room but it was discreetly locked. But Ty, the most temperamental of the three of them, hadn't thought that far ahead. Alice crept into his diggings. There before her she saw Ty's first pair of imported English shoes. She knew them on sight because Ty had already proudly displayed them to her and even boasted that he had gone berserk and paid thirty-five dollars for them. Another telephone call and Miss Faye had a hammer and nails in hand. Five or six neat blows and Mr. Powers' beautiful dog-coverings were fastened tight to the floor. They didn't show it. They sat there slyly waiting for the moment when Tyrone, the 3rd, would put his feet in them and attempt to walk away. For that moment Alice also left a note on Ty's mirror. It merely said, "Thanks, kids."

After that, there was no stopping them. There was always two against one, though in different

(Continued on page 283)

SPENCER and HEDY—

New patterns of cinema romance created by these latest members of the Hollywood Teamsters' Union —Tracy and Lamarr of M-G-M's "I Take This Woman"; Dunne and Boyer of RKO's "Love Affair"

Box office's King and Queen hold court again on the M-G-M lot, and here is the first picture on the first day, with a newcomer admitted to the charmed circle. This time it's Walter Pidgeon in "Too Hot to Handle" who completes the trio instead of Spencer Tracy of "Test Pilot" fame

BEHAVIOR

BY BOGART

Once you get to know Hollywood's most ornery cuss

you're a friend for life—just ask his ex-wives!

BY RUTH RANKIN

Because he's in love, there is, for the time being, a "new Bogart"—a mellow sort of fellow with a house, a garden and some dogs. But, when he reverts to type, not even his bride-to-be, Mayo Methot (below with "Bogie" and the Lester Stoeffens), will be one whit disillusioned

MAMA, that Bogey-man is here again. There is some talk that Humphrey Bogart, or Bogey—Bo, if you want to get tough about it—was born in the hottest part of Hell's Kitchen with a very dirty sneer on his face, and grew up to be the leading liquidator for Lefty Louie's gang. . . .

Bogey has not put himself out in the least to dispel this illusion. He kind of keeps it for a pet, the way snake charmers cuddle their boa constrictors, and for much the same reason: both of them use their pets in their work.

The fact that Bogey actually was born (1900) in an unimpeachable section of New York; that he looked like any other baby except to his mother (an illustrator of distinction for fashion magazines) and to his father (a well-known surgeon); and that he prepped at Andover, are all things he will admit, under pressure.

What he will admit without any pressure at all is that he has been getting into trouble all his life, and still is. It was just a short step further to put this talent to work and become the leading screen heavy.

Every friendship Bogey ever made started out with a hell-roaring fight, even up to and including his marriages. He says once he and his acquaintances go through the initial baptism of fire, they are friends for life and stick faster than adhesive to a blister.

"Nobody," he claims, matter-of-factly, "*nobody* likes me on sight. I suppose that's why I'm a heavy, or vice versa. There must be something about the tone of my voice, or this arrogant face—something that antagonizes everybody. I can't even get in a mild discussion that doesn't turn into an argument." And from the pleased way he looks when he says it, you get the impression that Bogey is awfully happy about the whole thing.

"The thing is, I can't understand why people get mad. You can't live in a vacuum, and you can't have a discussion without two sides. If you don't agree with the other fellow, that's what makes it a discussion. I'd feel like a sap, starting things by throwing in with my opponent and saying, 'Well, of course you may be right,' and 'You know more about it than I do,' and all the other half-baked compromises the tact-and-diplomacy boys use.

"My idea of honest discussion (maybe the word *is* argument) is to begin by declaring my opinion. Then, when the other fellow says, 'Why, you're nothing but a —— —— fool,' things begin to move and we can get somewhere. Or, all right then, I'm the one who generally pulls that line on him. So they tell me. Anyway, it's a line that gets lots of action.

"All over Hollywood, they are continually advising me, 'Oh, you mustn't say *that*. That'll get you in a lot of trouble,' when I remark that

(Continued on page 284)

FAMILY GROUP Mr. and Mrs. H. W. Powell and their son William, in the first picture taken together since fame and the family name became synonymous. He's Willie to his mother but his father calls him Bill. Wherever he lives, he makes arrangements for his parents to be near him. When he had a mansion in Beverly Hills they lived in a little house on the grounds. Now he's in a smaller place—but the family still lives near by

"Prosit . . ." hail the laughter boys as they knock glasses in their latest comedy, "The Devil's Brother." Oliver and Stan can really laugh at life's little jokes now for they went through plenty on their way up. But, look out, Laurel's likely to burst out cryin' any minute all over his nice bib

Tear-Stained Laughter

WHERE did Laurel and Hardy find out that tears could be made to pay—as comedy material? How did this inimitable team learn to splice weeping with laughter?

The roars of laughter that greet even their names as they are flashed on the screen are, in a sense, echoes of the poverty, hunger, rebuffs, all but death-dealing blows that made this laughter possible.

Stan and Oliver were total strangers to the kindly fates until Lady Luck made them screen partners. The lives of each are almost as alike as two peas except that Laurel's started in England and Hardy's in America.

Stan was trained in the same school as Charlie Chaplin. The English music 'alls. When barely in his 'teens, Stan trouped with the renowned Charlie in the vehicle that took them both to America—and world fame. Oliver's stage "prep" school was minstrel shows in the "sticks," and small-time vaudeville.

When Stan Laurel's well-to-do father in England sternly said "no" to his becoming a "comic," the boy ran away, determined to arrive on his own.

Because Oliver Hardy's widowed mother down in Georgia had to slave to support five offspring, he joined a barnstorming troupe to ease her burden.

Their persistent jinxes seldom lost sight of either lad after that.

Even today, secure as they are in the cinema's arena of plenty, tears well in Stan's sad eyes as he recalls the times when, penniless in strange lands, he felt his frail body couldn't cling to life

By E. R. Moak

against continued hunger, while a lump rises in Oliver's silvery throat as he speaks of how he, alone and "broke," lay fever-ridden in a cheap lodging house, awaiting the end he believed inevitable.

The smell of grease paint was in Stan's nostrils almost from his first "howling" appearance as a "blessed event" in Ulverson, England, 1895. As a true child of show folks, Stanley Jefferson made his stage début in a carried-on part. Dressing-rooms were his nursery, theater alleys his playground.

AT ten came the urge for a comedy career. The "governor," who was acquiring a chain of theaters throughout Britain, had other plans for his son.

But the fledgling took wing, short-changing his name to Stan Laurel, and bummed his way to London. Here his grit was immediately put to the test.

A clever pantomimist despite his tender age, Stan was limited in his search for work by his father's wide acquaintance among theatrical people. He knew they would report his whereabouts to his family. For twenty months he battled starvation with occasional work. London park benches became his beds. He soon learned where and when the bread-lines formed.

Stan thought he glimpsed sunbeams peeping through the fog when he was signed for a tent show in Holland. But, so eager was he for the opportunity, he failed to notice a clause in the contract—no salaries in case of rain.

And the skies belched water for three whole weeks after his arrival in the land of windmills and wooden shoes!

It took years of heartbreak and hard knocks to give Laurel and Hardy the gift for packing them in with "pathos behind the smile"

A mere kid, stranded, he couldn't speak the language. His back was against the wall. He stood in shop doorways through long, wet nights with odors from bakery basements aggravating his gnawing emptiness. The lad remembered his vision became blurred. Then he collapsed. He came back to consciousness in a hospital. As food restored him to strength, Stan discovered the Dutch authorities intended to deport him. Knowing that this move would restore him to paternal custody, he fled and panhandled his way across the Channel.

Back in London, Stan tripped over a new stumbling block. His father had a private detective agency looking for him. He could look for work only in the very out-of-the-way places.

But, as the fuss over his disappearance let down, Stan got his break with Fred Karno's English Comedians, with Chaplin featured. The pay was only three shillings a day—but he could eat on that. His idea of disguise fooled his dad's sleuths.

OLIVER HARDY came into the world in 1892 in a setting very close to show business, or at least very much part of "trouping"—a small hotel in Madison, Georgia, owned by his father. It was his baby home for only eighteen months when his father died. His mother tried to run the business, but mortgage payments far outdistanced the meager receipts. So she took her brood to Atlanta.

When Oliver was five, life handed him his first severe jolt, the start of a long series. His mother had always made her children believe that Santa Claus was a most generous soul, for up to then she had been able, by dint of hard work, to decorate their Christmas tree with several gifts for each. But the sugar bowl bank was empty. Now she was forced to tell them the dream-blasting truth!

"Mother did what she thought was the square thing," Oliver sadly reminisced, "but we were so young to be disillusioned—and there were so many blows awaiting us later on."

The incident stands out to Hardy, the man, as vividly as it did to Oliver, the child. It accounts for the loads of presents he now sends to Los Angeles orphanages every Christmas!

At six he was a newsboy in Atlanta, collecting extra pennies singing for his customers. At ten a roving minstrel outfit billed him as "the boy tenor."

Beaten and starved by drunken members of the company, the boy was not a minstrel long. He stood the abuse as long as he could because of his mother's urgent need for his contributions. But, when his chunky body became a mass of bruises and cuts, he took French leave, returning to Atlanta in a box car.

WITH his mother employed and his brothers and sisters doing odd jobs, Oliver was able to go back to school. But his vacations were spent in vaudeville.

Oliver's bulk belied his young years, so he had fairly frequent singing jobs in Atlanta cabarets. They helped him through high school and two years of law study in the University of Georgia.

He had not yet attained voting age when the family money problem made him put away his law books and head for New York in search of gold on the stage.

Broadway stage doors opened to him for try-outs which didn't become engagements, so he turned movieward as an extra.

Fifteen months old, and wasn't this chubby fellow already hinting at the Oliver Hardy of today?

Stan Laurel posed for this at the ripe age of two. But even then didn't he show a hint of the picked-on Stan who's such a riot today?

Hiking through a blizzard from a studio to save the carfare that meant cheese and crackers to him, he caught a heavy cold, awakening next morning in his five by seven hall room, too sick to lift his head off the roll of clothing that served as pillow. There he fought off delirium as his condition grew worse. He was afraid to call for help; the hawk-faced landlady would demand the already overdue rent.

For seventy-two hours he tossed on the hard, narrow bed, his temperature mounting rapidly, his parched throat craving water that was not to be had. Then he lapsed into unconsciousness.

In that grim plight a pal, in New York for a holiday, found him, and rushed for a doctor. Pneumonia had almost got him.

In 1911 Karno booked passage on a cattle boat for his fourteen comedians, including Chaplin and Laurel, and sent them to America. Stan's pay jumped

[PLEASE TURN TO PAGE 287]

74   July 1930

IT'S hard to believe, but in this sequence Ethel Merman is trying to convince Eddie (Harum-scarum) Cantor that she is his mother. Eddie says if this is mother love, he pities the poor orphan! All of Ethel's maternal instincts, it seems, have been aroused by the fact that Eddie has lots and lots of money! It's a scene from his movie, "Kid Millions"

YOUNG
in Heart

That's our own Child Roland—who dotes on canes, and doodles the dippiest drawings in Cinema City

BY SARA HAMILTON

THERE is a saying in Hollywood to the effect that when very very bad little writers die, they go to Roland Young—for an interview; the obvious implication being that they must pay for their sins on earth and, therefore, deserve the punishment of trying to probe from Mr. Young a few plain statements of fact. Or even fiction; they'll settle for anything. It isn't that Mr. Young is annoyed or even surprised at the shades in action, for as *Topper* he's been haunted by the loveliest, and is quite used to it. Nor is it that Mr. Young is exactly unwilling to impart information. The truth is he is most co-operative, even eager to aid in every way. Only nothing concrete *ever* materializes.

That, you see, is the HELL of it.

His inborn English reticence (he'll scoff) is constantly at war with his willingness to be noised about (if he must be) and the result is plain fantastic. The writer, pad in hand, begins:

"Mr. Young, I believe, you were born—"

"Yes, but I wouldn't bring that in. I mean—couldn't we just sort of work around that?" interrupts the actor.

Instantly, the writer senses that something special in the way of whimsey-pooh has just blown her way and she had better take a firm hand in the beginning.

"Mr. Young, I am not going to work around your birth anything of the sort," she says. "Either you were born or you weren't. It's your duty to tell the public which."

Mr. Young quietly picks up a pad and pencil and draws the picture of a bee—in profile.

This strange interruption over, the writer proceeds. "Mr. Young," she begins, hoping to spur him into action of some sort, "you are supposed to be a very funny man. Say something witty, please."

Mr. Young turns the paper over and draws a picture of a bee—full face. It's the image of Marie Wilson in a Dutch cap.

Then Mr. Young smiles that smile of bland innocence for all the world like the White Knight in "Alice in Wonderland." In fact, the idea that maybe Mr. Young is somebody from the "Alice" world grips one's fancy. He's as dressy as the White Rabbit, as smugly resigned to his fate as the Frog footman and as tea-time struck as the Mad Hatter. Finally, we decide that with a pair of tusks Mr. Young would make as pretty and as cute a Walrus as ever walked

hand in hand with a Carpenter and ate up little oysters. But all this time, mind you, we're afraid to say a word, a single word, for fear he'll begin his drawing.

He does anyhow. This time, it's an elephant with an extended rear leg upon which is perched a canary.

"A female," Mr. Young explains, admiring the bird on its peculiar perch. Which reminds us of his never-to-be-forgotten verse in his own book, "Not for Children":

Here comes the happy bounding flea
You cannot tell the HE from SHE
The sexes look alike you see,
But SHE can tell and so can HE.

IN an attempt to get the interview on a working basis, we make a list of every fact he thinks (and

(Continued on page 289)

No telling what chief Roland and Benchley are pl at left! It's c to be bloodcu

Not fugitives f hangover, these little beasties – examples of wh innocent Young viewer is up a

TROUBLE

"JOHNNY GET YOUR HAIR CUT"

"MY BOY"

"BOY OF FLANDERS"

"BUTTONS"

"OLIVER TWIST"

"HOME ON THE RANGE"

"LONG LIVE THE KING"

THE
KID"

THE
BUGLE
CALL"

"OLD
CLOTHES"

DRAWING BY VINCENTINI

"THE LAW IS ON OUR SIDE . . . NONE OF THAT MONEY HE EARNED BELONGS TO HIM."
—From a statement by Arthur L. Bernstein

Robbing *the* Cradle *for* STARS

Captivating Shirley Temple, the most popular actress in Hollywood today, was the first little life-saver for jaded Moviedom and movie-goers. But she earned her success by hard early training

Mickey Rooney is eleven, and thereby practically the grandpappy of "cradle stars." He is the clown of the lot, and steals pictures from adults

NINE times out of ten Hollywood gets what it asks for. And this time it asked, begged, even sat up and howled for youth, youth and more youth. And lo, youth was there!

But what youth! Not even Hollywood expected such an answer to its plea. For, marching along to fame, little feet stepping high, eyes shining brightly, little faces beaming, comes the "New Youth" to Hollywood.

Mere babes they are, but what babes!

Yes, Hollywood asked for youth and got it in Shirley Temple, David Holt, Baby LeRoy, Cora Sue Collins, Baby Jane Quigley, Jane Preston, Mickey Rooney, Scotty Beckett, Richard Ralston Arlen, Virginia Weidler, Carmencita Johnson, Ronnie Cosby, Spanky MacFarland, Buster Phelps, Edith Fellows, Billy Lee, Dickie Moore. And more, with the parade not over by any means. Others, perhaps just as talented, are

Cora Sue Collins faced many hardships before that "break" finally showed up

storming the gates. The way things are going it looks as if Hollywood will soon be a Gulliver in the hands of the Lilliputians.

What's more, they came at the psychological moment, these little life-savers. People were fed up with the old bill of fare. Nothing gave them a kick. Then out stepped Shirley Temple and the tired old public sat up with a gasp and begged for more.

And Hollywood, quick to take a hint after

With assurance and an amazing ability, babes in the Hollywoods are carrying the brunt of box-office business on their little shoulders

By Jane Hampton

a brick or two had been dropped on its badly dented head, is giving them more and more and more. And even allowing these mere babes, as it were, to carry the tremendous load of a motion picture success on their own baby shoulders.

And are they carrying through? Well, where would "Baby Take A Bow" be without Shirley Temple? And where would "Little Miss Marker" be without Shirley Temple? And where would "You Belong to Me" be without David Holt? And where would we all be without Baby LeRoy?

I shudder to think.

It's ancient history, of course, how little Shirley Temple, unknown to the vast majority of film fans, suddenly stepped out before an amazed audience in "Stand Up and Cheer," sang her little song, and did her little dance.

Things have never been the same. I doubt if they ever will.

But mind you, not without serving her apprenticeship did this little five-year-old lamb pie win her laurels.

Baby Jane Quigley, a three-year-old, spoke right out to Claudette Colbert and told the adult star just how and where she muffed her lines

Helen Mack, in the center (no, she's *not* a baby star) is holding that promising youngster, David Holt, the masculine Shirley Temple when it comes to emoting. His sister, Betty (right) also wants to act

Baby LeRoy, about the youngest of the babes, has made all his rôles, like that leg he's gnawing on, talk big turkey

A new discovery in the starlet heavens, Billy Lee, at the grand age of three. Billy is making his bow in the Paramount film, "Wagon Wheels"

For two years Shirley worked long and hard in those short kid pictures over at Educational Studios. It was there she laid the foundation for her success.

They rather knew it was coming, however, for in the palm of her little right hand is a peculiar marking. It was the first thing the nurses noticed the day Shirley was escorted into the world.

"What does it mean, I wonder?" they asked. And then someone said in a rather awed [PLEASE TURN TO PAGE 304]

Otto Dyar

LITTLE Shirley Temple revives a favorite childhood pastime of—
well, it just seems ages ago, doesn't it? Now, one wonders where
she found that clay pipe to blow bubbles. And the public just can't get
enough of Shirley. She took a rest after making "Now and Forever" for
Paramount, while Fox kept a job waiting for her, in "Bright Eyes"

Ferenc

DICKIE MOORE is mad as mad can be. The director wanted him to cry and said if Dickie didn't he was going to get another boy to play the part in "Slice of Life." "Let him get Jackie Cooper for all I care," mused Dickie. "What's the use of Christmas presents if you never get time to play with them?"

Deanna Durbin has found fame and has paid fame's price—for no little girl can accept an adult's world at fourteen without heartache

By **KAY PROCTOR**

It's Lonely

BEING A CHILD PRODIGY

A FEW weeks ago a little girl stood outside the stage entrance of a Hollywood theater. It was on a Sunday night and a wet rain had pelted down upon her, drenching her in the long minutes she had stood trying to get up courage to knock on that closed door. Finally, poised for flight she rapped timidly.

Inside the door stood another little girl, the center of admiring attention and flattery. She wore a pretty frock and was accepting compliments with a sweet but shy courtesy.

The doorman opened the door to the knock. The small waiting figure slid from the shadows into the beam of light.

"I would like to see Edna Mae Dur——I mean Deanna Durbin," she said, hesitantly.

"Are you expected?" the man asked, the routine gruffness in his voice tempered at the sight of the child's obvious timidity

"Er—a—no," she admitted, "but I think maybe she'll say it's all right. I'm Paula." She was told to wait a moment.

In a flash the door was flung wide. Two little girls ecstatically hugged each other while tears of happiness mingled on their faces.

Thus the paths of Deanna Durbin and Paula Jenkins her best friend, crossed for the first time in well over a year; Paula, the average little American girl who lives in an unpretentious bungalow in a middle-class part of Los Angeles, and Deanna, the fourteen-year-old sensation of Hollywood, star of "Three Smart Girls," and radio discovery of the year.

"And Mother," Deanna said, in relating the eventful meeting later, "just imagine, Paula said she and the other girls were all so proud of me! Isn't that wonderful?"

Only Mrs. Durbin knew why praise from that humble source meant so much to her suddenly famous daughter. Meant, in all truth far more than the lavish words and laudation heaped on her by important critics everywhere, knew with a catch in her heart.

DEANNA'S story begins back in 1923. Deanna, christened Edna Mae, then a baby one-year-old, came to Los Angeles with her mother, father, and older sister, Edith. The family home had been in Winnipeg, Canada, where Mr. Durbin was a moderately successful contractor. The boom in Southern California real estate drew them south.

From the day of their arrival [PLEASE TURN TO PAGE 122]

No longer a joyous game of tennis with her particular chums after school. Instead—a serious study of music, with Leo- pold Stokowski, for her next picture and (opposite page) personal appearances with Jimmy Wallington and Eddie Cantor

THE greatest actress of them all, Hollywood's most sought-after person. Facing sixty, Marie Dressler remains younger than a flapper and modern as next year's hat. She's just finished "Politics."

The Greatest Actress

ZaSu Pitts gave a fine performance as Lew Ayres' mother in "All Quiet." But a preview crowd tittered, and she was replaced

in Hollywood, says Von Stroheim, is ZaSu Pitts. But the audience laughs when she appears on the screen

Lew Ayres and the mother we saw on the screen, Beryl Mercer, in a scene from "All Quiet." She replaced ZaSu Pitts in the rôle

ERIC VON STROHEIM, whom Hollywood calls its greatest directorial genius (and then makes it hard for him to get a job) says that ZaSu Pitts is the greatest actress of the motion picture and one of its few great tragediennes.

Incidentally, and modestly, PHOTOPLAY proclaimed this ten years ago.

Backing up his judgment with action, Von Stroheim chose ZaSu for important rôles in his masterpieces, "Greed" and "The Wedding March."

But Hollywood persists in typing her as a comic.

Lewis Milestone chose her to play Lew Ayres' mother in "All Quiet on the Western Front." She gave a great performance. But she has played comedy parts so much that when "All Quiet" was previewed in a Los Angeles theater the audience tittered at her most tragic scenes. Panic-stricken, the producers retook all her scenes, using Beryl Mercer, a middle-aged character woman who is another great actress, in the part.

WHEN ZaSu Pitts came to Hollywood she was a funny looking girl who rode a bicycle and ate apples and didn't have any sex appeal. At least, that was the rumor around town.

She lived at the Studio Club and kept the girls there in hysterics whenever she moved those long hands of hers.

And then, one night, she met and danced with Tom Gallery and he thought she had sex appeal. The romance flourished and they were married.

Von Stroheim had never seen ZaSu. He didn't know that in the

The unforgettable beaten bride of "Greed"—the girl who triumphed in the limping "Wedding March" — the trouper who has stolen a hundred pictures from great stars—ZaSu Pitts. It's the sad and wistful face of a true tragedienne, yet audiences remember her comedy—and laugh!

stereotyped minds of the producers she was a comedienne. But had he known, he would not have cared a Teutonic toot.

In spite of all the mumblings of the producers—"that ridiculous Von Stroheim again, putting a comic in a dramatic rôle"—ZaSu was given the part of *Trina* in "Greed." It was during the time she worked for him that Von realized her sublimity as an actress.

"But," he said, "you've never seen her on the screen as I saw her. I consider that I've only made one real picture in my life and nobody saw that. Its poor, mangled, mutilated form you saw in a theater one evening and it was called 'Greed.' "

THERE are a handful of men who still speak in hushed tones of a terrific experience that occurred to them in a projection room when the first cut of "Greed" was shown.

It ran for ten hours.

And it was in this picture, Von Stroheim's greatest, the picture you never saw, that ZaSu Pitts did the magnificent work you never saw.

"The average person thinks she is funny looking," says Von Stroheim. "I think she is beautiful, more beautiful than the famous beauties of the screen, for I have seen in her eyes all the vital forces of the universe and I have seen in her sensitive mouth all of the suppressions of humankind. I've seen her lifted to the heights of great acting. Art must weep when ZaSu Pitts plays a comedy rôle.

"She should not be in comedy for she is the greatest of all tragediennes."

Bredell

December 1934

THE further she has advanced, the more her blood has warmed to the ancient philosophy of China, says Anna May Wong. Anna was born in Los Angeles of Chinese parentage, boosted along in pictures by Douglas Fairbanks, acclaimed in Berlin, lionized by England's aristocracy, and now is back in Hollywood, making "Limehouse Nights"

REYES

IT *SHOULD* REQUIRE REHEARSING—

DRINKING A *GALLON*
OF ORANGE JUICE!

● Edward Arnold can wear as many diamonds as Jim
Brady even if he can't drink as much orange juice. Jim himself tossed off a gallon without blinking an eye! Arnold,
who closely resembles the Brady of the gay nineties, plays
the rôle of the famous figure in Universal's "Diamond Jim"

Six-feet-four of English manho[od] and a microphone chang[e] Arthur Treacher ("Pips" to pals) from a suave gentlem[an] to an even suaver "Jeeve[s]"

Dignified is the word for C. Aubrey Smith in his screen rôles ("Hurricane," for example), but in real life his wife has another name for him

Roundup of CHARACTERS

Not a star in the carload—but facts

aplenty (famous and funny) about

those modest marvels, the bit players

BY SARA HAMILTON

THERE exists in Hollywood a delightful group of people known as character actors. "Only some of us are completely characterless," one wag grins. "Oh, completely."

Although the names of these chosen few seldom gleam from theater marquees in letters two miles, or even inches high, they do shine—and definitely—in the hearts of movie fans everywhere. "Oh look," thousands of fans may be saying at this very minute, "Funnyface Mowbray is playing tonight. Let's go see *his* picture." Undoubtedly Miss Big Name would melt if she knew. Or does she suspect, one wonders.

Minus the trappings and deliriums of stardom, these performers become something like kinfolk to their fans. They are as cozily familiar as the neighbor next door. And like good neighbors they have made a place for themselves in our hearts that couldn't be filled by anyone else. So, PHOTOPLAY has decided, like the Walrus, that the time has come to talk of many things. Of many things about our old friends, the character actors.

Of course, we can't tell you all about them. That would take books and books. But we can give you some facts about them that we hope modestly will bring you into closer understanding with these friends who have brought you so much downright enjoyment.

And so, dear reader, we give you . . .

Helen Broderick:

"It's the figure, not the face, that counts in this world of mice and men."

"So far, my movie dialogue has seemed to me to be just so much verbal dysentery."

"I'd pay seventy-five dollars for a lamp shade, maybe. But the woman who pays over ten dollars for a hat is a nitwit."

Quoting, if you please, from Hollywood's paradoxical comic—Miss Helen Broderick, who clowned so beautifully in "She's Got Everything." A paradox is Helen, because, of all the things in the world Helen never wanted to be, it was an actress. And of all the things she still doesn't want to be—it's an actress.

"If I thought I'd ever turn out to be one of those old has-been stars with grease paint up their noses so far they sniffle like Bernhardt instead of breathe, I'd end it all now. May I turn into a caterpillar if ever I begin dragging out ancient press notices or telling about the time I stopped the show in Cincinnati.

"From a fate such as that, dear heaven deliver me."

Back in New Jersey some years ago, Helen just fourteen years of age, decided to run away from home because her mother, a comic opera star, was forever talking stage.

But the catch was that the only people Helen knew were theatrical people, and to them the young vagabond had to turn for help. So they promptly landed Helen, who ran away to get away from it, on the stage. In the chorus. On the stage. And was she awful. Just terrible.

Of course, Broadway didn't think so many years later, when Helen spoke almost the identical lines in exactly that same devastating tone of voice—but that's another story.

Once in a while, they'd throw her a line to say—like throwing a fish to a seal—and she'd think, "Well, here I go." But the next day she'd pop out from the chorus to say her line of "Oh well, bridegrooms are always nervous," only to have the stage director leap back like a wounded mountain lion and moan, "My gawd, who said that?"

And they'd take her line away from her. And such a good line, too, she felt.

Things grew more and more terrible only a little time later. Helen was made understud[y] to Ina Claire in the play, "Jumping Jupiter," which sounds all right and was all right unti[l] one night—and this is really awful—Ina couldn't[

Herman Bing has made an asset out of an accent, a hobby out of a habit, more laughs for "Bluebeard's Eighth Wife"

Do-nuts and coffee on the "Merrily We Live" set made Alan Mowbray forsake his long-standing "no contract" policy

Edward Everett Horton took up college dramatics, Helen Broderick did a pinch-hit for Ina Claire, Eric Blore met Bart Marshall — three innocent events which eventually made them Hollywood's pet rib-ticklers s u p r e m e

play the lead and Helen gallumped on and tried to be ingenuish, fluttering butterflyishly about as did la Claire, tripping lightly o'er the stage like a bay mare with the bewildered leading man in dazed pursuit.

Dazed, because at this point the audience was only rolling in the aisles. That's all. Just rolling. When Helen began her song, "Cuddle Near Me All Day Long," it was the end. People, nice people, had to be led from the place in spasms.

So the manager promptly sent Helen out on the road as the permanent lead, and overnight "Jumping Jupiter" became, instead of a romantic musical, a sidesplitting comedy.

Helen married the leading man who groped so wistfully after her on that first awful night. She's still married to him. True, tried and happily.

With her new husband, she then formed a team and went into vaudeville. Bad vaudeville at first. Then a little better. Then to the circuit where people didn't actually throw things but would have loved to.

Then big time, and suddenly Broadway discovered, in that voice that once cried from the chorus, "Oh well, bridegrooms are always nervous," the panic of the year.

"Fifty Million Frenchmen" couldn't be wrong —not with Helen as its leading comic. For seventy-two months she caroused in that laugh riot, "Stand Up And Cheer," and then migrated to movies—which she tolerates a shade less than she does the stage. She's constantly awaiting the day her bankbook says so much, and then back to the farm for Helen.

"What people can't understand," she says, "is that I'm still the same person I was before Broadway and success. They seem to think fame is reason for people becoming artificial and putting on a new front or a new personality.

"I'm just me. Exactly the same as I always was."

Out in the valley, she and her husband live on a one-acre ranch—a heaven on earth to Helen. "What's this song, 'Roses in December,' all about?" she keeps asking. "I have roses in December right out in my back yard.

"Working in Hollywood may not be an actor's idea of heaven, but the guy who says he wouldn't rather live here—aside from the work —is plain nuts."

Her lack of any trace of the theatrical in her make-up and her genuine honest humanness enslave all who come to know her. The tone in her voice when she speaks of Broderick, her son, is something that causes people to gulp three times in rapid succession.

"I feel I never want to try anything else on Broadway again. I may not prove worthy to be Broderick's mother. My performance after his marvelous work in 'Of Mice and Men' may shame him. It may be shoddy or half-baked.

"When I read his notices the day after his show opened I thought to myself, 'This is it. This is what you've always wanted to achieve. Not success for yourself—you know, old girl, you haven't cared that much about it—but success through him. And now you've achieved it, Broderick. Through your boy.'"

One other thing—the "hey you lady" of the

(Continued on page 290)

PICTURES THEY WISH THEY'D
NEVER POSED FOR—

Above: This misty-eyed young thing is now one of the most sophisticated and sirenish stars. When this picture was taken, she didn't use an "e" to her name. **Right:** She used to play slant-eyed Oriental seductress rôles, today she is the ideal screen wife. **Center:** She is divorced from the scion of a screen royal family, and is now happily remarried to a popular star. **Top right:** She's very much on her toes today, and recently divorced. **Bottom right:** Here's the hardest. If you remember your Horace Greeley, you've got it.

92   *[Answers are on page 331]*

LOVE LIFE OF A VILLAIN

Basil Rathbone, by the star's own admission, has a secret—it's about a woman—a redhead named Ouida

BY KIRTLEY BASKETTE

"MY secret," said Basil Rathbone, "is a woman. She is small. She is vital. She has red hair. Her name is Ouida. She is my wife.

"Without her I would be nothing; with her I can be everything. Without her I would be miserable. With her I am the happiest man in the world.

"Of course," he added, "behind the success of every man there is some woman. But it isn't often we give them any credit. That's why my confession may be a little startling. Everything I have achieved—everything I may be today or hope for tomorrow—I owe my wife, Ouida."

For an hour I listened to the most amazing earnest tribute to a Hollywood wife I had ever heard.

It came from a man who is viewed throughout the world as the very incarnation of conceit and masculine arrogance.

The epitome of self-confidence on the screen, he revealed himself as emancipated from a blighting inferiority complex only by the patient love of his wife. Celebrated as a charming conversationalist, he confessed to a tongue-tied ineptitude until she brought him out of it. Respected as a shrewd career man, he revealed how a woman had launched that career, steered it, and secured it—at the sacrifice of her own.

He did all this eagerly, humbly, happily.

WE talked of a perfect marriage, oddly enough, in the house where a prize fighter, Jack Dempsey, had once lived in stormy domesticity with his former wife, Estelle Taylor. It was in the calm of a lovely evening. The Los Feliz Hills above Hollywood were blue and the air soft. Everything in the setting suggested a prelude to a pleasant story. Basil Rathbone, just in from a romp with his six dogs, brimmed with good nature. Somehow, Basil always reminds me of a race horse, lean, long, nervous, trim. He lit a cigarette and blew the smoke to the ceiling. He talks fast and with an electric charm.

"I haven't told this before," he said, "but right now it seems particularly timely. Because, rightly or wrongly, Ouida considers her job with me done now. She thinks I am established at last and capable of looking after myself. She feels she can relax now and return to writing, the career she abandoned to see me through. And

For what she has done for Rodion, his son (top, second left); for what she has done for his career and for the man himself, Sir Guy of "Robin Hood" sheds his screen villainy to pay humble homage to the lady of his heart

it was she who saw me through—because, if I hadn't met my wife, I honestly don't know what would have happened to me, for until then my life had had no direction. Certainly, I could never have caught on to Hollywood without her.

"I wonder how many of us here in Hollywood would be where we are without the help of some woman who loves us. Think of the tremendous influence Dixie Lee Crosby has had on Bing. Of the vast importance of Bella Muni to her extremely talented and sensitive husband, Paul. There are dozens of cases—and you don't have

to stop in Hollywood, of course.

"It's even intriguing to wonder just how gre[at] some historic figures would have been witho[ut] their wives. Disraeli, Napoleon, Washingto[n.] Can you imagine Robert Browning witho[ut] Elizabeth Barrett?"

"But speaking of the Rathbones . . ." I inte[r]rupted.

Basil smiled. "Right!" he said. "I'm getti[ng] out of my district.

"Well—Ouida came into my life two yea[rs] (Continued on page 29)

LIVING AND WORKING IN MOVIELAND

Hollywood

The community and state of mind that were Hollywood had crystallized in world consciousness before the period treated in this book begins. Implanted in the public eye in the Twenties as a land of milk and honey, of gin and sex, of big money and small passions, its image altered little till the arrival of the era of television, and of international production, deprived it of much of its magic. It has not lost all of that magic yet, nor will it yet awhile. Lacking a satisfactory equivalent elsewhere, Hollywood remains the twentieth-century symbol of the place where the caveman within us gets everything he wants—and of what happens to him after he gets it.

But by 1930, Hollywood had settled into a mold. The days of the great scandals, the wilder flamboyance, had passed. As Mae Murray put it, "We got used to the money." Those who stayed on top after the coming of sound, and those who followed them, noticeably drew in their horns. The new people especially were smaller and smarter and played it much safer than the outsize gods and goddesses of the silence that had been so golden. Too much was at stake to let the peccadilloes show. As another Mae, Miss West herself, summed up the new dispensation: "Hollywood is the only town where you can say come up and see me some time and not get taken up on it."

In these circumstances, the job of those whose work it was to keep the picture colony's image more dreamlike than a dream was full of problems. Hollywood had to go on being the land of the beautiful people and the sweet life, but—because of the Depression, because of Will Hays—it had to be decorous too. How to solve this conundrum—especially in the face of an increasingly sophisticated public? The scholar in every fan knew by now that "Hollywood," like its parent Los Angeles, was just a collection of crossroads. The physical plant which enclosed the *genius loci* was as garish as the rest of southern California

and could not be made to add up to more than a carnival version of dreamland. The Sunset Strip was a midway, the studios and their sound stages looked like a collection of warehouses, and even far-famed Malibu was scarcely distinguishable in outward appearance from Far Rockaway. Glamour and fun, dramatizable, picturable glamour and fun, had to reside not in the place itself but in the people and what they did there.

But what was that to be, for PHOTOPLAY's purposes? Not primarily the making of movies, long since reduced to a routine of fifty pictures a year from each of the major companies. For maximum excitement it had to be off-the-set stuff, and here studios and stars cooperated enthusiastically. The institutionalized social life of the Hollywood of the early Thirties was invented and staged with at least half an eye on the necessity to provide continuous fodder for the fan magazines. The Mayfair Club Ball, originated as a counterweight to the snobbish dances in Los Angeles and Pasadena which excluded picture people, was the opera-glove affair of the year, the Academy Awards (still localized and pretty small potatoes) its professional highlight. Between these two events, stars could be seen and photographed at the Cocoanut Grove, longest-lived of Hollywood rendezvous, and at the Brown Derby, whose patrons were all but given numbers to hang around their necks in indication of their standing in the pecking order. And, marking the progress of the seasons and the release schedule, there were the "permeers" (the corruption soon replaced the original, in print as well as in everybody's mouth) of the biggest, or at least the most expensive, new films. These were attended by "everybody," meaning every professional from star to bit player who could get in, and also by a mob which did not even hope to get in, a vast crowd of fans and nuts, the all-American rabble described by Nathanael West in *Day of the Locust*. Such were their numbers that photographs of the great occasion were often disappointing, resembling more than anything else the sleazily unglamorous photographs of, say, Valentino's funeral. PHOTOPLAY solved this neatly by lavish use of that fetching device of the infancy of pictorial journalism, the composite photograph. By this means the anonymous unwashed were blotted out in favor of any number of famous faces, massed together in a limbo which never existed except perhaps in the fourth dimension, where Hollywood itself had its true being.

But famous though the faces were they were always the same faces. Indeed, a zealous fan armed with a magnifying glass would have soon discovered that even the anonymous faces in the permeer crowds were often the same. It became apparent that Hollywood, far from possessing the ambience of a cosmopolitan capital, was permeated by an atmosphere far more familiar to the fan—a hometown atmosphere, his own. Despite its sprawling physical extent its population was that of a village, and it had the interests of a village. That primarily, as in all villages, was talk, whispers—gossip. Not, of course, the gossip of the barber shops, who's laying who—not in the fan magazines, not then. It was more like the talk of the bridge clubs: what blonde star has gone high-hat? Who's feuding with whom and why? What star's ex-wives have formed a cabal against him? Who's broke, in spite of the flashy front she puts up? This, because largely malicious, was engrossing and exhilarating and best of all, familiar; it put the fans on the same level as the, by now, ex-divine and human, all too human stars. In the beauty shops (*and* the barber shops) of the country, Hollywood gossip came to mingle with local gossip, inextricably and almost indistinguishably.

This was heady stuff, but it wasn't enough. Sex was still tabu—sex neat, that is, as distinguished from the standard fan magazine compound, "love." And the absence of sex left an aching void in talk about Hollywood, as it would have indeed in small-town gossip. A partial answer to the lack appeared in 1934 in the unlikely form of the candid camera. At first the fast-action shutter was used merely to catch stars in awkward or embarrassing poses, and the magazine cover-lines trumpeted "hundreds of off guard photos," taken by "our own photographer," fearless, intrepid in his exploration of the nightclubs—but every scoop eyed by stars and studios just the same. There was the rub: the companies were not about to allow

wholesale photographic disillusionment. Censorship was instituted, and excommunication from the lots was the fate of the cameraman who failed to clear his trophies with the stars before he showed them to an editor. PHOTOPLAY's "own" photographer, Hymie Fink, had little difficulty in beating the system, or rather inventing his own way round it. A Hollywood veteran, he had long since established rapport with the stars, and he conspired with his subjects to produce what can only be described as staged candid, or candid staged, shots which did the stars no harm while seeming to meet the requirements of neo-pseudo-realism.

The candidness of candid camerawork turned out to provide another plus for the fan magazines —another way of getting round the *verboten*. A shot of two stars having unretouched fun at poolside or in nightclub could be accompanied by a caption implying that the pair were contemplating heading straight from where they were to the nearest bed. The studios were at first aghast at this, but since the picture-caption unit delivered its charge by innuendo only, à la Walter Winchell, the always-desperate publicity departments decided that this development was something to be exploited rather than suppressed. In his researches for his monumental study, *Hollywood*, Leo C. Rosten discovered that in 1937 and 1938 the Misses Loretta Young, Sonja Henie, Simone Simon and Arleen Whelan and the Messrs. Tyrone Power, Cesar Romero, Richard Greene and Michael Brooke were engaged in a "libidinal round-robin" which, in the fan magazines, paired them off with one another successively, interchangeably, and continuously. By no coincidence whatever, all eight players were under contract to 20th Century-Fox, whose publicity department had stage-managed the entire two-year game of musical chairs. It was simple; you did it all with pictures.

This charade was repeated ad nauseam by every studio for the reason that nobody could think of anything else to replace it. Ever since Will Hays imposed a Code on the magazines to match his Production Code for the content of pictures themselves, film publicity had been in a state of stalemate. What the fans wanted to know about was sex in Hollywood, which they suspected was more hectic than anywhere else, and that was precisely what studios and magazines were forbidden to tell them about. Editors and writers fumed at the gutted stories they had to concoct, but with Mr. Hays firmly at the helm throughout the Thirties, no one who valued continued employment kicked over the traces. Then, in 1939, Ruth Waterbury, ambitiously expanding PHOTOPLAY, decided to dare all. The result was "Hollywood's Unmarried Husbands and Wives" (page 130). That almost brought the pillars of the temple down on her head, and she had to eat full-page crow in the next issue. The only consequence of her—it seems now—timid experiment was that the dictatorship of virtue clamped down more stringently than ever, into the war years and beyond.

With frankness about Hollywood's sex life virtually blocked off, PHOTOPLAY and its rivals turned increasingly to the fans' second gut interest, money. Meaning the unbelievable money the stars made, and how they flung it around, and their largely futile efforts to hang on to some of it. That led to gambling, always an occupational hazard of actors, and its Hollywood manifestation, characteristically larger than life—not just betting on the horses but also their ruinous ownership. As to the hanging on to money, that was more difficult to dress up, and not only because "wise investments" made dull copy. Stars and fans alike doubted the permanent wisdom of those investments, doubted still more that, even if wise, they would compensate the fallen star for his fallenness.

For there in their midst sat a *memento mori,* Mary Pickford, richer than any of them would ever be, eating her heart out at Pickfair, trying to console herself for her loss of popularity, and of Douglas Fairbanks, with the production of pictures starring other people—and with Buddy Rogers. If the aftermath of stardom was wormwood to her, what would it be to her juniors and inferiors? Strange to say, the magazines did not shirk these forebodings. Under the saga of sunny success which formed the staple content of PHOTOPLAY, there ran an obbligato of misfortune, a threnody to the loser. The plight of the extras, the ones who never made it, was obsessively dramatized, and that of the has-beens, the ones who made it and lost it, was dwelt on with equal morbidity. Perhaps these tales of woe added spice to the chronicle of dizzy triumph. In any case, the magazines knew that readers would not be put off by them. Whatever it cost to be part of Hollywood, even for a little while, it was worth it. A fan writer of the period called one of his stories "The Crowded Hour," and he dared to quote Sir Walter Scott: ". . . To all the sensuous world proclaim / One crowded hour of glorious life / Is worth an age without a name."

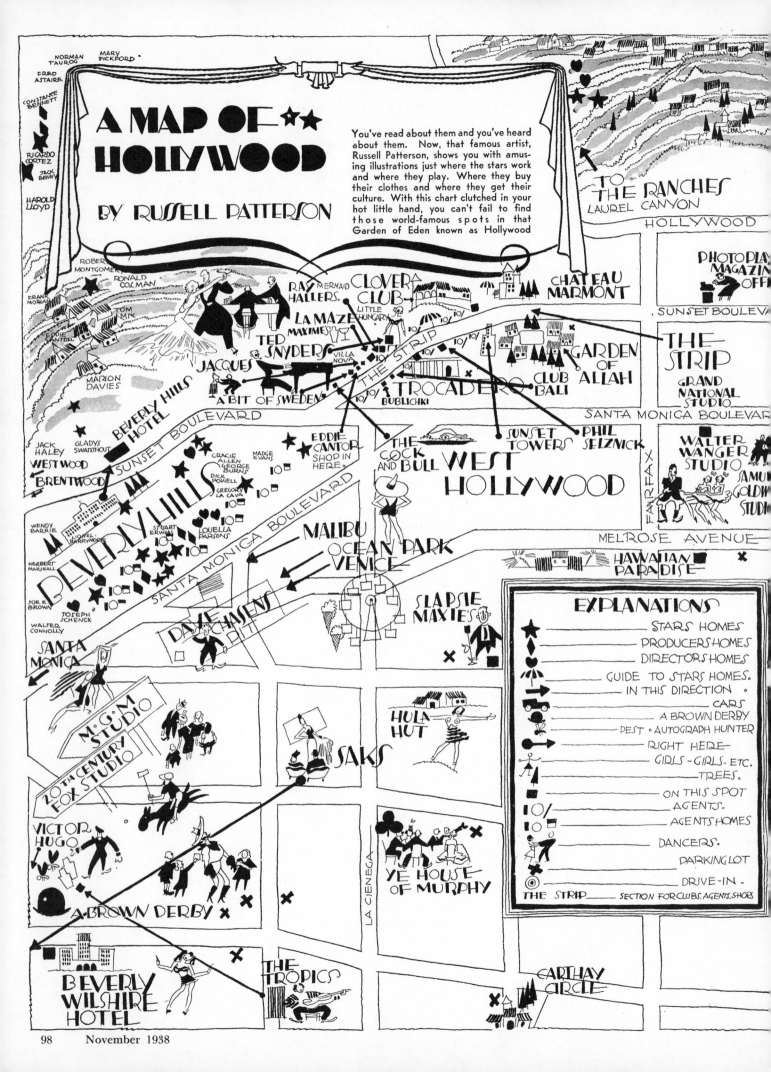

A MAP OF HOLLYWOOD

BY RUSSELL PATTERSON

You've read about them and you've heard about them. Now, that famous artist, Russell Patterson, shows you with amusing illustrations just where the stars work and where they play. Where they buy their clothes and where they get their culture. With this chart clutched in your hot little hand, you can't fail to find those world-famous spots in that Garden of Eden known as Hollywood

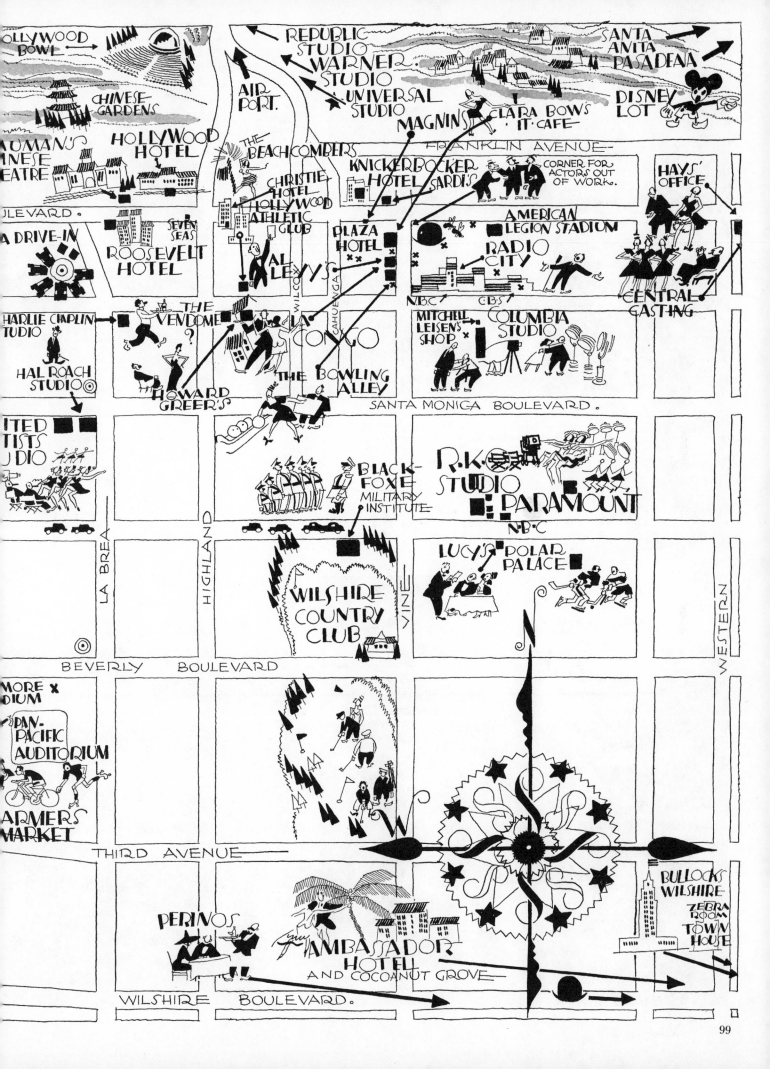

A resort hotel? No, just the little nest that provides shelter for the Fredric Marches and their two children

HOME IS WHERE THE

A Holmby Hillbilly—this showplace houses Constance Bennett and her young son, Peter

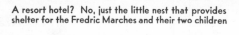

The house that radio built belongs to incorrigible Andy (Charles Correll) of "Amos 'n' Andy"

Breathing space is what Claudette Colbert wanted when she planned her charming home

High on a hilltop overlooking Beverly Hills is the magnificent establishment of Sam Goldwyn

HEART IS

EXCLUSIVE PICTURES TAKEN FROM THE AIR BY CAPTAIN C. W. EHRMAN

Nestled in a heavily wooded section of Bel-Air is Warner Baxter's English country home

KNOW HOLLYWOOD

CROSSROADS. Where stars are made, debts are paid and actors are a dime a dozen. The Times Square of Cinematown—Vine Street crosses Hollywood Boulevard. Left: Ken starts his camera cruise by a shot of Alice Faye, his co-actor in Universal's "You're a Sweetheart"

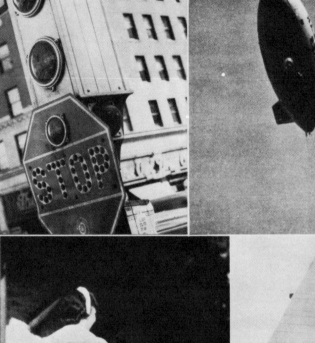

Taken especially for Photoplay by actor Ken Murray were these pictures of that fabulous town where a chariot race or Lady Godiva is a commonplace occurrence

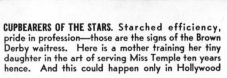

LANDMARK. The original Brown Derby on Wilshire Boulevard dozes placidly in the afternoon sun. Started by Herb Somborn (ex-husband of Gloria Swanson), it was an outgrowth of his desire for bigger and better strawberry shortcake and hamburgers. It gained rapid popularity, is now the scene of many big off-record deals

CUPBEARERS OF THE STARS. Starched efficiency, pride in profession—those are the signs of the Brown Derby waitress. Here is a mother training her tiny daughter in the art of serving Miss Temple ten years hence. And this could happen only in Hollywood

SKY TOUR. The Goodyear blimp with its sight-seeing cargo circles the spire of the famous Church of the Blessed Sacrament on Sunset. Night and day, over Santa Monica's beaches, Pasadena's Rose Bowl, Hollywood high spots, this sky tour goes on

HOLLYWOOD PISA. Many an unsuspecting tourist gapes at the brave man atop this wavering pile of old tires. A competent come-on for this particular business, his job holds no terrors for him: he is the dummy the movie hero used to throw over the cliff

MODERN CONVENIENCE. In the Farmer's Market, where many of the stars do their own domestic shopping, is this novel wheeled wicker receptacle for a tagging Junior who rebels at staying h o m e

STRICTLY BUSINESS. I n s i d e this m o n u - mental Sphinx goes the wondering tourist, finds therein a thriving real-estate office, often emerges the proud possessor of a "hilltop home" or a dozen orange groves

TEXAS IN TOWN. In the midst of the bustle of busy LaBrea Boulevard is this working oil well. Traffic darts deftly right and left around it, the tourist stands amazed, the native gives it not a glance— for of such modern miracles is this Hollywood made

COMEBACK TRAIL. From a Nevada ranch, Clara Bow, with husband Rex Bell, comes back to Hollywood to hang her restaurant shingle among Vine Street bright lights. There she mingles with those friends she used to know, meets as guests the stars of new-found fame

Hollywood
at Play
At Mayfair

TWO ladies of the screen's blood royal meet for a chat just outside the ballroom at the Biltmore Hotel where Hollywood's Mayfair party is booming along. In short, Mary Pickford and Gloria Swanson take time out from dancing to talk things over. They're telling each other the ball's a success. Our Mary's white frock is heavy with beads—and she wore the cape all evening. Gloria's gown is brown chiffon, and the jewelry's jade. The cigarette is nonchalant

MARION DAVIES gave a kiddie party and among the Hollywood children who came to eat ice cream and cake, all dressed up in their party clothes, were little Joan Crawford and Connie Bennett. Shame on you, Joan, for bringing your hoop to a party. Put it right outside the door or you won't get a single drop of gin

Can you name them?
Try; then see page
302. Photo by Stagg

Hollywood *at Play*

I T'S
Tuesday
night. The night
of nights. The stepping
out night of the movie village.

And Hollywood, the town of glitter and
glamour, goes out to play. With the cares of the
day behind, the burning Klieg lights, the grease
paint, the difficult scenes, shattered hopes and
broken dreams—all forgotten for the moment.
Hollywood dons its best low-in-the-back frock,
its immaculate dinner coat, and off it trots.

It's the Cocoanut Grove at the Ambassador
Hotel.

Behind a waving stick, a steady smile and a

Charlie Farrell and Virginia Valli stroll in after a while. Charlie follows the head waiter to a little table reserved for them at one side. He glances around casually and his eyes suddenly light up. There's little Janet Gaynor at a table near the edge. Charlie gets up and asks Janet to dance; Janet's escort bows to Virginia Valli and they step out on the floor.

And again the ever-alert Phil Harris smiles his approval.

Off in a corner, behind a stately palm, sit Clarence Brown and Alice Joyce, at dinner. Night after night. And why not? They've announced their marriage now.

An occasional glance from Phil reveals that all is well. The lights melt softly into an amber glow as the rhythm of the music changes.

Suddenly, at the top of the steps leading into the Grove, is a tiny flutter of excitement.

Joan Crawford comes trailing in with Franchot Tone. Immediately, Phil swings into Joan's favorite, "Melancholy Baby."

It's Joan who knows all the newest songs in advance. "Have you heard 'Night [PLEASE TURN TO PAGE 302]

deep red carnation, stands Phil Harris, the orchestra leader, looking down. On Hollywood at play. The smile beams, the stick flutters and the keen blue eyes of Phil Harris spot the romances, the shattered ones and the budding ones, of the movie stars, while the strains of the lilting music float gently upward to the astonished little stuffed monkeys hanging tail downward in the cocoanut palms.

Lew Ayres sits alone at one of the tables. Across the room Lola Lane, his recently divorced spouse, makes merry with a group of people. And Phil Harris, sensing something, waves his baton and the orchestra plays, in its most appealing manner, "Maybe It's Because I Love You Too Much." ...

By Sara Hamilton

Hollywood's Greatest First Night

"STRANGE INTERLUDE" brought them out in droves. It was undoubtedly Hollywood's greatest first night and our indefatigable photographer, Stagg, caught the real spirit of the event in these pictures. You can easily identify Connie Bennett in the foreground talking with George Fitzmaurice. Then there is Jean Harlow dividing her attention between Paul Bern, her new hubby (left), and Harry Cohn whom she also embraces. Directly behind this group you see Mary Pickford, but the chap reading the paper seems to be pulling a "cover-up" act. Take that paper away from your nose, Jimmy Durante, we know you.

"STRANGE INTERLUDE"

Clark Gable and the Mrs. directly above. It was Mrs. Gable who startled the first nighters by wearing the only woolen gown in a sea of silk, satin and velvet. And last, but most important of all, the star of the picture, Norma Shearer

When the stars turn out, so do the fans. Above is a cross section of the twenty-five thousand people who thronged the streets around the Chinese Theater for blocks. Police were unable to handle the mob. Many were hurt in the crush

Mad, Merry Malibu

The cradle of the beach pajama and the home of the $5,000-a-week beachcomber. The most interesting and goofiest stretch of sand in the world, where the antics of the stars make the sea-gulls dizzy

Malibu—the craziest community in the world, bounded on the south by Wesley Ruggles and on the north by Connie Bennett. That's her shack nearest to you. The road is from Hollywood. Stars go here to "get away from it all," and build their houses this close together. Note garages and tennis courts in back of homes

MALIBU. Hey, hey.
A row of houses on a sandy shore. Bound by Connie Bennett on the north and Wesley Ruggles on the south. With Louise Fazenda smack in the middle.

The spray ground of the stars. Hollywood gone pajama. The gay, hysterical Hollywood of old, moved twenty miles north and twenty times goofier.

The place where stars go to get away from it all only to get in deeper and slightly wet to boot. And love it.

"What's become of the good old Hollywood?" incoming writers mourn. "The gay, mad spirit that made Hollywood, Hollywood? Where is it?"

Calm down, stranger. It's still here. Just a few miles farther north on a damp and sandy shore. All here. Everything, including Lew Cody.

Hi there, Malibu.

A half mile stretch of delirium tremens architecture along an astounded Pacific Ocean.

Even the fish can't get over it. And the sea-gulls fly dizzily around. Squawking for help and a bit more imported caviar.

Where people build seventy-five thousand dollar houses on a thirty foot lot they can never own. And pay a dollar a day for the privilege.

The freak property of the world.

"What, sell my land," cries the owner, "when people, hundreds of people, pay me one dollar every day just for the privilege of living on it? For just ten years? Be your ladylike self."

Malibu. Where everything is dated from the fires.

"Now, let's see. When was it Jack got his divorce from

By Sara Hamilton

Mabel? Was it right after the big fire or just before the little one? No, remember Fred got sunburned and peeled all over everything just after the little fire, so it must have been the medium one. Yes, that's right. It was just after the medium fire. Only seven houses (contents included) burned that time."

Where the white stone mansion of Miss Ringe, the owner of Malibu's golden sand, sets high above the movie colony on a nearby hill and looks down. Wondering, wondering, wondering.

A good half mile strip of houses. With a tiny three feet between. A Swiss chalet next to a Southern manse. With bell ringers and yodeling in one house and banjo strumming in the other.

A Spanish fandango with a tamale front next door to an up and down board shack. Like the Mulligan's, across the track.

The red and white mansion of Lil Tashman. And a Mexican adobe shack with a water jar (never touched) and two scandals each season.

A suburban type home with *green grass in the front yard, geraniums, palm trees and shrubs. On a sandy shore.* I ask you, ladies and gentlemen of the jury, I ask you.

And all this next door to a sand-drifted front yard, with the sand sweeping across a completely hidden fence into the jellied consommé.

Chiffon curtains to an ocean-sprayed window. Cretonne, next door. Oriental rugs. With grass ones on the other side. Every house screaming out the personality of the owner. A dead giveaway.

"Here am I. A Spanish complex with a slight leaning to Bank of Italy architecture. Look."

We look.

But no matter the style or period of any house they all have that triangular glass windbreaker on the northwest corner of the fence. There is such a thing as an ocean breeze overdoing it.

It began, this Malibu, with Anna Q. Nilsson, a desire to rest, and a tiny board hut. And, year by year, it has grown bigger and bigger, and madder and madder, and gayer and gayer.

111

Joan Bennett's house has a color scheme of blue and white both inside and out. The bedrooms are off the balcony

In this little red and white nest, buffet supper may start at 7 P. M. Friday and finish around 10 Tuesday morning. It belongs to Eddie Lowe and Lil Tashman. And there are mine host and mine hostess, themselves, snatching a short, quiet sun bath. Lil's bathing suit and Eddie's robe are red and white to match the house. And, you ask, who are those folks at the back door? Oh, just a few droppers-in

People once paraded in old sweaters and corduroy. And now look. If you have a strong constitution, that is.

A 3 by 6, red and white awning on a front porch on Monday, means three new red, white *and blue* 6 by 9 awnings on Tuesday, four red, white, blue *and orange* 9 by 12 awnings by Wednesday and on and on, until the next Monday the original awning-putter-out thinks up another one to slap the neighbors silly. It's grand.

And styles. At the beginning of each season all the Malibu-ites gather up last season's clothes and swear this year they'll wear out their old things at the beach. What's a beach for but to wear out old clothes, they demand?

Then, the first warm Sunday, Lil Tashman or Connie Bennett strolls, oh so nonchalantly, up the beach, and the riot is on. A bright green bathing suit, backless on Monday, means four brighter green backless suits on Tuesday. On Wednesday, there are seventeen of the brightest green suits full of wide open spaces ever viewed by mankind. And are they viewed? Until the next Sunday someone thinks up something else.

GOOD old Malibu. Where everything is different from an everyday world. Elsewhere rents go down. In Malibu, they go up. Like a fevered temperature.

Seven hundred and fifty dollars a month for a yellow frame cottage. Including dog kennels, of course. Seventeen hundred and fifty dollars a month for a bilious looking stucco with four master bedrooms, a ping-pong table and quantities of leftover aspirin.

And people claw each other for the privilege of living on the poorest beach along the coast, where the rip tide rips, the under-tow tows, Jack Gilbert entertains Hawaiian princesses and everything finally burns down, anyhow.

Where Violet Love walks to her bedroom window and sniffs, "My Gawd, smell. Peggy Pretty is using Coty tonight and last night it was Feu Follet. Where does she get all that perfume, is what I'd like to know."

Or a famous blonde glances through an open window to another open window and sneers, "Humph. Call that real lace

Photos
By
Stagg

Here's the lad who stands guard over Malibu, at the main road. A kidnapper or a casual whoopee-maker with seven or eight too many under his belt wouldn't have a chance against hard-boiled Bill Barber, who shoots a mean forty-five, if the occasion arises. Bill knows who has and who hasn't the right to ca-vort on Malibu sands

Welcome—if you're invited—to the brand new home of Marie Prevost. Right on the sandy front yard there's a small strip of garden. And what a grand sun porch for bridge playing. But does Marie have any privacy? Just see how close her next-door neighbor's house is. That's Malibu!

The general store at Malibu looks just like the one at Hicktown, except that R. L. Bills, the proprietor, sells more caviar and *pate de fois gras* than pecks of potatoes and turnips. John Boles, in typical Malibu costume — white cap, white sweater and open shirt — does the family marketing for his missus just like you and I do

on those stepins? Ridiculous. Simply ridiculous, if you ask me."

A stone wall along the coast highway protects Malibu from the outside world. At the gateway stands a small white hut. The post office. With old-time open boxes and names printed beneath. And what names! Connie Bennett, Chico Marx, Warner Baxter, Estelle Taylor, Leila Hyams, George O'Brien, Eddie Lowe, Louise Fazenda and dozens of others as famous.

"My dear, there's that same bill for Susan Bigname again. See, sticking out of her box. Well, the way some people don't pay their bills has me under."

Just a village post office where world-famous people gather every day for mail and gossip. Just as thousands of others do, the world over.

A gateman is posted here who halts every incoming car of strangers. "All right, where are you going? You expected? Just a minute." As we now have telephones in some houses, the gateman phones. "You expecting visitors from Sedalia, today? Two women, one man, four children, one with the whooping cough, and four guinea pigs? *No? Okay.*

"Out please, and make it snappy. You're not expected."

And the informal visitors are on their way. Out.

A kidnapper wouldn't have a chance to ply his trade here.

A straight road leads down from the main highway to the settlement. From the back road all that can be seen is a row of garages and a low black fence marked, "Visitors for number fifty-three park here. Visitors for sixty-eight park here, etc." The owners' Chevrolets, Rolls Royces, Packards, Fords are all tucked away in the small garages.

Seven patrolmen are on duty night and day. Protecting the homes from gate crashers that may have gotten past the gateman, souvenir seekers, over-eager fans and yes, gangsters. Then too, there's the ever-present danger of fire.

After the first fire, when fourteen houses burned to the ground, a new fire engine was [PLEASE TURN TO PAGE 307]

Why Constance *Is Unpopular In* Hollywood

By Ruth Biery

Read Hollywood's side and Miss Bennett's side and judge for yourself

I DOUBT if any woman was ever as thoroughly disliked by Hollywood as Constance Bennett.

I doubt if anyone ever thoroughly disliked Hollywood as does Constance Bennett.

I do not mean pictures. Connie likes her work. I mean she hates that mythical, fourth-dimension social place made famous by picture people. She once asked me, "Did you ever know such a *dull* town?"

On the other hand, dozens speak of her as, "That conceited, ungracious, high-hat, snooty, independent, hateful Constance Bennett!" Not only magazine and newspaper people but actors, actresses, electricians, extras and all the other components of our heterogeneous city.

Now, there are two sides to every question. Matrimony; politics; prohibition—anything controversial has a *pro* and *con* angle.

So there is Hollywood's *and* Constance Bennett's!

I am going to attempt to give each impartially and let you judge. Only I must warn you, as a lawyer warning a jury, Constance Bennett has never lost an argument in her life. Producers have learned that! Now, they give her the price she asks *first* so they won't have to pay *more* later.

Even Connie's wedding could not proceed to a smooth, made-in-heaven conclusion. Everything went well until that crucial moment when the groom gently places the ring upon the bride's finger. At this point the Marquis fumbled. The ring wouldn't go on. He tried to push it on her finger. And at this point Connie's language was—well, it wasn't the sort of language you'd expect the suave, smooth Connie to use.

But the ring at last went on and the ceremony proceeded.

Came the wedding reception and Connie didn't like the attitude of several of her guests. Without more ado she proceeded to tell them so, which is something I was always led to believe a blushing bride does not do on her nuptial day.

Hollywood made much of those incidents. Embellished them thoroughly. "That's Constance Bennett for you. Couldn't get through her own wedding without having a row!"

Incidentally, Connie is being criticized on another score. Newspaper photographers and reporters huddled out in the cold awaiting an opportunity to do their duty: get the news of an international wedding. She did not invite them inside. They froze and awaited her pleasure.

It just happens that Connie had notified her publicity department twenty-four hours in advance. Diana Fitzmaurice, in whose home the ceremony was performed, had said she could not have the photographers and newspaper folk. She didn't have room. Connie had said they couldn't be accommodated because her wedding was to be *private*. One syndicate had answered that argument: "What! A private wedding for a public woman like Constance Bennett!"

Now, Connie doesn't consider herself a public woman. She thinks of herself as a *person* rather than a personage and claims

Constance knew the news cameraman was taking this picture, but she was so interested in the polo game she didn't give a hoot that the camera caught a few wrinkles in her forehead

Henri is really a fine chap and there is one thing sure about his marriage to Miss Bennett. He'll never have a dull moment

she is entitled to certain personal rights exactly as any woman. She had arranged for the publicity department to send out a photographer and one writer who would impartially distribute pictures and information. If the newspapers wouldn't take those (incidentally the publicity department slipped and failed to notify the papers of Connie's orders) it was none of her business. *Her wedding was to be private!* It was. And those who dislike her have made public scandal of her treatment of cold men huddled on the front lawn.

She had difficulty with both the M-G-M and First National publicity departments. At Metro, she was accused of refusing to take the proper number of stills for "The Easiest Way." Stills are important; they are the photographs by which studios advertise pictures.

She didn't refuse to take the stills; she simply refused to take *certain* stills. One in particular. They wanted her in a teddy bear she wore in the production. "No! Five years from now when I am married and have a family, I don't want pictures of me in underwear staring at me from the 'Police Gazette.' "

Connie was right, but they tried to argue. They didn't realize you can never *argue* with a Bennett. She counter-offered with a negligée. There was a scene. Connie promised to appear for the other stills on a Saturday morning. She was ill. Undoubtedly, they didn't believe her. They insisted she never gave them enough stills; she insists she did.

THEN she went to First National. The publicity department asked her to pose with her father, who was playing in "Bought," looking into a make-up box.

"Now, isn't that original?" Connie asked demurely. "When you get something *new* I'll be glad to pose for you!"

First National also wanted stills. They had heard the M-G-M story. They asked Connie to reserve a day for them. "I will be there from two until five on Saturday."

"We would prefer you at ten, Miss Bennett!"

"I will be there from two until five, I said. And when I say I'll do anything, I do it!" (Which is true, by the way. As we'll prove later.)

"But we can't get enough. We want an entire day. If you'll come at ten—"

"You can get a hundred stills between two and five. I'll be there at two!" She was right again, and by this time the well-known Bennett dander was up.

Darryl Zanuck and other officials walked onto the set. The publicity man turned to them, mentioned the Metro situation; said he needed Miss Bennett at ten—

Connie heard. "You keep still, young man. When you have any experience to talk from, you can talk. What happened at another studio is none of your business. I said I'd be here at two—" There was more; much more. The officials backed Miss Bennett. They had learned, by being forced to pay her income tax on top of her salary when they first demurred at the figure, not to argue with a Bennett.

Evelyn Mulhall (Mrs. Jack) and Kathryn Carver Menjou (Mrs. Adolphe) were among those who disliked *la* Bennett. One evening, at a party, they told her so.

"Why?" Constance demanded instantly.

"Oh, the way you hold your head; look down your nose at people; speak—"

"CAN I help the way I look?" Connie asked quietly. "If I learned to hold my head high as a child, to carry myself in a certain way, is it my fault? If I speak a broad A, as I was taught, am I supposed to change it because others in Hollywood don't use it? Now, be fair, girls. You don't *know* me; how can you dislike me?"

Certainly, they're friends—good friends, today. They couldn't win an argument with a Bennett.

A writer had an appointment to interview Miss Bennett on the set of her present picture, "Lady With a Past." A publicity man took her down—the two waited. For several hours! Miss Bennett made no move toward them. Finally, in desperation, the publicity man went to her and said, "Miss So and So has been waiting for several hours—"

"And how should I know that? I've never met her. Am I supposed to know everyone whom you bring down? Why didn't you bring her over?"

"But you had an appointment, Miss Bennett."

"How did I know she was the appointment?" Rah; rah; rah. A whole line of them.

Constance Bennett does not take things for granted. She must be told. Her publicity department knows this, of course. Undoubtedly, this man should have announced the writer; equally surely, he was afraid to approach Miss Bennett until she had given him some recognition.

The writer was furious. I chanced to meet her when she left. "I was raised to be a lady! Constance Bennett is not a lady!"

Connie was passing through Albuquerque recently. Twenty-five hundred people were on the platform to greet her. She wanted to send a telegram and do several other things in the ten minutes the train would be in the station. She stepped from a train; a little child [PLEASE TURN TO PAGE 308]

"Gentlemen, a toast. We toss off the first forkful to our mutual wife!" Husbands Nos. 1, 2 and 3: "To Gloria!"

The scene is the Brown Derby Restaurant, on Vine Street, Hollywood—a thriving venture in which Mr. Herbert Somborn, No. 2, is happily interested. The other characters at the meeting are Mr. Wallace Beery, No. 1, and M. Henri, Marquis de la Falaise de la Falaise de la Falaise, No. 3. The current Mr. Swanson, No. 4, is enjoying his honeymoon in foreign parts. The three boy friends are assembled around a table in the restaurant, and getting their share of stares you may be sure. Mr. Beery is the biggest. Mr. de la etc. is the handsomest, and Mr. Somborn is very nearly, if not quite, the most prosperous-looking.

MR. BEERY—Well, boys, the club might as well come to order. As a starter I recommend that Henri, here, as the newest member, be voted into the chair.

M. HENRI—But no! It is only fitting that Mr. Beery, the senior member, should preside! Name of a name! But yes!

MR. SOMBORN—Now, no bickering, fellows! I really think you rate the chair Wally! After all, you date 'way back to the Mack Sennett days. So I vote with Hank here.

MR. BEERY—(simpering becomingly, if you can imagine Mr. Beery simpering at all)—Well, all I can say, men, is thank you. It is a great honor to preside at the first regular meeting of the Ex-Mr. Swanson Club. And now I move that we have a nice *filet mignon* all round and get down to business.

MR. SOMBORN—I'll second that motion—Hank, you don't even have to vote, as we've got a quorum already. Gus—three of those special filets, and they should be succulent.

NERVOUS OLD LADY FROM MIDWEST—(I almost forgot about her)—Gracious sakes, Madge, what three fine looking men those be!

MADGE—Sh, Auntie! They all used to be married to Gloria Swanson!

NERVOUS OLD LADY—Gracious sakes! And they act so friendly like!

MADGE—Ah, they have a Bond!

MR. BEERY—(rapping on his water tumbler with a fork and causing six jobless extras, working as waiters, to choke on their boneless sole)—Now, men, let's get down to brass tacks. What is the pleasure of the meeting?

M. HENRI—I think, messieurs, we should dispatch the cablegram to that so gallant Mique de Farmer—our distinguished successor. Yes? No? *Que voulez vous? Oui? Non?*

MR. SOMBORN—Hank, it's a great idea! I move that our

distinguished president write a cable right here on the table-cloth—I'll pay the laundry bill with pleasure. Wally, it is the sense of this meeting that you compose a wire to Mr. Michael Farmer, No. 4, here and now, and we'll split the toll three ways. Right, Hank?

M. HENRI—Okay keed.

MR. BEERY—Boys, I take this commission in the spirit in which it is offered. How about this? Dear Mike comma congratulations and best wishes for a wonderful honeymoon period You have undertaken a great and noble career and one that will demand all your fortitude period We all wish you better luck than we had period Love and kisses from the Swanson alumni meeting at the Brown Derby.

MR. SOMBORN—Wally, it's a pip. I bet that will cheer Mike up all right! Oh my goodness, boys—what a woman!

MR. BEERY—You said it, Herb! What a woman!

M. HENRI—*Eh bien! Quel femme!*

MR. SOMBORN—Oh boy, eh?

MR. BEERY—Yes sir—oh boy!

M. HENRI—*Ma fois! Oh garcon!*

MR. BEERY—Well, it was a great experience, men. Mere chit of a girl when I up and married her—back in the old Essanay days, that was. Gosh, it makes me feel old! The truth is, I don't remember her very well, but I've seen her in pictures.

MR. SOMBORN—Well, Wally, you date pretty far back. She was a star when I married her, you know. Boy what days those were in the movies! Why, money lay around loose in the streets!

M. HENRI—(Feeling slightly faint)—*Mon Dieu!*

MR. SOMBORN—Fact! You came along pretty late, Hank! Things around here had slowed up a lot by the time you blew in.

MR. BEERY—(rubbing his hands as the chow arrives)—Heigho! Here come the filets. Gentlemen, a toast! We toss off the first forkful to our mutual wife!

(All stand, with poised forks. The restaurant is largely agog.)

MR. BEERY—To Gloria!

MR. SOMBORN—To Gloria, God bless her!

M. HENRI—To that so handsome, that so charmant M. Farmer!

MR. BEERY—Down the hatch!

(The three gentlemen bolt the first forkful of *filet mignon* and then throw the forks at the

Being a fairly incorrect report of a meeting of The Boys Who Used to Be Married to Gloria

The Ex-Mr. Swanson Club

"Who are those nice looking men?" asked the Nervous Old Lady from the Midwest. "Sh, Auntie," said her niece, "they all married Gloria"

nervous old lady from the Midwest, who falls in a dead faint, accompanied by her niece.)

MR. BEERY—(sitting down)—Boys, did I ever tell you about the time Gloria—I think it was in '19—was walking down Hollywood Boulevard—it was all lined with pepper trees in those days, and—

M. HENRI—Ah, those days in Paris, when we were young and charming. The trees in the Bois, the music at the Reetz, the cocktails at Zelli's! Ah, that night when Gloria took off her shoes and went—what you call wading—

MR. SOMBORN—Speaking of wading, reminds me of the time Gloria was on location at Santa Monica. It seems that a big leading man named Hector Glutz, or Glitz, or something was—

MR. BEERY—Heigho! Them *was* the days! Why, when Gloria wore that Sennett bathing suit the cops used to—

MR. SOMBORN—(shaking his head reminiscently and wiping away a tear with a roll)—Dear little "Bunny"!

MR. BEERY—(stopping short and glaring at Mr. Somborn)—I beg your pardon, Herb. You're wrong. Gloria's pet name is "Toots"!

MR. SOMBORN—(trading him a particularly nasty glare)—Mr. Beery, I said "Bunny," and "Bunny" it was and it is. DEAR LITTLE "BUNNY"!

M. HENRI—(leaping to his feet and waving a butter knife)—Messieurs! My fraaaans! Who should know better than I that Gloria's name is "Snookums"! Such strange names sadden me. Please, gentlemen! Darleeeeng leeeetle "Snookums"!

MR. BEERY—"Toots"!

MR. SOMBORN—"Bunny"!

M. HENRI—"Snookums"!

(Mr. Beery winds up and lets go with a boiled potato. Mr. Somborn sees that and raises it with two hard rolls. M. Henri, not to be outdone, wafts a salt shaker and sings the "Marseillaise." The firing then becomes general.)

By Leonard Hall

ILLUSTRATED BY VAN ARSDALE

"Boys, did I ever tell you about the time Gloria—"

The Man all Hollywood FEARS

He has made more stars unhappy than can all the studio executives

By Kirtley Baskette

HE has Hollywood—all of Hollywood—scared half to death!

He causes more bad dreams than Boris Karloff, more headaches than Will Hays. In a caste ridden town he topples sacred cows right and left. Moguls and minions alike are his targets. He says "No" to yes-men and "Yes" to no-men. He goes out of his way to plunge the greatest stars, directors, executives, celebrities, and the Lord only knows who else, into quivering confusion.

He is the scourge of filmland.

Yet he looks quite as harmless as a June-bug. A short, roly-poly little man with a shining bald head, wind wing ears, and an absurd mustache perched over a tremendous rubber-elastic Hapsburg lip.

If you met him on the street, you would probably politely turn your head to snicker, as you do when you see him on the screen. And if you met him at a party, as you probably would in Hollywood, you would count him the last person possible in the room to hand you an inferiority complex—but that's his specialty.

Vince Barnett is Hollywood's champion "ribber," a professional purveyor of insults (rates on request). He has been getting in Hollywood's hair for five years now, ever since he first tested producer Jack Warner's nonchalance by telling him he should learn the fundamentals of making pictures.

During that time, he has made life miserable for everyone you have ever heard of, and miraculously escaped death or serious injury. For three years, he devoted all of his energies to dishing out insults at parties, banquets and special occasions, at so much the insult, and made quite a good thing out of it until "Scarface" came along and made him one of your favorite comedians, and one of the busiest actors on the screen.

His list of victims is bound by the cover of Hollywood's blue book.

Mary Pickford was one of the first. At a beach party, Vince, who is as Irish as Paddy's pig, was introduced as a German exhibitor. It was right after a German orchestra had played "The Star Spangled Banner," after a private showing of one of Mary's pictures.

In broken English, Vince congratulated her on her publicity sense. Mary didn't understand.

"Didn't you pay der orchestra?" asked Vince.

Then he proceeded to insult all her guests. He told Elsie Janis she had gone to war as a publicity stunt. Mary thought he needed conversion to altruism. She asked him outside to talk it over.

"I nefer leave a party mit a married voman," huffed Vince, indignantly—and then Douglas Fairbanks mercifully exposed the joke.

Raoul Walsh, the director, brought him to a party where four hundred of filmdom's élite were assembled. Vince made the rounds as "head waiter," accused everyone of stealing the silver, snatched plates from under their noses, and generally made a mess of the party. He bawled out Charlie Chaplin for trying to attract attention, and when Winston Churchill, a distinguished guest, placed his arm on a chair in which a young lady sat, Vince batted it off reproachfully.

"We have rooms upstairs for that," he admonished. Tom Mix blushed crimson with the same accusation when his arm was lifted unceremoniously from Lupe Velez' chair. Only Tom, more impetuous, set about choking the insulter, and forced Walsh to give the joke away to save Vince's good health.

INCREDIBLY enough, Barnett "ribbed" Mix successfully four different times. He had already accomplished the feat thrice in various poses, when he mentioned the fact one day to Carl Laemmle, Jr. The producer scoffed, there was a bet, and just then Tom arrived. He had been to the sheriff's office and he remarked that there were more men in the Los Angeles jail than in a certain small South American republic.

"You're a liar," said Vince calmly.

"What!" thundered Tom, turning pale.

"You're a liar," repeated Vince. "It's not true."

"In my country," gritted Mix, doubling his fists, "we don't take that."

"Then why don't you go back to your country?" countered Vince, "whatever it is."

Mix choked, "I'm an American, you—"

"I nefer leave a party mit a married voman," huffed Vince. Thus Mary Pickford was indignantly admonished

"In my country we don't take that," gritted Tom Mix, showing his fists to the man who had called him a liar

Jones' drive rolled to edge of the green. The "Terror" sniffed, "Sarazen would have gotten on!"

"I don't believe it. Prove it!"

This to Tom Mix, who had served in three wars, was too much. As he saw red, the joke was tactfully disclosed and Barnett collected!

Maurice Chevalier took his "ribbing" at a cocktail party which Marion Davies gave with Vince in the rôle of butler.

Serving the cocktails, butler Barnett hovered around the polite Parisian with his hors d'oeuvres and tinkling glasses, purposely missing him. When Maurice, still mannerly but longing for a drink, would reach for a glass, Vince would draw away the tray until the nervous Gaul was fit to be tied. And he never got a cocktail, although Barnett openly upbraided him for being greedy when all the glasses were empty.

Clark Gable is the only star who actually lost control of himself and went into action upon the irritating ribber. Usually posing as a foreign executive, or important exhibitor, Vince was frequently saved from bodily harm, because even stars hesitated to commit mayhem on one who bought their pictures. Gable didn't let that stop him.

IT was at one of Joan Crawford's parties. Vince was talking to Doug, Jr. and Heather Thatcher. Clark, alone at the other end of the mantel, passed by. Vince grabbed him.

"What do you mean," he demanded angrily, "walking away when I'm talking to you?"

Gable was nonplussed, but protested.

"You weren't talking to me, my man."

"Your man," sneered Vince. "I'm not your man—and just because you're the Great Gable—"

"Don't call me 'the Great Gable'—"

And so it flamed until Clark set his jaw and turned to the rest of the guests.

"Ladies and gentlemen, I apologize in advance for this," he said, and then swung one from the floor.

Luckily Vince ducked.

Norma Shearer called out the servant reserves and had them give Vince the bum's rush when he badgered her at one of her parties. She ventured an opinion on a business matter to the pseudo-Eastern executive Barnett, who promptly told her to mind her own business.

"House wives," he insulted, "shouldn't discuss business. If you paid attention to your house it wouldn't look so lousy."

Norma rang the bell and the door slammed from the inside.

And Mae West won't ask Vince Barnett to "come up sometime" after the one he pulled on her on a trip to New York when she was playing in "Diamond Lil."

Posing as a member of the vice [PLEASE TURN TO PAGE 309]

Here's the "Terror" himself. The man Hollywood fears as Italy fears Mussolini. Cartoon by Dobias

"Retire or else take voice lessons from Texas Guinan," so Richard Barthelmess was advised

"No smoking!" And with that the cigar was snatched from Dempsey's mouth at Dempsey's own party

Wera Engels was pale with anger when thus scolded: "You let yourself go in Paris. You got very fat"

The Girl They Tried To Forget

Everyone but Bette Davis raised a hullabaloo about Bette's being almost left out when the Motion Picture Academy made its awards

THE least disturbed by all that thunder in the West—still reverberating—over the Academy of Motion Picture Arts and Sciences' annual awards is that little blonde center-of-it-all, Bette Davis.

She's the least disturbed by the fact that the Academy gave her belated recognition for the dramatic greatness she uncovered in her characterization of the cruel, destroying *Mildred* in "Of Human Bondage," because she cares least about such honors.

Not that she isn't appreciative of the startling flood of indignation with which her staunch supporters inundated the august Academy, nor is she unaware of the fact that a stirring write-in campaign to put her in her rightful place was made and which brought about the "special award."

But, Bette just doesn't give a hoot about such things. As a matter of fact, Bette wasn't even in town when the repercussions began to echo the length and breadth of Cinemaland.

She was away on her idea of a perfectly marvelous vacation.

She was five hundred miles north of Hollywood, up towards San Francisco, in a roadside auto camp with her husband, frying his morning eggs, burning the toast, and worrying far more about her Scottie, which had a boil on its ear, than about the even more painful irritation the Academy had started.

Bette isn't even a member of the Academy. In fact, she has never attended one of the annual Award Banquets at which that congress hands out gold statuettes to various screen artists—including one actor and one actress—saying, in effect, "You're the top. This means that in 1934 you delivered the best individual acting performance on the screen."

BUT this year—well, it was rather taken for granted that Bette would be at least one of the select three to be nominated in accordance with a custom that has endured since the Academy was born. But Bette wasn't even nominated. You remember those nominated were Norma Shearer, Grace Moore and Claudette Colbert, with the final award going to Miss Colbert. And no one will honestly question that final choice, for "It Happened One Night" was grand entertainment—an excellent story with acting that superbly sustained it. No, I think no one is quarreling with the decision, but here is the question that has been raised: why, when nominations were

under consideration, the mental lapse, not only as concerns Bette Davis, but also with regard to Myrna Loy, who climaxed a year of exceptional achievement with her engaging brilliance in "The Thin Man"? And why were Robert Donat's "Count of Monte Cristo," and George Arliss' "Rothschild" overlooked?

The howls, were, however, the loudest concerning the alleged slight to Bette, who is neither "politically" strong nor ever has been handed too much prestige in Hollywood.

Hollywood championed her so vigorously that for a while the whole town seemed to be one giant indignation meeting. Editorials, articles, telegrams, telephone calls bombarded the austere Academy until, I am sure, like the bewildered author in "Once In a Lifetime," its members eventually concluded that "It couldn't *all* be a typographical error."

EVEN my postman lingered the other morning on the doorstep and pushed back his cap from a puckered brow.

"My son and I have been talking about this Academy nearly passing up Bette Davis. It's a darn outrage," he said heatedly, "and I think PHOTOPLAY ought to give 'em the devil!"

What my postman failed to notice was that the Academy, possibly for the second time in its career, had already experienced a goodly dose of "the devil." And it started early, on the posting of the nominations, because after a few days of being on the receiving end of unleavened brickbats, it took pains to announce that the voting for the main award would be free for all. That's when the write-in campaign for Bette started, followed, sometime later, by the "special award" for Bette.

Heretofore, in case you don't know, each acting member of the organization was supposed to have three votes. The three resulting nominations closed the voting—tight.

Not because Bette Davis needed any extra champions. The woods were full of 'em. It was because PHOTOPLAY knew it would be interesting to see how Hollywood's Number One Forgotten Woman felt about suddenly becoming the object of Hollywood heated affections that I dashed on a thousand-mile round trip jaunt to the auto camp, to see her. This auto camp was just south of San Francisco, where Bette, whose weekly pay check does her very, very nicely, was keeping house for her lord and master, Harmon O. Nelson, in Spartan simplicity.

- Bette Davis and her husband, Harmon O. Nelson, live in Spartan simplicity in an auto camp south of San Francisco—and it's no gag

- She was blissfully unaware that thousands were yowling because the Academy forgot her *Mildred* when making the annual awards

- Ham's work is near-by and Bette has a quaint idea that her place is with him. She knows too he won't be supported by a movie-star wife

- She's been forgotten before! Besides, she's busy enjoying life with Ham, learning how to broil lamb chops and make the toast

by KIRTLEY BASKETTE

It's only fair to confess herewith that I, pretty much in common with all the rest of Hollywood, had regarded this auto camp business with a jaundiced eye.

After all, when a Hollywood actress cashes a check for three or four figures of the best every week, and then chooses to stop indefinitely at an auto court, it's news—such unnatural news that it stirs suspicions of a publicity "gag."

But it just happens that the Nelsons live on a budget predicated both on Bette's income and Harmon's income, which last, of course, is not movie money. When she's not working, she lives on his paycheck, and, I might truthfully add—loves it.

"Ham," as she calls him, heads an orchestra in a nearby night club, and Bette has a quaint conviction that a wife's place is with her husband.

She greeted me wearing slacks, and the worried look of a lady whose Scottie is a surgical problem.

I remembered talking to Bette Davis right after "Of Human Bondage" had been released. Like everyone else, I had been tremendously impressed with the genius she had revealed in painting *Mildred*, that vicious, anaemic little trollop of Somerset Maugham's play. Rather reverently I had asked her what in the world had happened to her to give such a performance.

And she answered, "Nothing."

So I should have been prepared for her rejoinder when I informed her importantly, as if [PLEASE TURN TO PAGE 278]

HEDY LAMARR

And Other Dangero[us]

BY BARBARA HAYES

While Hedy Lamarr (top) is the newest uncontested glamour girl, two other brunette beauties, Patricia Morison and Dorothy Lamour, are having a battle royal that has to do with mathematics—strictly speaking, figures

JOAN BENNETT is in Hedy Lamarr's hair—but distinctly.

For while Hedy is the uncontested newest glamour girl, the allure woman of the present season and the oomph gamble of M-G-M, the youngest Bennett has a gleam in her eye and a part in her coiffure that is driving Hedy crazy.

To say that Hedy is piqued by the situation is putting it mildly. The only thing that prevents a violent feud actually developing between them is that pretty Joan won't play. Joan isn't having any feud. She is merely sitting back, impudently smiling, acting the perfect lady that she always is—and if any attitude is more calculated to drive another woman wild, female research is yet to unearth it.

Actually Hollywood doesn't have many feuds any more, all things considered. Good old knock-'em-down, drag-'em-out fights such as Gloria Swanson and Pola Negri used to indulge in are all but outlawed today. As the town has grown larger, it has, perversely, become smaller in its social doings. You simply can't keep a good feud burning if you have to meet your rival five times a week at dinner.

Of course, you can't call the passages at arms that went on between Joan Crawford and Norma Shearer during the making of "The Women" any little friendship binders. Nor are the engagements that currently are being indulged in by Dorothy Lamour and Patricia Morison of the type that exactly cement devotion, and all the catty things Bette Davis and Miriam Hopkins are said to have said to each other during the filming of "The Old Maid" were not in the script. But still and for all, today's stars tend to keep their temperamental clashes to themselves, not nearly so much because they are angels, as because they have to. From picture to picture you can never tell whom you are going to be cast with and even a fine actor finds it difficult to do love scenes opposite a person with whom he has quarreled. (If you don't believe that, recall the chill that lay over the love scenes between Sonja Henie and Ty Power in "Second Fiddle.")

IT'S undoubtedly because Hedy is still rather a stranger around Hollywood that she is being as outspoken as she is about Joan, but at that, her situation is really irksome.

To begin with, Hedy was discovered and put into pictures by Walter Wanger, Joan Bennett's most devoted escort. She had, of course, been brought to this country by M-G-M after making the sensational "Ecstasy," but until Walter cast her in "Algiers," she was wasting her beauty on the desert air of Culver City. With the showing of "Algiers," she proved to be the biggest sensation to hit the movie business since Garbo, and everything looked set for her to become the greatest of new stars. M-G-M hurriedly put her in "I Take This Woman." The name "Lamarr" was used as synonymous with sex appeal, come-hither, charm and all the other desirable attributes of enchantment, but "I Take This Woman" was shelved and, after a long delay, "Lady of the Tropics" was started.

Meanwhile, Joan Bennett had changed her hair from the light blonde she had always worn it on the screen to a dark brown, and then she had proceeded to part that dark brown hair right smack in the middle. Certainly she had a perfect right to do so if she chose to, and you wouldn't expect anything so simple as that to start a revolution, except that when you looked at Joan, you saw that in dark hair she looked enough like Hedy Lamarr to be her twin. Also while Hedy, through no fault of her own, was

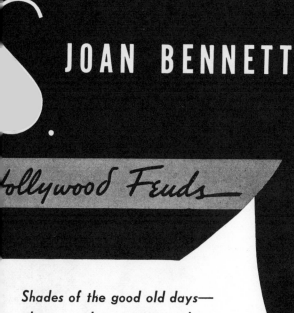

JOAN BENNETT

Hollywood Feuds

Shades of the good old days—glamour girl wars against glamour girl on the Hollywood front

waiting around for a second picture, Joan made the highly successful "Trade Winds," and followed that up, still dark-haired, by the even more successful "Man in the Iron Mask." In other words, Joan looked like Lamarr and acted like the daughter of five generations of good actors which is just what she is, and a very neat combination that does make, too.

Right about then, Joan, who was interested in Hedy because Wanger had discovered her, proceeded to introduce Miss Lamarr to Gene Markey, who is Joan's ex-husband. Hedy called Joan up the next day to say that Gene was fascinating (which he is), and Joan called Gene to say that he had scored a terrific hit with Hedy (which he had), and the next thing you know Mr. Markey and Miss Lamarr were man and wife, with Reggie Gardiner, who had been Hedy's escort up until that time, left very much out in the cold.

Enter, then, the person of Miss Melinda Markey, the very beautiful, very provocative and very small daughter of Gene Markey and Joan Bennett.

Now Joan Bennett is one of those girls who has a genuine passion for maternity. Give her the choice between love, wealth, a career or her daughters and she would not waver for an instant. She would take her children if she had to sacrifice the whole world for them. In fact it was to support her first baby and bring her up magnificently that Joan went out into the world —a divorcee, at eighteen— and literally went hungry until she got her first big break in pictures. There is not one detail of the lives of Ditty, the older daughter, or Melinda, the younger, that Joan does not supervise. Nothing from their diet, to their posture, their schooling, or their clothes is left to chance.

So, therefore, when Joan, in response to Gene's request, said that she preferred not to have Melinda visit his new home because she felt a five-year-old was much too young to understand about "Daddy's new

(Continued on page 310)

La Bennett won't play. She's having no part in a violent feud. But worse revolutions have been started for less than what Joan has done. In the meantime, Hollywood's having its day

Norma—intelligent, calm, reserved. Joan—impulsive, generous, warm. Theirs is that eternal conflict between mind and emotions —and a bitter one, too

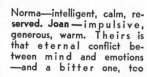

The trail is dark and hidden (by the publicity department) in the Bette Davis-Miriam Hopkins battle—but we were the profiteers in the feud that went on during the making of "The Old Maid"

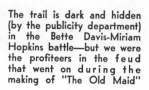

THE *Camera* SPEAKS

Turn the page and get a welcome to the Darryl Zanucks' party just as hearty as the one W. C. Fields is giving Fanny Brice—a salute from one Ziegfeld graduate to another!

The place: The Gables' Valley ranch. The time: Any day between takes of "G.W.T.W." and "Vigil in the Night." The people: Leaders of Hollywood's fast-growing station wagon set—Clark and Carole

Carpenter

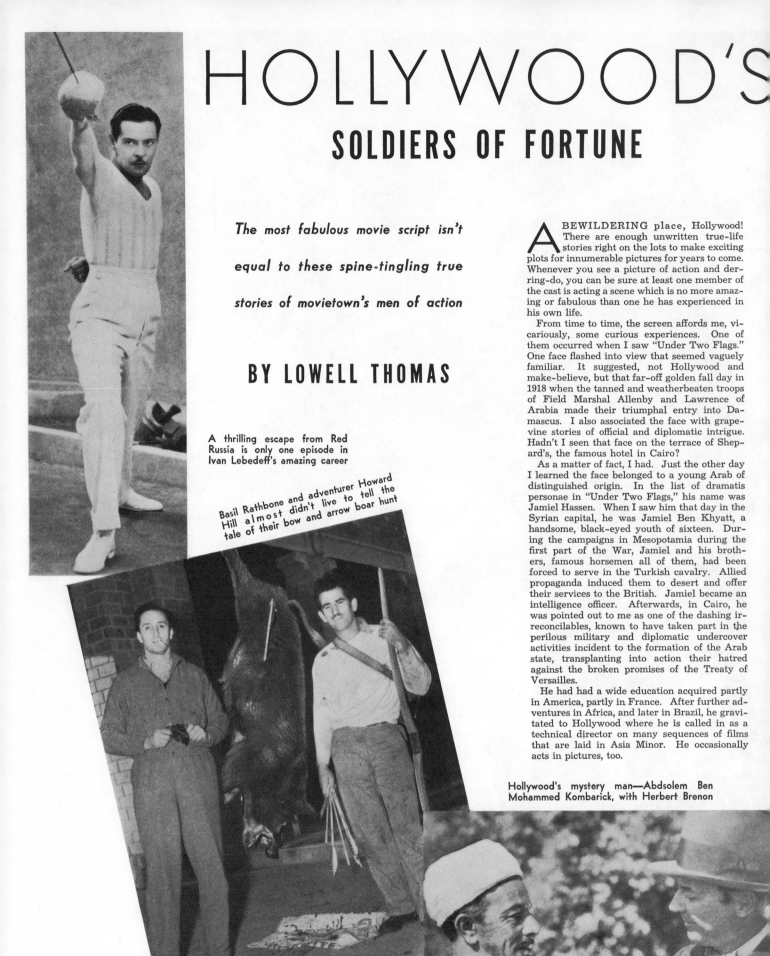

HOLLYWOOD'S
SOLDIERS OF FORTUNE

*The most fabulous movie script isn't
equal to these spine-tingling true
stories of movietown's men of action*

BY LOWELL THOMAS

A thrilling escape from Red
Russia is only one episode in
Ivan Lebedeff's amazing career

Basil Rathbone and adventurer Howard
Hill almost didn't live to tell the
tale of their bow and arrow boar hunt

A BEWILDERING place, Hollywood! There are enough unwritten true-life stories right on the lots to make exciting plots for innumerable pictures for years to come. Whenever you see a picture of action and derring-do, you can be sure at least one member of the cast is acting a scene which is no more amazing or fabulous than one he has experienced in his own life.

From time to time, the screen affords me, vicariously, some curious experiences. One of them occurred when I saw "Under Two Flags." One face flashed into view that seemed vaguely familiar. It suggested, not Hollywood and make-believe, but that far-off golden fall day in 1918 when the tanned and weatherbeaten troops of Field Marshal Allenby and Lawrence of Arabia made their triumphal entry into Damascus. I also associated the face with grapevine stories of official and diplomatic intrigue. Hadn't I seen that face on the terrace of Shepard's, the famous hotel in Cairo?

As a matter of fact, I had. Just the other day I learned the face belonged to a young Arab of distinguished origin. In the list of dramatis personae in "Under Two Flags," his name was Jamiel Hassen. When I saw him that day in the Syrian capital, he was Jamiel Ben Khyatt, a handsome, black-eyed youth of sixteen. During the campaigns in Mesopotamia during the first part of the War, Jamiel and his brothers, famous horsemen all of them, had been forced to serve in the Turkish cavalry. Allied propaganda induced them to desert and offer their services to the British. Jamiel became an intelligence officer. Afterwards, in Cairo, he was pointed out to me as one of the dashing irreconcilables, known to have taken part in the perilous military and diplomatic undercover activities incident to the formation of the Arab state, transplanting into action their hatred against the broken promises of the Treaty of Versailles.

He had had a wide education acquired partly in America, partly in France. After further adventures in Africa, and later in Brazil, he gravitated to Hollywood where he is called in as a technical director on many sequences of films that are laid in Asia Minor. He occasionally acts in pictures, too.

Hollywood's mystery man—Abdsolem Ben
Mohammed Kombarick, with Herbert Brenon

Two sons of Erin who share a lust for life. Above, Errol Flynn, most famed of Hollywood's daredevils . . .

. . . and, left, George Brent, who had a price set on his head in the days of the Irish Rebellion

Victor McLaglen (right) takes any fighting or soldiering rôle in his stride. He knows!

One day, working on the set of "Under Two Flags," a member of the cast came up and said to him:

"Weren't you a Turkish cavalry officer in the Mesopotamian campaign?"

"Why, yes—yes, I was," answered the surprised Jamiel.

"And during a bitter skirmish near Bagdad, weren't you in command of a detachment which nearly captured a British officer?" continued the actor.

"That's right," said the puzzled Jamiel. "We fired several shots at him but he escaped over a wall. But how did you know?"

"I was the British officer," said the actor.

The actor was Victor McLaglen.

QUITE as varied as the Arab's is the saga of Victor McLaglen. The rôle of the bitter, fighting Irish patriot in "The Informer" and the wise-cracking, genial sergeant in "Wee Willie Winkie" —in fact, any rôle which includes fighting or soldiering, McLaglen takes in his stride. He knows.

It is strange to think McLaglen was born in a humdrum London suburb, a rectory, to boot. Six feet four in height, he says he's the "runt" of the family, which includes eight enormous brothers and one sister. When Victor was fourteen, the Rev. McLaglen became Colonial Bishop of South Africa. Then the Boer War broke out. The strapping fourteen-year-oldster had little trouble persuading the Recruiting Sergeant that he was old enough to fight. After the War, he worked in the gold mines of the Rand, the diamond mines of Kimberly. Even that was too tame. Footloose, he drifted to America, took up prize fighting and wrestling, won the heavyweight championship of Eastern Canada. In between bouts, he worked as a stevedore. (Remember him not long ago in "The Magnificent Brute," heaving the huge ladle of molten steel into the vast maw of fiery furnaces below him?)

Once McLaglen even turned copper. He looks back upon that experience with reasonable pride, for he was no ordinary harness bull but Chief of the Railway Police at Owens Sound where he pulled off exploits of real value for the law, including the arrest and imprisonment of a fur-stealing gang.

He finally gave up the ring to join a medicine show, left that to travel with a Wild West outfit. When that palled, he shipped aboard a tramp steamer bound for Fiji and Australia. He landed in Perth just as the gold rush to the Kal-goorie field was beginning. It was inevitable that he should join this expedition, but McLaglen was one of the thousands who found more experience than gold. Aboard another tramp steamer to Ceylon and Bombay. Since his boyhood in the rectory, the tales of Rudyard Kipling had aroused in him an ambition to go through the jealously guarded Kyber Pass. It was no journey for a tourist, but McLaglen accomplished it.

During the War he was in Mesopotamia with the Irish Fusileers, was decorated for bravery in action against the Turks and the Germans. He eventually became Prevost Marshal with the rank of Captain.

It was in England that Captain McLaglen first got into pictures. British films in those days were pretty poor affairs, but they were the means of his eventually going to Hollywood. Since "What Price Glory," the Laurence Stallings-Maxwell Anderson war play in which McLaglen could practically make up his own lines he knew them so well, his career has been easy sailing. Today he lives on one of the most enviable estates in California, surrounded by horses and dogs, served by an Arabian valet, (Continued on page 313)

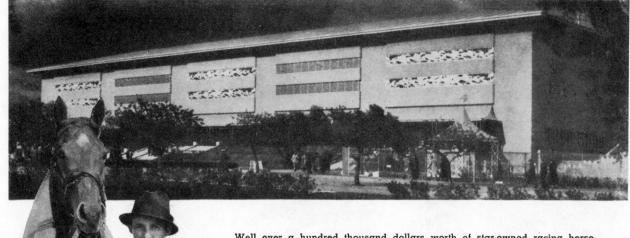

Well over a hundred thousand dollars worth of star-owned racing horse-flesh awaits its destiny at popular Santa Anita race track, shown above

Now—It's Horses

"They're off!" Who's off, mister? The horses or the movie stars? Well, it's the latest enthusiasm

By Kirtley Baskette

Bing Crosby keeps his prancing pets down on his ranch at Rancho Santa Fe. He's put his hopes in Khayam, above, to lead them home at Churchill Downs in a year or so

There's always bound to be a gay crowd at Santa Anita, watching the races. Right, Sally Eilers, Sharon Lynn, and Ann Alvarado are waiting for the start

Look at 'em! Who has a ticket on the winning horse? We'd say Ben Bernie. Arline Judge, husband Wesley Ruggles and his brother Charlie don't look quite so lucky as ye maestro

"**T**HEY'RE off!" blares the loud-speaker.

It is Christmas Day at Santa Anita and across the purple velvet of the Sierra Madres the afternoon pennons of a California sun slant on the taut tendons and slick sides of a bunch of bobtailed nags.

"They're off!" echo the jam-packed stands where the rays proceed to highlight hundreds of faces any moviegoer could pick out of the crowd with no trouble at all.

It is Christmas Day at Santa Anita, and if you could rise above the color and excitement of this auspicious opening of Hollywood's second big racing season, you might calmly and reasonably question,

"Who's off, mister? The horses or the movie stars?"

For that fevered babble you hear of "selling platers," and "speed burners," "morning glories" and "mudders;" that hectic glow that reddens a famous face when the jockeys boot 'em home—they are merely symptoms of a seasonal madness, a delirium into which Hollywood has gradually been whipped, en masse, by the mighty *virus equus*, or "horse bug" to you.

They get a new enthusiasm every season

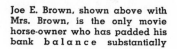

Among the many stars who are to be found at Santa Anita every year, Jack Holt is one you'll surely see. Above, it's Lady's Man and Charming Lois Wilson

or so, these movie stars. They've had it for cars. They've had it for yachts. They went crazy for tennis, for badminton, for the desert, for bicycles. But horses are killing them.

Last year the siege was comparatively mild, but this year it's an epidemic, fanned into fury by stacks of Hollywood greenbacks invested in thoroughbred horseflesh, by records of betting clean-ups (and clean-outs), by pages of systems, dope-sheets and rival hometown riding silks.

Last year horseracing was new and a little frightening to most of the stars. They stood on the side like a country boy taking his first spring swim, and tested gingerly the exhilarating current—but this year beginners' luck has all run out and practically everyone you know or ever heard of it—at least in his own estimation—a wise and experienced old railbird, set to plunge ahead on into the Sport of Kings.

And that "plunge" is more than a figure of speech. It signifies a deep dive into stellar pockets for the stuff that makes a horse race interesting. They didn't name it the Sport of Kings because a jockey happened to wear a purple shirt. "They're off!" also means the lids are off the Hollywood coffers as they have never before been off for purely sporting purposes. Even those investments for a comfortable old age which have been concerning the heavy sugar makers of late, will have to wait while the ponies run.

Last season fifteen million dollars poured through the betting machines of Santa Anita. It wasn't all from the wallets of the colony, of course, but they did their bit. This season much more than a wagering interest glues Hollywood to the track.

Well over a hundred thousand dollars worth of star-owned racing horseflesh, bought, trained and groomed for the past year with Santa Anita in mind faces the barriers this year carrying the silks of sports minded stars.

Last year Clark Gable created something of a mild sensation by actually buying a racehorse, one Beverly Hills, of whom

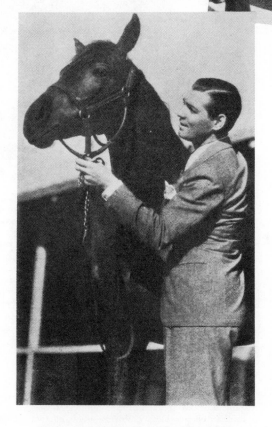

Clark Gable's Beverly Hills (there they are above) won his first big race. But then—well, read a neat bit of racing luck

Joe E. Brown, shown above with Mrs. Brown, is the only movie horse-owner who has padded his bank balance substantially

there is more to tell later on. Connie Bennett, not to be outdone, responded with Rattlebrain. And after consistently backing a nondescript nag named Bing Crosby, who had a forlorn habit of eating dust, the real Bing decided to toss sentiment to the winds and risk his roll on horses he could keep an eye on. Whereupon he claimed one Zombie after a claiming race and started the most famous movie stable to date, one in fact, which may someday give the Whitneys and the Bradleys and the Dodge-Sloans and the Vanderbilts a respectable run for their money, if Bing's dream comes true.

For from Zombie, whose sinister name somehow seemed to scare the rest of the horses into running right away from him, the Crosby stables have grown to impressive proportions.

Before the season closed last year, Bing had gathered seven bangtails under his blue and gold colors, picked, you know, from his former radio theme song, "When The Blue Of The Night Meets The Gold Of The Day." Like Zombie they were no Man O' Wars. They set him back around $1500 apiece, the original price tag on Zombie.

Today Bing counts sixteen horses in his rapidly multiplying thoroughbred family. They represent an investment of around eighteen thousand dollars, and Bing figures that each horse costs him roughly $100 a month to keep. $1600 a month is an item if you call it a hobby. But [PLEASE TURN TO PAGE 316]

HOLLYWOOD'S UNMARRIED

"Just friends" to the world at

large—yet nowhere has domesticity

taken on so unique a character

as in this unconventional fold

The romance of Clark Gable and Carole Lombard is an interesting manifestation of how famous untied twosomes take to one another's hobbies. But calling the case of Paulette Goddard and Charlie Chaplin (top) is something else again. Did they take the vows on Charlie's yacht? Even Hollywood wonders

BY KIRTLEY BASKETTE

EVERY afternoon, for the past three years, a little meat market on Larchmont Avenue, near Paramount studios in Hollywood, has received a telephone call from a woman ordering a choice New York cut steak.

Sometimes she orders it sent to the Brown Derby, sometimes to an apartment penthouse on Rossmore Street, sometimes to the studio.

Wherever George Raft happens to be dining.

The woman who sees that George Raft has his favorite evening meal, no matter where he may be, is Virginia Pine. She is not George's wife, although there's little doubt that she would be if George's long-estranged wife would give him a divorce.

Carole Lombard is not Clark Gable's wife, either. Still she has remodeled her whole Hollywood life for him. She calls him "Pappy," goes hunting with him, copies his hobbies, makes his interests dominate hers.

Barbara Stanwyck is not Mrs. Robert Taylor. But she and Bob have built ranch homes next to each other. Regularly, once a week, they visit Bob's mother, Mrs. Brugh, for dinner. Regularly, once a week, too, Barbara freezes homemade ice cream for Bob from a recipe his mother gave her.

Nowhere has domesticity, outside the marital state, reached such a full flower as in Hollywood. Nowhere are there so many famous unmarried husbands and wives.

To the outside world Clark Gable and Carole Lombard might as well be married. So might Bob Taylor and Barbara. Or George Raft and Virginia Pine, Charlie Chaplin and Paulette Goddard. Unwed couples they might be termed. But they go everywhere together; do everything in pairs. No hostess would think of inviting them separately, or pairing them with another. They solve one another's problems, handle each other's business affairs.

They build houses near each other, buy land in bunches, take up each other's hobbies, father or mother each other's children—even correct each other's clothes—each other's personalities! Yet, to the world, their official status is "just friends." No more.

Yet George Raft, a one-woman man if there ever was one, is as true to Virginia Pine as a model husband would be. He has been, for three years. He has just bought her an expensive home in Beverly Hills. Recently, when they had a slight tiff, George took out some other girls, but was plainly so torch-burdened he could hardly stand it. He has never seriously looked at anyone else. Nor has Virginia.

Consider the results—strictly out of wedlock.

Before they met and fell in love, George was the easiest "touch" in Hollywood. He made big and easy money and just so easily did it slip through his fingers and into the outstretched palms of his myriad down-and-out friends. George, who came up the hard way, still has a heart as big as a casaba melon and as soft inside. But he is more careful with his money now. He invests it—and well.

Before he met Virginia, George's civic interests ventured little further than Hollywood and Vine, the fights, and a few of the hotter night spots. Now George Raft has his finger in a dozen Los Angeles business ventures and community interests. He is a solid citizen.

Before George and Virginia teamed up as a tight little twosome, George gloried in flashy, extremely-cut clothes. His suits, always immaculately knife-edge creased, had trousers with the highest waistlines in town. His coats were tight across the shoulders, narrowed extremely at the waist. His shoes were narrow, pointed and Cuban-heeled. He was Mister Broadway.

Virginia talked him into seeing Watson, one of Hollywood's most exclusive tailors. What's more, she talked him out of the theatrical clothes and into a more conservative taste.

All this is called "settling down." It usually happens to people after they've been married. Only George and Virginia still aren't married. He lives at the El Royale Apartments and Virginia lives in another building up the street. They just go together. But she orders his meals. And he spoils her little girl to death.

HUSBANDS AND WIVES

Gilbert Roland (top) has been Connie Bennett's devoted slave for years, while Connie's titled husband remains in Europe. Just "going together" are Virginia Pine and George Raft—but she orders his meals and he fathers her little daughter, Joan

Another "almost perfect" domestic picture—Barbara Stanwyck (top, with her son Dion) and Robert Taylor. Interests—deep, expensive, permanent—merged when Bob bought the knoll adjoining Barbara's Northridge ranch. Marriage couldn't have worked more of a change

No real father could be more infatuated than George with Virginia's five-year-old daughter, Joan. Nor would you call George the perfect picture of a family man, either. He has already paid up an insurance policy that will guarantee Joan a nice little stake when she is ready for college. He seems to lie awake nights planning something new and delightful to surprise her with whenever he sees Virginia, and that's usually all the time.

One of the stories the salesgirls still tell down at Bullock's-Wilshire, Los Angeles' swankiest store, is about the day Virginia Pine and little Joan came into the shop. Joan spied something she wanted right then. But Virginia, wishing to impress upon her daughter that a person isn't

always able to have what he or she likes in this world, said, "But, Joan, you can't have that. You haven't the money to pay for it."

"Oh, that's all right," stated Joan in a loud, clear voice. "Just charge it to George Raft!"

When Bob Taylor docked in New York from England and "A Yank At Oxford," he waited around a couple of hours for a load of stuff he had bought over there to clear customs. Most of it was for—not Bob—but Barbara Stanwyck and her little son, Dion.

They've been practically a family since Bob bought his ranch estate in Northridge and built a house there.

Northridge, itself, is an interesting manifestation of how Hollywood's untied twosomes

buy and build together. It lies in a far corner of the San Fernando Valley, fairly remote from Hollywood, all of fifteen miles from Bob's studio, Metro-Goldwyn-Mayer. No coincidence can possibly explain his choosing that site, pleasant and open though it is, right beside Barbara Stanwyck's place.

Barbara was there first. With the Zeppo Marxes, she established Marwyck Ranch to breed thoroughbred horses. She built a handsome ranch house and moved out. Bob Taylor had never been especially interested in either ranch life or horses until he started going with Barbara. But witness how quickly their interests—deep and expensive, *permanent* interests

(Continued on page 320)

A HEART-TO-HEART TALK

WE REGRET that it is necessary for us to have this heart-to-heart talk with our readers and our friends in Hollywood.

For more than twenty-five years PHOTOPLAY has stood as a friend and champion of the motion-picture industry and has demonstrated consistently, we believe, its eagerness to play fair with our readers, the stars and the industry as a whole.

Unintentionally, we have been made to appear to step out of this character upon which we so pride ourselves.

Last month, we published in PHOTOPLAY a story in which we described friendships existing between prominent men and women in Hollywood, friendships which are well known to our readers and the public through articles that have appeared here and elsewhere for some time.

The purpose of our story was to show that these relationships in their companionable and mutually helpful aspects were so worth while that it was our hope that they could eventually culminate in happy marriages.

We regret that the purpose of this story was misinterpreted in certain newspapers. Excerpts were republished without permission and removed from the context, making these friendships appear in a light far from our original intention.

Such an interpretation is unfair, not only to this magazine but to the stars involved. We must stand on our reputation of solid and constructive publishing history when we assure the stars mentioned in the story, as well as their studios, that we genuinely regret these unfortunate interpretations of our meaning and motive. This article was intended merely to portray some of the finest friendships we have ever known.

Hired to double, she literally became the Swedish star

Greta Garbo herself—The white flame of Sweden. Note the uncanny resemblance of the extra girl opposite to the popular star

Geraldine De Vorak — Greta's double. The resemblance is remarkable. Physically she is the same to the half-inch in measurement

The Girl who Played Greta Garbo

By Lois Shirley

"GOTT! She looks like me!"

Greta Garbo, seated in the dark projection room, saw her exact likeness flashed across the screen. The gowns made for her newest picture were being modeled by her double.

"You like this frock, Miss Garbo?" the costume designer asked.

"Oh, yes, O.K." she said absently. Her interest was not in the way the dresses hung, nor how the colors photographed. She was held by the amazing likeness she saw before her. "Dot girl! Gott, don't she look like me?"

There are two Garbos in Hollywood.

One is the white flame from Sweden.

The other is Geraldine De Vorak, her double.

Geraldine's duties consist in having gowns fitted on her, in making wardrobe tests and in standing in front of the camera until the lights are ready. Occasionally she is used for a long shot to save the star's energy.

She has assumed more specific duties than these. Having become a figment of her own imagination, she has taken it upon herself to play the rôle of Garbo. She is what Garbo should be and isn't.

She is Greta Garbo's private life.

Her physical requirements are exact. Greta and Geraldine measure the same to the half inch, weigh the same to the half pound. Their faces are shaped alike.

Geraldine has everything that Garbo has except *whatever it is that Garbo has*. To the latter has been given a great, vital talent. To the other an imagination only. An imagination so demanding that she has been able to re-create herself in the likeness of the Garbo.

Psychologically, the thing is sound.

Garbo's own private life does not suit the silver sheet lady of passion. The off-screen Garbo is hopelessly young, as *gauche* as a farmer boy and as timid as a younger sister. Her tweed coats are the despair of the modistes. She wears her little sports hats pulled tight down over her ears.

Her dislike of grandeur amounts to a passion. It is her delight to pass up limousines in her shiny little Ford. She has attended but one *premiere*. She has never crossed the sacred

portal of Eddie Brandstatter's Montmartre Cafe. A publicity man's camera is a red signal for flight.

These outward manifestations she leaves, ironically enough, to an extra girl on a forty dollar a week salary. Greta takes the cash and Geraldine the credit.

The paraphernalia of stardom is anathema to Garbo. At heart she is a simple Swedish girl, and the sudden success that now surrounds her is not worth a single white-capped wave on a Scandinavian sea.

She is, I'm afraid, a bitter disappointment to the executives at the studio. Not from a box office standpoint, mind you. The shekels she has brought in are of bright, true gold. But she has failed as a private life star.

Such a dazzling personality on the screen! She might see her picture in every paper in every city every day. But she refuses to do anything to put it there. She leaves the studio at night and goes straight home. She pulls her little sports hat over her eyes and travels the world incognito.

STARDOM bores her, so she leaves her glittering, dazzling, successful garments at the studio. And there Geraldine De Vorak finds them and puts them on.

Strange—that to the one should be given the divine gift and to the other only the desire.

Garbo is the actress. De Vorak, the star.

Geraldine is everything that a star should be.

Tweed coats and little sports hats? There's not a one in her wardrobe. She wears what Garbo should wear. Small, interesting toques. Clinging velvet gowns. Furs.

Her hair is combed back off her face like Garbo's. She walks majestically into the studio commissary and sits alone at a table. She has grace, where Garbo is awkward. She cups her chin in her hands and imagines that she is Garbo.

Strange—that two women should be made in the same mould. They are alike, completely alike, physically. But one has, in some inexplicable manner, clasped a feather of the bird of beauty.

Geraldine, living in a world of her own making, ignores the difference in their stations. To Garbo the acclaim is nothing. She doesn't care a Swedish herring [PLEASE TURN TO PAGE 309]

WHEN THEY WERE

TWO-BIT

In 1925, the misses Myrna Loy (top) and Lucille LeSeuer (right), supporting glamorous star Zasu Pitts in "Pretty Ladies," burst upon a public, which, unfortunately, didn't notice them. The future Joan Crawford is the Japanese lady at the far right on the stage; Myrna is draped over the left end of the bamboo bridge

In "Dancing Lady," way back in 1933, a blond young man was hired to appear in just one scene in which he was to sing to the heroine. He did his job thoroughly, made a hasty exit. His name, new to the fans, was Nelson Eddy

The tense look on the face of this young bit player may be the result of his proximity to that gangster (see above) On the other hand, it may be his way of making the most of his few scenes in "Don't Bet on Blondes," starring Claire Dodd. Presenting Errol Flynn —who, one year later, was to shoot to stardom in "Captain Blood"

This young man haunted Central Casting until, in desperation, they got him a job. As a bit player in "The Collegians" in 1929, the future King of the Movies started the upward climb via the now-famous Gable grin, which flashed, then, without benefit of make-up man

he's dynamite for Paramount today, ut in 1928 she was just a minor femi- ine foil for Bill Boyd in Pathe's Power." It was all just "good, clean omedy," though, and, despite the fact hat her name was the last on the cast, Iiss Lombard enjoyed her bit part im- ensely, went to town as "A Flapper"

A small brunette took time off from a college career to act a bit in "Words and Music," starring Lois Moran; liked it so well she gave up mathematics for the movies; was rewarded by marriage to Joel McCrea, and a lead in Para- mount's "Wells Fargo": it's Frances Dee

"The Love Parade" of 1929 excited the critics because: 1, it was All Talkie (!); 2, it boasted Jeanette MacDonald, an "eye feast." They ignored the other eye feast, cast simply as "Second Lady in Waiting"—Virginia Bruce

The Tragedy

OUTSIDE the gates of the studio stand a large group of people, waiting. From all walks of life they come. The ex-vaudeville actor, the ex-jockey, former businessmen, Chinese girls, one-time millionaires, hobos, young men, old men, girls, old women—and still more heart-rending, former stars and featured players discarded by the changing movies.

All hoping against hope that some miracle will happen and they will find themselves inside the gates, headed for the casting office.

"Had any luck lately?" I asked a slim, young girl.

She smiled. "One day's work in seven months. I'm used to having a tough time, though. But see that guy up there with the blue flannel jacket? I can remember when he was an important casting director, himself."

Hollywood we know as a bright and tinseled land of romance. But now beneath its surface boils and bubbles a mass of trouble which threatens to burst through the glamour-coated crust of Moviedom and cover Hollywood with a lava of grief.

For, fifteen thousand people in Hollywood's motion picture industry will soon find themselves completely cut off from any chance of earning a living there. Their earnings were always meager enough! Mostly they lived on hope. And now that is being taken from them, too. Hope. Hope . . Hope . . .

It's the watchword of thousands who call themselves extras in this business of making motion pictures. It's the thing that keeps them going on day after day, hungry, anxious, tired, waiting in the hot sun or standing in the rain outside the studio gates, wearing a fixed, false smile because a director, an assistant director, a producer, anyone, someone, might notice the smile and beckon them into the magic portals of the motion picture studio.

And now, for fifteen thousand, that hope is being taken away.

For, there are 17,541 people registered at the Central Casting Office as extras. And the list now is being cut down to approximately fifteen hundred names. A mere pencil mark, and fifteen thousand would-be actors and actresses will be flung out of the world of motion pictures forever, into the streets of Hollywood.

These two girls came to Hollywood and found jobs in the studios as extras. But now, after months of unemployment, they are living in a tent, clinging desperately to the hope that by some stroke of magic the studio gates will open to them again

Weary after a day of shooting, the extras on location wait to be paid off. These were working in M-G-M's "The Tide of Empire." Since the spectacle picture has given way to the simpler drama, scenes like the above are becoming very rare

of 15,000 Extras

Struggling to win a place in the cinema sun, hungry, dispirited, they must put behind them forever their dreams of screen success

By Sara Hamilton

What will Hollywood do with this mass of hungry, hopeless people?

And who is to blame for the tragedy?

Strangely enough, the extras themselves are greatly to blame for their own pitiful plight.

Tossed out of other work by the recent depression, attracted by the false stories of Hollywood's squanderings and extravagances, excited by the thrill of living and working in the same town and the same industry with world famous personalities, they drifted to Hollywood and attached themselves to the motion picture industry. They registered with the Central Casting Bureau, and joined the great army of extras.

The Central Casting Bureau, bewildered and harassed by the ever-increasing demands for work, overburdened with the growing army of ambitious, inexperienced extras, looked about for some solution.

It was the extras themselves who offered the solution.

Not the drifted-in extras. But the men and women who for years have made the business of being an extra their life work.

[PLEASE TURN TO PAGE 331]

Dreams of stardom and living in a palace have vanished for the little group of extras who have begun to build themselves a shantytown near Universal City out of junked lumber and tin. In the film colony there is now no way for them to earn a living

When a studio asks for extras, here's the answer. Thousands wait day after day, hungry but ever hopeful that a casting director will call for them. Before long, 15,000 extras will be cut off the lists of the Central Casting Bureau. Then *all* hope will be gone

What price has Griffith got for so much glory? He denies he is "broke"

By Mildred Mastin

the names on the signs were different. Next week they will be changed again."

It was a theatrical statement, made by a man who has a talent for expressing simple truths in a melodramatic way.

The man was David Wark Griffith.

Recently, a columnist wrote that the director is broke, in need. If that is true, Griffith does not admit it. He points with pride to several rare pieces of antique furniture in his apartment; to his library, its walls lined with finely bound books. He speaks casually of a winter vacation in Florida, of the pleasant, leisurely hours he is spending now, rewriting some plays.

Thus, subtly, he denies rumors that he needs financial help. For he is intensely proud.

Griffith should be wealthy today. He is not, because, like most artists, he lacks good business sense.

Many major improvements in picture making were invented or initiated by David Wark Griffith. A clever business man would be collecting royalties. Griffith collects nothing—except occasional praise, when someone is feeling sentimental.

There was a time when motion

When David Wark Griffith was a great man in movies. This rare picture reveals him directing a scene for "Hearts of the World," in 1918. Billy Bitzer is on the camera stoop

The Star-Maker Whose Dreams Turned to Dust

AT the window of a tall Manhattan hotel, a man stood looking down at Broadway. From the window, twenty-two stories above the street, he watched hundreds of dancing, burning electric signs, screaming the names of movies and their stars.

For twenty years the man had been the outstanding creative genius in motion pictures. He was idle now. Out of the game.

"Movies," he commented slowly, "are written in sand. Applauded today, forgotten tomorrow. Last week

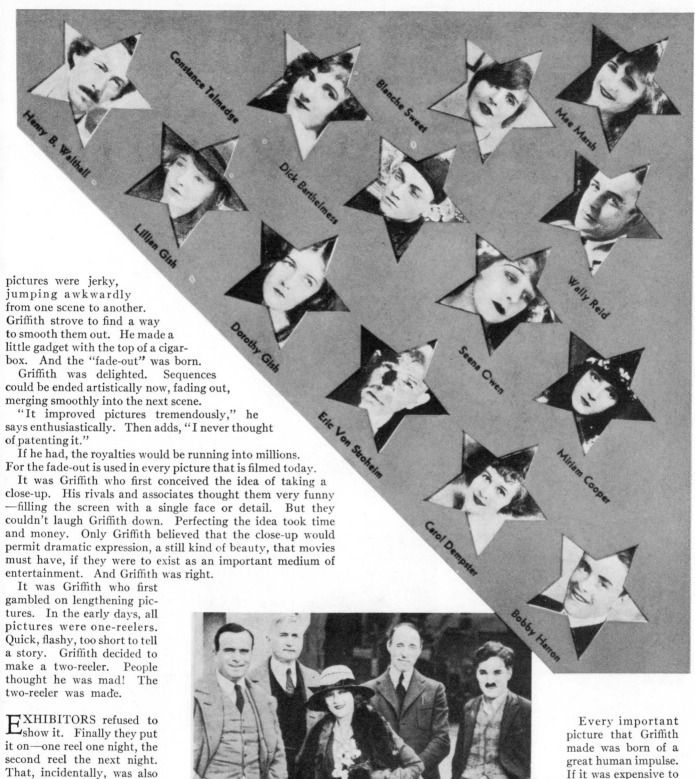

pictures were jerky, jumping awkwardly from one scene to another. Griffith strove to find a way to smooth them out. He made a little gadget with the top of a cigar-box. And the "fade-out" was born.

Griffith was delighted. Sequences could be ended artistically now, fading out, merging smoothly into the next scene.

"It improved pictures tremendously," he says enthusiastically. Then adds, "I never thought of patenting it."

If he had, the royalties would be running into millions. For the fade-out is used in every picture that is filmed today.

It was Griffith who first conceived the idea of taking a close-up. His rivals and associates thought them very funny —filling the screen with a single face or detail. But they couldn't laugh Griffith down. Perfecting the idea took time and money. Only Griffith believed that the close-up would permit dramatic expression, a still kind of beauty, that movies must have, if they were to exist as an important medium of entertainment. And Griffith was right.

It was Griffith who first gambled on lengthening pictures. In the early days, all pictures were one-reelers. Quick, flashy, too short to tell a story. Griffith decided to make a two-reeler. People thought he was mad! The two-reeler was made.

EXHIBITORS refused to show it. Finally they put it on—one reel one night, the second reel the next night. That, incidentally, was also the beginning of the serial.

The first picture that might properly be called of epic dimensions was a Griffith gamble—"The Birth of a Nation." Griffith did not produce that picture because he thought it would make money. (And, of course, he got little money out of it. He doesn't even own the film today.) He planned it because, he says, he wanted to tell the North the truth about the South. As a child he had sat in a Kentucky schoolhouse and read, with bitter resentment, the story of the Civil War, always written by a Northerner. Some day, he promised himself, *he*, a Southerner, would tell the story.

Remember when these outstanding celebrities organized the United Artists Association? Left to right: Doug Fairbanks, Oscar A. Price (Association president), Mary Pickford, Griffith, Chaplin

Every important picture that Griffith made was born of a great human impulse. If it was expensive to express the thing he had to say, Griffith did not economize. But he was never extravagant in the spectacular, superficial way that some others have been.

He produced over four hundred films. And the total cost of making them was approximately twelve million dollars. The gross profits from the pictures were five times that—slightly over sixty millions. Only a small part of these profits ever found their way back to Griffith. When they did, he usually tossed the money, with reckless courage, into another picture. [PLEASE TURN TO PAGE 332]

Ralph Graves, once a movie hero, is now a writer. This picture was taken after he married the late Marjorie Seaman, left. The other lady is Colleen Moore

startled into semi-shame at its own forgetfulness, looks around to check up on the lost legion of stars that were. At such times when a player, whose name once was a toast and still is a tradition, bobs up shorn of the glittering robes of stardom.

True, some of those who tasted glory are doing well enough in careers far removed from greasepaint. Others are having a hard, heart-breaking time of it, trying to stay in the profession which remains their very life's blood. Some have new philosophies—others live in the past. But all prove that Fate, where careers are concerned, plays few favorites in Hollywood.

Fifteen years or so ago, the biggest star on the Universal lot was pretty Ella Hall, still remembered for the film, "Jewel."

Today, Ella Hall is a saleswoman at the most exclusive women's dress shop on Hollywood Boulevard. And she's a very good one, too—so good that all the stars' trade contacts are in her charge.

Ella was said to have been in love with Director Robert Leonard, but vivacious Mae Murray, coming out from the "Follies" stole him away.

W HEN Clara Kimball Young was discovered recently living in a shabby, four-family flat in Los Angeles, financially pressed for the necessities of comfortable existence, Hollywood shuddered when it recalled the Clara Kimball Young of only yesterday.

Then she was the magnificent star whose city estate was one of the show places of Los Angeles. Then she was the best dressed actress in Hollywood, whose $50,000 chin-chilla coat established a legend of sartorial splendor.

It seemed that Clara had suddenly been harshly dealt with by life, by the Fates of Hollywood who spin destinies with small regard for feelings. But, of course, it wasn't sudden at all—just seemingly to Hollywood, which is so busy with exciting affairs of the moment that it hasn't time to look back very often.

Someone outside of Hollywood had to tell Hollywood about Clara Kimball Young. From that she got her first screen job in many, many months—the part of Jackie Coogan's mother in Jackie's film comeback. It was a job she needed badly.

It is at times like this that Hollywood,

Clara Kimball Young, at one time most glamorous of stars, was recently discovered in a shabby Los Angeles flat. The old fellow receiving the drink is George Fawcett, once famous for his grumpy rôles

STARS

Read the roll of famous names of other days. What do we find these folk doing now?

By Kirtley Baskette

So Ella married Emory Johnson, an actor-director, who failed of complete success. When their children needed additional support, she took a job behind the counter and made good.

When Bebe Daniels and Mrs. Skeets Gallagher opened their new dress shop in Westwood Village, they wanted Ella to take charge of it. But her employer wouldn't let her go. She was too valuable. She was reckoned a star again—but this time a star saleswoman.

Business always has attracted stars to whom the screen seemed to offer nothing

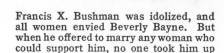

Francis X. Bushman was idolized, and all women envied Beverly Bayne. But when he offered to marry any woman who could support him, no one took him up

further. Some have developed latent trade talent and achieved success. To others, the venture has meant the loss of what financial security they had left.

Kathleen Clifford, "Pretty Kitty" Clifford, who at one time was Hollywood's most beautiful blonde ingénue and, later, leading lady, started and operated a chain of florist establishments in Hollywood and Beverly Hills until the depression came along and forced her to give them up. Now she runs a beauty shop, a more modest business, but one which she is making yield her a living.

Katherine MacDonald, the stately "American Beauty," whom President Woodrow Wilson nominated as his favorite of all screen stars, launched her own cosmetic shop with some success, while Florence Lawrence, the famous old "Biograph Girl," who was the biggest star of the biggest company of its day—even before Mary Pickford had ascended to her throne—failed not long ago in a beauty salon venture. Now she lives in an obscure section of Hollywood, completely out of the scintillating world.

Many will never forget Milton Sills and Katherine MacDonald in "The Woman Thou Gavest Me." Her movie days over, Katherine went into the cosmetic business. Sills died in 1930, after a heart attack

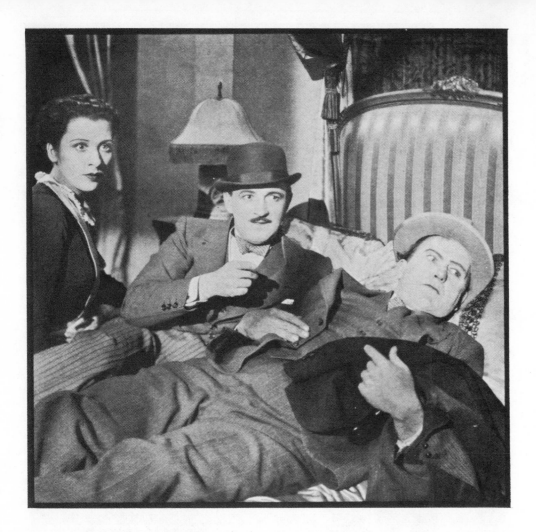

[PLEASE TURN TO PAGE 337]

Raymond Griffith (center) was a favorite in pre-talkie days. His inaudible voice hurtled him from top-rank. Now he is Zanuck's ace writer at 20th Century

Dorothy Davenport Reid was a big star when her much more famous husband, the late Wallace Reid, was doing bit parts. As he ascended in the movie firmament, she retired to the real life rôle of wife and mother, but, upon his death, emerged again. With the substantial means left by Wally she added to her personal fortune, but made the mistake which has spelled ruin for more than one star. She turned producer and took heavy losses, which ate up her fortune, and forced her to make a living managing an apartment house in which she had a half-interest.

Of late, her ambition has been to mold the screen career of Wally Reid, Jr.; and as for herself, she has fought back to a place in Hollywood as a scenarist and director, recently directing "The Woman Condemned" for Willis Kent, an independent producer.

YOU recall how Charlie Ray lost a large fortune producing "The Courtship of Miles Standish." The "Ince wonder boy," who had a tremendous following as America's country cousin, had suddenly gone sophisticate, donned tails and a top hat —and failed. He tried again and again. Several times during the past few years he has attempted a feeble comeback, but Hollywood has turned a cold shoulder in his direction. Vaudeville engagements keep him alive, although every year a rumor trickles through that Charlie is about to stage a comeback. Now no one even believes the rumor.

But even before Charlie had definitely arrived as a star, Monroe Salisbury was devastating hearts as the screen's perfect lover. Marguerite Clark sought him for her leading man in several of her pictures, and Marguerite Clark, you will remember, was running right along-side of Mary Pickford.

Today, Monroe is night clerk at the Warner-Kelton hotel in Hollywood (owned by Pert's folks) and at one time had an interest in the place, while Marguerite, retired for many years, is the wife of a wealthy New Orleans man, and her Southern mansion with its carved glass door on magnolia-scented St. Charles Street has few things in it to remind her of her star days.

Marguerite Clark was the sweet, nice girl of those early days,

but the wicked vampire, the sensuous siren, was Louise Glaum, another Thomas Ince star who scored a sensation in a sticky picture called "Sweetheart of the Doomed."

Luring men to their downfall was her forte for the camera then, but today it's luring customers to the box-office, for Louise with her husband operates a movie theater in National City, California, not far removed from the honky-tonks of Tia Juana.

They don't make much money, because there aren't very many people in National City, but there, where Louise is said to be happy and healthy, there isn't the tragedy of hanging on when the crowd has passed by.

Perhaps the most pathetic side of Hollywood is presented by those who stand in the extra lines and sit on the set watching new stars receive the adulation—the attention that once went to them. Ethel Clayton has stayed in Hollywood, turning to the studios when bad fortune overtook her. Can a star of her former importance relish the tiny bits she must play?

Recently, on the set of "Bolero" at Paramount, Elinor Fair, the beautiful girl who played with Bill Boyd in the memorable "Volga Boatman" and then married him, and Julanne Johnston, once Douglas Fairbanks' leading lady, sat practically unnoticed in their extra-bit capacities while Carole Lombard and George Raft held the spotlight they used to know.

Mae Busch, Mary MacLaren,

Today, Francis Ford works as extra, when he gets a part, and watches others in leads he used to play

LIVING AND WORKING IN MOVIELAND

On the Set

From the start of the movies, a perennial debate had raged over how much of what went on behind the scenes it was "wise" to allow the public to see. The technical wizards were reluctant to have the tricks which made up movie magic, such as "back-projection" (see *The Mummy*, next page) exposed to a believing public. Stars were leery of off-camera shots which might reveal the extent to which their screen glamour was a paste-up job, put together by make-up men and the artists of light, photography and costume. All these fears were rationalized by the theory that the public wasn't interested in "technical stuff" anyway. How much better to confine on-the-set photographs to the studied poses taken by the publicity department and winnowed by all concerned before their inclusion in the batches of stills routinely sent out to publicize new films as they came off the assembly line.

The directing intelligence behind PHOTOPLAY was not about to accept this attitude. Quirk knew that *his* public, the fans, were so fascinated by every aspect of the movies that they were more than willing to accept disillusion in exchange for information. Certainly they were not to be deprived of at least a glimpse of the flash-point of movie-making, what happened on the set. Besides, they knew so much already that a squib of set gossip, or an informal photograph, could hardly shatter their dreams. The revelation that the regally tall Gloria Swanson of the screen was in fact tiny was no revelation at all; the fans already knew from the Answer Man (page 171) that she was exactly five feet tall. Quirk had insisted from the beginning that the studios shoot special stills for PHOTOPLAY according to his specifications. Later, by determined persistence, he insinuated his own cameraman onto sets where other journalists and photographers had given up trying to gain admittance. His perseverance—and his muscle—gained PHOTOPLAY a certain competitive advantage. Less well-connected editors, bored by the routine "production shots" sent them by the studios, had come to consider such material as fillers. PHOTOPLAY's consistent use of them, by the law of averages, netted a goodly percentage of scoops (page 152).

The Great Pyramids Move to Hollywood

THE name of this picture is "The Mummy" —weird fantasy of the miracle-makers of Hollywood. Boris Karloff, who terrified you as the monster in "Frankenstein," will play in this, his first starring rôle, the part of an Egyptian mummy that comes to life.

This is much more than an ordinary studio scene, and when you see this production screened, you will be amazed by the transformation.

The cab in which are seated David Manners and the Hungarian star, Zita Johann, with

Boris Karloff opening the door and Noble Johnson peering in the window, will be standing in the highway beside the camels.

Universal has brought to the making of this picture an amazing new technical process, unlike any hitherto used. A cameraman was sent

And an Egyptian Mummy Comes to Life!

from Universal's Berlin office to Egypt to obtain the authentic atmospheric shots.

The large screen on the left hand page behind the actors and the movable cab interior is of frosted glass. On it we see the Egyptian background scenes being projected from the portable projection booth in the rear. The process is such that the actors in the studio actually appear as an integral part of the Egyptian setting.

Karloff achieves one of the greatest feats of screen make-up yet known. He was covered from head to foot in dampened cotton and collodion over which the make-up was applied. When it was completed, he was unable to move a muscle of his withered face! All of this preparation for only three minutes on the screen!

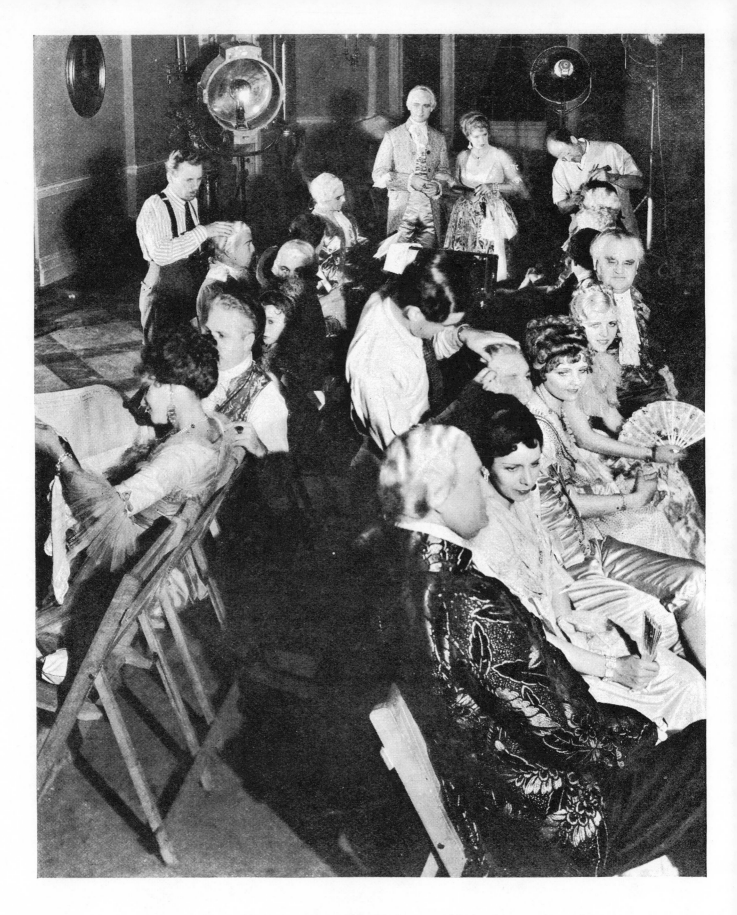

WHAT do the extras and "bit" players think about when they
sit for hours like this while the make-up experts get them ready
for the director's call?   Here is an interesting scene caught by
PHOTOPLAY's cameraman behind the "Alexander Hamilton" set
at the Warner Bros. studio.   Note the girl on the left perusing
the stock market pages and also the swell lookers on the right

natt

THIS scene from "Rasputin and the Empress" (latest title) is perfect in its artistry. In the palace of the czar, at this mystic hour of the night, what is John Barrymore saying to czarina Ethel? "Get rid of that monk, *Rasputin!*" might be a safe guess. And Ethel for the moment has a doubt. But, careful John, there's eaves-dropping going on! Don't you see that huge "mike" overhead?

Filming Helen Hayes' most solemn scene

HERE we glimpse some of the tender care and unflagging attention to detail which went into portraying Helen Hayes ready to take her vow as a nun, for the talking picture version of the well-known novel, "The White Sister," written by F. Marion Crawford. It was the silent version with Lillian Gish, you may remember, that many think really made Ronald Colman on the screen, away back in 1923, and also wrote a chapter in the history of outstanding screen successes by playing to crowds when reshown several years after its première.

Judging from this picture, we may expect an equally notable rendition in this version, now being done by M-G-M. Note that instead of merely filling the area visible to the camera, the producers have provided a full company, with complete detail and action to the most remote corner on either side of the camera. Note too the perfection of feeling shown by May Robson

Photo by Stagg

April 1933

in a new version of "The White Sister"

and Sarah Padden, playing the two nuns accompanying Helen. And while Director Victor Fleming—visible just over the watching officer's head—scans each principal, his assistant, Cullen "Hezzy" Tate, is keeping a vigilant eye upon every member of the supporting company, from a post just beneath the camera, while the producing staff is grouped about, alert to catch every command and the full values of the portrayal.

Now just a word about that officer, visible in the foreground. He is watching from off set, and is not playing in this scene. He is *Giovanni*, Helen's youthful sweetheart. But beneath that make-up you may or may not recognize him as—Clark Gable.

Throughout this and other scenes embodying church ritual and ceremony, everything was done under the guidance of two priests, who traveled extensively in Italy before undertaking the task.

Irving Berlin admits he can't keep his eyes on the piano keys when playing for Ginger Rogers and Fred Astaire to dance. The famous songwriter is rehearsing with the pair for a scene in the RKO-Radio musical, "Top Hat." Berlin has written some grand tunes for the film

Earl Cronkv

LORETTA YOUNG takes directions from Cecil B. DeMille for a
scene in Paramount's "The Crusades." Talking to Anna Demetrio,
who is in the scene with Loretta, is Henry Wilcoxon, *Richard the
Lion Hearted* in the elaborate film of the exciting and gripping era

You Can't Get On These Sets!

GRIMES

To PHOTOPLAY'S knowledge, this is the first candid picture of Greta Garbo taken on her set. In "Anna Karenina," Greta plays croquet with Fredric March, and enjoys it so much, she plays it between scenes. It's a mean game!

All visitors, while the vital scenes of "Anna Karenina" and "The Flame Within" are being shot, are forbidden, or, at least, kept distant

Take one! Greta Garbo's first scene, with Basil Rathbone, for "Anna Karenina." Director Clarence Brown is in a pensive mood. He has done six of Garbo's pictures, which is a world's record. But Cameraman Daniels has handled nineteen of Garbo's twenty films!

The emotional scenes in "The Flame Within" are being photographed to the tempo of the musical score, instead of scoring the picture after it is completed, as customary. Edmund Goulding (in white trousers) directs a scene with the aid of Jerome Kern, dean of American composers (with script in hand). In the scene are Margaret Seddon, Herbert Marshall, Maureen O'Sullivan, Louis Hayward, a stage "find," and the blonde Miss Harding

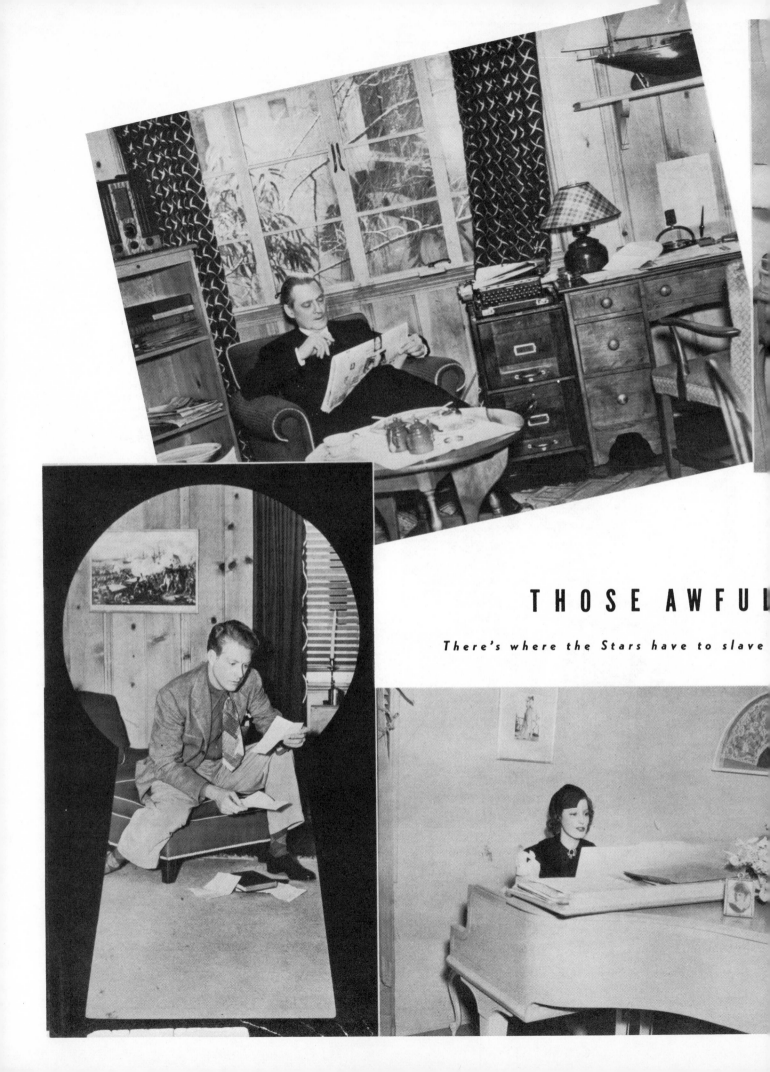

THOSE AWFU

There's where the Stars have to slave

FACTORIES

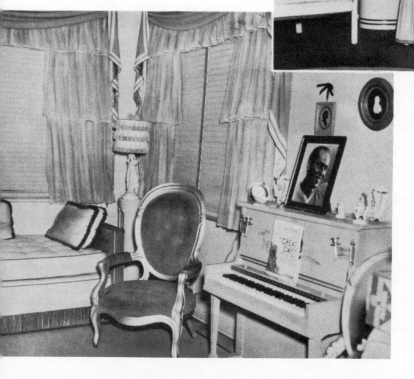

Presenting that glorified institution of the Hollywood proletariat—the star's dressing room. Nelson Eddy, in a knotty-pine atmosphere, relaxes on a soft chaise lounge; Lionel Barrymore, at ease with his newspaper, is proud of his ship model (hobby hangover from "Captains Courageous"). The feminine contingent has other ideas of soul-soothing decoration. Jeanette MacDonald chooses an all-white piano to match her all-white room; Ginger Rogers likes old ivory work and peach satin; Ann Sothern goes for blue dots and taffeta upholstery; but Joan Crawford's forte is that big picture of Franchot Tone enthroned on her piano.

THE *Screen Test*

THAT BROUGHT FAME TO FRANCES FARMER

Test No. 567 — August 9, 1935

FRANCES FARMER

in scenes from

"The Second Man"
and "The Lake"

Age 21   Height . . . . . 5' 6¼"

Eyes . . . . . Hazel   Hair . . . . . Blonde

Today Frances Farmer is talked of as the greatest "find" since Garbo. But, when a scout arranged her tryout at Paramount late in 1935, this hazel-eyed young co-ed had had no acting experience except college theatricals. Her test was a severe one for any actress—scenes from "The Lake" which Hepburn played on the stage, and from Lynn Fontanne's play, "The Second Man" (left and below). The studio took one look, signed Frances to a long-term contract.

LIVING AND WORKING IN MOVIELAND

Behind the Camera

Ruth Waterbury's editorial on the following page is remarkable for its timidity. It would never have occurred to the freewheeling James Quirk in his day to apologize out loud for discussing production problems and politics in his "corner" of PHOTO- PLAY. But even he was aware that the space given such matters must be proportionate to reader interest in them, and that that interest was strictly limited. The stars were the focus of fan fascination and, when the chips were down, all the rest of the complicated marvel of movie-making and marketing so much excess baggage. All the magazines strove to vary the star formula, but every attempt to do so by covering movie personalities outside the stars themselves ran into a stone wall of reader indifference.

In part this resulted from a certain modesty on the part of the fans. Whatever other functions they performed, the magazines had primarily to be vehicles of reader identification. Fans might with some realism picture themselves in routine movie jobs (see page 160); granted the miracle of transportation to Valhalla, they could possibly qualify as studio stenographers or prop-men, or serve in some capacity in the publicity department; God knows the magazines had given them all advanced courses in publicity methods. But if they were to make the leap into fantasy, they preferred to jump the whole way and see themselves magically transformed into stars. They did not dream of becoming powers behind the scenes, of rising to the over-lordship of a great studio—even though that might provide a ready-made seraglio—still less of actually *making* the films which so deeply enchanted them. That was work, work was a thing they knew something about, and they knew damned well that this kind of work they were not individually capable of doing. To be struck by the lightning of publicity might make a nobody into a star, but it wouldn't make him a producer, a director, or even a make-up expert.

Fans were aware that the director was the most important single individual in the making of a film, some of the brighter because they had deduced it from what they saw on the screen, most simply because they had been told. But so long as they remained fans simple as opposed to fans complex, their interest in direction was immutably tepid. (Dorothy Arzner was an exception; because she was, *mirabile dictu*, a woman, she got a good deal more fan publicity than her rather spotty career warranted.) Occasionally a tribute to a Griffith or a DeMille appeared in "Brickbats and Bouquets," but directors chiefly appeared in the pages of PHOTOPLAY as the husbands, former husbands or husbands-to-be of female stars. In one other role were they tolerated, that of star-maker. The lengthy article about John Ford on page 166, one of a short-lived series on directors, undoubtedly got by the editorial shears because of its title. The meteoric rise of Frank Capra in the Thirties was signaled in the magazine, nominally because he had directed everybody's favorite, *It Happened One Night*, but really, from a fan viewpoint, because he had "made" a star of Barbara Stanwyck and salvaged the faltering careers of Claudette Colbert and Clark Gable. As for Ernst Lubitsch, he achieved and retained fan identification as the director all the stars wanted to work for "because they loved him so much." Mr. Lubitsch, it may have been remarked, was a very wise man.

close ups and long shots

BY RUTH WATERBURY

LUBITSCH is out of Paramount. Dietrich has returned to Europe. Mae West has gone to sign with Ben Schulberg—which means that her pictures will probably be released henceforth through Columbia.

Winfield Sheehan who used to be head of Fox is heading toward Paramount. Already several of those who worked closest to him in the old outfit have Paramount appointments.

At Universal no one knows positively from day to day who owns the studio. The Laemmles are reported out then reported in again.

At Warners the actors are in a rage. James Cagney became so disturbed over the threat to his career he believed five pictures yearly to be that he took his troubles to court, got himself declared a free lance, or, in other words, free to act where he liked, as rôles called him, and not forced to work out his existing contract. The Brothers Warner promptly announced that they would appeal this decision in an effort to force Jimmy back on the payroll, which, considering that the fiery James gets $4,500 every week, is wanting him very much indeed. Meanwhile, Pat O'Brien is on suspension for refusing to play the same rôle Jimmy refused to play. Ann Dvorak has lost in the court battle and must go back to work, whether or not she likes it.

The Screen Actors' Guild openly boycotts the Academy and a junior guild is in rapid process of formation, which promises to take every extra off a set where stars, not members of the guild, try to perform.

Dudley Nichols, who was given the 1935 Academy writing award a few weeks ago for adapting "The Informer" for the screen, turns back the statue with a polite nod to the effect that he cannot accept the honor, being a member of the Screen Writers Guild and, therefore, not approving of the Academy.

Never has Hollywood been in more of a turmoil.

AND yet, reversely, never has Hollywood been making better pictures.

FOR several years now this war between the actors and producers has been seething. From the angle of an impartial observer like myself this argument has its two faces. Just as I have never known an author who was satisfied with his publisher, just so is the actor who is satisfied with his producer a rare phenomenon. Temperament, passion, beauty make a bad mixture with the cold intelligence that must be used to run a business.

Actors are natural vagabonds; like all creative people, natural rebels, when they begin to talk in terms of their second million, it's more apt than not to muddle them up.

THE situation is considerably complicated by the rise of the Hollywood agent Being on commission, it is to his advantage to get his client the highest possible wage, which is agony to the producer. The agent tells the client to hold out a certain sum at option time; if producer A won't give it to him, says the agent, producer B will. Producers A and B have a pact not to raid each other's stars, but a good star is money in the bank and there the trouble starts.

To me the most hopeful note in the whole thing is the matter of lending stars from one organization to another; this tends to keep everyone reasonably happy and it certainly makes for better productions.

The most money grubbing star will usually exchange a smaller salary for a better part, and, with rôles tailored to fit, they seldom care where they play them, all other conditions being equal.

TWENTIETH CENTURY-FOX and Metro have a particularly successful working arrangement and Metro with some inner genius seems to understand better than any other organization how to keep its players happy. These two companies have most recently used Janet Gaynor as a basis of exchange for Robert Taylor. Paramount exchanged Carole Lombard with Universal to get Margaret Sullavan. The dollar element in these transactions is not nearly so important as the personality factor. Already the edict has gone out that new discovery, James Stewart, is too valuable to be loaned out for a while.

It is amusing to think of actors being figured out like cargo shipments of sugar as opposed to rubber, or what have you, like the export-import trade, but this is actually how the scheme operates.

Recently I am told that Pioneer offered $500,000 for Fred Astaire for six weeks and didn't get him. Radio isn't a gold mine, but Mr. Astaire as their exclusive property was worth more than the half million to them. But if Pioneer had had an Elisabeth Bergner to exchange to play the rôle of *Queen Elizabeth* in "Mary of Scotland," let's say, the situation would have been very different. Pioneer had only money, and here is a case where money wasn't enough.

IF I bore you by giving you here the inside on the motion picture "business," the actual wheels within wheels that make this amazing industry go round, you have only to write and tell me so and I will stop writing about it, but it fascinates me as much as the personality stories that rightly appear on PHOTOPLAY's other pages. Here in my corner I feel I may tell you the other aspects of Hollywood, those secret factors that go on behind the scenes that really make it a world power.

On the next few pages of this issue you will see several stories in which I have attempted to keep my word to you, given months ago, when I took over the editorship of this magazine; I promised to give you "big name" writers and important news stories on Hollywood. In the "big name" class I have in these five months given you James Hilton, Dorothy Speare, Channing Pollock, Adela Rogers St. Johns, Hagar Wilde and now, in this issue, Hugh Walpole.

Although he has been a Hollywood resident for almost two years, this has been the first time any magazine has been able to get Mr. Walpole to write about the movie world.

AS for news stories, in this issue are three I was told we couldn't get. "They" said Dick Powell wouldn't talk about Joan Blondell, that Henry Fonda wouldn't talk about Margaret Sullavan, and that positively Joan Crawford would not discuss her second marriage. So the talented PHOTOPLAY staff went to work and we got all three.

They DON'T Want To Be Stars!

By
Robert Fender

IT used to be "If a Man Bites a Dog—That's News!" But now you can tuck that one away with the lavender and old lace. Hollywood, birthplace of most new things, has delivered a bouncing, brand-new definition of that word. Suppose you read further.

Out here in this country of manly chests and feminine twitters, they have a little industry called the movies. A magic business it is, which makes princes out of poor men and lady princes out of poor gals over night. Everyone in town today is eligible to be a star tomorrow. No effort. No nothing.

All we do out here is take sun baths and play black-jack until that best guy in the wide, wide world, The Producer, says: "I want you to be a star for my company at seven thousand a week." Then we catch up on our eating and place an order for that blue Rolls we've had our eye on for so long. It's really very exciting. None of us knows when the good news is coming to us.

The point, minus furbelows, is that everyone in Hollywood considers himself good movie material. Star material, in fact, and is just waiting around, doing this and that, until the great day when the casting directors will come to their senses and realize it, too. Scratch a truck driver here and you'll find a

Johnny Engstead bangs out publicity about the Paramount stars. Honestly, now, isn't he as handsome as any juvenile on the lot? But Johnny prefers his trusty old typewriter

Charles Welborn, a dashing young studio still cameraman, fights off picture chances. "My end of the camera is best," says he

bozo who'll confide that he can do everything Karl Dane does (wasn't *he* a truck driver once?). Make a pal of the soft drink engineer at the nearest drug store and he'll confess that everyone tells him he's funnier than Jack Oakie and would screen better.

Get the confidence of your landlady and the poor dear will let you in on the way she would play Marie Dressler rôles if she ever got the chance. Tell your postman he's a good guy and he'll come right back with: "Do you think I'd make good in the movies?" The situation, in short, is that Hollywood's population may be classed as: 1—Those already in the movies, and 2—Those waiting to get in.

What a job, then, to find someone in the hamlet who could act in the movies if he wanted to but doesn't want to! Not someone who thinks he has a chance before the cameras but one who's actually had the chance, chances in fact, and has openly sneered at the idea.

Many of Hollywood's smart and handsome boys and girls prefer to work back of the camera, thank you

That's the little assignment I gave myself the other day, a little assignment that would make Jason give up all ideas of winning the Golden Fleece and go back to his old Greek tumbling act. None too anxious to start the job, I strolled around one of the studios lately in search of a pleasanter subject.

And there, on a movie lot, of all places, came my first lead. A young man was needed to do a "bit" in a certain picture. The director, happening to be short a player, turned to a

Margery Prevost, Marie's sister, came from the "Follies" to try picture acting. But she was more interested in interior decorating and found true happiness in a studio art department

good looking "still" camerman by his side. "Jump in there, Scotty, and do it," he said. I drew closer to see how "Scotty" would take it. This was the way stars were made and I wanted a ringside seat to witness "Scotty's" opportunity. This was the stuff dreams, Hollywood dreams, were made of. "Scotty," whoever he was, now had his chance. What, I wondered, would he do with it?

I looked at "Scotty." He was smiling a dry smile. He was speaking. "Do you mean to say," he drawled, "that you want me to get out there in front of the camera?" The director assured him that that was exactly what he meant to say. "Scotty" laughed. "And be a movie actor?" he snorted. "Sure!" came the reply, "Why not?" Then "Scotty" howled. "Oh, no!" he managed between chuckles. "I'm awfully sorry," he continued, "but no, thanks!"

My throat grew dry. The studio walls, I felt, would topple down any minute now. The sun, I was sure, had

stopped in its course and sailors at sea were battling sudden storms. My head whirled. I found a cot and lay down.

The shock of seeing and hearing someone actually turn down a chance to be in the movies nearly proved fatal. Next day, feeling stronger, I hunted up this "Scotty" person. I wanted to talk with him. If possible, I wanted to touch him.

His name, I learned, is Charles Welborn and he has photographed almost every important person in the world, not excluding Calvin Coolidge and Douglas Fairbanks. He is convinced that he has the best job in the world and the best mother (he lives with her) and the best motorboat. Known about the studio as the best looking guy out of pictures, "Scotty," nevertheless, is firm in his resolve never to turn romantic screen lover.

"Once, between pictures," he told me, "I was out of work for six months and plenty broke. They offered me a job doing dance routines and playing around in a big revue, but I told 'em I'd rather go hungry. I've had other chances to act, too, but why get started in that stuff? Give me a job where I can earn my dough!"

CHEERED by "Scotty's" confession I knocked around at other studios in search of a boy or girl who, although eligible for the screen, will have none of it. At Fox I found beautiful Noreen Phillips, private secretary to E. W. Butcher of that lot. Miss Phillips knows all about acting in the movies for the very good reason that she has acted in 'em. No sooner had she taken her job as secretary when she was besieged with requests to take a film test.

Victor Schertzinger finally turned the trick, and for two years Noreen played this part and that. She got along swimmingly and was even given an important rôle as sister to Olive Borden in "The Secret Studio," when she asked for her old job back. She's private secretarying again and tickled to death to be away from the cameras.

"To my mind," she told me, "acting in films is sure death. There's nothing real about it, nothing genuine. The waiting and constant dilly-dallying kills all incentive. You begin to drift and lose all sense of security. [PLEASE TURN TO PAGE 308]

Oh, what a blonde! Noreen Phillips knows all about picture acting. She did it for two years. But she's much happier as a secretary on the Fox lot

"Quiet!" When These Folks

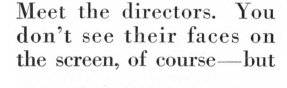

Meet the directors. You don't see their faces on the screen, of course—but

Dorothy Arzner—once a script girl, but now the only active woman director

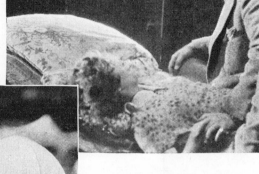

Frank Borzage, famed for "7th Heaven" and "Bad Girl," rehearsing Charlie Farrell and Marian Nixon in "After Tomorrow"

Von Sternberg at the "location" microphone. He directs Dietrich

Clarence Brown directing Clark Gable and Joan Crawford in "Possessed"

Stephen R. Roberts, who was responsible for that thrilling film, "Sky Bride"

Speak, Great Stars Listen

Without them there would be no movies. They're powers behind the camera

The great Lubitsch and his cigar, with George Cukor. These two guided Maurice Chevalier through "One Hour With You"

Norman Taurog knows all about children and his skill produced "Skippy"

Mervyn LeRoy, youngest director of hits. "Lit le Caesar" was one of his

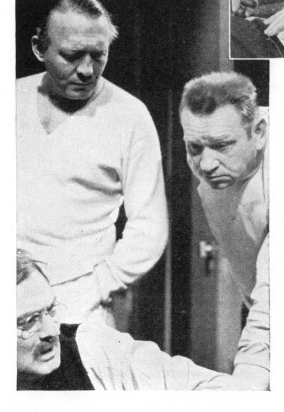

Director Goulding, Lionel Barrymore and Wallace Beery in "Grand Hotel"

Al Santell directing Marian Nixon in "Rebecca of Sunnybrook Farm"

"All Women Are Sirens at Heart"

says Mister Lubitsch

To May Allison Quirk

The great director analyzes some famous screen personalities

Ernst Lubitsch, creator of stars, believes that charm is the most important thing in the world to a woman. That, given proper setting and opportunity, every woman desires to be a seductress

NIGHTLY in Hollywood, there are big stars and little starlets who pray, in pajamas and other things, "Oh, dear Lord, let me make a picture with Lubitsch before it is too late."

For Ernst Lubitsch is a molder of personalities. No screen player has ever passed through his direction without emerging a more vital actor or actress.

His ability to breathe life into a character that would be drab in other hands; his ability to make phlegmatic personalities suddenly seem subtle and brilliant, has always had something of the Svengali touch about it.

I cannot recall a single piece of bad acting given under his direction.

From the time, about fourteen years ago, that he led Pola Negri through the torturous, dramatic heights of the German-made picture, "Passion," right down to Miriam Hopkins' scintillating performance in "Trouble in Paradise," his record is unbroken. "Passion" brought Pola international fame and gave them both Hollywood contracts.

Lubitsch was born in Berlin, Germany, about forty-one years ago. He was brought up in his native city, received all his early training as an actor in the theater there, and directed his first motion pictures in Germany.

Yet his fundamental qualities are as un-Germanic as is the lissome body of Marlene Dietrich.

LUBITSCH'S handling of risqué situations is French in its subtlety. His sense of humor and play might be Gaelic. His worship of beauty, whether it be in a human being, a landscape, or an exquisite bar of music, might easily come from some early Latin lineage.

I have heard him search for words to describe his emotions over a purple sunset in the desert canyons of Palm Springs, or the dark massive line of oak trees silhouetted against the gray dawn of a new day.

Furthermore, he knows more about feminine psychology than any man I have ever met. That, in itself, is disconcerting.

But one day recently I took courage in hand and obtained an interview. I wanted to learn more about his special brand of wizardry.

"How is it that every actress acquires unsuspected sex allure under your direction?"

He grinned at me and then scored one with his answer. He knows the frailties of our sex, that man.

"All women are sirens at heart," he said. "No matter how unemotional, how stolid, a woman may be, she has moments when her greatest desire is to be—shall we call it, a courtesan, siren or seductress? The exactly proper emotional condition and environment will bring it to the surface.

"If I manage to develop some quality in a player that the public has been unaware of, it is [PLEASE TURN TO PAGE 338]

May Robson

Barbara Stanwyck

Walter Connolly

Nils Asther

Claudette Colbert

Jean Parker

Frank Capra guides screen unknowns into prominence, and gives new life to fading stars

Clark Gable

Hollywood's New Miracle Man

The magic of Capra's direction has turned out an amazing string of hits for Columbia

By Kirtley Baskette

HOLLYWOOD has a modern Merlin — a master magician — in a quiet, self-effacing man who lays no loud claims to his obvious genius.

Yet, a leading producer told a group of other top executives:

"I'd give a million dollars for the contracts of Frank Capra, Bob Riskin and Sam Briskin!" (Riskin is the scenarist and Briskin the supervisor on Director Capra's pictures.)

One million dollars for the privilege of hiring somebody!

What makes it more fantastic is that this modern magician has no deep and mysterious secret by which he works. He has one rule. You'll grin as you read it. It is this:

"A dull scene is just so much footage and holds a picture back. Some form of entertainment must be put in."

But, Frank Capra, by the soft spell of his directorial instruc-tions in following his rule, has guided screen unknowns into prominence, and into waning screen greats he has breathed new life.

What is even more important, by the magic of his sure, inspired direction he has created an unbroken line of pro-gressively sensational box-office produc-tions—each one to be long remembered.

The result is that Capra's pictures have raised Columbia Studios from a subordinate independent producing organ-ization to the outstanding major studio it is today.

If there is any secret to his genius, it is an indefinable one that permits him to put realism, humaneness, and an understand-able naturalness into his pictures.

Looking into the background and the youthful tastes and ideals of this remark-able man gives a clue to the "how come" of his developed genius.

First off, let me say, Frank Capra today sports no high-sounding prefixes to his family name. He affects no spectacular mode of dress or swaggering movie mannerisms. He never has raised the heavens with temperamental bellowings—on the set or off the set.

Physically, he is short and stocky, and he has a mild, pleasing manner. His olive skin, flash— [PLEASE TURN TO PAGE 339]

The Star Creators of Hollywood

The first of a series of brilliant articles about the men whose genius lifts pictures and personalities to fame—the directors. This month, John Ford

By HOWARD SHARPE

EDITOR'S NOTE: Late last winter, in its search to bring you new and different material about Hollywood, PHOTOPLAY started that amazing series of articles called "The Private Life of a Talking Picture," a study of the technical side of the motion picture industry.

That series brought such an immediate response from intelligent readers, and upon its completion created such a demand for more original material that, in response to your requests, PHOTOPLAY is here starting a series on the men who make pictures.

Hollywood calls these men directors. The term is guilty of understatement. Their task is one of creation, since no single portion or phase of any motion picture is independent of their touch; and the success or failure of any production is primarily due to them, secondarily to the actors.

In this series, written by the same brilliant author who wrote "The Private Life of a Talking Picture," PHOTOPLAY's objective is not so much to bring you a personal history of these men, but rather a detailed analysis of the work they do; so that in the end you may, for yourself, understand the complicated processes of the directing and molding of a modern movie. Also, to see Hollywood not in the phoney light of stars' "love lives" but rather in the full glory of its undeniable influence upon the thought of our times.

RUTH WATERBURY

sightless, boarded windows were in deep shadow; from nowhere the oily Irish fog ribboned in. There was gloom in the air, and terror.

Ford, casual in old pants and old shoes and old shirt, said, "Come on now, me lads. Double quick!" and the three stumbling, frightened rebels began to dodge along the cobblestones and barricaded sidewalks.

"All right. When you go past that window, Preston, be careful. It's going to break and there might be glass flying around."

"Okay," Foster and the other two said together.

"Try it again," Ford said, sitting back. To the cameraman, in a low voice, he murmured, "*Now!*"

The three shabby refugees began their action again in what was to them the second rehearsal. But the film was clicking silently past the lens.

Sincerity is the keynote of Ford and his work. Above, he fought the studio for years to make "The Informer." It won the Academy Award! In 1928 he directed "Four Sons." It was a four handkerchief picture and remains one of the screen's greatest miracles

OUT at RKO, just now, a company is making that symphony of courage and hate and love called "Plough and the Stars," under the direction of one Sean O'Fienne—a tall and typical Irishman whose beautiful name was Anglicized by an unfeeling Saxon people to Jack Feeney and later changed by himself (he is a simple man) to John Ford. I chose him as the object of my first bombardment of questions because he made "The Informer," which is the greatest motion picture ever filmed, and because in himself he represents all that is the best of Hollywood and its industry.

The set I walked into was an entire section of Dublin enclosed by a sound stage; from the asphalt studio street to the cobblestones of this Irish square was only a step or two, but the difference in mood was an ocean and eight thousand miles. Ford had a couple of scenes to finish before he could settle into a chair and bite through a pipestem and analyze his technique, so I sat and watched—and learned almost as much about him as I did later from his own introspective conversation.

The sequence was one in which Preston Foster, and one of the imported Abbey Players, were to help a wounded companion (the picture is set during the 1916 "Uprising") down a street and around a corner and into an alley; meanwhile machine guns and snipers were to create peril and terrific din. The miserable little shops, the tenements, the sullen dirty brick walls and the

Out of the careful set silence there sounded the sudden, fearful clatter of a machine gun. Foster and his companions, really surprised and for a moment really terrified, scurried around a corner and past the plate glass window Ford had warned them about.

Six shots burst through it, crashing in quick succession. Sharp slivers spattered through the fog. Echoes bounced.

The three soldiers looked back, aghast, and then ran for their lives.

"Wasn't that a pip?" Ford said delightedly to the script girl.

"You'll have to replace the window for the take," Preston said, coming up. He wiped his forehead.

"That was the take," Ford told him sweetly.

THERE'S very little news available about the private life of this Sean O'Fienne. He may have led a sort of "Anthony Adverse" existence, and probably has, since occasionally he mentions (in a noncommittal tone) that he saw this war in China or that revolution in Mexico, and that such and such a thing happened to him in the South Seas. But he will tell you, if you ask long enough, merely that he was born of Irish parents in Portland, Maine, and that he went to school there, and that after graduation he came to Hollywood to join his famous brother, Francis Ford. [PLEASE TURN TO PAGE 333]

THE only woman who ever became a topnotch talkie director. Starting as a stenographer on the Paramount lot, she's still with the same company. She's had to resign four times to get recognition, and was scared stiff at the responsibilities. But now she's sitting pretty, as you can see in this fine study of Dorothy Arzner and her faithful camera

1. PHOTOPLAY cover, July 1929. (Bessie Love)

2. PHOTOPLAY cover, December 1929. (Norma Talmadge)

THE FANS AND THEIR MAGAZINE

In PHOTOPLAY, James R. Quirk had created the standard format of the fan magazine. Its skeleton consisted of a series of service departments: "Casts of Current Photoplays"; "The Answer Man," who supplied the stars' vital statistics; "Addresses of the Stars," for the thousands who wanted to write to them; "Brickbats and Bouquets"—later changed to the less abrasive "Boos and Bouquets"—for those who wanted to air their views in the magazine itself; "The Fan Club Corner"; "Screen Memories from PHOTOPLAY," nostalgia for the dwindling number of oldsters in the readership—and contests, contests, contests. This standard circulation-getter took the form, in PHOTOPLAY, of testing readers' memories, not only for faces, but for parts of faces. These departments were aimed at the basic rather than the casual fan, the hard-core buyer or subscriber to the magazine. Contrary to widespread belief, the most important part of the fan magazine readership was not to be found in beauty parlors. In round numbers, beauty parlor patrons may have made up the largest proportion of casual readers, but the beauty establishments played the same role in the fan magazine economy as doctors' waiting rooms did in that of the NATIONAL GEOGRAPHIC. The real reader, the one who plunked down the money, did not want to read her favorite magazine in public; she was far more apt to shut herself up in her bedroom and proceed, in the words of one of them, to memorize its contents. It was she at whom advertising was aimed, she who swayed the bias of editorial policy.

Who was she, in her millions? For as long as he could, James Quirk pumped up the illusion that his readership was the whole family. But by the "new decade of the Thirties," era of talking pictures, long skirts, legal drinking—and Depression—it was no longer possible to pretend that every member of the family had an equal interest in motion pictures. All might enjoy the escape that movies continued to provide, but not enough to read about them month after month. Mom and Pop had worries, and Brother had never been a dependable fan; it was Sister who continued to support the magazines with her avid interest. That interest was kept avid because she thought she could get something out of them. In dawning teenhood, she vaguely thrilled to the thought of becoming one of those gorgeous creatures, the stars, or at least of getting close to them—what would it be like to actually *meet* one? But as her teens wore on, less and less did she dream of herself achieving Hollywood, discovery, and assumption into the heaven of the great. The magazines had taught her too much. But she did know, and also from them, that many of those who had been touched by the magic wand were not overwhelmingly her superior in intelligence, education, "background" or even, in some cases, in looks. How did they get so far on so little? This was a question the magazines were eager to answer, with Quirk and his successors in the lead. The blanket reply was, there are tricks to the star trade, and if you study them and learn them and practice them they will give you a better-than-average chance to get what you're after in that station in life to which it has pleased God to call you. Carolyn Van Wyck, presiding over "PHOTOPLAY's Hollywood Beauty Shop," explained carefully every month that if you used make-up to enlarge your eyes like Greta Garbo, or your mouth like Joan Crawford, you would become, not Crawford or Garbo exactly, but at least a lot better-looking than you used to be. Miss Van Wyck was a conduit for such professional make-up secrets as the Hollywood experts chose to let out, but PHOTOPLAY's oracle on diet, exercise, posture and other forms of self-policing was herself an expert, none other than Sylvia of Hollywood, masseuse extraordinary to the greatest stars. Acquiring her as a monthly columnist was a real coup for the magazine. Sylvia's advice was genuine and she was a hard taskmistress; no doubt she did much to improve the general feminine landscape. But it is to be wondered at that her photograph was published beside each column. It could only plant doubts as to the efficacy of *any* regimen in improving the unimprovable.

Fashion was obligatory for the magazines too, but fashion was just brief, double-barreled grief. Editors knew that fashions, if they were to be anything but pictures of actresses in good-looking clothes, must anticipate the style six to eight months in advance, a practical impossibility. Moreover, current modes had to be altered drastically in both color and line for the black-and-white screen, with results, in still photographs, which made smart women smile. PHOTOPLAY rationalized *that* by boasting that Hollywood had supplanted Paris as the fashion lawgiver—a boast that eventually came true. But granting that you had the nerve, in Sauk Center, to wear an ermine-and-black-satin "afternoon ensemble" created by Chanel for Gloria Swanson, and cut it out yourself from the pattern furnished by PHOTOPLAY, where, in Sauk Center, would you buy the materials? Much the same dilemma confronted the readers of the articles on food and cooking. How to duplicate the Basil Rathbones' epicurean dinners with groceries from the supermarket—or Norma Shearer's cookout at Malibu, for that matter? More successful were what were amazingly called in the trade the "psychological" articles—how to slay the stag line,

how to get your man and hold him, how to *behave*. Such material was attractive not only to Sister at home, but also to the beauty parlor matrons, the stenographers and shopgirls, who made up the big fan audience. Women had been borrowing and passing on such lore for a long time; the fan magazines were just a new and more exciting transmission belt.

Ludicrous as all this seemed to those a step or two higher on the cultural ladder, the fan magazines in the Thirties did move things forward a bit. The composite Miss Photoplay (page 200) might be, in print, a strange conglomerate of Hedy Lamarr's beauty, Connie Bennett's ritziness, Dietrich's mystery, Ginger Rogers' gosh-darn-humanness and Garbo's soul. Her actual counterpart was more likely to be seized of Jean Arthur's common sense. She learned what she could from the screen and its popular interpreters, and let the rest go hang. In the process of learning, she was cured of the middle-class vice of suffocating gentility. No more would Alice Adams suffer silent anguish over burnt roast and slattern maid. She'd dispense with the maid, cook the roast herself, and if she burnt it, laugh at herself—like Myrna Loy. Cecil B. DeMille used to say that the Crane Corporation owed him a proportion of its profits for what he had done for the American bathroom. Somebody, maybe American men, owes the fan magazines more than they know.

ASK THE ANSWER MAN

A tall dark man is coming into your lives, girls. Bob Taylor is his name. Watch him in "Times Square Lady" and "West Point of the Air"

ANOTHER tall, dark and handsome hero has been acclaimed. The girls have just gone crazy about Robert Taylor, one of the outstanding of the new leading men.

Bob's real name is S. Arlington Brugh. He was born in Filley, Nebr., August 5, 1911. Is 6 feet, ½ inch tall; weighs 165 and has brown hair and blue eyes. He is of Scotch, Dutch and English descent.

Bob entered pictures about a year ago, playing in "Handy Andy" with Will Rogers. That was shortly after he graduated from Pomona College. His second picture was "There's Always Tomorrow" for Universal and then came "A Wicked Woman" for M-G-M. His latest pictures are "Times Square Lady" and "West Point of the Air," both for Metro.

Most of his leisure hours Bob spends playing tennis. When not thus engaged he likes to take in movies. He says his hobby is clothes, especially sweaters. So girls, get out your knitting needles.

EILEEN KOCH, NEW YORK CITY, N. Y.—The following stars were born in November: Frances Dee, the 26th; James Dunn, the 2nd; Joel McCrea, the 5th; Dorothy Wilson and Dick Powell, the 14th; Will Rogers, the 4th and Raquel Torres, the 11th. Kent Taylor was born on May 11, 1907.

PEGGY STONE, DES MOINES, IOWA.—Billie Dove made a number of talkie pictures before she married Bob Kenaston and retired from the screen. Among them were "Her Private Life," "The Painted Angel," "Sweethearts and Wives," "A Notorious Affair," "The Other Tomorrow," "The Age of Love," "Cock of the Air," and "Blondie of the Follies."

MARY KOELZER, CHICAGO, ILL.—Elizabeth Patterson was born in Savannah, Tenn. Do you still think she is the same one you used to know?

HELEN WANNAMAKER, CHERAW, S. C.—Gene Raymond was born in New York City on August 13, 1908. His favorite sport is horseback riding.

N. M. E., PRINCETON, IND.—Clark Gable was born on February 1, 1901. He has been married twice. Last marriage took place on June 29, 1931. George Raft has been counting birthdays since September 26, 1903.

BONNIE JUNE ROHLAND, OAKLAND, CALIF.—You're not so bad either on thinking up questions, Bonnie. But then I love to answer them. Gene Raymond, and how the girls fall for that lad, was born on August 13, 1908. At this writing he isn't married and isn't even engaged. Francis Lederer was born in Prague, Czecho-Slovakia, November 6, 1906. He was married and divorced several years ago in Europe. I don't believe Joe E. Brown's son is married. He is about eighteen years of age.

B. D., DAYTON, OHIO.—Lanny Ross was born in Seattle, Wash., on January 19, 1906. His real name is Launcelot Patrick Ross. He is 6 feet tall, weighs 160 and has light brown hair and gray eyes. He was educated at the Taft School in Watertown, Conn., and at Yale University. He also studied law at Columbia. Lanny is not particular about staying in pictures. He prefers his radio work.

R. B., SYRACUSE, N. Y.—Eddie Nugent was born in New York City on February 7, 1904. He is 6 feet, 1 inch tall; weighs 155 and has dark brown hair and green eyes. His first important picture was "Our Dancing Daughters." Did you see him in "Lost in the Stratosphere"?

JOE R., CHICAGO, ILL.—Frankie Darro is a hometowner of yours, Joe. He was been celebrating birthdays on December 22nd, since 1917. His real name is Frankie Johnson. Can't give you his measurements because he is still growing. His latest picture is "Little Men."

KATHLEEN DONNELLY, PEORIA, ILL.—Hope you will continue to like my little column, Kitty. Robert Young's real name is Robert George Young. Ginger Rogers' is Virginia Katherine McMath. In private life she is now Mrs. Lew Ayres. Jean Parker's real name is Mae Green. She was born in Montana August 11, 1915. Is 5 feet, 3 inches tall; weighs 106 and has dark brown hair and hazel eyes. She is still single. Some of her pictures are "Little Women," "Two Alone," "Lazy River," "Operator 13," "Have a Heart," "A Wicked Woman," "Limehouse Blues," and "Sequoia." Don't miss this last one when it comes to your part of the country.

JUST a word of complete approval of your fine magazine and its lack of sticky gossip and fan-lure.

Your photographs are always excellent—which means Mr. Hyman Fink must be a whiz at the shutter. I, too, am a picturetaker of sorts and am interested in all points of photography. That short bit about photography advice by Mr. Fink should be enlarged into a department in your magazine. My job is to photograph portraits and activities of the students at this college for American Indians, the only college for Indians in the world.

I'm positive that any advice from Mr. Fink would be worth while. Why not think it over? Incidentally, I'm thinking of enlarging my attic, in order to find more room to store away PHOTO-PLAY, which I have bought for years.

EDMUND C. SHAW,
Bacone College, Bacone, Oklahoma.

We appreciate Reader Shaw's praise and trust he will be pleased to see the new department, "Movies in Your Home," on Page 70. This will be an occasional feature and any camera addict should find many new pointers which will be helpful.

P. S.—Mr. Fink is a whiz at the shutter.

EASY COME, EASY GO

YES, Hedy Lamarr is gorgeous and glamorous, but can she act? All she did in "Algiers" was look alluring in close-up after close-up and certainly that's easy enough with her glorious face. Of course, one must admit that she reacted nicely to Charles Boyer's passionate glances, but who wouldn't? No, unless Hedy can prove that besides her haunting loveliness she can also act, she will be doomed to failure, for the public is tired of "glamour girls" and their eternal posturings and posings. Dietrich lost out and Garbo's appeal is certainly on the wane, so if Miss Lamarr has nothing to offer us but her exoticness, she too will fade into obscurity, for, to be an actress, one must be more than just "a thing of beauty."

MARGARET LEMWORTH,
New York City.

Hedy Lamarr's next picture will be "I Take This Woman" with Spencer Tracy and Walter Pidgeon at M-G-M, the studio which lent her out to Walter Wanger for "Algiers." The director is Frank Borzage, the man who was responsible for Janet Gaynor's sensational work in "Seventh Heaven" in 1927—the picture, you recall, which really made Miss Gaynor a star. As for Miss Lamarr's acting, it is hard to judge from one picture. Shall we give the gal a chance?

RULES FOR WRITING TO A STAR

I'VE long enjoyed your magazine and look upon you as a true friend. I am a star's secretary, which is why I must regretfully withhold my name. Every year a new crop of fan-mail writers appears and I'm sure that many of them need a few pointers. Here they are: please write legibly—print the name and address if your handwriting isn't legible—and don't squeeze your name and address into one small corner. What a blessed relief it is to see a typewritten letter turn up!

Please don't write five-page letters, if your handwriting isn't legible. Please write in ink. Some letters come a long way and are so pencil-smeared when they arrive at the studio they are practically illegible.

Please put your address on the letter itself and not refer the reader to the envelope.

Please write a letter, if possible, and not a card. The cards come in with postmarks all over the back and front and often it is impos-

Most Talked-of Comeback of the Year—Lew Ayres'! "Holiday" started him on the upgrade; "Cousin Henry" in "Rich Man, Poor Girl" added momentum; then—the first of a series of starring pictures, "Young Dr. Kildare" (above), with Lionel Barrymore

sible to make out names and addresses because of this.

Please don't ask the star to do you a favor. He can't get you a job, nor can he get you into the studios to look around, much as he would like to help you. Don't pry into his private life, tell him all your troubles, or ask for his home address.

Most of the mail is very nice and interesting and both my employer and myself enjoy reading it, but some of it isn't, hence this letter. Thank you for your time and trouble.

PRIVATE SECRETARY,
Hollywood, Calif.

DOUBLE, DOUBLE, TOIL AND TROUBLE

SINCE the early "nickelodeon" days, I've been an avid moviegoer. I've seen two and sometimes three pictures a week. I'm quite in accord with the slogan "Motion Pictures Are Your Best Entertainment"—but, now I'm through. When the double-feature nuisance came into being, I began shopping for my movies, only to find that this necessitated either a 5:30 dinner, hurriedly eaten (in order to be at the theater by 6:10), or losing a couple of hours' sleep because the second show wasn't out until midnight. Then

came Bingo, under the various titles of Screeno, Bank Night, or what-have-you. That, I could avoid and did, but it meant that I often missed a picture I very much wanted to see. But now an even more deadly menace is rearing its head—stage shows, and theater managers have the effrontery to tell you (and right in the midst of the "Motion Pictures Are Your Best Entertainment" campaign) that they are trying to bring back vaudeville.

I don't want vaudeville; I don't want Bingo; all I want is one good picture an evening. So, I'm through until theater owners and managers get back to the fundamental purpose of a motion-picture theater.

GRETCHEN MANNING,
Pittsburgh, Pa.

This brings to mind another problem—that of change of titles. After the studio has exploited pictures for months under one title, it is confusing, to say the least, when one keeps looking in the newspapers for a picture to come to town, only to find out it's been in town the week before under another title. Has this bothered you? If so, can you think of a solution?

Nelson Eddy, opera and radio star, and the golden-voiced Jeanette MacDonald in that dramatic pageant of song, "Naughty Marietta"

The Winner!

Photoplay's Gold Medal for the Best Picture of 1935 Goes to—"Naughty Marietta"

ENTHUSIASTICALLY we announce that that musical masterpiece in which Jeanette MacDonald and Nelson Eddy were starred, "Naughty Marietta," wins PHOTOPLAY's fifteenth annual award for the best picture of 1935, by a large majority of votes!

Who can forget this lovely tuneful operetta of Victor Herbert's with its pirates, convents, marriage auctions, soldiers and Indians against the colorful background of old New Orleans? Who doesn't remember Nelson Eddy's magnificent marching song, "Tramp, Tramp, Tramp" or both the stars' voices blended in the thrilling "Ah, Sweet Mystery of Life"?

Withal a sweeping personal triumph for the stars, the honors are also shared by M-G-M who produced the picture (this is the second successive year they have been responsible for our Prize Winner), by W. S. Van Dyke for his usual brilliant direction; by Herbert Stothart, the musical supervisor; by the whole cast which included such well-known figures as Frank Morgan, Douglas Dumbrille, Elsa Lanchester and Joseph Cawthorn. That this operetta marked a huge advance in the technique of the recording itself, is acknowledged by the motion picture industry itself which awarded Charles Steincamp the Academy of Motion Picture Arts and Sciences prize for the recording of "Naughty Marietta."

Among our thousands of diversified votes, "Mutiny on the Bounty," also an Academy Winner, won second place; "David Copperfield" was third, and "The Informer" which won the critic's prize was fourth.

We are pleased that our readers evinced such an ardent interest in music. Their overwhelming choice of this glorious production for the Best Picture of 1935 thereby adds the first musical film to the growing list of distinguished PHOTOPLAY GOLD MEDAL Winners

Photoplay Magazine's New $5,000 Cut Puzzle Contest

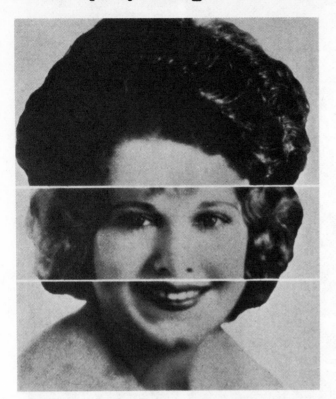

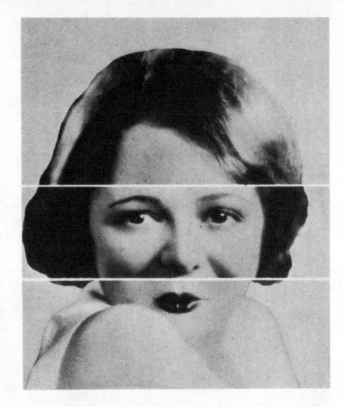

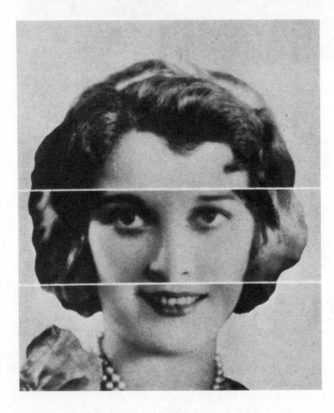

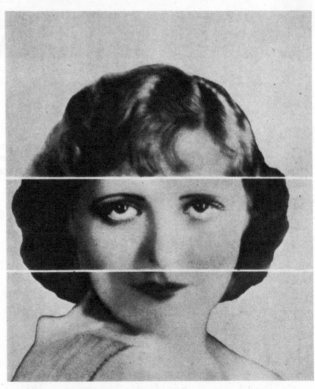

The hair is so red that it typifies It,
The eyes to a true blonde belong;
The mouth made her hit in a story that told
Of a heaven where plenty went wrong!

The hair in the city of Quakers was born,
The eyes now direct a director;
The mouth shone so bright in the film, "Peter Pan"—
That they had to deflect the reflector!

The hair, from old Philly, once played on the stage,
The eyes have been, always, with Fox;
The mouth has a lure that has brought her world fame,
(Though her ears some folk just long to box!)

The hair is New England (but only by birth),
The eyes won a contest for fame;
The mouth studied dancing and art for two years,
Will this help you to locate her name?

RESUME
Two blondes and two red heads, two pairs of brown eyes,
Two married, and two unengaged!
And all of them talented to a degree
That has made them headlined, and front paged.
Five-six is the tallest—five-three is the least—
And all four young ladies came out of the East.

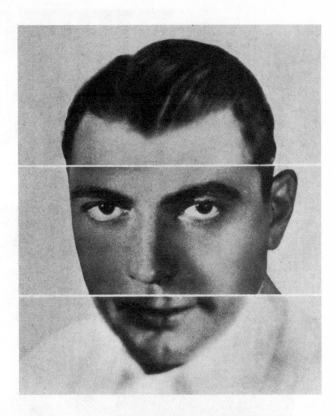

The hair is adept at all Indian roles,
The eyes have made war less than hell;
The mouth has a wife who once played on the screen,
(But her new part, as wife, she does well!)

The hair is a father, he's handsome and dark,
The eyes took a college degree;
The mouth owns Montana as his natal state,
But his boyhood was spent o'er the sea!

The hair was a cowboy—he rode for his health—
The eyes to a dancer was married;
The mouth is a popular bachelor and
They do say, by the girls he is harried!

The hair has a name which once stood for green hats
The eyes played on good old Broadway,
The mouth, though divorced, is now married again
To a most charming widow, they say.

RESUME
They all have dark hair, but just two have dark eyes,
And three are quite tall—and one's not;
And all four were college boys once on a time—
You can't guess the learning they've got!
Two of them are married—and two have fought shy,
And most of the girls in this land wonder why!

Answers are on page 276   175

PHOTOPLAY'S
Memory Album

Edited By Frederick L. Collins

Lawrence Tibbett's "The Rogue Song" raised the cry of "The movie-going public wants no hi-falutin' music!"

Garbo had the movie world jittery when she sprang her first "I tank I go home." Above, when she returned

Jeanette MacDonald, darling of the musical comedy stage, became Chevalier's partner

Warners set the world agog with talkies. Al Jolson and May McAvoy in "The Jazz Singer"

Above, Charles Farrell and Janet Gaynor became the leading screen lovers in the film "Seventh Heaven"

Above, the Farrell-Gaynor team scored again in "Street Angel." But within a year came a new order—the talkies

Probably the most popular screen pair of the day was Mr. Rin-Tin-Tin and his very comely spouse, named Nanette

Studio vied with studio in the new medium—articulate movies. M-G-M's bid—a dozen beauties as a living curtain in "The Broadway Melody"

Harry Carey and Edwina Booth in "Trader Horn," the film which sent Miss Booth on her daring adventure to Darkest Africa

Eddie Cantor, with the "It" girl, Clara Bow, in his first movie, "Kid Boots." Critics saw him as "promising material"

"Hell's Angels" introduced a sensation, Jean Harlow (with Ben Lyon), and platinum as a shade of hair

"The Tower of Lies" had in it the new star, Norma Shearer (with Bill Haines), and Lon Chaney without make-up

The prize picture of 1931 was the great epic "Cimarron," with Richard Dix in the leading rôle of Yancey Cravat

Right, Charles Rogers with Clara Bow in "Wings." He had not yet been nicknamed Buddy

Ruth Chatterton (above with Ulrich Haupt) in "Madame X." No less a personage than Lionel Barrymore directed her

Left, Doug Fairbanks, Jr., and Edward G. Robinson from the classic "Little Caesar." It made movie history

CAL YORK

Announcing-

The Prince of Wales looking for a horse? No, it is our bonnie prince Charlie in the outfit he wore while boar hunting with the Duke of Westminster. He ate off the mantel for two days after that historic event

First picture of Harold and Mildred Lloyd, and young Harold, Jr., who from a three-pound incubator baby at birth has grown to an eight-pounder in three months. "Bud," as the world's most publicized baby is known to his dad, took his first experience before the camera as if born to the studio

BLONDE Miriam Hopkins and Brunette Claudette Colbert met in the full glare of the kliegs and gave each other slap for slap at Paramount's Eastern studio.

It was a scene from Chevalier's "Smiling Lieutenant" megaphoned by Herr Lubitsch.

Miriam's part was more outstanding, more showy, than Claudette's.

Miriam did not attempt to hide her satisfaction.

Came the day for the face-slapping scene—the big scene of the picture when the girls fight over Chevalier.

The cameras cranked. The girls went to it with a will.

On the sidelines Lubitsch chuckled. "All for the good of the picture," quoth he. But as take after take brought bigger and better slaps the "crew" were a little worried. By the time the foreign version takes were reached, things were at their merriest.

"Cut!" commanded Lubitsch. He went over to the girls, congratulated them on their fine work and induced them to shake hands and smile prettily at each other.

A VISITOR asked little Robert Coogan, who played *Sooky* in "Skippy," if he wanted to be an actor.

"Not when I grow up. All actors are really crazy," he answered.

OUR old friend Pola Negri is in Hollywood on a very sporting chance. She ardently desires to make good in talkies—and whether or not she makes a picture for RKO-Pathe depends on the success of a test she's taking on the Coast.

She traveled 6,000 miles to take that test!

I called on Negri in New York. She looks the same—a little heavier, perhaps, and certainly a little tamer. Since we saw her last, nearly three years ago, she's been divorced, and from an artistic point of view pretty much out of the spotlight.

The Perilous Pole is still a beautiful woman—and still, in her heart, the queen of queens. The death of her popularity in American pictures in 1928, her divorce—nothing has bowed that regal spirit.

POLA'S going to a new Hollywood—where queens are out of fashion. Now it's a place where a lot of hard-working men and women live. She'll work hard, because she's very ambitious. But she probably won't find a loose throne around the place.

Negri's voice is rich and deep. Of course,

there's a notable accent, but accents are pretty much the fashion in pictures now.

Pola talks freely enough about her recent divorce from Serge Mdivani. And about love and marriage in general.

"Happy marriage must begin calmly," she says. "Mental stimulus, not passion, should be the basis. I shall choose an older, understanding man next time, and we shall live happily ever after."

A MOVING picture producer is quoted as saying:

"All this talk about Marlene Dietrich and Greta Garbo being alike is wrong. Garbo is photographed from the hips up. Dietrich is photographed from the hips down."

HOWARD HUGHES' offer to Walter Winchell, New York tabloid gossip writer, to play the part of *Whitey*, the reporter with a

The Monthly Broadcast
of
Hollywood
Goings-On!

Undaunted by her old box-office toboggan, Pola is back in Hollywood wooing the microphone for a contract. She's off passionate love forever, she says. Ah me, Pola, how can love live without you?

The be-sweatered Nordic in the center is the closest double for Greta Garbo found in a search of all Sweden. The girls on either side won second and third prizes. Now, you Garbomaniacs, be kind to them. They do not threaten your idol's throne nor declare themselves also of the royal blood

nose for glamorous living as well as news, in "Queer People," is no longer a rumor. It's a definite thing.

It carries such a wad of money with it that no one expects Walter to refuse.

As Winchell's newspaper contract calls for a daily column, his Broadway friends are chuckling over the prospect of the columns he would write during the seven weeks it would be necessary for him to be in Hollywood.

As Walter, himself, likes to be known as Little Boy Peep, the Great Gabbo, Big Ears and Vulture Vinchell, some of the names irate victims of his gossip have called him, Hollywood, as one man, would have to lock itself in during his stay.

NOW, let's get down to the love, marriage and divorce news of the month. There's plenty of it.

But don't fail to follow this department through to the back pages or you'll miss something you can tell at the next meeting of the Ladies' Aid Society.

AS this issue goes to press, the matrimonial battle of Estelle Taylor and Jack Dempsey is in high—with shot and shell flying from both camps.

Jack has established a residence near Reno, with the avowed purpose of seeking a divorce under the generous Nevada laws.

According to best reports, Estelle, in Hollywood, has been closeted with her attorneys drawing up a suit which she intends filing—charging mental cruelty.

Estelle, in statements to the press, has said that she didn't care for the ex-champ's pals, and that he was terrifically jealous, and that there was nothing she wanted more than babies.

A few months ago she was quoted as saying, "Babies—never!"

Jack, in the very little talking he has done,

has hinted that Estelle's insistence on a film career, to the exclusion of downright domesticity, has caused him great tribulation.

AND as matters now stand, both are suing. If Estelle wins, it means she will get quite a share of Jack's hard-earned fortune.

Rumors that all was not well at the Dempsey place have been common for several years. In the spring of 1929, for instance, the sure-thing gamblers of Hollywood were willing to wager almost anything that the marriage would not last through the year.

Now the long, sad story is out, with its charges and counter-charges, and another marriage is over.

PAULINE STARKE and her husband, Jack White, producer of comedies, are on the outs and bound for the divorce courts. Recently Jack sent word to Pauline that if she insisted on demanding one-half of his worldly possessions, according to the California community property law, he'd start saying things himself.

THE "lowdown" on Olive Borden's recent elopement with Theodore Spector, 31-year-old Paterson, N. J., stock broker, is an interesting tid-bit. Olive, it seems, was one of the guests that Ricardo Salecedo, Latin playwright, was entertaining at a farewell party for Anna May Wong in a smart Fifth Avenue Hotel.

The phone rang and a voice asked for Olive, who, upon answering it, relayed the message that her mother was very ill and she would have to leave immediately.

Wide World

That grand old trouper, Marie Dressler, on the way to the set, escorted by her faithful maid. She has about recovered from her recent illness and worked hard on her latest release, "Prosperity," whose funny rôles she shares with pal Polly Moran

Tom Gallery doesn't seem discouraged by that divorce from ZaSu Pitts. He's looking pleased to have Madge Evans by his side. Rumor says there's romance in the air

GEORGE BRENT, that erstwhile nice Irish lad who's married to Ruth Chatterton, constantly ignores the publicity department's requests. Has his marriage gone to his head? And if so, we wonder why. And isn't it a pity?

THE Ethel Barrymore wit is hitting on all twelve these days. A visitor remarked to a studio official: "Pardon me, but you're a supervisor, aren't you?" Whereupon Ethel commented, "Don't they smile when they call them that?"

JANET GAYNOR has gone Garbo—even though the public won't let her play rôles of sophistication.

And now—the company stops at five o'clock sharp. No matter what's going on, little Miss Gaynor walks away on the dot.

Okay, Janet—you're making more at the box-office than Garbo.

JANET is so big, dramatically speaking, that they had a tough time getting a leading man for her in "Tess of the Storm Country." The boy's part isn't very big. Not much chance for individual honors.

Lew Ayres was first choice. He demurred and Universal did not lend him. Alexander Kirkland was second. He also demurred. He was under contract to Fox and told to take his twelve week lay-off at once as chastisement. Actors are supposed to take what they are given, you know.

Then Joel McCrea. But he didn't like the idea of being second fiddle, either.

Charlie Farrell up and volunteered. He'd like to play with Janet in anything. *He* didn't care how big or small the part was. And since the public was begging for Charlie and Janet to play together, anyway—

HOLLYWOOD doesn't expect Greta Garbo back until after the first of the year. Manager Harry Edington is ill in the hospital, but we understand he plans to leave for Sweden soon after he recovers, to fetch his famous protégé.

They're keeping the Garbo dressing-room dusted each day at Metro, ready for an any-moment surprise appearance of this always-surprising woman. And her name appears each month on Metro's star list.

And every new story is looked over as a "Garbo possibility."

Just a kind old lady who trusts everybody. Now stand by for a shock. This is Clive Brook, disguised as that immortal detective, Sherlock Holmes

WITH Al Jolson saying she won't and George Jessel saying she will, Norma Talmadge's friends are wondering if she really will return to the screen in "Wunderbar."

Jessel insists he has the screen rights to the piece and Jolson says he hasn't.

The feud between Jessel and Jolson, if it could be called a feud, dates from, "The Jazz Singer."

That was Jessel's outstanding stage hit, but when Warners planned to make it into a picture, he demanded so much money that Jolson was put in the rôle as a sort of second choice.

WHILE Director Michael Curtiz was working his company for "Twenty Thousand Years in Sing Sing" twenty nights out of twenty-four, John Barrymore attended a dance marathon at Santa Monica. The manager rushed up and asked him if he would have his photograph taken with one of two remaining couples.

"Certainly!" Jack was gracious.

The manager dragged the weary couple to Jack. They were nearly asleep on each other's shoulders. Jack shuddered. "Say, have you folks been working with Curtiz?"

GARY COOPER asked the powers-that-be for permission to go to New York and the very next morning these powers read in their morning papers that Gary had left by airplane with the Countess di Frasso and Mary Pickford. Of course, retakes for "A Farewell to Arms" were supposed to be over, but the picture hadn't been previewed yet and there might be changes needed. Well, the ladies are as important as health. And Mary and the Countess wanted to get going.

A débutante and her escort. Shirley Temple is the lady, and Eugene Butler the young man in the case. They are playing in the Educational comedy, "Glad Rags to Riches"

A pair whose voices and sheer nonsense have won a big place in the hearts of all radio listeners—George Burns and Gracie Allen. They've made personal appearances, but everybody can see them now in Paramount's "The Big Broadcast"

TAP, TAP, TAP. That very refined tapping from a certain Hollywood studio these days is just the terribly ultra Constance Bennett learning to tap dance.

FOGS and rain descended on "The Kid From Spain" set when the bull fight was only half completed. And the overhead was mounting.

Sam Goldwyn walked down to the set to talk it over with Eddie Cantor and Director Leo McCarey.

"It's terrible," Sam groaned. "This thing is costing too much. Something will have to be done. I'm worried sick."

"You do look a bit drawn," Eddie sympathized.

"Drawn?" the Irish director said. "Why, Sam, you actually look over-drawn."

And even Goldwyn laughed.

POOR Virginia Bruce had a tough honeymoon.

She was working in "Kongo." And if you ever saw a *dirty* picture, it was that. Taken in mud. Even the interior shots were largely in huts with dirt floors.

Virginia's hair was stringy. Her nails were uncut.

She went to Director Bill Cowan with tears in her eyes.

"Can't I have a shampoo and a facial and a manicure just for the week-end?"

"Absolutely not. You might not get the dirt back in the same proportions."

"But I want to go out with Jack—"

As new-hubby Jack Gilbert is noted for wanting his women fastidiously groomed, no wonder the bride decided to give up her career and spend all her time being a little home body.

THE romance between Toby Wing and Jack Oakie is still flaming.

And the Loretta Young-Louis Calhern affair is really looking serious.

Lyda Roberti, the Polish hot-cha, won't be bothered with beaus. Lyda goes everywhere alone. Lives alone, travels alone and sits off in corners alone.

And Lyda did it before Garbo ever thought of it, we're told.

But Billie Dove doesn't go solo if Phillips Holmes can help it.

Yep, it's a new romance.

Eugene Robert Richee

Beware, men — the "panther woman"! Kathleen Burke is the winner out of sixty thousand girls in Paramount's nation-wide contest for the coveted rôle

HOLLYWOOD'S best story of the month: Joan Bennett arrived late at Winfield R. Sheehan's birthday party for Janet Gaynor. In the last-moment rush, Joan had forgotten her glasses.

Near-sighted, you know.

Gene Markey led her by the hand around the buffet supper tables. Joan started ahead with her plate. She ran into an extra chair, and sat down.

The roomful of already-eating people gasped. Some audibly.

Joan had taken a seat next to her ex-fiance, John Considine, Jr. Then she couldn't very well leave.

And if Joan had planned it, she couldn't very well have devised a better stunt to take the limelight from Janet.

All eyes were focused upon Joan's table from that moment.

EDDIE CANTOR has a daughter, aged six. One evening when he returned from work at the studio he found her busy over an original drawing.

"What are you drawing?" Eddie asked.

"A picture of the funniest comedian, daddy. You see," holding up the picture, "he has your eyes, Jimmy Durante's nose and Joe E. Brown's mouth."

JUST a few of George Raft's girl friends: Virginia Cherrill, Billie Dove, Shirley Grey, Constance Cummings.

He went down to see Connie off when she left for New York; he took Shirley out the next night and he says Billie Dove is one of the loveliest creatures he's ever seen.

Again, place your own bet.

PHOTOPLAY'S Hollywood

*All the Beauty tricks
of all the stars Brought
to you each month*

Gloria Swanson did not have glamour in 1926. But today—her smile is unforgettable and even her nose is fascinating. Her eyes, too, reflect the spirit of her great battle for self-beauty

In five years Norma Shearer has developed from a sweet-faced girl into a lovely lady. She has learned to reveal her perfect hairline, to emphasize her mouth's appealing curves. Yet the change is not entirely physical. Self-analysis, determination and work are largely responsible

HERE I am in Hollywood again! The Embassy at the luncheon hour! The Chinese Theater for the opening of "Mata Hari"! The Mayfair Room of the Biltmore!

These are some of the play haunts of Hollywood's beauty—beauty so glamorous, so perfect, that you gasp and ask yourself, is it real? It is real.

It is almost unbelievably real. For it is beauty that has been worked for, made sometimes from almost nothing. This beauty is the fruit of sacrifice in some way. It has been suffered for, paid for dearly in time and dollars and self-discipline.

It is the highest priced beauty in the world.

Contrary to general opinion, Hollywood beauty is not skin deep. It is not alone the rose-textured skin of sixteen or the gold of youthful curls. Hollywood beauty is, however,

Beauty Shop

Conducted By
Carolyn
Van Wyck

Was it heartache or ambition that changed Greta Garbo from this unkempt child into a national figure of romance? Certainly masterful eye make-up has done its part

Joan, does that beautiful strength in mouth and chin tell the story of your transfiguration, too? Compare the butterfly with the grub. Can you believe they are the same?

largely the result of self-study, of effort and determination to correct a fault and a development of personal allure which can sometimes make you feel beauty where literally there is none.

Shown on these pages are four of the most glamorous faces in Hollywood! A comparison between past and present portraits is more eloquent than words. You can see the results of effort and development in these faces, and you would be amazed at some of the beauty barriers these actresses have overcome.

Every star has her own little beauty secrets, her tricks of overcoming this and that weakness which you and I and the rest of the world possess. Beauty like theirs is yours, too, if you want it and will work for it like the stars do. Nature does a good job in one out of fifty; with the rest good looks is a personal achievement.

Don't Go Platinum Yet! *Read before you* Dye!

By May Allerton

LISTEN carefully, you girls who have gazed in wonderment, perhaps tinged with a touch of envy, at the glistening white locks of Jean Harlow and other stars and players of the screen.

Wait, all you thousands of girls who have written PHOTOPLAY that you are considering going the limit in light coloring and asking for information about "platinum blonde."

You are going to get that information here and now, every enlightening and every bitter fact.

Then, if you must go platinum, be it upon your own head. It will be anyhow. But do not say that PHOTOPLAY did not warn you.

Jean Harlow started the fad, for *fad* it is, in "Hell's Angels." In that picture she played the rôle of a seductive, irresistible charmer before whom men fell as if they were mown down by a machine gun.

Capitalizing on the public interest in the girl in that rôle, producers vied with each other to cast her in similar rôles in other pictures; always the platinum bullet that shattered masculine life and honor; the epitome of sex appeal in the parts she played, the clothes she wore.

It was natural, therefore, that the startlingly white hair should be taken as a symbol of devastating femininity.

It is not the first time in motion picture history that a distinctive style of hair became of world-wide interest. Nearly two score years ago Irene Castle's motion pictures sent millions of girls scurrying into the hair dressing parlors of the world to have their long locks shorn to a short bob. Garbo's longish bob, reaching to the shoulder, and curled on the end, cost hairdressers millions of dollars, when old and young alike permitted their hair to grow again.

EVEN men were not immune to the screen influence. Valentino's sleek hair, brushed straight back, and glistening with pomade, made millions of dollars for the manufacturers of men's hair dressings, and created the "sheik" type, adding a new meaning to the word in our language.

Although Jean Harlow started the fad you cannot blame her for it. She is a natural blonde of the lightest type. The platinum coloring of her hair gives it life and vibrancy when struck by the incandescent lamps, and its photographic effect is so startling that several stars have made use of it.

Joan Crawford used something like it in "This Modern Age," but discarded it, and permitted her hair to regain its natural coloring. Lola Lane (now Mrs. Lew Ayres) is one screen beauty who frankly admits she has gone platinum. Her hair was naturally a very light brown, but she found that the platinum color softened the hair line on her forehead and gave her a better screen result.

The best hairdressers of New York and Hollywood, as well as cities in other sections of the country, report that thousands and thousands of women, young and old, have come into their establishments intent on becoming platinum blondes,

In nearly every case these women have been warned that,

Here is the stark truth about the new fad. PHOTOPLAY warns its readers that it is suitable to only one woman in a thousand, and, inexpertly done, is a hazardous proceeding which may be followed by the keenest regret

except for one woman in a thousand, it is a hazardous proceeding which may be followed by regret, and even disastrous results. Inexpertly done, it can result in complete, if temporary, baldness.

The majority of reputable beauty shop proprietors and operators positively refuse to attempt it except for those with hair so light in coloring that it requires little extra bleaching.

In its effort to learn all there was to be learned about platinum hair PHOTOPLAY representatives interviewed thirty of the best and most reputable hairdressers of New York, Chicago and Hollywood.

We learned details that will make your hair stand on end.

"Platinum blonde" is really almost white hair with a faint blueish-lavender tint. The effect is secured by a thorough bleaching of the hair in a treatment that may last four or five hours, a whole day, or even longer, depending on how dark the hair is to begin with. Extra strength peroxide, with a few drops of strong ammonia added, is applied to the hair and allowed to dry. This is repeated over and over until every bit of color is extracted from the hair.

Some beauty shops mix the peroxide and ammonia into a white paste which contains magnesium and this is called a "white henna," but it's the peroxide and ammonia which do the bleaching. Making a paste out of it is merely to prevent the bleach from running, and is effective when "touching up" the roots of the hair later on. A preparation made by the dye manufacturers is also used for bleaching in many shops.

After the hair has been thoroughly bleached, the platinum rinse is applied as the finishing touch. This rinse is a definite dye, just as much so as a dye used for black or brown hair. Simply taking the color out of the hair does not make a platinum blonde. If this were true, every woman with snow-white hair would be platinum. Nor does just a rinse of simple French blueing do the work.

THERE is danger and even physical suffering if you get an operator who does not understand exactly what is to be done. If the scalp is sensitive, the pain is excruciating when the bleach is applied. This does not last long, however, unless there is a scalp abrasion. Then the results might be serious.

All this sounds discouraging, doesn't it? That's just what we intended it to be. But you haven't heard anything yet.

There's a little matter of upkeep I want to mention.

The cost of the original platinum process, followed by the necessary shampoo and wave, will be anywhere from $7.50 to $50, depending on the color of the hair to start, and the exclusiveness of the shop doing the work. That pretty item, however, is only the beginning of weekly expenditures to keep your platinum head looking well groomed.

Unless the hair is very light to start with, it will need a "touch up" once a week or the roots will begin to look dark. "Touch ups" vary in different [PLEASE TURN TO PAGE 340]

She Started
It All

JEAN HARLOW is responsible for the Platinum Blonde vogue. Beauty specialists warn women in this issue that only those gifted with her naturally light coloring, transparent skin, white teeth, should consider it.

Here it is—the new type! Marlene Dietrich's lack-lustre eyes say everything to be said

And Tallulah Bankhead's style whets sharply the imagination

While Garbo is the symbol of everything mysterious in woman. She started it

CHARM? No! No! You

THE movies have done it again!

They've introduced a new word into ordinary conversation, started a new fad, begun a new cycle, created a new standard.

The movies are good at that.

The new word is "glamour," the new fad is glamorousness, the new cycle is more glamour and the new standard is more of the same thing.

The ingénue with her friendly, hurt smile, her bird-like gestures, her coy maidenliness is as old-fashioned as a hansom cab. In a word, if you want to be popular—be glamorous.

For years the Elinor Glyns and Beatrice Fairfaxes have been writing about charm. They've told young women with social ambitions that that vague quality was essential. But the word has now been passed into the limbo of forgotten things. The new one, the all-consuming word of the moment, is "glamour."

If you don't believe me (and you wouldn't be the first), take a look at the present roster of film stars. Take a couple of looks—they're worth it. Marlene Dietrich, of the heavy-lidded, inscrutable eyes, the sullen mouth. Garbo (who really, I believe, started it all), of the languorous, pale body. Tallulah Bankhead, also heavy lidded, also inscrutable. Joan Crawford, the exponent of the neurotic younger generation. Constance Bennett, long limbed and fluid, a woman to pique the imagination. Lilyan Tashman, decked in sophistication and Paris gowns. Elissa Landi, mysterious as a supervisor's idea. And the very new one—Lil Dagover, a rapturous beauty who came to American before her time, was sent back and now returns to spread glamour. And many, many more come to mind—but I'm running out of adjectives.

Although the new school has been gathering momentum for some time,

The once popular vamp — straight, direct but never subtle. Example, Theda Bara

Paramount really fired the first shot when they dropped from their contract list Mary Brian, Jean Arthur and Fay Wray. Now here were three charming, sweet, whimsical little girls who, so everybody thought, had a good sized fan following. But, according to statistics, they simply didn't draw at the old box-office.

The glamour gals were beating them hands (and eyelashes) down.

These girls were the exponents of the charm school. Charm simply oozed—but they had no glamour.

But Mary Brian is being smart. After some futile little girl tears, when she was told her name was to be struck from the list, she packed her trunks and left Hollywood for her first European trip. She went in search of sophistication.

After six years of "the little girl who lives next door" rôles, she's out to become a woman capable of stealing the husband of the little woman who lives next door.

Mary, for six years a good draw, suddenly found herself, like a number of others, one of that vast horde of disappearing ingénues for which you, you and you have no use.

WHAT brought about the drastic change? Your guess is as good as mine.

It all goes in cycles anyhow. Remember the Theda Baras, the Nita Naldis, the Virginia Pearsons, the Louise Glaums?

For them "vamp" was coined. "Glamour" has now been introduced into the average vocabulary. Their kingdoms toppled when Sweetness and Light showed through.

For years the nice girl had her day. Her screen path was clear. She must neither drink, nor smoke. She must be chaste, nay almost prudish. She must be kind to old ladies, children and stray cats. Her clothes must be

The Mary Pickford of long ago exemplified girlish charm. Now that's too tame

Mary Brian says she will never look like this again and she means it

Young, pretty, nice Jean Arthur. But the fans demand something different. Can she give it?

Must Have GLAMOUR

By Katherine Albert

neat but not gaudy. And the only appeal admitted was that vague, spiritual quality that does things to man's Better Nature.

But now—whoops—the new brigade. Why, the Dietrichs, the Garbos, the Bankheads, the Landis (and have you noted that they're all blonde, which was formerly virtue's symbol) may kick old ladies in the face and tie tin cans to dogs' tails. They may steal other women's husbands and bathe in champagne—and the fans love it.

These women possess the new and vital commodity—glamour!

Norma Shearer is the outstanding example of cultivated glamour. Think way, way back to the Norma who was. I remember years ago when I worked in her studio, there was a story under consideration for little Shearer. It was finally, I believe, called "The Devil's Circus." And the climax was—I hope I'm still right—the seduction of the girl in the story.

Well, they pondered for weeks. Could they allow that rare exponent of girlish charm and simplicity, Norma Shearer, one teeny, weeny [PLEASE TURN TO PAGE 343]

Can This Be The Same Girl?

Norma Shearer, classic example of a woman who follows the personality trend. When all was sweet and pure Norma was the young lady at the left. Came glamour, and wise Shearer changed her style. At right as she was in "The Divorcée"

Beauty and Personality

Bette Davis has a lovely figure. But Sylvia tells us the trim little star has some faults that should be remedied. For one thing, her eyes are too staring. Such mannerisms can be corrected with a bit of persistence

The cords in Bette's neck are accentuated by incorrect head posture, Sylvia says. But she has lots of charm, as hubby Harmon Nelson is aware

Over Frisco" and I wondered why you would let the studios give you such an unsympathetic rôle. While I was still wondering, you stepped out in "Of Human Bondage" in another terrifically unsympathetic part but one in which you did such magnificent acting that I stood up and cheered. And you're winning a reputation as a real actress in these new rôles. So you must be on the right track.

Now maybe you think I'm stepping out of *my* rôle as beauty doctor when I tell you that in this letter I want to talk to you about your personality. Really, I'm not, for beauty and personality are inseparable. The mental and the physical are as close together as a rose and its perfume.

DEAR BETTE: For the last few years I've watched your career. And I've seen an amazing thing happen to you. I've seen you go from ingénue to extremist, and then to a wonderful character actress. In "The Working Man" you were grand. Then I saw you in "Fog

are Inseparable

Sylvia tells Bette Davis

Faulty mannerisms are fatal to charm. If you have any, write to Sylvia.

Sylvia

Your mental attitude shows on your face, Bette Davis. The mental attitude of every woman shows on her face and makes her beautiful or homely, appealing or hard. If you're going to continue to play unsympathetic rôles (and I must say I admire your courage in taking the rôle of *Mildred* and making it sit up and beg), you've got to show me—and the rest of the world —that you're not like that in real life. That you're not actually hard and bitter and cynical. And you must pepper your career with a few sympathetic parts.

I know what you've been through, Bette. I know how you came to Hollywood and got shoved from one stupid rôle to another. So you stuck out your chin and said, "I'll show 'em." You showed 'em by changing your type. But don't make a mistake, baby. Don't let that hardness of the parts you play show on your face. Don't let it keep you from being as lovely as you can be.

I want you to heed my advice. And I want every girl in the world who has, in the struggle for existence, grown cynical, to learn how to turn that bitterness into lovely, feminine appeal.

Look at yourself in the mirror, Bette. Your figure is lovely, isn't it? You're a cute, slim little thing. But, darling, your neck has its faults. Your eyes are too staring. Your jaw line is too prominent. And you can, if you will, do wonders with the shape of your nose. You have an ample mouth. I like that, but often you make it up to look too extreme.

Now that we know where we stand I'm going to tell you—and all the rest of my readers—how that face and neck can be remodeled.

One night, Bette, I heard you over the radio. It was one of the most intelligent talks that has ever come out of Hollywood. That intelligence manifested itself in "Of Human Bondage." You've shown in that picture what a wonderful actress you are. You are right among

Bette can play a harsh rôle superbly, but Sylvia urges her to forego the appearance of cynicism off the screen. And a different mouth make-up is suggested, too

Miss Davis' intelligence shows in her forehead, and her determination in her jaw. But Sylvia advises her to affect a somewhat "softer" appearance

the big shots of Hollywood. Now you can fight for a few sympathetic rôles.

God gave you your intelligence. I can see that in your expressive forehead. But it isn't always wise, in Hollywood (or anywhere else in the business world), to show it too pronouncedly. So make that intelligent forehead look softer by bringing your hair forward, over it. In the October PHOTOPLAY, you were pictured with half-a-dozen highly becoming coiffures. You should stick to them, or something similar.

Hollywood has made you determined, Bette. That's why you stick your chin out and, thereby, give your jaw a line that it shouldn't have. It's a mannerism — a bad habit you've got to break, because when you carry your head in that [PLEASE TURN TO PAGE 344]

See These Latest Chanel

ANOTHER big fashion "scoop" for PHOTOPLAY! Once again we are able to give you an exclusive preview of the Chanel-designed clothes that you will see Gloria Swanson wear in "Tonight or Never." And, according to our reviewers, Samuel Goldwyn has made a picture worthy of the clothes.

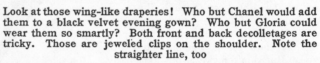

Look at those wing-like draperies! Who but Chanel would add them to a black velvet evening gown? Who but Gloria could wear them so smartly? Both front and back decolletages are tricky. Those are jeweled clips on the shoulder. Note the straighter line, too

Chanel goes in for sleeves in a big way, it seems. Huge muffs of fur match a face-framing collar on the short satin jacket which accompanies this regal white satin evening gown. That train is dramatic, isn't it?

STYLES IN Gloria's Picture

Chanel has caught all the glamour that surrounds an opera singer in these clothes she has designed for Gloria's operatic screen rôle. Look at this afternoon ensemble in black satin and ermine. Every line of it is distinctive. The coat is long and slightly fitted. Barrel cuffs of ermine trim the sleeves, while a double collar of the fur rises about the face. The dress depends upon intricate seaming for its chic. Bands of ermine trim the surplice neckline. A barrel muff echoes the sleeve detail and a pert turban tops the unusual costume

Longer and more elegant goes the trend in evening wraps *a la* Chanel. This gorgeous satin one is lavishly trimmed with that precious fur, chinchilla. Again the unusual cuff detail that marks all these "Tonight or Never" costumes

Hollywood
Snubs Paris

Movie capital is self-reliant as a style center. Designer no longer looks to "shabby" Paris for ideas

By William P. Gaines

Travis Banton, designer of those stunning gowns worn by Paramount stars. He omitted his seasonal Paris visit, finding home more inspiring

FOR the first time in nine years, Travis Banton, designer of dresses for the beautiful women of Paramount, is not making a seasonal visit to Paris.

Because Banton does not think Paris can show Hollywood anything more of importance in the way of costuming. Not this year, anyway.

Hollywood, as a style center, has become self-reliant.

Oh, a man like Travis Banton, who creates such a quantity of fluffs and ruffles for such ravishing *femmes* as Colbert, Lombard, Dietrich, Hopkins and West, needs a bit of brushing up on his ideas now and then.

It's good for him to get around to the cities and resorts where women are fashionable without being in the movies.

Paris might have been one of these cities once upon a time —as long ago as 1932.

But Banton went back to Paris last year and found it "shabby." What style there was across the ocean, he observed, was in London.

This year, Banton, in search of design inspirations, stopped at New York. Then, for sunshiny frills, he turned South to see what women with money were wearing in Palm Beach.

So, if the French capital wants to get back in the style swim, it might do well to look over some of the Travis Banton creations in forthcoming Paramount productions. Paris can see how the smart women of New York and Palm Beach may influence one of the superior designers of Hollywood—and that, today, means of the world.

As for the Parisian influence manifest in what the women of New York

In fact, Paris borrows from Banton. The way he dresses Mae West excites forty million Frenchmen. Here he is being flamboyant

are wearing, Banton sees it growing less pronounced, year by year.

"New York designers have become adult and adept in their art. When they draw the lines of a dress, they no longer peer apologetically across the ocean and ask the French: 'Is this all right?'"

The fact is evident that Hollywood now influences New York much more than Paris does, and the trends which come across the continent from the West far exceed New York's influence on Hollywood.

For some line or ornament that New York offers Hollywood, it takes in return a raging Princess Eugenie hat from a Greta Garbo picture,

Claudette Colbert has a "perfect figure for the designer," Banton says. Such a pleasure to sketch Claudette's frock!

football player shoulders from a Joan Crawford picture, a splash of the plumed and décolleté past from a Mae West picture.

Even Paris went into a frenzy, trying to simulate the Mae West ensembles, and it took certain details from Deitrich—*coq* feathers, for instance.

Banton thinks prohibition repeal had much to do with New York's fashion circles putting Paris to shame.

"Women would wear any old thing to sneak into Tony's or '21,' during the speakeasy era. But with repeal, 'dining out' returned to favor. The grand entrance is back in style. Women know they will be seen, and they enjoy being seen at their best."

BRINGING gaiety into the open, and a generally more cheerful attitude toward conditions are responsible for the elaboration and intricacy of the new gowns, Banton believes. Dress expresses a people's spirit.

He is favoring a fairly straight silhouette. The skirt suggests the natural curves of the body, with some concern for drapery. More than ever before is there a distinction between day and evening dress, the skirt from eight to eleven inches off the floor for daytime, and long—even with train, after sundown. Banton is splitting some of his skirts.

Some of his most fascinating creations are worn by Marlene Dietrich in "Scarlet Empress." This is a costume picture, to be sure—a story of Catherine the Great of Russia; but there always is the possibility of some detail of dress or coiffure, when exhibited by such a favorite as Dietrich in such a picture, starting a widespread fad.

Who can say, yet? Perhaps every little high school girl in the country soon will be imitating the Dietrich headdress arranged by Banton. It is simple, surely; something similar always has been worn by girls in school. Just a ribbon from the back, with the bow on top, and bangs—but it's the little Dietrich-Banton touch that makes it different. Slightly more elaborate is the fillet of flowers which Marlene wears in the same manner, in the same picture.

SOMETHING else to watch for from "Scarlet Empress" is the ruche. Will women go for this neck treatment on a grand scale? Such speculations must be exciting to a designer of screen dress, although Banton modestly insists he creates for each picture alone, and not with an eye for what effect might be copied from it.

Keeping the stars becomingly gowned is a job that drains a man's resourcefulness, but, says Banton, it affords many delights to the designer. These women—even if they care much more for acting than playing the clothes horse—are grand models. Their personalities are a constant spur to ingenuity.

"Only on very rare occasions do I have any trouble with temperament. The first time I do a woman's clothes, there is apt to be a struggle. But when she learns to have faith in me, we get along splendidly."

Banton says he has gained too much wisdom to talk about "the best dressed woman in Hollywood," but he sees no danger in sprinkling his comments more generally.

Such a lovely Hollywood creation as this one by Banton, worn by Marlene Dietrich in "Scarlet Empress," may influence our styles more than Paris can today

Every high school girl soon may copy this ribbon headdress arranged by Banton for the new Dietrich film

Marlene, so innocent looking to be the "Scarlet Empress," has a Banton-designed fillet of flowers to wear, too

"Lilyan Tashman is dress conscious. She exaggerates everything and is not a model for the average woman to follow. But, in her individual way, she really dresses beautifully.

"Carole Lombard has great natural chic. She wears clothes beautifully; can put them on and forget about them.

"Claudette Colbert has the perfect figure from the designer's viewpoint.

"Norma Shearer dresses in excellent taste.

"Joan Crawford's gowns are terribly effective.

"Marlene Dietrich is the most natural dresser of any woman I have known. Everything she puts on is sublimated by the Dietrich personality."

Banton thinks the coming of the talkies was the greatest factor in making Hollywood the style center it is today.

"Taste has improved a hundred per cent in the last five years.

"Hollywood was too isolated, too provincial, before talkies brought a great number of New York stage people to the West Coast. They came with their Fifth Avenue fashions, and the movie colony accepted the challenge."

Banton himself was a New York designer [PLEASE TURN TO PAGE 347]

Those virtuosos of rhythm, Ginger Rogers and Fred Astaire, dancing in "Follow the Fleet"

Ginger Rogers

Rules for Slaying

NO girl," Ginger Rogers said to me emphatically, "no girl is a born belle-of-the-ball—just as no girl is a born wallflower. There's nothing mysterious about the way some girls are always rushed to death by the stag line and others aren't. You *learn* to be popular at a dance just like you learn anything else. A few fast rules plus a few feminine secrets and—well, it's simple, really."

If anybody should know about that Ginger should. I think I can safely say that no young lady in these forty-eight states could step onto a dance floor anywhere in any one of them and rate a bigger rush than the beautiful Rogers. Her recent pictures with Fred Astaire have established her beauty, charm and dancing ability. She is the top in any stag line's language.

And yet, when it comes right down to the technique of slaying the stags, *Ginger Rogers hasn't got a thing you haven't got or that you can't develop if you want to!* She told me the simple secrets that have made her America's Belle-of-the-Ball Number One.

"Before we start," Ginger reminded me, "don't forget that I'm not basing my ideas on my screen work alone. Heavens! because I've danced in pictures it wouldn't necessarily indicate that I'd know the problems of the girl at a college prom or on the floor at her country club. But, I know those problems first-hand. I've had them myself. I've danced all my life . . ."

Ginger went back to the very beginning of the dancing care that was to take her from Texas to vaudeville to New York Hollywood, from high school hops to débutante parties, dink night spots to the outstandingly fashionable clubs througho the country.

"And naturally," she said, "when you make a career of dan ing you're bound to learn a lot about it. One of the thin I'm surest of is that the old saw about 'the strange social cher istry of the ballroom that seems to inevitably divide its fa guests into two classes—the sought-after and the wallflowers' just an old saw! There's no reason why belles-of-the-ball *shou* be few, but there are a lot of reasons, apparently, why they *ar*

"I've held up a few walls myself, frankly. I believe every g has at some time or other if she's gone out very much. But m early experiences taught me one helpful thing: 'Wallflowe are self-made!' "

We were sitting at tea in the Rogers' suite in a Manhatt hotel. Ginger, weary and actually footsore from her rece completion of some several hundred hours dancing in the ma ing of "Follow the Fleet," wore a pale gold hostess gown t color of her hair and a nice ridiculous, squashy pair of soft-sol

This team has perfected the most graceful ballroom dancing since Irene and Vernon Castle

the Stag Line

The technique of getting a huge rush instead of just a big one isn't only in knowing the latest steps

By Mary Watkins Reeves

moccasins.   She'd come on to New York for a few days of rest and fun before beginning her next picture.

"With these worn-out tootsies of mine," she laughed, "I'm fine one to gab about belles-of-the-ball! I don't think I could last three dances at a prom this minute—but I could sit up here with my feet propped on this hassock and *talk* about it to you for hours!

"First of all, a girl just can't allow herself to be a poor dancer. I say allow because I believe the ability to follow readily and gracefully is born in every girl and only needs to be cultivated enough.

"Nine times out of ten a bad dancer is bad through sheer neglect.   It always has struck me as odd that so many girls will work hard to perfect their bridge or tennis or personal attractiveness and neglect their dancing.   I think they expect to go to a dance and get a rush on the strength of their looks alone.   Well, maybe. But even the loveliest face in the world can look like a nightmare to the poor man who's struggling around with a clumsy partner.

"Men don't demand that a girl be a *swell* dancer, but they certainly do justly demand that she be a *good* one.   Good enough to follow the current steps and fads, to readily adapt herself to being led by a variety of partners.   A Texan and a New Yorker, for instance, may do the same simple waltz step in entirely individual ways; if you've ever travelled about the country you know how true that is.   A really good follower can quickly adapt herself to any type of leading; a poor follower is up against it when her partner doesn't dance exactly like the rest of the home-state boys.

"The stag line demands simply that a girl stay on her own toes and be more like a feather than a lump of lead.   That's all And those two things any girl can do if she wants to.

"Dancing lessons?   Why not?   If you can afford them and will apply yourself to instructions they can do wonders for you. But, if necessary, entirely on your own, you can do a lot to improve yourself   [PLEASE TURN TO PAGE 345]

Who Is Your Husband's Favorite Actress?

And What Are You Going To Do About It?

By Ruth Rankin

Many a quiet, stay-at-home man goes crazy over Harlow. If your husband comes out of the theater raving about Jean's radiant loveliness and bare shoulders, you should do something about it. And you had better not waste much time

Does the man you love walk a mile to see Gaynor on the screen? If he does, look into your own past and present, and govern your future accordingly. There's a reason for his preference, and it's very important to you

DOES your husband go out of the theater doing a rave about Mae West or Greta Garbo or Janet Gaynor? Does he keep it up all the way home? And does it quietly burn you to a handsome brown crisp or show up the electrical sparks like a blown-out fuse?

Come on now, girls. Don't deny it. I know better. If you don't get mad, either inwardly or visibly, you simply are not human. And if you weren't human, you wouldn't have a man, or go to a movie. Case dismissed.

The less you resemble the actress who rates the rave, the madder the whole business makes you. If you are a little bit like her, it's apt to be quite flattering. I know a man who can snap his wife out of her worst peeve by saying, "Take off those whiskers, Joan Crawford, I know you!"

The sages tell us it is fatal to analyze too closely those who have our devotion. So don't put your husband on the pan. Analyze *yourself* and the woman on the screen who has his admiration. Remember, you can change practically everything else in this life, but you can't change a man.

Why not regard your man's enchantment at the hands of his favorite picture-girl as a break for you?

It is certainly a perfect indication of his choice, a barometer of his likes and dislikes. Instead of being incensed about it, why not be guided by it?

For instance, there is a certain brawny gentleman (you all

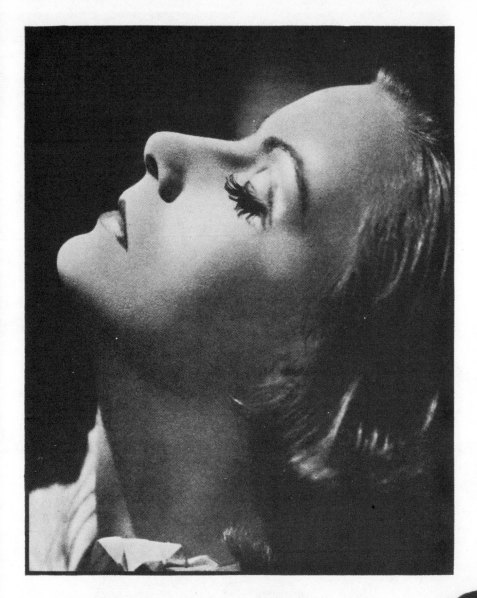

when he had the situation in hand and was permitted to be protective. Then she will know that his enchantment is in reality an indirect compliment to her.

This one happens to be a case-history with an obvious solution. There are many which offer more of a problem—in fact, there are several which seem beyond hope at the first diagnosis.

A perfectly charming merchant, who seems quite well-balanced in every other respect—has gone ga-ga, *non compos mentis*, in plain American—*nuts*—about Greta Garbo. He admits it without a blush, the rogue. He will drive to Pasadena in a pouring rain to see a Garbo picture for the third time.

To make the situation practically hopeless, his wife is a bouncing athletic girl with all the glamour of a bowl of wholesome baked beans.

She pretends to be amused about it, but it annoys her. If she had eyelashes as long as Garbo's, she would trip over them, and her eyes snap and sparkle in place of her rival's troubled languor. But all is not lost. She has two natural assets which would safely eliminate the accusation of imitating Garbo, and she could use them to advantage . . .

One is a long free stride and the other is a gorgeous [PLEASE TURN TO PAGE 347]

Maybe you are one of those wholesome-as-bread-and-butter women, and your husband does emotional cartwheels at the mention of the glamorous, languorous-eyed Garbo. However, don't be incensed by his raves over Greta. Be guided by them

know one just like him) who has a yen for Janet Gaynor, which leaves his wife fit to be tied.

It has not yet dawned on Mrs. S—— that five years ago, when she married Bill S—— she was a cuddly little thing who made him feel big and strong and wonderful. Bill had some kind of an idea that he was going to be head of his own house—but five years have changed all that. Mrs. S—— has developed a regrettable air of positiveness, and is about as helpless as an armored tank.

Some day she will get around to the realization that papa is crazy about Janet because Janet reminds him of the days

A surprising number of men suffer with Colbert trouble. If your husband has been smitten by Claudette, don't take it as a joke. The poor man may crave bangs

197

BIOGRAPH GIRL: Her adorers of 1909 didn't know her by the name of Florence Lawrence

THE VAMP: She gave the public a taste for leopard skins, couches and seductive wiles—the screen's first siren, the incomparable Theda Bara

AMERICA'S SWEET-HEART: Like her kitten, Mary Pickford held us all in the palm of her hand

ECSTASY GIRL: Outstanding example of modern glamour—the pulse-quickening Hedy Lamarr

THE ORCHID LADY: Patrician beauty of the early '20's; essence of refinement —lovely Corinne Griffith

from

PLATINUM BLONDE: The crowning glory of glorious Jean Harlow made history

IT GIRL: The rah-rah era personified by the wink of titian-headed Clara Bow

SARONG GIRL: A minimum of clothes gave Dorothy Lamour a maximum of fame and a title she wants changed

Since the screen's infant days,

the "It" girls have made names

for themselves—as Photoplay's

history of titled ladies reveals

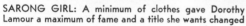

"VAMP" TO "Oomph"

OOMPH GIRL: Sultry sex returns in the shape of the shapely siren, Annie Sheridan

PRESENTING
Miss PHOTOPLAY

CREATED BY THE GREAT AMERICAN ARTIST

JOHN LA GATTA

HER CREDO:

She would appreciate a combination of Clark Gable, Gary Cooper and Bill Powell for romance's sake, and she would like a "Thin Man" marriage, and a Shirley Temple daughter

She would love to own Connie Bennett's custom Rolls Royce but would be satisfied with the fast little roadster Luise Rainer drives

She would like her nails to be as long and as perfectly kept as Marlene Dietrich's but if they break off in a badminton game, that's all right too

She's at home in a drawing room and happy in a penthouse and congenial in a shanty. Likes hamburgers and crêpes suzette

She would rather dance with Fred Astaire than have a new dress and he probably would tell her that she was very good which would be true

She wants Claudette Colbert's charm, Myrna Loy's poise, Alice Faye's voice and the indefinable something that Jean Arthur has

She enjoys Bing Crosby, is rapt over Benny Goodman and does a nose dive when Nelson Eddy sings. She laughs well

Above all, she is intelligently honest

The National Guide to Motion Pictures

PHOTOPLAY N.S.E.

JANUARY
25 CENTS

CLARA
BOW

Earl Christy

"QUIT PICKING
on me" says
CLARA BOW

Winners
of $5,000.
Puzzle Contest

FOUND AT LAST
The One Contented Man
IN HOLLYWOOD

3.   PHOTOPLAY cover, January 1931.   (Clara Bow)

4. PHOTOPLAY cover, December 1931. (Jean Harlow)

PICTURES AND TRENDS

The Talkies, the Depression and "Decency"

They couldn't believe it would happen because it had been tried so often before. Thomas A. Edison had seen the motion picture primarily as a visual complement to his earlier phonograph, and that was his chief interest in it. He and others had introduced talking pictures in 1895, 1900, 1905, 1907, 1912 and 1915, the last time on a very elaborate scale. The 1915 talkies were better synchronized than their primitive predecessors, but still very poorly amplified, and the public rejected them completely—probably because the silent movie had just reached its first peak of eloquence and passion in *The Birth of a Nation.* By comparison, these tinny talkies seemed meagre and thin, a side show to what was obviously the main event. In a year they were forgotten.

By the time the desperate Warner Brothers reintroduced sound in 1926, the movie people had acquired a vested interest in silence. They knew that the art world and much of the rest of the entertainment world laughed at the movies for their commercial flatulence. But they also knew that the silent art, such as it was, was entirely their own invention, and instinct told them that if silence was threatened, they were threatened. So they resisted the tide of sound with a Canute-like obstinacy—chiefly by delay, and a species of self-hypnosis. It was the public which made them know that the tide was irresistible. A vocal minority of the audience deplored sound—but the voice-less majority cast the deciding vote by making every sound picture, no matter how bad, a howling success, and every silent picture, no matter how excellent, a relative failure. That was clear by the end of 1928, and that was that.

James R. Quirk of PHOTOPLAY shared the Hollywood outlook and was one of the early intransigents. His review of *The Jazz Singer,* buried in the back pages of the magazine, noted the introduction of Al Jolson's songs into this otherwise silent film, but predicted failure because Jolson couldn't act! Inside knowledge of the events which followed helped Quirk see the light before his readers did, and he set to work with a will to ease the abrasions of the transition period. The magazine gave due coverage to the marvels of sound—but still greater space to its casualties. Quirk knew that the principal concern of the fans of 1928–30 was the fate of the great silent stars in the new medium. That it was his own concern as well is evidenced by his departure from standard editorial policy in the case of John Gilbert, a close personal friend. After the resounding failure of his first talkie, *His Glorious Night,* Gilbert's doom was obviously sealed, but PHOTOPLAY went on discussing his future in optimistic terms as long as possible —and a good deal beyond. In the six pictures Gilbert made for M-G-M after *His Glorious Night,* Quirk's reviewers found virtues invisible—and inaudible—to the rest of the world. When, through

---

The Shadow Stage

THE JAZZ SINGER—*Warners*

AL JOLSON with Vitaphone noises. Jolson is no movie actor. Without his Broadway reputation, he wouldn't rate as a minor player. The only interest in the picture is his six songs. The story is a fairly good tear-jerker about a Jewish boy who prefers jazz to the songs of his race. In the end, he returns to the fold and sings *Kol Nidre* on the Day of Atonement. It's the best scene in the film.

Greta Garbo's intervention, Gilbert seemed restored to studio favor, PHOTOPLAY trumpeted triumph. What happened then demonstrated conclusively that not even Miss Garbo, let alone a fan magazine, could save a career when the public had made up its mind. Gilbert's performance in Garbo's *Queen Christina* was excellent, and his subsequent work in that interesting film *The Captain Hates the Sea* was even better, but to no avail. The movie audience had silently consigned him to the silent past.

The novelty of the talkies—how great that novelty was, it is difficult to convey today—carried the movies to new levels of success, despite the crash of 1929; Wall Streeters began to speak of them as a depression-proof industry. Unemployment itself at first upheld the box office; the hopeless job-seeker sneaked into the movie houses in the daytime, for temporary refuge and solace, and to kill time. But by 1931, savings as well as hope were gone. People stayed home and listened to free entertainment on the radio. The theatres, like the streets, were empty.

The studios reacted to plunging grosses in the immemorial manner of show business, by ever-increasing resort to sex and violence. It seemed at the time to come about very naturally. When he became arbiter of film morals in 1924, Will Hays had made known that by and large he frowned on adaptation of current plays to the screen—and indeed the average Broadway play of the boom period was apt to be tin-pot pornography. But the technical requirements of early sound seemed to dictate the use of stage material. So *Strange Interlude* came to the screen. The success of two silent films, *Underworld* and *The Racket,* and the flood of gangster headlines in the Capone period, produced a comparable flood of racketeer movies. In the first two years of the Thirties, there were months when it was very difficult to find anything but a gangster picture to go to. In addition to these derivates, the screen invented a sort of genre of its own, centering around the whore as heroine. Except for *Anna Christie,* this was without precedent in American dramatic tradition, and justifying it taxed the ingenuity of the film-makers to the limit. A reviewer of one of these films was moved to say, "One can imagine the producers of *Faithless* asking themselves the question, 'Under what circumstances could a woman take to the streets and not only be forgiven by her husband but also win from him a compliment on her nobility of character?' The answer offered is, when the young wife hustles in order to buy food and medicine for her ailing spouse. What manner of hero are they offering us on the screen today?" The movie, this critic noted, exemplified "the current screen doctrine that it's not what you do that counts, but what you can get away with."

It certainly was. But there was danger in it for PHOTOPLAY. On the one hand, the box office said that these gamey films were enormously pleasing to what was left of the movie audience. On the other, PHOTOPLAY was still officially a family magazine, dedicated to the rule of right reason and with close links to the Puritan establishment. Quirk did his best to steer around the rocks, ignoring the spreading prurience as much as he could and playing it down all he could. It is noteworthy that Edward G. Robinson and James Cagney, top favorites of the period, received scant recognition in PHOTOPLAY of their vast popularity, and that Jean Harlow was both snubbed and scolded, apparently for the crime of being Jean Harlow. But letters from conservative readers warned the editor that this blindered caution was not enough. In the circumstances, about all he could do about it was print the letters and hope for better times.

Better times came for PHOTOPLAY, though in strange guise. Their harbinger, or *agent provocateur,* was, of all people, Mae West. Miss West was not one of the "new shady dames" of the screen, a heroine who lost her virtue in a fit of absentmindedness and atoned for her sins, and her penthouse and mink, by the shedding of copious tears which glittered as brightly in the camera's eye as the diamonds around her neck. Mae was Diamond Lil herself, and diamonds, she said, were her career. It was that openness, termed brazenness by the righteous, which made Mae her enormous hit and also brought about her downfall. Sin, the righteous agreed, was a fact of life, but it was no laughing matter, and the Mae West films rocked the whole nation with laughter. Between Miss West's first starring vehicle, *She Done Him Wrong,* and her second, *I'm No Angel,* the Legion of Decency had been formed, the Production Code Administration set up, and producers put on notice that sin was no longer "in." By the time her third picture, *It Ain't No Sin,* was ready for release, the title had to be hastily changed to *Belle of the Nineties,* though advertising under the original name had already been printed.

James Quirk died while this storm was still gathering. His successor, Kathryn Dougherty, faced it bravely and perhaps with secret relief. Will Hays—"drunk with power," as Miss West would put it—had added to his Production Code a Fan Magazine Code of similar provisions and purport. This was an advantage to Miss Dougherty. While PHOTOPLAY had trod the path of quasi-respectability during the period of Depression cynicism, other fan magazines had sought to recapture lost circulation through outright scandalmongering. Now all were brought into line by decree, and PHOTOPLAY, under feminine leadership, could enter a new era in which, at least officially, the gangster and the shady dame were banished—as was the pervasive implication, endemic in all films of the period, that American business and politics, like love itself, were little better than a racket. Who and what were to succeed them, none could say.

PHOTOPLAY Inaugurates Its New Special

HEART TO HEART—
First National

THE BATTLE OF THE SEXES—
United Artists

THIS is one of those rare comedies. It is the last co-starring picture of Mary Astor and Lloyd Hughes for First National. Louise Fazenda and Lucien Littlefield draw honors for the rib-ticklers. The scene is one of those little towns where an angular spinster matches her tongue against the weekly newspaper. A real princess comes to visit! But—more of the story would spoil the treat in store for you. Don't miss it.

A LIGHT-HEAVYWEIGHT drama, not as belligerent as the title implies, but human, sophisticated and worth while. Jean Hersholt as a business mogul greatly distresses a happy family by becoming entangled with a gold-digging blonde, Phyllis Haver. Don Alvarado is good as the power behind the blonde, and Belle Bennett adds suspense to suicide as the distraught wife. Worth your while.

THE MYS-TERIOUS LADY— M.-G.-M.

THE WHIP— First National

THE first reel lays on the Garbo slinking sinuousness with lavish hand. She will win no lady friends with that! And men don't want their "It" served so obviously, either. Otherwise the picture is okay. Fred Niblo gives us a gripping story of war intrigue. Garbo is a great spy as well as a great lover, and Conrad Nagel proves Madame Glyn was right when she said he had IT. So see it.

DOROTHY MACKAILL'S first independent starring vehicle is a beautiful production depicting the sportsman-life of the English gentleman. But, despite the beauty of fox hunts, the excitement of Ascot races and a thrilling battle between Ralph Forbes and Lowell Sherman, it misses being a big picture through slow movement and jerky interludes. However, it is worth seeing.

LADIES OF THE MOB— Paramount

JUST MARRIED— Paramount

THE IT girl turns dramatic. Clara Bow steps right into stark melodrama with a fistful of firearms and proves by her fine handling of this tense rôle that she has been "holding out" on us. The author of this story is a life termer in a California prison, and creates a vivid picture of gunmen and their "molls"—not cheerful but strangely sympathetic. You will scold yourself a long time if you fail to see Clara in this.

A CATCH-ME-IF-YOU-CAN stateroom farce, from Ann Nichols' play, beautifully acted, directed, and titled. It concerns the pre and post marital complications of six young things aboard a transatlantic liner, and they certainly do rock the boat. Ruth Taylor is pleasing enough as a synthetic heroine, but James Hall has turned out to be a super-comedian. Sophisticated comedy with the lid off.

Department Devoted to Sound Film Reviews

WHILE THE CITY SLEEPS— M.-G.-M.

LOVE OVER NIGHT— Pathe

NOW and then Lon Chaney tosses his make-up kit over the fence and acts like a human being. He appears "as is" in this picture, which shows crook stuff at its highest tempo, dwarfing "The Big City" to the size of a newsreel, and proving that an occasional straight rôle is fine balance for big character actors. He gives a remarkable characterization of a tough dick. A well-knit story, exceptionally cast and directed.

ANOTHER mystery-comedy, which Rod La Rocque plays with such seriousness that it is uproariously funny. Jeanette Loff is again his leading woman. The picture is filled with comedy business, much of which is provided by Tom Kennedy, who plays a dumb but persistent detective. Some of the situations are excruciatingly funny and the entire picture is splendid entertainment.

Sound Pictures

GEORGE BERNARD SHAW— Fox Movietone

THE LION AND THE MOUSE— Warner Vitaphone

THIS picture is the wow of the talkies and the most talked about release of the season. It is the first time that Bernard Shaw ever has talked directly and face to face with the American public. What a voice and what a face! Although over seventy years old, Shaw is built like an athlete. He moves as gracefully as Jack Dempsey. And he has so much sex appeal that he leaves the gals limp.

The all-too-short reel opens in Shaw's garden with birds singing—tweet, tweet—in the distance. Then Shaw appears and you hear his footsteps—scrunch, scrunch—on the path. He walks close to the camera and goes into his monologue. The high spot is his imitation of Mussolini. Be sure to see this reel, even if you have to travel to the next town to do it.

THE FAMILY PICNIC—Fox Movietone

THIS is the first picture done all in Movietone, with dialogue, squawking children and all the bedlam of modern life.

The story—if any—tells the adventure of a terrible family out for a horrible picnic. As a pleasure jaunt, it is just one long agony. And you laugh because you remember some such ghastly party. The reel proves that natural lines, without any attempt to be literary or dramatic, are effective just because they are natural. And ordinary noises—a stalled engine or the honking of horns—are funny because they are so completely true to life.

So see this picture, just as a novelty and just to find out what Movietone can do.

THIS old Charles Klein melodrama is spotted with dialogue. It is not an all-talkie, since it preceded "Lights of New York" from the Warner Vitaphonic plant.

The story is old-fashioned, reeking of another dramatic day. *Ready Money Rider*, the powerful plutocrat, wrecks an honest judge because of a judicial decision. The story deals with the romance between the son and daughter of these two enemies. The dialogue, since it was lifted from the creaky old play, reeks of mothballs. However, Alec Francis, as the judge, and Lionel Barrymore, as the millionaire, do excellently with their lines, particularly Mr. Francis. May McAvoy and Willie Collier, Jr., come out of the affair with far less honors. You will probably find it highly interesting.

LIGHTS OF NEW YORK—Warner Vitaphone

ANNOUNCED as the first all-talkie, this melodrama of Manhattan night life aroused a lot of attention from the New York critics. The Warners originally intended this to be a short talkie subject, then they got enthusiastic and enlarged it to seven feature reels. It's full of murder and attempted crime.

The cast, headed by Helene Costello, Wheeler Oakman, Cullen Landis and Gladys Brockwell, struggles hard with the pioneer problems of sound filming. None of the players emerge with particular glory. Sound films will have to work out a better technique to advance—and, of course, they will. This film, however, is a landmark of the sound movie.

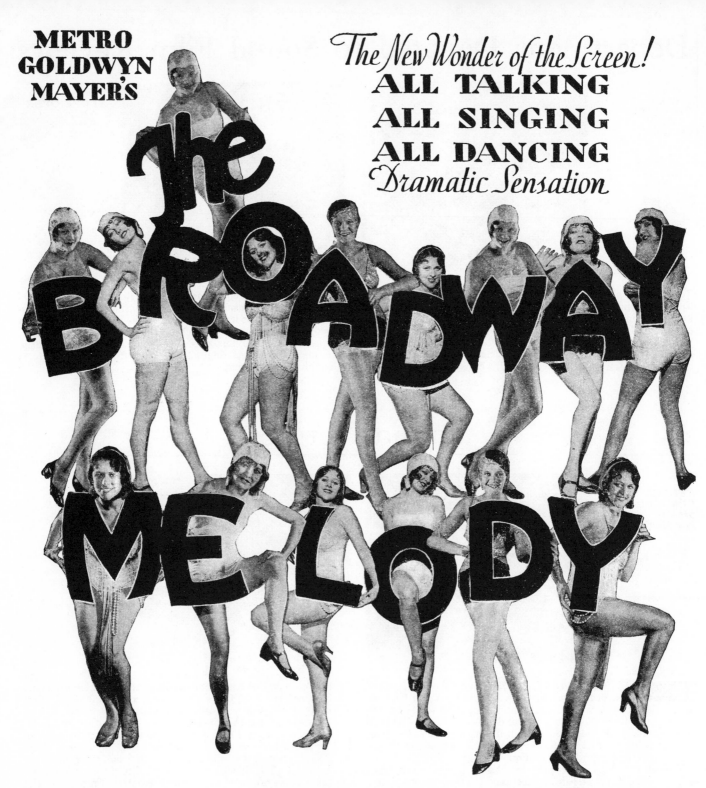

METRO GOLDWYN MAYER'S

The New Wonder of the Screen!
ALL TALKING
ALL SINGING
ALL DANCING
Dramatic Sensation

THE BROADWAY MELODY

with
CHARLES KING
ANITA PAGE
BESSIE LOVE
Directed by
HARRY BEAUMONT
Story by Edmund Goulding
Continuity by Sarah Y. Mason
Music by Nacio Herb Brown
Lyrics by Arthur Freed
Dialogue by Norman Houston
and James Gleason, author of "Is Zat So?"

FROM COAST TO COAST has swept the fame of the newest miracle of the films. All the magic of Broadway's stageland, stars, song hits, choruses of sensuous beauty, thrilling drama are woven into the Greatest Entertainment of our time. Metro-Goldwyn-Mayer, the leader in production of silent pictures, now achieves supremacy of the Talking Screen as well. See "The Broadway Melody" simultaneous with its sensational $2 showings in New York, Los Angeles and elsewhere.

METRO-GOLDWYN-MA

"More Stars than there are in Heaven"

THE METRO-GOLDWYN-MAYER LION GREATEST STAR ON THE SCREEN

New York *in* 1980!

BUILDINGS 250 stories high! . . . Traffic on nine levels . . . Rockets that shoot from star to star . . . Airplanes that land on the roofs of buildings . . . A whole meal in a capsule that can be swallowed at one gulp . . . No—this isn't a Jules Verne dream induced by a welsh rarebit . . . It's New York in 1980, as foretold in the new Fox picture, "Just Imagine!" . . . A picture of the great set showing the metropolis fifty years hence—the most intricate setting ever created for pictures . . . It took 205 engineers and craftsmen five months to build it, at a cost of $168,000 . . . It was designed after long conferences with noted artists and scientists who dare peer far into the future . . . The set stands in a balloon hangar at a former Army flying field twenty miles from Hollywood. . . .

Seventy-four 5,000,000 candle power sun arcs light the set from above . . . Fifteen thousand electric light bulbs illuminate its buildings and streets . . . DeSylva, Brown and Henderson, the trio responsible for "Sunny Side Up," conceived "Just Imagine!" . . . The leads are played by John Garrick, Maureen O'Sullivan, El Brendel and Kenneth Thomson . . . In 1980—people have serial numbers, not names . . . Marriages are all arranged by the courts . . . Prohibition is still an issue . . . Men's clothes have but one pocket. That's on the hip . . . But there's still love! . . . Don't laugh! Our granddaddies laughed at the thought that men might fly! Fantastic? Certainly—but stranger things have come to pass than those which have been portrayed in this dream New York of A. D. 1980!

The TRUTH About

Laura La Plante did not really sing or play the banjo in "Show Boat." Doubling in another voice was easy, but Miss La Plante had to study banjo strumming so that her work would look right

When you hear your favorite star sing in the talkies, don't be too sure about it. Here are all the facts about sound doubling, and how it is done

Laura La Plante did not sing and play the banjo in "Show Boat"—at least not for all of the songs. Two doubles helped her. One played the banjo, the other sang.

And so it goes, *ad infinitum*.

THERE are voice doubles in Hollywood today just as there are stunt doubles. One is not so romantic as the other, perhaps, but certainly just as necessary.

Those who create movies will probably not cheer as we make this announcement. In fact, they may resent our frankness. They may even have the Academy of Motion Picture Arts and Sciences write letters to PHOTOPLAY about it.

Richard Barthelmess received what he considered rather embarrassing publicity in connection with the song he did not sing in "Weary River." And, as a result of that, persons who undoubtedly know say that he is effecting a change of policy regarding future pictures. I was told on good authority that he informed Al Rockett, who heads First National's studios in Burbank, that he did not choose to

LIGHT travels 186,000 miles per second, but nobody cares. Sound pokes along at approximately a thousand feet per second, and still nobody cares.

But when Richard Barthelmess, who is famed as a film star and not as a singer, bursts into song in "Weary River," playing his own accompaniment, folks begin to prick up their ears.

And when Corinne Griffith plays a harp in "The Divine Lady" and acquits herself vocally, with the grace of an opera singer, people commence asking pointed questions.

And when Barry Norton does a popular number to his own accompaniment in "Mother Knows Best," a quizzical light appears in the public's eye.

Then, too, when Laura La Plante strums the banjo in "Show Boat" and renders negro spirituals in below the Mason and Dixon line style, the public breaks out in an acute rash of curiosity which can be cured only by disclosing state secrets of the cinema.

Richard Barthelmess did not sing and play the piano in "Weary River." A double did it.

Corinne Griffith did not sing or play the harp in "The Divine Lady." A double did it.

Barry Norton did not sing in "Mother Knows Best." A double did it. He did, however, play the piano.

Everybody knows now that Richard Barthelmess did not sing in "Weary River." And, of course, he didn't play the piano. Johnny Murray sang "Weary River" into a "mike" out of range of the camera while Frank Churchill played the accompaniment. It was done very neatly

Voice Doubling

By Mark Larkin

Lawford Davidson, who gets $500 a week as Paul Lukas' voice double. Lukas has a heavy accent

Eva Olivotti, who did Laura La Plante's singing in "Show Boat" and did it very well, indeed

Johnny Murray, Dick Barthelmess' voice double. He's under contract to be Dick's voice for all 1929

sing in forthcoming photoplays. "I am not a song and dance man," he explained, "and I don't want any pictures that feature me as such."

Nevertheless, Richard will sing — or rather someone will sing for him—in his forthcoming feature, titled at present, "Drag." That is, he will have a voice double unless they change the story. One never knows, you know, until the picture is released. There's many a slip between the screen and the cutting-room floor!

But Dick will not be seen actually in the act of singing as was the case in "Weary River." Probably there will be only his shadow, and the expression of the man for whom he is singing, this man—in the rôle of a song producer—registering reactions to the song.

If you saw "Weary River," you will remember that Dick sat at a piano and played and also sang. The means by which this was accomplished was ingenious, to say the least.

YOU will remember that it was a grand piano. Mr. Barthelmess faced the audience. You did not see his hands upon the keys, yet you saw him go through the motions of playing and singing. And you heard what you thought was his voice. But it was not his voice.

Many persons have said that it was the voice of Frank Withers. But it was not. It was the voice of Johnny Murray, former cornetist at the Cocoanut Grove, and now under contract to First National to sing for Richard Barthelmess. He is a real, dyed-in-the-wool voice double, Johnny is.

There was much enthusiasm on the set the day Johnny Murray put over the song, "Weary River." Dick threw his arm around Johnny's shoulder and said something like this: "Don't you ever die, young fella, or go East, or get run over, or anything!" And they both laughed.

Dick faced the audience during the filming of the scenes at the piano so as to conceal his hands. It has been said that a dummy keyboard was built on the side of the piano at which Dick sat, but that is not so. But the strings of the instrument were deadened with felt so that when Dick struck the keys the strings would give forth no sound. And Frank Churchill, pianist in a Hollywood theater orchestra, sat at a real piano off stage and played the accompaniment while Johnny

Murray sang. The recording microphone was close to them and nowhere near Barthelmess. Dick merely faked the singing and playing, but he did it so beautifully that the results were convincing beyond doubt.

Probably the highest paid voice double in pictures is Lawford Davidson, who doubles [PLEASE TURN TO PAGE 348]

It may surprise film fans who saw "The Divine Lady" to realize that Corinne Griffith neither sang nor played the harp. Miss Griffith did study the fingering of harp strings to get the correct illusion

★ *THE LOVE PARADE—Paramount*

SPARKLING as Burgundy, and almost as intoxicating, "The Love Parade" is one of the outstanding pictures of the year. It is Lubitsch's most brilliant effort since "The Marriage Circle." The little director here conquers light opera!

After the dashing nobleman marries the *Queen of Sylvania*, he gets durned tired of constantly obeying. So he bludgeons the queen into letting him be head man.

Maurice Chevalier, a great favorite after his first American picture, despite a weak story, is grand as the prince. His songs are triumphs. Jeanette MacDonald is an eye-feast as the queen, and sings well. Lupino Lane amuses.

The music is relatively unimportant, although "Dream Lover" and "Nobody's Using It Now" may be popular. Don't miss "The Love Parade." *All Talkie.*

The Shadow Stage

A Review of the New Pictures

★ *THE TRESPASSER—United Artists*

YOU'LL paste this baby in your memory book. Gloria Swanson, in her first all-talkie, is a sensation.

After the "Queen Kelly" disaster, it became imperative for Gloria to rush a phonoplay into the market. Edmund Goulding and the star hurled this picture into production. The breakneck speed with which it was made might have ruined it. Instead, it gave "The Trespasser" superb pace.

But the star! The glorious one never looked more beautiful. Her voice does every trick demanded of it, and she sings two songs like a meadow lark. And what clothes!

Swanson plays *Marion Donnell*, a business girl who is snatched from the side of her husband, a wealthy youngster, by his father, soon after the wedding. She and the resulting infant have lean days until her millionaire employer takes her under his protection. Crisis follows crisis, until she finds happiness in the arms of the estranged husband. The story reeks with hokum, but nobody minds.

Gloria gives the greatest performance in her career. The whole cast is keyed high, too. Kay Hammond is stunning as a crippled wife. William Holden is the best heavy father in history. Robert Ames, Henry Walthall, Purnell Pratt—all good. And Wally Albright, last in "Wonder of Women," is a stage kid you don't want to strangle.

"The Trespasser" is an achievement. *All Talkie.*

★ *THEY HAD TO SEE PARIS—Fox*

"A HORSE doctor's gotta be smarter than any other kind of doctor because a horse can't tell you where it hurts" —that's one of Will Rogers' punch lines. The real Will Rogers steps before the microphone and you'll have to forgive him for all those silent efforts. He's great!

The story concerns a suddenly rich Oklahoma family who bear down on Paris for culture and background.

In this Rogers is reunited to Irene Rich, his first leading lady, who gives an elegant performance. Marguerite Churchill, as the daughter, is a gal who bears watching, but the feminine hit is a real French "mamselle," one Fifi Dorsay.

This is big entertainment, with Will Rogers giving some of our first rate emotional actors a run for their Saturday night remittance. *All Talkie.*

SAVES YOUR PICTURE TIME AND MONEY

The Best Pictures of the Month

THE TRESPASSER   SUNNY SIDE UP
THE LOVE PARADE
THEY HAD TO SEE PARIS   THE LADY LIES
FOOTLIGHTS AND FOOLS   FARO NELL
BLACKMAIL   YOUNG NOWHERES
DISRAELI

The Best Performances of the Month

Gloria Swanson in "The Trespasser"
Janet Gaynor in "Sunny Side Up"
Marjorie White in "Sunny Side Up"
Maurice Chevalier in "The Love Parade"
Jeanette MacDonald in "The Love Parade"
Will Rogers in "They Had to See Paris"
Irene Rich in "They Had to See Paris"
Walter Huston in "The Lady Lies"
Claudette Colbert in "The Lady Lies"
Colleen Moore in "Footlights and Fools"
Louise Fazenda in "Faro Nell"
Donald Calthrop in "Blackmail"
Richard Barthelmess in "Young Nowheres"
Marian Nixon in "Young Nowheres"
George Arliss in "Disraeli"

★ *THE LADY LIES—Paramount*

THIS magnificently staged and acted drawing room comedy is another milestone in the talkie's progress. Critics of the baby talking picture said the phonoplay would be good only for action melodramas and the more obvious sort of story. This picture makes them look silly.

Here is a smart, sophisticated little comedy of New York life that tingles with punch, done with much imagination by Director Hobart Henley. It is the story of how two growing children hurled themselves into the lives of their father and his pretty shopgirl sweetheart. It has stinging drama and it has a storm of laughs—many furnished by Charles Ruggles as a gently stewed friend of the family. Walter Huston and the beautiful Claudette Colbert are stunning as the lovers. Claudette wears gorgeous duds. *All Talkie.*

★ *SUNNY SIDE UP—Fox*

YOU'LL eat this one up, and it furnishes its own cream and sugar. Janet Gaynor turns loose her cute little singing and speaking voices in a story of high life and low in New York, and Charles Farrell is on hand to woo her with more than gestures.

"Sunny Side Up" is another Cinderella yarn, with the rich young Farrell finding the poor young Gaynor at a block party on the New York East Side. This will never do, thinks Charlie. Before you know it, Janet has cut out the rich girl friend, played by Sharon Lynn, and the Gaynor-Farrell love team scores a thumping old touchdown in the last minute of play.

El Brendel, Fox favorite, furnishes a lot of laughs, as does Marjorie White, a pert little piece from the musical comedy stage. The De Sylva, Brown and Henderson music is particularly gay. Janet pipes the theme song, and nearly everybody has a tune or two in his system.

Something new for Janet and Charlie, after their royal line of sobby little love stories. But they came through like good troupers, and you'll care for the result.

The bright little picture shows that we can have our songs, dances and loves without going backstage for them. And don't forget to keep your eye on the White girl. She should go far. *All Talkie.*

★ *FOOTLIGHTS AND FOOLS—First National*

UNQUESTIONABLY this is Colleen Moore's best picture since "We Moderns." Talkies have given her a curious break which she's taken big.

Her voice is pleasant and versatile, and the story standards raised by talking films permit her to chuck the synthetic program stuff and turn to something bigger. This is it. The story, by Katherine Brush, is a skilful combination of sophisticated humor and poignant emotional drama.

New York's musical comedy sensation, *Mlle. Fifi d'Auray,* is a temperamental French whirlwind before the footlights. Offstage, she's little *Betty Murphy,* who loves a boy who's a rotter. As *Fifi,* Colleen wears a hundred mad gowns and wigs, and sings French songs with a naughty lilt. As *Betty,* her piquant self. Both ways, gorgeous! *All Talkie.*

Is JACK GILBERT *Through?*

Read to the end of this great story of a great star menaced by the talkies—and you'll find out!

By Katherine Albert

WHEN beautiful Ida Adair, second-rate actress in a traveling theatrical troupe, bore an unwanted, unloved man child in Logan, Utah, she didn't know that some day he would hold the fate of two enormous studios in the hollow of his hand.

She didn't know that the little boy, cradled in the top of a trunk, lulled to sleep by the clicking of wheels over rails, would grow up to be one of the most glamorous contemporary figures.

Lovely Ida, as profligate as a Winter wind, as vivid as a sunset, called her son John. It was a plain name for a plain little boy—a sullen child who resented life before he could talk and who looked upon the world into which he had been unfortunate enough to be born with a growing distaste.

Jack Gilbert, erstwhile soldier of fortune, erstwhile rubber salesman, extra boy, director, writer, itinerant actor, has become one of the most exciting personalities that ever flashed across a screen.

He holds one of the most unusual contracts ever given a star. And it's an iron-bound contract, without options!

In two years he will be paid, as salary, one million dollars! His studio bungalow is more elaborate than most of the homes in Hollywood. His fame has spread around the world. Thousands of women who have never seen him are in love with him.

AND now Hollywood says that the great Gilbert, the amazing lover of the screen, is through—has failed at the very height of his career.

It says that his enemies (and he has plenty) are glad. But that the studio officials who must pay him a million dollars in two years, whether his pictures play to vacant seats or not, are turning white-haired over night.

Is Jack Gilbert finished? Is his art but dust and ashes? Let us consider the facts in this amazing case.

The signing of the name John Gilbert to a little piece of paper was of utmost importance to a fifty million dollar deal. Jack was more or less of a pawn. He didn't realize how vital he was to the financial gods.

He had been discontented, miserable—as he usually is, except when he is radiant, enthusiastic—with his lot at the Metro-Goldwyn-Mayer studios. He had argued with the producers about stories and characterizations. United Artists had made him an offer. He decided to accept.

But forces of which he knew nothing were working around him. The West Coast officials had heard only rumors of the Fox-M-G-M merger, or rather, the sale of the controlling interest of Loew's Inc. to the Fox organization.

But the New York powers knew of the deal and they also knew that if Gilbert, one of the most important stars, slipped through their fingers, the deal might not go through. Fox wanted M-G-M, but it needed all their stars.

GRETA GARBO was safely bound under a long-term contract. Lon Chaney, Marion Davies, Billy Haines, Ramon Novarro, Joan Crawford were all secure. Only Gilbert showed signs of leaving.

Gilbert and his manager went to New York and the executives there told him that he must remain with M-G-M. Gilbert refused. At last he was asked, "But what will make you stay?"

His manager answered. He outlined a contract so absurd, so preposterous that he expected only loud guffaws. But the executive didn't laugh. He knew that if Gilbert didn't sign, the tremendous deal might fall through.

"You will stay on those terms?" asked the executive. "Very well, I will draw up such a contract."

And such a contract! It is for two years, two pictures a year at $250,000 a picture or about $10,000 a week. Gilbert has the right to O.K. or N.G. all stories. He was given an enormous dressing room bungalow, second to

[PLEASE TURN TO PAGE 351]

Jack Gilbert in his first talking picture, "Redemption." He was nervous, too highly keyed, self-conscious. The studio says it is "temporarily shelved." Will it ever be shown?

"Now I Help You,"
says GARBO *to* Gilbert

in one of the most amazing "turnabouts" of picture history

Here she is—Queen Garbo shaking hands with the first American actor who helped her. Now she's returning the favor, with ample interest

The Swedish girl had done well in "The Torrent" and in her next, "The Temptress." Gilbert was popular enough to "carry" anyone, however little her name might mean. Why not use her in his new "Flesh and the Devil"?

Not an unusual decision in movie casting—but what Gilbert did *was* unusual.

Most "kings" would have pouted—if indeed they didn't roar to high heaven—over being given "untried" support.

Gilbert made his supporting lady feel welcome and appreciated as a fellow artist. Garbo speaks of it yet.

More than that: Garbo could have as much publicity as her work might command. No trying to grab it all for himself.

No need to tell you the result—how everyone woke almost overnight to hail a new queen of the cinema. Garbo's star shot up to the heights. The acid test of the talkies only made it twinkle the brighter.

Meanwhile, poor Jack! Faced with talkies, he incautiously thought all he needed to do was talk. The result, with a voice that sounded a bit creaky, practically laughed him off the screen.

WHO says that royalty knows no gratitude—or that Garbo is an aloof, mysterious embodiment of perfect screen art, without inner warmth of human feeling? Listen.

Eight years ago last July, a scared, none-too-well-dressed Swedish girl landed in New York, in tow of the great Swedish director, Mauritz Stiller. Brought because Stiller insisted she must come if he did—and ignored as merely part of the price for getting him.

The studio, not much interested, used her in "The Torrent." But no prairies were set afire; the lonely visitor, at whose English people smiled, knew discouragement to its bitter full.

Meanwhile a comparatively new star—an amazingly bright one—was blazing in the movieland firmament. Jack Gilbert, no less, movie idol of nearly every woman throughout our fair land.

Now the studio got a bright idea.

FIVE years pass—years that Gilbert played in rôles which meant less and less—unable to live down that unfortunate talkie début.

Then Garbo's trip to Sweden—her return to play *Queen Christina*. The world rejoiced—and nobody thought of Jack. Nobody, that is, except Garbo.

Arrived in Hollywood, she went over the studio's plans for her film, pronounced everything satisfactory. But—

She'd prefer Jack Gilbert in the romantic male lead.

And Jack will do the lead, in place of the man previously selected. So now who will say that royalty knows no gratitude—or that Garbo lacks warm human feeling?

By Martin Stevers

Would You Quit

So she took the $250,000! When the microphone was not kind to Corinne Griffith, she wisely accepted First National's offer for the remainder of her term. Now the Orchid Lady rests

For years Monte Blue had labored as a Warner Brothers contract star —hard-working and careful with his wages. Not so long ago the company bought the unexpired portion of his contract for $50,000

Billie Dove's producers bought off her contract, but it isn't likely that the beauteous one is much perturbed. Now she's going to marry a multi-multi-millionaire. And, so why not say, "Attagirl, Billie"?

SUPPOSE your boss should walk up to you some morning and say:

"Lookahere, I'll give you a couple o' hundred thousand dollars in cold cash if you'll quit working for me right now!"

You know darned well that the first thing you'd do, after coming to, would be to phone the funny house and tell them to come with straight-jackets and things.

But, such things *do* happen!

Well, say you, it must be a crazy business where the boss pays somebody a houseful of money *not* to work. You're right. It's the movie business!

And just to show you how nutty it really is, nine times out of ten the person who's being paid *not* to work considers it an insult. Imagine getting mad because somebody wants to give you a quarter of a million to do nothing!

You think I'm lying? Look at Corinne Griffith. She got $250,000 not to make any more moving pictures for First National. First National paid it to her. Warner Brothers gave Monte Blue about $50,000 not to work for them any more. Jack Gilbert got mad when Metro-Goldwyn-Mayer offered him about a half million dollars to go away some place after "His Glorious Night" was finished. The picture, that is. Jack told M-G-M to take their half million and soak it in vinegar. More about that, later.

But all that's getting ahead of the yarn by a couple of jumps. You see, this is all about the jolly Hollywood pastime of contract-buying. You've probably read about producers buying up So-and-So's contract.

By Harry Lang

Maybe you wonder what it means. Well, briefly, it's like this: Some producer or executive sees a great future for some actor or actress on stage or screen. "That's a big bet for us," he tells himself, "so let's sign him up."

Bingo, a contract is drawn up and slapped down before the supposed-to-be-star. When the latter sees figures like $5,000 a week, he signs his name so quick that it looks like a fast-motion film. Then he goes to Hollywood.

There he gets a test. Not infrequently, the putative star flops like a wet towel. Sometimes they let him make a picture. This is worse than flopping on the test, because when he flops in a picture, strangers see it, and when he flops in a test, only a few studio executives see it. Anyway, when and if he flops, there is weeping and wailing in the *sancta sanctora* of the Big Bosses. "Who signed this lemon?" everybody asks. The outcome usually is: "Well, let's buy up his contract."

SO the star-that-wasn't is sitting pretty. He's got a contract which calls on the producer to pay him so much a week for so long. It's up to the producer to make it worth while for the fellow to break the contract. Usually, after parleying back and forth, some sort of settlement is effected—on anywhere from a twenty-five per cent basis up.

In other words, if the he-who-flopped holds a contract for twenty-six weeks at $5,000 a week, and accepts a fifty per cent settlement to call the contract off, he gets $65,000 cash.

The producer saves the other $65,000, plus the cost of producing pictures that wouldn't have made money.

And that's what they call buying up

Work *for* $250,000?

Corinne Griffith did! It's all part of the great game of contract-buying in filmland

somebody's contract.   Here are some examples—and some sidelights to show that you never can tell what it's all about.

Take the strange case of Ina Claire, for instance.

The gorgeous blonde had long been one of the bright spots of the speaking stage when the talkies began to churn Hollywood.   The producers hustled to sign up the legitimate stars. Pathe got Ina's name on the dotted line, and sat back feeling happy about it.   The contract said Ina was to do two pictures in nine months, and if Pathe liked her, a third picture after that.   For the first, she was to get $75,000; for the second, $100,000.   If a third, for that, then, $125,000.

INA made "The Awful Truth," as Picture No. 1, and drew her $75,000.   Then began the business of looking for the second story.   Things didn't go right—all sorts of things.   When at last Pathe bought "Holiday" for her, there wasn't really enough left of the nine-months' contract period to make "Holiday."   One thing after another went wrong, and finally they went into a huddle.   When it was over, Ann Harding was cast for the lead in "Holiday" and Ina Claire walked free with $55,000 as her bit for settling the contract in cash.

Now, here's the funny aftermath.   Pathe paid her $55,000 not to work—and at once, Paramount began negotiations with Ina.   The negotiations dragged and dragged, Paramount unwilling to pay what Ina asked.   So Ina called the turn.   She went on the stage in Los Angeles in Donald Ogden Stewart's play, "Rebound," which he had been trying for months to sell to the movies.   The opening night was one of those things —high-priced seats, all sorts of colored lights and arc lamps, the big shots of movieland all there in their swell clothes. The big shots, the critics, the public, all raved about "Rebound" and Ina Claire.

On the second day of the engagement, Paramount okayed Ina's figures and signed her to a contract.   She stars in "The Royal Family."   And the last laugh is Donald Ogden Stewart's. "Rebound," which one producer after another had turned down as no good for talkies, was bought—by Pathe!—for something in five figures, guesses running from $20,000 to $50,000.

THEN there's Corinne Griffith, who is as sagacious as she is beautiful—and that makes her a very, very wise girl.   Corinne was First National's big bet in silents and was drawing down about $7,500 a week, plus a percentage of the profits.   When the microphone broke into the studios, Corinne, like most other stars, had quite a hard time adapting herself to it. "Lilies of the Field" and "Back Pay" were not so hot.   Her voice did not register one hundred per cent.

Corinne had a clause in her contract which provided that she and her equally sagacious husband, Walter Morosco, approve stories, directors and everything in connection with her pictures.   She held out for stories of her own choice and directors who she thought could help her with her voice. Of course it was a futile battle.

Finally the First National executives said, "We've got to do something.   Let's offer Corinne a quarter of a million to settle her contract, and that may bring her to terms."

Corinne snapped up that quarter of a million so fast it made her head swim.   After ten years of hard work she was tired, anyway, and she and Walter thought a quarter of a million dollars was good pay for a vacation.

Corinne isn't one of those stars who are screen crazy, and she may or may not come back.

In the meantime she is studying voice, in case she does get something that suits her.   [PLEASE TURN TO PAGE 346]

A famous married pair which underwent some odd contract-juggling.   Jack Gilbert indignantly refused to sell his million-dollar contract when "His Glorious Night" failed, determined to make good in talkies.   Pathe bought up Ina Claire's contract for $55,000—then she signed with Paramount to make a very big picture

The Shadow Stage

A Review of the New Pictures

☆ *THE SECRET SIX—M-G-M*

NO, gangster pictures are not dead—not as long as they produce thrillers like this! A sequel to "The Big House," it is not as gruesome and has more humor. And, of course, not as new and unusual.

If good citizens combine secretly and work as energetically to destroy gangsters and crime as gangsters work to promote themselves and their work, law and order will win—that's the theme. Bootlegging, subsidizing of public officials and gun play are the crimes. You will see exactly how liquor is made; you will witness the most thrilling gangster chase ever pictured. Beautifully produced and directed by George Hill (assisted by Writer Frances Marion), the cast is splendid, including Wallace Beery, Lewis Stone, Clark Gable (watch this newcomer), Johnny Mack Brown and Jean Harlow.

☆ *QUICK MILLIONS—Fox*

IF you like gangster pictures, you'll like this one for its completely novel treatment. The film is as cold-blooded as the gangsters who are characterized, and this effect is gained by the remarkable use of apparently disjointed scenes that contrive to keep the thread of the story and your interest at the same time. It's a man's picture and is utterly lacking in wild histrionics.

Spencer Tracy is head-man, playing an erstwhile truck driver who becomes—sure, they always do!—leader of the racketeers. Although he tries to crash society, he remains a hoodlum and pays the penalty. He does his job perfectly. Sally Eilers gets first-lady honors, for Marguerite Churchill hasn't much to do. Recommended because it is the highest type, directorially and technically, of this breed of film.

☆ *SEED—Universal*

THIS picture should delight everyone—fans and producers alike.

It follows none of the formulas of present-day pictures; it has nothing sensational to recommend it; it is wholly without obvious sex appeal; it offers no preachment, yet it is one of the finest pictures turned out this year. Charles Norris will certainly rejoice that the lesson in his book is presented so forcefully and yet with such delicacy.

A writer of great promise marries early, quickly has five children, finds himself weighted down with family responsibility, and is forced to abandon his writing.

A former sweetheart returns, as a member of his firm, and she immediately sets about to restore his aspirations to write. His wife has only time for the children and her household duties. You foresee the inevitable triangle.

Lois Wilson, as the wife, has her first good opportunity in months. She gives a beautiful, sympathetic performance. Genevieve Tobin, as the former sweetheart, is lovely and justifies all predictions made for her, but the big surprise is John Boles, who doesn't sing but who walks away with a most difficult rôle. The children are all natural and lovable.

Director John Stahl deserves much credit for this excellent picture. If you miss it, you won't forgive yourself.

SAVES YOUR PICTURE TIME AND MONEY

The Best Pictures of the Month

SEED	THE MALTESE FALCON
THE SECRET SIX	QUICK MILLIONS
FAME	CITY STREETS

The Best Performances of the Month

John Boles in "Seed"
Lois Wilson in "Seed"
Ricardo Cortez in "The Maltese Falcon"
Wallace Beery in "The Secret Six"
Spencer Tracy in "Quick Millions"
Doris Kenyon in "Fame"
Sylvia Sidney in "City Streets"
Gary Cooper in "City Streets"
John Barrymore in "Svengali"
Ramon Novarro in "Daybreak"
John Gilbert in "Cheri Bibi"
Joan Crawford in "Complete Surrender"

☆ *FAME—First National*

EVERY once in a while there happens along a picture so splendidly played and directed that it stands out distinctively from the ruck. Such a one is "Fame."

It's an unspectacular story of what happens to the hopes and dreams of people—people like "you and me"—when those hopes and dreams collide with worldly needs. There are no sensational climaxes, no "big" scenes. Instead, there is a story so beautifully and humanly told that it will hold your rapt attention throughout. Director Robert Milton has instilled into this picture that same quality that made "Holiday" a grand job. And Doris Kenyon, in the leading rôle, proves a right to top ranking among today's screen players. A less capable one might easily have overacted the rôle to death. The rest of the cast is nearly perfect.

☆ *THE MALTESE FALCON—Warners*

ARE you one of those who delight in a fast-moving gripping mystery yarn? Does your spine tingle in response to the clever machinations of the screen detective?

Then this picture is your dish, and you'll love it. See if you can untangle the mystery before the last reel. It's a great game.

Ostensibly, this is a starring picture for Bebe Daniels, but her part isn't one, two, four, compared to that handed Mr. Ricardo Cortez, the sleek young gentleman who is now doing the best screen work of his career. What a performance Cortez gives in this picture, playing the demon detective who is also a first-rate Don Juan.

The story, made from the well-known novel of the same name, concerns the desire of several people to possess a jewel-encrusted statuette of an enameled falcon, worth fabulous sums. Cortez is the lad who turns the trick.

Bebe does excellent work in a part that doesn't give her nearly enough elbow-room. Cortez, as we've said, is thoroughly fine, and good helping performances are given by Una Merkel, Dudley Digges and Otto Matiesen.

This is as fine a piece of film mystery—with chills and thrills—as the screens have held in some months. You'll like it, you mystery fans!

☆ *CITY STREETS—Paramount*

SEVERAL things set this timely, fast-moving gang melodrama apart from the general run of such pictures.

First, it introduces to Paramount audiences a grand little actress named Sylvia Sidney, a product of the Broadway stage. She was rushed into the feminine lead of this picture when Clara Bow was taken out to rest after the De Voe trial, and Sylvia justifies the company's faith in her. Gary Cooper, too, does a first-rate job as an unsuspecting youth caught in the activities of a gang of beer-runners. It's a thriller that rings true.

The supporting cast—including Paul Lukas, Wynne Gibson and William Boyd—is great, and there isn't a dull minute in the picture. Chalk up a hit for Director Rouben Mamoulian.

By *Ruth Biery*

Joan Crawford as *Sadie Thompson* in "Rain" is at the height of her shady dame period in that film, "Letty Lynton" and "Grand Hotel." An actress of great dramatic power, but will she return to peppy, lovable rôles again?

HOLLYWOOD has created a new woman, a different type of heroine, a unique feminine personality. The leaders of the new school are Garbo, Marlene Dietrich, Tallulah Bankhead—and if you've seen "Letty Lynton"—Joan Crawford.

Girls younger at the picture game than these are following suit—Ann Dvorak, Karen Morley, little Frances Dean, whose first publicity picture you will find on these pages, and many, many others.

"Glamorous" and "mysterious" have been the adjectives that best described these women but it is something more than that, and just how deep-rooted it is, just how many girls

and women throughout the country are taking these screen stars as models, remains to be seen. I wonder if it is a good or bad influence.

You will realize that this new type is an outgrowth of modernity when you stop to consider the cinema head-liners of yesterday—Mary Pickford, Marguerite Clark, Mary Miles Minter, Lillian Gish, May Allison, Corinne Griffith, May McAvoy and dozens of others. These girls represent the sort of woman that men want to protect.

The new cinema heroine can take care of herself, thank you, since she combines, with her mysterious allure, many of the hard-headed attributes **and** even some of the physical characteristics — the tall, narrow-hipped, broad shouldered figure—of men.

You may tell me that yesterday's screen had its sirens. Surely it did —women like Theda Bara, Nita Naldi, Gladys Brockwell, Betty Blythe, who led a man to destruction and laughed—heh! heh!—at the plight of the poor, bewildered thing. But these women were vampires, heartless creatures, villainesses, and in the final reel the fallen hero always returned to the protecting arms of that sweet, golden-haired girl waiting for him in a halo of sunlight.

NOWADAYS it's the heroine who falls. These new vamps are not vamps in the strictest sense of the word, since they are the heroines of the picture.

The bad woman—the shady dame is today's heroine.

There is no point of contact between these glamour girls and their vampish predecessors. The vamp was all feminine allure. Whereas the children of mystery have, as I pointed out a paragraph or so ago, a man's viewpoint, and a man's ability to deal with brutal situations. Hence—the new sex. And because she is new, she is mysterious—this shady dame.

Look over the standardized cinema star—those thick, heavily made-up lips, sloe eyes, lashes heavy with mascara, hair sweeping in a hard wave from high forehead. That's the face. The body? Slender hips, broad shoulders, lithe slim lines. And now for the voice—deep, throaty, guttural. You know that voice.

In the days of Marguerite Clark a large mouth on a woman was considered ugly, so actresses who had large mouths rouged their lips in such a way that the line stopped before it reached the corner of the mouth.

But did you notice Joan Crawford's mouth in "Letty Lynton"? The lipstick extended beyond the corner and the mouth was greatly exaggerated in both thickness and length.

And her eyes—Joan's lovely, large, frank eyes, hidden by

DAMES" *of the Screen*

Will the vogue for these so-called glamorous heroines of Hollywood last?

live up to expectations? This same studio has high hopes for Jill Esmond, whom you saw in "State's Attorney."

Universal presents Tala Birell. She didn't have much of a chance in "The Doomed Battalion" but she has been promised an opportunity to be a shady dame in her next picture.

Fox thought Elissa Landi would measure up to specifications, but although Elissa has a strange background she has the characteristics of a straight-forward, intelligent Englishwoman, with a peach [PLEASE TURN TO PAGE 328]

Frances Dean, a lovely newcomer, already has felt the Garbo influence in make-up and mannerisms. Note how her young mouth has been thickened and lengthened with lip rouge to meet the new demand

weighted lashes. The eyes looked black, yet Joan's eyes are blue. The effect, so somebody told me, was attained by using a red filament over the camera lens in the close-ups.

The strange thing is that Garbo started the fad quite unintentionally. Garbo is naturally the type which all the others are trying to be. Her eyelashes are without benefit of false ones, more than an inch long. They curl naturally. Her eyelids droop of their own accord and her hair sweeps back from that high forehead with no *coiffeur* to guide it. Her shoulders are naturally broad, her hips slender and her voice low-pitched. That long, efficient, almost masculine stride, is her own. And because she seemed to combine subtly both feminine and masculine characteristics she was mysterious, alluring and glamorous.

PRODUCERS are not to be blamed for their sheeplike ways. Garbo brought money into their coffers. *Sic*—why wouldn't girls who copied Garbo's looks, her mannerisms and her clothes do likewise? The hunt for Garbo types has continued since box-office receipts from her first picture told the executives that the girl was a sensation.

Paramount discovered Marlene Dietrich, who brought her own brand of glamour to the screen. More lately, Tallulah Bankhead arrived. Now the studio is experimenting with Sari Maritza.

Radio Pictures sought for a long time. Gwili Andre, a Danish girl and at one time New York's highest paid artist's model, was the end of their hunting expedition. The powers of Radio **are** breathlessly awaiting the public's acceptance or rejection of Gwili. She looks the part. Will she

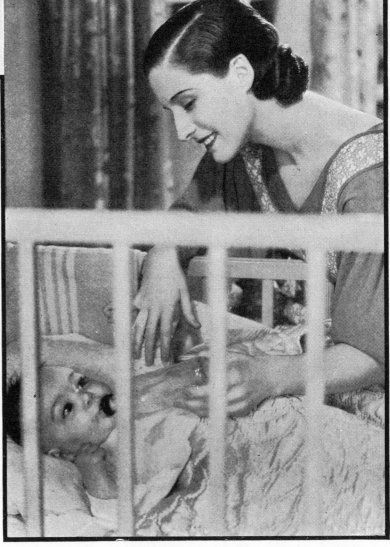

Norma Shearer has passed through her shady dame period and gone straight. Although she runs the gamut of emotions in "Strange Interlude," a scene from which you see above, "Smilin' Through"—her next—marks her return to the ultra sweet and charming

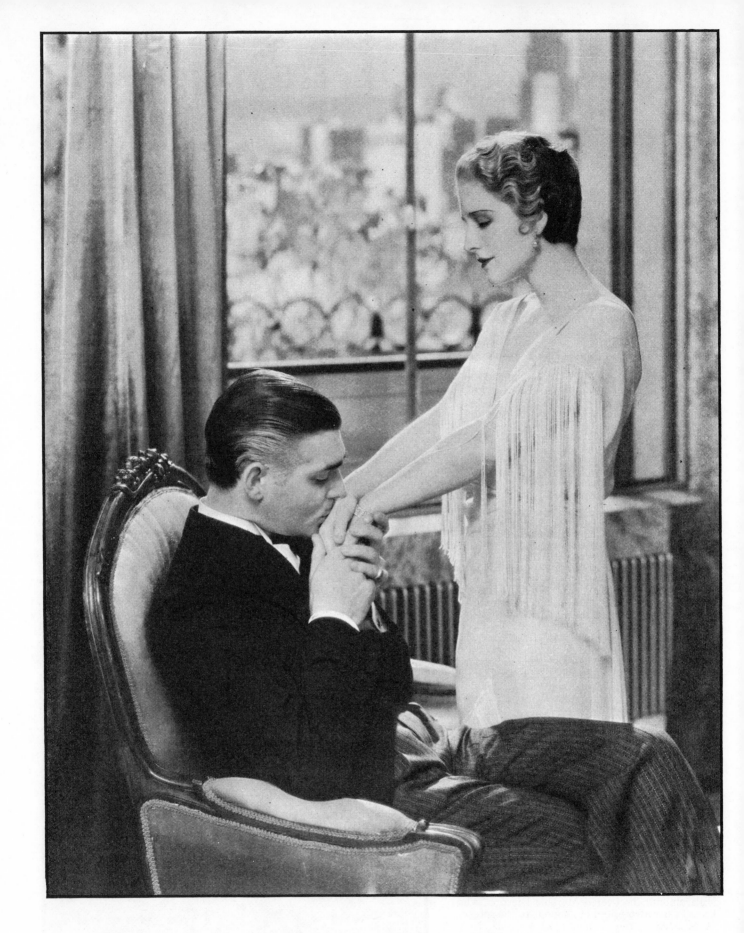

THOSE who have seen "Strange Interlude" say that Norma Shearer has realized her ambition and may now be classed with the greatest actresses of the day—Helen Hayes, Katherine Cornell, Lynn Fontanne. So it's no discredit to Clark Gable to say she steals the picture

MAE WEST

"IT AIN'T NO SIN"

with ROGER PRYOR, John Mack Brown, Duke Ellington & Band • Directed by Leo McCarey
If it's a PARAMOUNT PICTURE it's the best show in town!

PHOTOPLAY

Close-Ups *and* Long-Shots

By
Kathryn Dougherty

W HEN a big job needs doing, usually along comes the right man to do it. While the cry for reform of motion pictures has been going up throughout the land, a revolution has been taking place within the inner circles of the industry itself.

In Hollywood sits Joe Breen, a crusading, determined Irishman, who has been delegated by the Motion Picture Producers and Distributors of America to make a thorough, non-compromising clean-up of the screen and Breen is taking his mission with the grimmest seriousness. So is his superior, Will Hays.

Codes have been drawn up in the past, but supervisors, directors and others have shown a latitude at times in observing them. Perhaps we should not blame them much. Americans are notorious as a people for enacting and then forgetting laws. Besides, the making of a picture is an amazingly involved process—a score of persons influence its course. What comes out of the hopper is not always the idea that went in.

S INCE he became "czar" of the movies in 1922—in reality but a newspaper title —Will Hays has done much to keep the industry within bounds. But it must be remembered that Mr. Hays' power is not absolute; he can only suggest or argue; he cannot command. Able and influential as he is, in the final analysis he is an employee of the motion picture industry. Yet without his guiding hand the industry would long ago have got into serious trouble. He has again and again set his foot down upon practices likely to bring unfavorable public reaction. I am pretty certain that had he had undisputed control the present wave of reform would not be rolling across the land.

B UT the producers have suddenly become submissive to the Hays influence. And that is why Joe Breen, in charge of studio relations, is watching every step of every film production like a hawk.

The reform is so wide sweeping that not a single foot of film may be released without Joe Breen's stamp of approval.

This means that he first must have thoroughly read the story from which the script is to be made; that he must approve the script; that he or his representatives must see all the rushes as the production progresses; that he must recommend cuts and retakes where he thinks necessary; and that he must follow through every change. When the picture is ready for the theaters he must see the final print. Appeal is permitted, but the machinery for that is a new set-up altogether removed from the Hollywood studio heads. If the system doesn't work it won't be the fault of Will Hays or Joe Breen.

PICTURES AND TRENDS

History and Literature, Musicals, Screwball Comedy

Screen cycles of the Thirties, though they seemed to audiences to spring full-panoplied from the head of Jove, were actually the product of considerable calculation. Opportunist the studios might be and wish to be, but the talkies had so lengthened production schedules that the movie-makers found themselves, for the first time, trying to guess the mood of next year's audiences, not this year's. Often this act of divination was strictly an act, but in the case of the Decency fervor they had unpleasantly tangible guidelines to follow. Long before the Catholic bishops and their Protestant supporters actually promulgated the Legion of Decency, church groups had made known their displeasure at what was being shown on the screen to bankers—and bankers' wives—and in 1932, banks were the dominant power in an industry which seemed headed for wholesale receivership. The producers were caught in a dilemma which had the feel of a straitjacket. The churchgoers, who disliked sex and violence on the screen, didn't go to the movies; the rabble, which loved both, did. And nobody in Hollywood seemed able to conjure up a viable box office alternative to the strange frieze of vice, crime and decay which had become the movies' picture of American life. But the pressures from above grew ever greater, somebody had to take a chance, and David Selznick did it. About a month after the announcement of the Legion of Decency, *Little Women* appeared. Its instant success handed the reformers priceless evidence for the argument that the public really did want "good" films—and it seemed as if a docile Hollywood had snapped to attention the minute the Legion barked its commands. In fact, of course, *Little Women* had been conceived and slated for production a year earlier.

Selznick's inspiration provided a path for the Hollywood sheep to follow. History and literature, that was the ticket, and especially the history and literature of Victoria's time, age of repression, high-mindedness and sweet romance. Dickens, Thackeray, Scott and Bulwer-Lytton temporarily overran the screen, and their influence was long-lived. This was as safe as houses, and it had many unforeseen advantages. For example, whoring and sadistic violence could still find place in Victorian movies because these sins were committed by people who were safely dead and didn't count any more. That was important. More than to overt sex and crime in the films of the preceding years, the righteous and the rich had objected to the *tone* of these films, a tone which over and over again implied that there was something radically wrong with present-day American institutions and the American view of things—that, in fact, the whole mess stank. The shift from the contemporary to the more or less barbarous past made everything okay.

There were other pluses in the backward look. History brought back spectacle, which had been substantially abandoned since the coming of sound had made location shooting difficult. It was at this moment, too, that the trick film reappeared, in the form of escapist science-fiction like *King Kong* and *The Invisible Man,* and in that unique spoof of the supernatural, the *Topper* series. From 1933 onward, the camera was pointed at virtually every spot in the universe except the spot under the audience's nose.

The audience responded positively. In spite of radio and recessions, the box office slowly climbed through the rest of the Thirties, though it never reached the heights of 1929 until the Second World War. This fact has been seen by some as an example of successful mass-manipulation, by others as proof that the audience has no real choice because it can only choose from what is offered it. Both interpretations miss the great fact of the change in the life of the country, in its mood, which coincided with the coming of Decency. It would have been futile to introduce sweetness and light into films in 1931 or 1932, backed by no matter how vociferous decent legions. But after Roosevelt's inauguration, people were determined to believe if they possibly could that happy days were here again, and equally determined no longer to be afraid of the big bad wolf. It was not, really, a matter of moral reform, of pressure from on high. Audiences *wanted* to believe in goodness and happiness again.

The musical was the least problematic element in the era of screen optimism which followed Roosevelt's inaugural. Life did not have to be sweetened up and prettied up for this film form; life was simply jettisoned outright in favor of pure fantasy. Especially was this true of the films of Busby Berkeley. The first musicals of the early talkie days had been mere copies of the stage, photographed straight on, and these the public soon rejected. With some dim idea of curing this, of making his song-and-dance routines "cinematic," Berkeley photographed his chorines vertically rather than horizontally, in geometrical patterns, and deployed them in "Broadway" night clubs, stages and rehearsal halls such as never were on land or sea. To film buffs of the period, though not to the general public, Berkeley's films seemed poor and thin, a tin-pot vulgarization of the fantasias of Florenz Ziegfeld. Today's buffs regard them as original, spontaneous creations, an indigenous American counterpart of the violins, ruins and draperies of European Surrealist imagery. No doubt that is how they will look in the future to an unprejudiced eye.

Parallel to these surrogates of musical comedy, the operetta tradition maintained itself throughout the Thirties, at first in the Maurice Chevalier pictures, later in the greatly popular, sickly-sweet confections centering around Jeanette MacDonald and Nelson Eddy. There was also a brief vogue of operatic films based on the equally brief popularity of Grace Moore—whose *Love Me Forever* prompted the embittered Otis Ferguson to call his review "Love Me Some Other Time." This poisoned reaction suggests an actual division of audience taste at the period; the majority of the majority loved the standard musicals; the rest ignored them. But no one was indifferent to the musicals which Fred Astaire, with the help of Ginger Rogers, created out of himself from 1933 on. Astaire and his partner were products of the stage, and they were frequently assisted by stage talent such as George Gershwin and Irving Berlin. But what Astaire made happen on the screen had never happened anywhere else, nor did it have a movie counterpart. Astaire and his films had no detractors; in this, as in so many other respects, they were unique.

Calculated though some screen cycles were, producers simply blundered into others. When Harry Cohn filmed the stage success *Twentieth Century* in 1934, Hollywood was aghast. The picture was too full of show-business "in" jokes; worse, the two leading characters were animated by the basest of motives and were unredeemed by "sympathy"; worst of all, what was to happen to Carole Lombard's "glamour" when the fans saw her in rough-and-tumble fights with her co-star, John Barrymore? But before *Twentieth Century* was released, Cohn's judgment had been vindicated in advance by the unexpected success of two pictures also dimly regarded by the pros—*It Happened One Night,* which had been launched as the last of a mini-cycle of cross-country-bus films, and *The Thin Man,* which M-G-M had put on the drawing-board as an inexpensive "B" vehicle for the fading William Powell and the rising but not-yet-topnotch Myrna Loy. *It Happened One Night* and *The Thin Man* were not only smash hits in first-run, they were rebooked, sometimes three and four times, by virtually every theatre in the country, an accolade accorded no other films of the Thirties with the exception of the first Mae West, a few of the Astaire-Rogers, and Disney's *The Three Little Pigs.*

As for Miss Lombard's glamour, it took such a

beating from there on in that her latecoming devotees were incredulous that she could ever have been one of the glazed and brittle goddesses of the early decade. On the other hand, the cream of the jest in Irene Dunne's case was the incongruity of such an obvious lady getting mixed up in the lowdown goings-on of "screwball comedy." The essence of the screwball premise was to show the world turned on its ear. Perhaps that was the way the world looked to most audiences by 1935.

The Depression was officially over—but it was still hard to get a job and almost as hard to hold one. War was over the horizon, and it visibly and audibly marched closer year by year, month by month. You couldn't count on anything any more. So, since you couldn't build a home of your own, why not just play house? The screwball comedies persuaded their public, with very little arm-twisting, that everyday life was a form of make-believe.

THE other ladies at the party were very grand in lace-trimmed satin and velvet gowns, but none was so winsome as *Jo March*, clad in a simple dress of black alpaca. *Laurie* thought so, too. And *Jo* never lacked a dancing partner. It was *Laurie*, the wealthy boy next door, who gave the *March* girls (poor as church mice!) a glimpse of "high society." The rôle of *Jo* is played by Katharine Hepburn

SCULDUGGERY in the offing! And it must be bad if it scares a
pirate! *Jim Hawkins* (Jackie Cooper), young hero of "Treasure
Island," offers his assistance to *Billie Bones* (Lionel Barrymore). *Billie*,
in modern lingo, is "on the spot!" Robert Louis Stevenson's much loved
adventure story of a search for treasure is being filmed by M·G·M

"The Charge o

Warner's magnificent $2,00
000 picturization of Tennyso
famed poem, "The Charge
the Light Brigade," is expect
to make screen history, a
add more laurels to the cro
of Errol Flynn who stars in

the gallant Captain of the
Lancers, leader of the "six
dred," dashing handsome
l Flynn has a rôle only he
ld play. Opposite him is
via de Havilland, who won
heart in "Captain Blood"

229

Bull

PHOTOPLAY brings you the first pictures of M-G-M's screen version of Shakespeare's immortal story, "Romeo and Juliet." Norma Shearer portrays the sensitive Juliet and Leslie Howard is Romeo

What Power Can Save Them?

Introducing you to just one of Fay Wray's bad moments in that new hair-raiser, "King Kong"

Yes, this is just one sample of what happens to Fay and Bruce Cabot, in RKO-Radio's new nightmare about dinosaurs and the monster ape that suddenly start ripping New York City apart. And what will happen a moment from now, when *King Kong* has drawn them relentlessly back from their desperate attempt to escape? Well, we can't say—but we do think this shows you some of the weird thrills you can expect from this new super-shocker

hollywood faces the far East

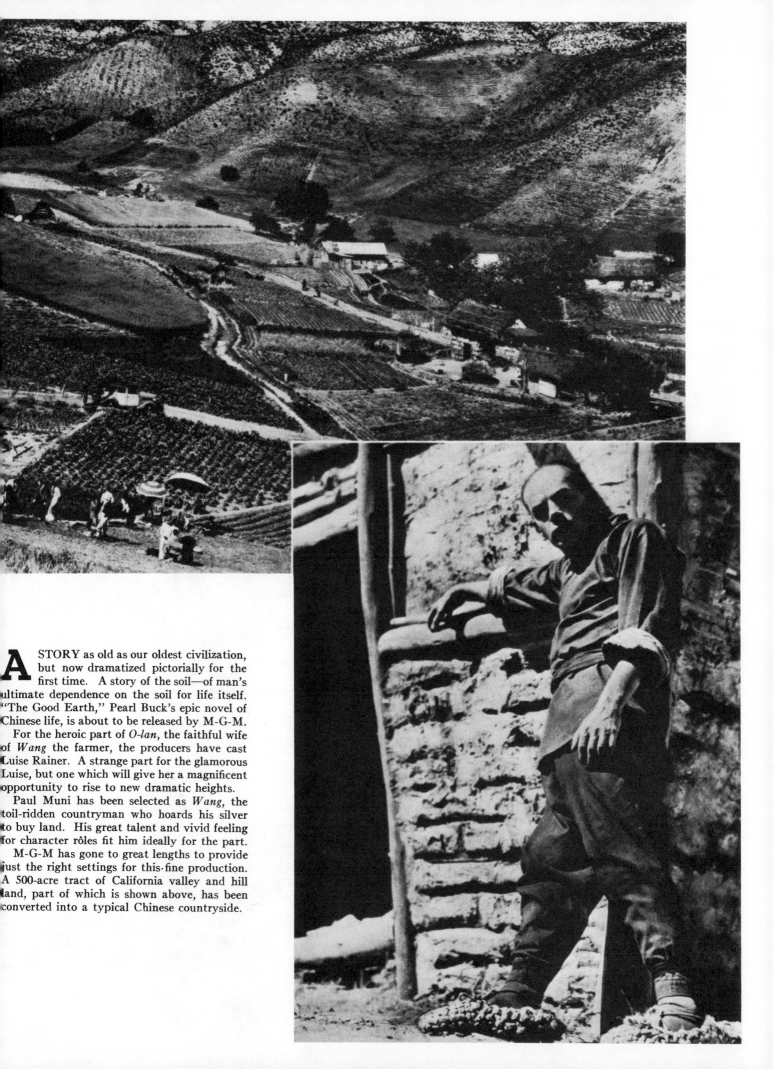

A STORY as old as our oldest civilization, but now dramatized pictorially for the first time. A story of the soil—of man's ultimate dependence on the soil for life itself. "The Good Earth," Pearl Buck's epic novel of Chinese life, is about to be released by M-G-M.

For the heroic part of *O-lan*, the faithful wife of *Wang* the farmer, the producers have cast Luise Rainer. A strange part for the glamorous Luise, but one which will give her a magnificent opportunity to rise to new dramatic heights.

Paul Muni has been selected as *Wang*, the toil-ridden countryman who hoards his silver to buy land. His great talent and vivid feeling for character rôles fit him ideally for the part.

M-G-M has gone to great lengths to provide just the right settings for this fine production. A 500-acre tract of California valley and hill land, part of which is shown above, has been converted into a typical Chinese countryside.

Dottie and Bob spot a ship coming to their rescue—and their expressions tell you just what they think of it

Typhoon

It's a new team but the same old sarong (breaking out in a different print). Dottie's latest beau is that skyrocket of "Union Pacific," Robert Preston. This time Lamour's a Dutch East Indie beauty and Bob's a chap who been shipwrecked on her island —presumably by Dottie's eyes

Ah! "Typhoon!" solves that old problem of whom to take to a desert isle!

Richee

December 1939

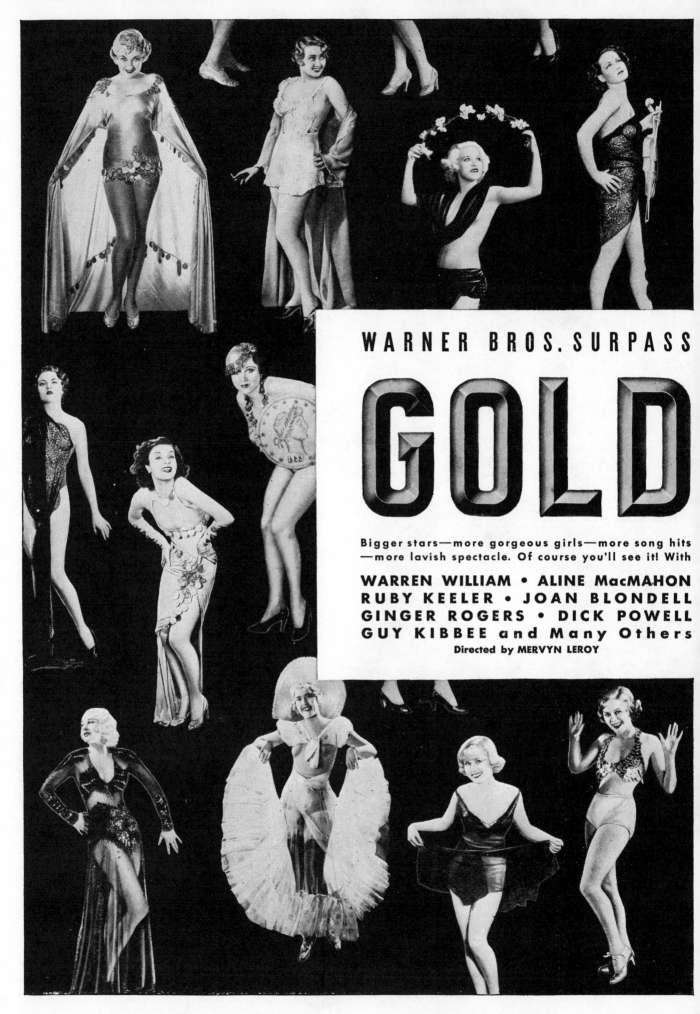

WARNER BROS. SURPASS

GOLD

Bigger stars—more gorgeous girls—more song hits —more lavish spectacle. Of course you'll see it! With

**WARREN WILLIAM • ALINE MacMAHON
RUBY KEELER • JOAN BLONDELL
GINGER ROGERS • DICK POWELL
GUY KIBBEE and Many Others**
Directed by MERVYN LEROY

THE GLORIES OF "42nd STREET" WITH
DIGGERS OF 1933

WARNER BROS.' "GOLD DIGGERS" FOR 1934!

"DAMES"

With 14 Noted Stars Including

RUBY KEELER • DICK POWELL
JOAN BLONDELL • ZASU PITTS
GUY KIBBEE • HUGH HERBERT

And Hundreds of Glorious Busby Berkeley Beauties

★

Directed by RAY ENRIGHT of "20 Million Sweethearts" Fame

★

Sumptuous Musical Presentations Created and Arranged by BUSBY BERKELEY

★

Five New Song Successes by WARREN & DUBIN • KAHAL & FAIN • WRUBEL & DIXON

WITH A WALTZ IN YOUR HEART

Surrender to the happy seduction of Ernst Lubitsch's most glorious picture holiday! When Maurice Chevalier with delicious gaiety flirts, sings, conquers Jeanette MacDonald, the rich and merry widow, it's your big new screen thrill! Because Franz Lehar's romance is the greatest operetta of our time M=G=M has spared no expense to make it memorably magnificent! With the stars and director of "The Love Parade".

In the hush of a lilac=perfumed night to the soft sobbing of gypsy violins . . . they danced the dance of love . . . the "Merry Widow Waltz".

MAURICE
CHEVALIER
JEANETTE
MacDONALD

an **ERNST LUBITSCH** Production

THE *Merry Widow*

with

EDWARD EVERETT HORTON · **UNA MERKEL**
GEORGE BARBIER · · · **MINNA GOMBELL**
Screen Play by Ernest Vajda and Samson Raphaelson

A METRO-GOLDWYN-MAYER PICTURE

jeanette - nelson

Nelson Eddy and Jeanette MacDonald in "Rose Marie," M-G-M's timely
response to the universal shout of acclaim (still resounding, by the way)
for Eddy's and Miss MacDonald's vocalizing in "Naughty Marietta"

The exhilarating screen progress of the dancing meteor who has personality to boot! Top left, "The Dancing Lady" with Joan Crawford, his first film. Remember the Carioca with Dolores del Rio (top) in "Flying Down to Rio" and with Ginger in the same film? "The Gay Divorcee" (below) made everybody Continental conscious

An Outline of Astaire

He gave you dreamy waltzes in "Roberta," white tie and tails in "Top Hat" (below), joined the Navy for "Follow the Fleet," was a spatted dandy in "Swing Time" (above) his latest picture, but he's always Astaire, just Astaire, the world's best hoofer. His astounding agility, his rippling rhythm will soon enhance "Stepping Toes"

Irving Lippman

TEMPERAMENT and temper run riot in this scene between Carole Lombard and John Barrymore—one of many high-spirited moments in Columbia's "Twentieth Century." In this adaptation from a stage comedy of last season, Barrymore is the eccentric producer who snares Carole, a Broadway star and his ex-flame, into signing a new contract

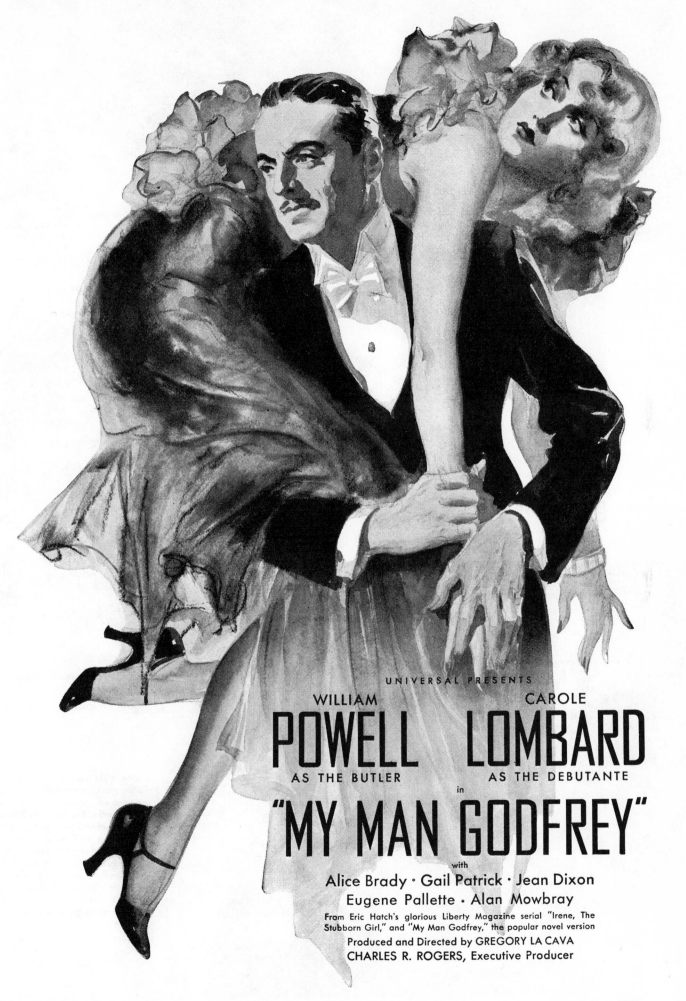

UNIVERSAL PRESENTS

WILLIAM · CAROLE
POWELL · LOMBARD

AS THE BUTLER · AS THE DEBUTANTE

in

"MY MAN GODFREY"

with

Alice Brady · Gail Patrick · Jean Dixon
Eugene Pallette · Alan Mowbray

From Eric Hatch's glorious Liberty Magazine serial "Irene, The
Stubborn Girl," and "My Man Godfrey," the popular novel version

Produced and Directed by GREGORY LA CAVA
CHARLES R. ROGERS, Executive Producer

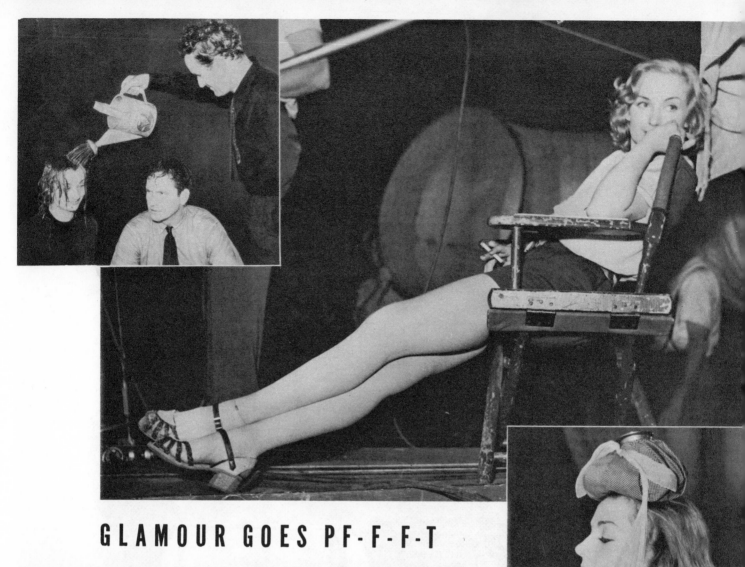

GLAMOUR GOES PF-F-F-T

Drama in her bare feet, stringy hair via the sprinkling can method—these our exponent of allure goes for in typical Lombard fashion. She'll show her legs (and nice ones, too) and don an ice bag with aplomb. She'll beef a bit and scowl if necessary, for dignity is dropped when Bill Wellman directs Carole and Freddie March in "Nothing Sacred," the Selznick cinema in which glamour, with much gusto, goes pf-f-f-t

STAGE DOOR

Hollywood has proved that it can take a kidding and can even kid itself—but when Margaret Sullavan's New York stage success of last winter hits the screen little more than the name will be intact. After all, a serious drayma that's so obviously a slap in the face at Hollywood—well, that's asking too much. Rumors of bitter feelings between Katharine Hepburn and Ginger Rogers evaporated into thin air when the costars got going on this story of stagestruck girls in a theatrical boardinghouse, with Director Gregory LaCava at the helm; Adolphe Menjou, Constance Collier and Gail Patrick to lend support

After a ducking by MacMurray, Lombard looked just like a left-over Christmas tree in February—but Lombard got her man!

Romance via the wet-toe route: Dick Powell courts pneumonia and Rosemary Lane in "Hollywood Hotel"—and seems to like it

This is the "how to be enticing though spanked" method, used by Claudette on Gary Cooper in "Bluebeard's Eighth Wife"

FASHIONS
IN
PASSIONS

Maybe you movie queens can get away with it, but what about us ordinary gals who must win our men, too?

BY RUTH WATERBURY

DEAR Carole:—
  Dear Miss Dunne (I don't know you really well enough to call you Irene):—
Dear Miss Hepburn (I'll stay formal with you, knowing how you feel about interviewers—remember that time we flew across the continent together, dear?):
Dear Claudette (hi, there, toots!):
Dear Runners-Up:—
  I come to you girls for help. You alone can guide me. For years, I have believed in all of you as examples of how to get on in this world. For many seasons I have used you as mentors,

An open letter to Lombard, Dunne, Colbert, Hepburn and all other heroines of the "A kick in the slats is the best way to romance" school!

The Hepburn system of sitting down in water worked on Cary Grant (but why?) in "Bringing Up Baby"

The technique Irene Dunne used on Cary in "The Awful Truth" would ruin any off-screen siren's chances

figuring that by modelling myself after you—a long distance after, I admit, still I was there—I might finally become alluring; learn to wear my clothes with that certain something, get wise as to how to smile through my lonely tears, discover how to be a good sport and to act gallantly though my heart might be breaking.

Not that I wanted to do any of these things just for themselves, you understand. Just like you movie kiddies, all of that was a way to land my man—mine or anyone else's. But for guidance along such lines, I went to see you girls.

When you were being just straight glamorous, I could have hope.

I could follow your moves. After all, I, too, could order a yard of eyelashes from the drug store. I may have looked a bit like a water spaniel when I got them on, but get them on I could and have them cast shadows on my nose (which is better in a shadow than in a bright light anyway).

It wasn't such a stunt to imitate Joan Crawford's exotic lip make-up, even though it made my mouth feel as though it had been doused in cold starch. I could buy sweaters anyplace and learn to keep my shoulders back so that I had those visible points of interest all newcomers on movie lots are photographed revealing.

I could, by shopping like crazy, buy clips that at five hundred yards looked, for two and a half bucks, quite a bit like those all of you wear that cost from seven hundred dollars up. I could let my nails grow dagger-length like those of the glamorous Dietrich.

EVEN when Elisabeth Bergner first came over here and went coy in "Escape Me Never" (whatever became of her anyway?), with Luise Rainer following in "Escapade" and they both made love by being just darned cute, I could do that, too. You remember, girls, that Elisabeth went so far as to bend double and peer at the hero from between her outspread legs. I never quite tried that. Men upset me enough as it is without me turning myself inside out deliberately. But I did try Luise's trick of putting my head down on my left arm and gazing at my man very much on the slant. All he said, I must confess, was, "S'matter? Did you drop something?" I mean, it wasn't too effective in making him dizzy with nameless emotions, but at least I could do it and hope it would get him eventually.

But how to be a siren while goof-nuts—that's what baffles me. In the past couple of seasons everyone of you girls—beautiful, young, enchanting—have suddenly become bird-brained. You have changed your approach. But you end up in the same old way, right smack in the hero's arms. But for us little women in the audience, what a strain! Our particular objective sits there beside us at the theater, admiring you. He yells with laughter at you. He thinks you're keen. How can we expect to do anything with the old tricks like eyes shadowed beneath hat brims, mysterious smiles on our lips, or even that mouldy old line about their not thinking we are that kind of a girl, do they? Drag those techniques out this spring and it's about as effective as talking about the Oxford movement at the monkey house. And it's all your fault.

REALLY, Carole, you are the one I put it up to most because you started the slapstick route to romance two years ago in "My Man Godfrey." That was the one in which you first got your clothes torn and your hair messed up, but Bill Powell loved you just the same. You were a wow—a hit in excelsis. You followed that up with a lot of others, climaxing with Freddie March kicking you half way across the room *(Continued on page 321)*

THE *Camera* SPEAKS

Theodora goes wilder when Irene Dunne and Cary Grant go in for a bit of hi-jinks in that delightful domestic comedy, "The Awful Truth"

PICTURES AND TRENDS

The End of the Thirties

The Roosevelt Era was a time of contradictions in the movies. The Production Code still rode high, and its mandate was to enforce stability, conformity, non-controversiality—but the vital impulses kept pushing up around its edges. The gangster film had been banished because it glorified crime, but the love of violence found disguised expression in films about G-Men and T-Men (the Bureau of Internal Revenue was not yet universally detested) and the iniquities of the prison system. Sex found refuge in the screwball comedy, whose lovers were usually married but behaved as if they weren't. Politics was officially tabu, but writers, directors, and even a few producers pushed the making of "social" films which painted a mosaic picture of the country's political schisms whether they meant to or not.

This split between the official and the real pained the fan magazines. There was no way to paper over the contradictions except simply to ignore them—as the magazines tried to ignore the social-consciousness films. *Fury, Black Fury, Black Legion, Blockade, Pasteur, Zola, Juarez* were presented to the fans simply as "good stories," or in terms of the stars, such as Paul Muni, who perversely insisted upon appearing in such "danger-ous" vehicles. From such problems the magazines turned with relief and determination to new manifestations of the escape impulse. Concerned at the shrinkage of foreign markets due to the approach of war, producers of the late Thirties attempted to combat it by producing what were essentially Hollywood films in Europe. The result in pictures like *A Yank At Oxford* and *Goodbye, Mr. Chips* reflected an obsolescent European scene which provided perfect escape from reality for American and European audiences alike. But the escape-hatch supreme for the last three years of the Thirties was the publication of *Gone With the Wind*, its purchase for the movies by David O. Selznick, and the reverberating controversy, participated in by everyone alive, over its casting. The answer to Hitler was the question, who will play Scarlett? As the decade guttered out, *Gone With the Wind* at last appeared. PHOTOPLAY's review of it was almost routine. The subject had been sucked dry—and the spotlight stolen by the declaration of war three months earlier. The response of the magazines to the war itself was characteristic: which foreign stars will have to leave the screen and go and fight?

"The Hurricane"   A newsreel view of the Hindenburg disaster   A Mickey Mouse cartoon   "The Adventures of Tom Saw[...]

WHY WE ROOSEVELTS

On her trip to Hollywood, Mrs. Roosevelt formed impressions of many stars, from Temple to Taylor, studied the studios carefully. Now, in this article, she tells why she thinks the stars of today are popular and issues a challenge to producers of tomorrow

It is a pleasure and a privilege to see

Hollywood—stars, studios, films—

through the eyes of the First Lady of

our land and her White House family

IT is strange how for some of us our interest in people as individuals seems to tinge everything we do! The very best movies in the world might be shown in the White House and, if I have work to do, I would probably leave all my guests and sit at my desk all evening. If someone said to me however, " 'So and So,' whom you met last January at the Birthday Balls, and whom you liked so much, is in that movie," I would probably decide that my work could be done between eleven and one a. m. and sit through the movie and enjoy it. I would have to have that personal interest in an individual before I would be tempted to see the play. That is the secret of the great popularity of movie stars, I suppose.

The rest of the family do not seem to be affected to quite the same degree that I am, however. They are all just natural movie fans. Jimmy and Betsy will come in in the evening during their busy winter months and say, "We are going to the movies; don't you want to come with us?" I raise my hands in horror and say: "Heavens, when I have more than I can do on this desk, I certainly am not going to the movies!" They go gaily off, jeering at me.

When the children come home for holidays or week ends there is always a demand for movies in the White House and, of course, it is practically the one and only relaxation which my husband has and it is a rare thing that a week goes by without at least one movie being shown for him.

Of course, we always have newsreels and, even when I do not stay for the long movie, I

"The Life of Emile Zola"   "Snow White and the Seven Dwarfs"   A newsreel view of the Coronation   "Little Miss Broadway"

ARE MOVIE FANS

These are some of the movies requested at the White House—and the versatile Roosevelts had definite reactions to them all

BY ELEANOR ROOSEVELT

wait to see those, for they seem to bring the whole world before us. We can see things which happen hundreds of miles away just as though we were on the spot. I contend that seeing things is almost a necessity in this visual-minded period of our development, and the newsreels are probably doing as much as the radio, newspapers and magazines to make people world-minded today.

Sometime I hope they will go a step further and do an educational job by stepping back into history and bringing the past before us so that we may better understand the happenings of the present. I remember once being given a preview of a film which depicted present conditions in a foreign land. Interesting as it was to me, I realized all the way through that the average theater-goer would need to know what conditions had existed in that country for two or three hundred years before, or he could not really understand the story which the film was trying to tell. Perhaps we are going to find ourselves learning history and becoming better world neighbors someday as a result of new uses to which the movies may lend themselves.

The newsreels, interesting as they are however, are only the appetizer for the real film.

I THINK a little trip to Hollywood would make every movie-goer more appreciative of the films which he sees. I spent one morning seeing three of the big movie studios. My time was so limited that I could only get an impression of each one but it was a breath-taking experience.

From Warner Brothers I carried away the vision of real streets with buildings—in Paris, in Spain, East Side New York City—and of a research department where a whole wall was lined with hardware of different periods and reference books that were so enticing that I would have gladly offered myself as a candidate for a job among them!

From Metro-Goldwyn-Mayer, I think my impression was one of marked efficiency. A tremendous scene moved before my eyes and then I was shown how certain illusions can be created and I realized more vividly every minute how many skills may be used in the creating of moving pictures. I had thought of it first as largely acting and writing; when, as a matter of fact, it

is engineering and painting and a painstaking student's job.

At the Twentieth Century-Fox studio I was so taken up with Shirley Temple that I thought of little else, so I suppose what stayed with me there is the impression of the choice of the right person for the right film. After all, in the movies as in the legitimate theater, half the success is in the casting.

With this visit as background and the very pleasant acquaintanceships made at the time of the Birthday Balls each year when I have a chance to meet and talk with some of the movie stars, my interest is growing greater. I must see whatever films my acquaintances are in and I understand a little better all that goes into giving us this entertainment.

For the youngest members of the family it is never very hard to choose a film. Mickey Mouse always is successful and calls for much applause and squeals of joy, but the grandchildren are not the only ones who enjoy Mickey Mouse. The President never has an evening of his own planning without at last one Mickey Mouse film. Walt Disney's extraordinary film, "Snow White and the Seven Dwarfs," has charmed everyone, old and young alike. Some of the little children are frightened by the witch, to be sure, and they weep, but the older members of the family liked it from beginning to end. Even one hard-boiled columnist who has few enthusiasms wrote of it in glowing terms.

One of the movies which I shall never forget was "The Life of Emile Zola," very well acted by Paul Muni, I thought. "The Buccaneer" with Fredric March, "Tom Sawyer," "Arsene Lupin Returns," "Hurricane" and many others that I cannot recall have been given this winter at the White House and all of them, I think, were a pleasant evening's entertainment and well worth seeing.

OF course, as far as we are concerned, the movies are used purely as a method of relaxation and entertainment, but every one of us realizes that it is not only as an amusement that the movies are important. Here is something which may be used to shape public opinion, to bring before a tremendously wide audience a great variety of facts and thoughts which can be a powerful imaginative stimulus. I do not mean

that we are at present using it to the full extent to accomplish these ends, but that it may do all of this in the future is very possible.

There are undoubtedly many movies which have done great harm. I can remember years ago being dragged from my fireside in our cottage on Campobello Island, off the coast of Maine, to attend a movie in the little town of Eastport, Maine. I came away from that movie outraged, for society, spelled with a capital "S," was pictured not only as corrupt and immoral, but so unbelievably stupid that I could hardly stand having it looked upon as a true picture of any kind of life by the youth of our country. That old type of picture has practically disappeared, and also there is rapidly disappearing today the type of picture which glorifies the gangster and criminal. They made us more sympathetic with the rascal than with the righteous man. We do occasionally see this still. I do not feel so strongly about it as I should perhaps, for I have so often found in real life that the rascal was attractive and had charm that I am not so sure but what it is well to make this discovery both in literature and on the stage, in order that we may learn to look beneath the surface and not be taken in too easily by appearances.

However, it is harmful to make small boys want to be the head of a gang, and I am very glad we have begun to show that it is possible to have qualities that evoke admiration, and still be a policeman or a "G" man, or even an everyday good citizen. Every now and then, I also get letters filled with concern from mothers and teachers who feel that certain movies actually put into dull or criminally inclined minds methods of procedure, thus stimulating the imagination which has a criminal bent to practical action.

The answer is, of course, that the public demands excitement and sometimes seems decidedly sadistic, enjoying a cruelty and horror on the stage or in a film which they might not be able to stand in real life. This is a curious trait of human nature; but it is true that producers must, to a certain extent, cater to the demands of the public and that if we wish to change anything in the movies, on the radio, on the stage, in the newspapers, we must change

(Continued on page 325)

PAY BOY OF THE WESTERN WORLD

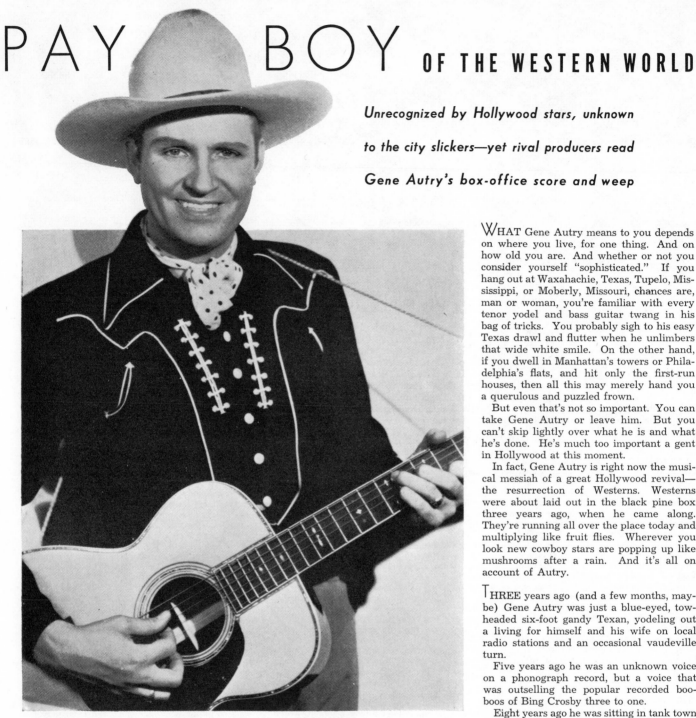

Unrecognized by Hollywood stars, unknown

to the city slickers—yet rival producers read

Gene Autry's box-office score and weep

This shy, ingratiating Texan becomes the messiah of a great revival

BY KIRTLEY BASKETTE

WHAT Gene Autry means to you depends on where you live, for one thing. And on how old you are. And whether or not you consider yourself "sophisticated." If you hang out at Waxahachie, Texas, Tupelo, Mississippi, or Moberly, Missouri, chances are, man or woman, you're familiar with every tenor yodel and bass guitar twang in his bag of tricks. You probably sigh to his easy Texas drawl and flutter when he unlimbers that wide white smile. On the other hand, if you dwell in Manhattan's towers or Philadelphia's flats, and hit only the first-run houses, then all this may merely hand you a querulous and puzzled frown.

But even that's not so important. You can take Gene Autry or leave him. But you can't skip lightly over what he is and what he's done. He's much too important a gent in Hollywood at this moment.

In fact, Gene Autry is right now the musical messiah of a great Hollywood revival— the resurrection of Westerns. Westerns were about laid out in the black pine box three years ago, when he came along. They're running all over the place today and multiplying like fruit flies. Wherever you look new cowboy stars are popping up like mushrooms after a rain. And it's all on account of Autry.

THREE years ago (and a few months, maybe) Gene Autry was just a blue-eyed, towheaded six-foot gandy Texan, yodeling out a living for himself and his wife on local radio stations and an occasional vaudeville turn.

Five years ago he was an unknown voice on a phonograph record, but a voice that was outselling the popular recorded booboos of Bing Crosby three to one.

Eight years ago he was sitting in tank town railroad depots in Oklahoma, Missouri and Texas tapping out telegraph messages and passing the empty hours making up cowboy songs.

Eighteen years ago, he dangled his cactus-scratched legs from the cattle loading platform of the Tioga, Texas station, waiting to help herd his dad's steers aboard the slow train. And while he waited he milled around with the older cowpokes and picked up the fret changes of the "gitter" and the lonely tunes of the range.

That might seem a dull dish of history to pass you at this point, but it planted the bonanza that started the Western gold rush today.

Because one night in Claremore, Oklahoma—you've heard of that place—a hometown boy with a maverick shock of grayish

(Continued on page 326)

MORE women adore him than Clark Gable. They write him more love letters than they write Robert Taylor.

More kids worship him than Shirley Temple. His screen voice thrills thousands more than Bing Crosby's husky notes, his grin cracks more masculine crusts than Jimmy Cagney's fists ever cracked, his daring deeds are more admired than Errol Flynn's.

Darryl Zanuck has just laid a cool half million on the line for his contract, and had

it laughed back in his lap. Zanuck wanted his magic draw to persuade people to sit through Shirley Temple and Eddie Cantor and Tyrone Power and Alice Faye—so they could see him in the second feature.

He's the most amazing young man in Hollywood—yet not a tenth of Hollywood has ever seen him. More than half of the beglamoured stars of the upper movie crust have never even heard of him—until quite lately. Maybe you haven't, either—or maybe he's the most notable man in your life.

M U N I ... MAN OF THE MONTH

Paul Muni, winner of this year's Academy Award, steps out and tops his "Louis Pasteur" performance with "The Life of Emile Zola." Born Muni Weisenfreud in Lemberg, Austria, forty years ago; educated in U. S. A., regards himself 100% American; stage debuted at 11, became Ghetto idol at Yiddish Art Theater where he met and married Bella Finkel 16 years ago; speaks seven languages; is interested in politics—American and European; is a fine violinist and adroit boxer; likes prize fights, hates parties; has unsuspected sense of humor; collects dictionaries of all sizes; lives simply in a Spanish farmhouse in San Fernando Valley—a swimming pool is the only Hollywood touch; threatens to retire in two years

From "The Grapes of Wrath": "Cars . . . wrecks . . . abandoned . . . What happened to the folks?"

"I'll work for food. The kids. You ought to see them . . ."

John Steinbeck

Nunnally Johnson

Darryl Zanuck

Even John Steinbeck, author of the year's most daring book, believed the picture would never be made. Here's the answer from this famous producer and writer who adapted it

BY NUNNALLY JOHNSON

EDITOR'S NOTE:
The most discussed book in many years is "Grapes of Wrath." The fact that its author, John Steinbeck, deals with a phase of American life in which great social injustice is apparent has led to the rumor that when Darryl Zanuck bought the motion picture rights forces more powerful than Zanuck would prevent his making the picture—at least with all the power and vigor contained in the original book. Many people are shocked by the startlingly realistic dialogue and situations painted ruthlessly by John Steinbeck and so the story has grown that "Grapes of Wrath" will never be filmed. Therefore I went to Nunnally Johnson, famous writer and producer, who was entrusted with the task of adapting the book to the movies, and asked him to give the readers of PHOTOPLAY a frank and fearless statement of the real facts. I am proud to be able to present it herewith.
—E. V. H.

LAST April, when Twentieth Century-Fox bought "The Grapes of Wrath," I went to New York to talk to John Steinbeck regarding its conversion into a screen play, and we had scarcely reached the olive in the first Martini when he asked me what the hell was this rumor that the company had got the story for the sole purpose of ditching it.

That was the first time I heard the report, but not the last by a long shot. The way it came to Steinbeck, the banks that finance the movies were putting the finger on the book by authorizing Darryl F. Zanuck, production head of Twentieth Century-Fox, to buy it and bury it and forget it, at any price and on the house.

Since the bankers who finance the movies were unlikely to let me in on any such Machiavellian maneuver as that, I hardly knew what to say. Odd things happen in Hollywood. But I doubted it. For one thing, my last recollection of Zanuck before I left the studio was that of a man shouting with excitement. For another, if the book were dead what was the point of adding to the cost of the funeral by assigning me and my pay to it? Once you've got the corpse set in the casket you don't go out and

BE SHELVED?

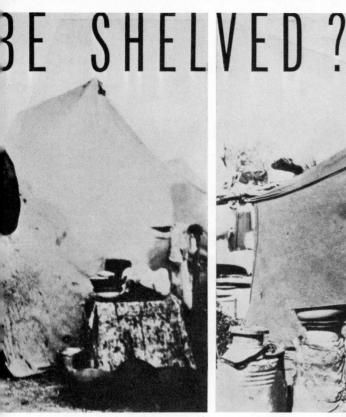

"...side each habitation some kind of automobile"

"Men who had never been hungry saw the eyes of the hungry"

Farm Security Administration Photographs

treat it to a spring wardrobe. For still a third, it wasn't a Book of the Month, and so I didn't see how a banker could have heard of it, much less read it.

But that was all I could tell Steinbeck, and I admit it wasn't much. So I suppose it goes without saying that he remained skeptical—polite, to be sure, but clearly skeptical. Nor, incidentally, has his skepticism ever abated, even when he read and approved the script of the screen play. And he'll still be dubious until he has seen the picture on the screen—for which, God knows, I don't blame him.

A dozen times I came on the rumor in New York and for months afterward in Hollywood, until here at the studio we became resigned to it, as a man with a harelip becomes resigned to his affliction. Movie gossip writers, working with that crystal ball which is standard equipment for slightly incompetent journalists, fed the campaign with dark and mysterious hints of information straight from the old feedbox. Zanuck was bluffing. Zanuck had to assign a writer to the story simply to save his face. Zanuck was going to fenagle Will Hays into banning it, for the same reason. Zanuck was secretly begging the Governor of California to intercede.

Parenthetically, I must say that Zanuck loved it. "Show me a man who can prove that I spent $70,000 for a book in order to shelve it," he said, "and I'll make a picture about *him!*" Nothing improves Zanuck's disposition like a good stiff rumor that he'll never do it. His spirits rise, soft drinks flow like water in his office, and it is a first-rate time to hit him for a raise or a vacation. Close parenthesis.

Since then, a number of agencies have indicated their antagonism to the book by passing resolutions against it and in some instances by barring it from public libraries. A woman writer, Ruth Comfort Mitchell, wife of former California State Senator Sangborn Young, has announced her intention to answer "The Grapes of Wrath" with a novel based on the odd premise that the California rancher is himself a tragic

figure in that he "faces a great problem in these homeless hordes of poverty-stricken dust-bowl refugees who camp on his property and beg for work." In her novel, she promises there will also be a pure love story. Behind her intention was the contention of many Californians, that Steinbeck's book was unjust to the conditions in that state.

FOR my part, I found only one implied charge in "The Grapes of Wrath" that was wholly indefensible. This was the wholesale recruiting of ignorant dust-bowl refugees by means of handbills and newspaper advertisements by unscrupulous labor agents. Who should bear the responsibility for these agents and their methods, I do not know. But I confirmed Steinbeck's charges regarding them by obtaining photostat copies of both handbills and advertisements. That they did lure many times as many men as they had jobs, as Steinbeck claimed, was clear on the surface.

But the company, purely as a mattter of precaution and for its own satisfaction, engaged a private investigation to check on conditions in the counties where the Okies have settled in California. Without distrusting Steinbeck's material, it was felt advisable to have at hand, in cases of attack, something more specific by way of answer than a book of fiction, however well documented. This investigation, while it found summer conditions somewhat better than they have been and may again be during winter, disclosed no reason why we should modify the tell-

(Continued on page 320)

"I seen a thing in the paper says they need folks to pick fruit" . . . "Look, it don't make no sense. This fella wants eight hunderd men . . . An' maybe two-three thousan' folks get movin' account a this here han'-bill." Here's proof of the ads and handbills which started the migration

261

To one woman
he gave his memories...
to another
he gave his dreams—
wild longings—
fierce desires
he dared not name...
for an interlude of
stolen love!
Could any woman
be content with
half a love?
Could any man
summon enough
for both?...
A vivid portrayal by

LESLIE HOWARD

star player extraordinary in

INTERMEZZO
A Love Story

SELZNICK INTERNATIONAL'S
great production introducing
the glamorous new Swedish star

INGRID BERGMAN

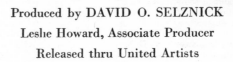

Produced by DAVID O. SELZNICK
Leslie Howard, Associate Producer
Released thru United Artists

"GONE WITH the WIND" Indeed!

By KIRTLEY BASKETTE

Call out the riot squad! A new Civil War is raging! Who will play the principals in the world's best seller?

TIME was when you could call a man a rat in Hollywood and get yourself a stiff poke in the nose. But now what you get is—"Rhett? *Rhett Butler?* Well—I don't know about that 'profile like an old coin' stuff, but I've been told I am rather masterful, and—"

Yes, and there was a day when you could call a woman scarlet in this town and find yourself looking into the business end of a male relative's shotgun. But now it's—"Scarlett? *Scarlett O'Hara?* Oh, do you really think so? Well, I wish you'd say that around Mr. Selznick. Of course, my eyes aren't exactly green, but unless they use Technicolor—"

Ever since that very small but very un-Reconstructed Rebel, Mistress Peggy Mitchell, of the Atlanta Mitchells, wrote a book called "Gone With the Wind," which went like a seventy-mile gale over the country and whipped up a grade-A tornado, a civil war, the like of which Jeff Davis never dreamed, has been raging uncontrolled 'way out in Hollywood.

Houses are divided, brother against brother, husband against wife, butler versus pantrymaid.

"Why, Judge," a woman told the court the other day, "this bum says the only man to play *Rhett Butler* is Warren William. How can I go on living with a cretin like that?"

"Yeah," countered the defendant, "and, Your Honor, she embarrassed me before my friends plugging for Ronald Colman. Ronald Colman—imagine! My business dropped off."

"Divorce granted," murmured the court, "although per-sonally I've always thought Gary Cooper would be a natural for the part."

What is considerably worse, actors and actresses who have never been South of the Slot in San Francisco or below Twenty-third Street in Manhattan, whose closest tie to Dixie in fact, is a faint resemblance to Virginia ham, wander around calling people "Honey" in a languid, molasses manner. Mugs who always thought Pickett's charge was a labor demonstration, now demand real mint in their grog. Even the high yellows down on Central Avenue are brushing up on their southern accents.

It's really pretty awful.

Of course if you haven't read the astounding book that has leaped clear out of the ordinary fiction league to become the marvel of modern American literature, all this may leave you as dizzy as a six-day bicycle rider. In that case, all I can say is that if you're around number sixty-seven on the waiting list and sound of wind and limb there is still hope.

But if you have, you'll understand why nerves are snapping from Burbank to Brentwood as the two juiciest parts in the history of Hollywood dangle like ripe luscious cherries just above tiptoe reach. For "Gone With the Wind" is all set to be made into the greatest moving picture of all time (they admit it). Only there isn't any *Scarlett O'Hara.* There isn't any *Rhett Butler.* The suspense is terrific.

Furthermore, the curious effect of this book, which now hovers around the million sales mark, is that the minute a gentle reader closes the back cover with the wistful hope that *Scarlett* will get another crack at *Rhett* someday, a crusading, militant, in fact belligerent one-man casting department is born. Yes Ma'am, and with a lusty squall.

So look what happens. Sixty thousand letters, wires, com-munications of all sorts, sent direct or forwarded by critics, columnists and radio commentators have poured in and keep pouring to sweep the excitement higher and higher The result

Clark Gable, everybody's choice, everywhere — but tied up

Freddie March, hero of one best seller, "Anthony Adverse"

RHETT BUTLERS

is the biggest screen sweepstakes of modern movie history. The prize: fame, fortune and the greatest eager, ready-made audience any star ever dreamed about.

Who will win? Well—here are the favorites, complete with clockings, handicaps, and pole positions. You pays your money and you takes your choice:

Ladies first, which means *Rhett Butler*—

Clark Gable is the odds on favorite. He probably will play the part. If he doesn't there may be a Revolution. The nation-wide choice, by a wide margin, he runs neck-and-neck with Warner Baxter in the South, which, incidentally, will have plenty to say about the casting of this picture. Gable is also the big Hollywood favorite, although if you can't see him you can't see him *at all*. It's that way. Letters have poured in threatening boycotts and reprisals (honest) if he's cast as *Rhett*. The same if he isn't.

Clark is the right age, the perfect build, the effective sex quotient. On a very touchy point—whether or not he can put on a southern accent and wear it becomingly—he is doubtful. He would give a year of his life to play *Rhett*—why not? It would be the biggest monkey gland his career could conceivably manage.

But—Gable is among the most jealously hoarded of M-G-M stars. And Selznick International, not M-G-M, copped this prize story of the century. M-G-M turned it down! Selznick International means John Hay Whitney and David Oliver Selznick. But again—David Oliver Selznick is married to Louis B. Mayer's daughter. Would Gable be available? What do you think?

Fredric March is the only factor so far officially tested for *Rhett*. Was the early choice, but seems to have faded in the back stretch. Would be available, eager and willing to play *Rhett* on a moment's notice. Runs about third in the terrific straw balloting which in-

Warner Baxter has amazing support. Enough sex appeal?

Ronald Colman, a strong contender— but he has handicaps

Tallulah Bankhead as southern as corn whiskey. Too blasé?

Miriam Hopkins, red hot choice, has a margin in her favor

creases every day. Is regarded by millions as a great actor—many others do not agree. Played the other great sensational best seller title part, "Anthony Adverse." Consensus of opinion is that Fredric would be an adequate *Rhett* but that's all. Lacks the sinister sex considered absolutely essential to a great performance.

Warner Baxter has surprising support from Atlanta and the deep South. Is the best "sympathy" actor in the race. His recent sock hit in "To Mary—With Love" is considered an apt build-up. Warner has the strong support of all who picture *Rhett Butler* as a man who suffered and suffered. Is keeping his fingers crossed day and night because if he landed it would be "In Old Arizona" all over again for him. His contract, of course, is with Twentieth Century-Fox, which makes him eligible. Darryl Zanuck who is a borrower of stars in the talent market wouldn't dare bite the hand that feeds him and keep him locked up in the closet. Warner, too, is about the right age, a little on the oldish side. His weakness, too, is no powerful sex appeal.

Ronald Colman popped into the running through an erroneous press dispatch. But once in has remained a strong contender. Chief advantage is his spot as long term contract star with Selznick International, his decided romantic charm, suavity, age and sympathetic personality. Chief disadvantage his ever-lovin' Britishness, hard for the folks down South to swallow when the story is almost a sectional issue.

Those are the favorites. But Cary Grant, Basil Rathbone, Edward Arnold haven't given up yet.

Now gents—it's your turn.

For *Scarlett O'Hara*—

Tallulah Bankhead—shared the same bum steer announce- [PLEASE TURN TO PAGE 350]

SCARLETT O'HARAS

Bette Davis, Hollywood's choice, but in the dog house now

Margaret Sullavan, a success in a former Civil War drama

GABLE AS RHETT

Drawings by Vincentini

PHOTOPLAY THROWS ITS HAT IN THE RING

Herewith we enter the Great Casting Battle of "Gone with the Wind," because to our mind there is but one Rhett—Clark Gable. So sure were we of our choice that we had Vincentini paint this portrait of Clark as we see him in the rôle: cool, impertinent, utterly charming. We like all the other handsome actors mentioned as Rhett—only we don't want them as Rhett. We want Gable and we're going to stick to that regardless

1889

Light up fifty candles on the cinema's birthday cake! My, how the baby has grown! From kinetoscope to television—and from kiss to kiss—well, you'd hardly recognize that little peep show which was such a sensation in 1889, when Edison invented it, but don't tell us you can't recognize a kiss when you see one!

TELEVISION TONIGHT.

People were simply scandalized by the daring of May Irwin and John C. Rice. Can you blame us for waiting breathlessly to see what television will bring?

The touching little opus at the upper right, daringly titled "The Kiss," was quite a shocker in its day— Wonder what they would have thought of Hedy Lamarr and Robert Taylor in "Lady of the Tropics"?

1939

JUBILEE!

CLOUDS OVER HOLLYWOOD

"**W**AR declared!" The words struck like a bombshell in the midst of Hollywood, uniting in one great bond of sympathy the many nationalities in the Melting Pot of the entertainment world.

The crowds were laughing as they emerged from the première of "The Women," gay with the sparkle of watching a gay, sparkling picture, happy with that sense of well-being within the industry which comes from the knowledge that another hit is born. Then, as they reached the street, the newsboys' cries reached their ears.

A stunned moment before the full impact of the news struck home. Bitter silence as realization came. Then a growing murmur of restlessness and fear and heartache for the many strangers within the gates who for so long now had been no longer strangers.

"What of Boyer?" "What of Niven?" "And Richard Greene?"

What of Niven, indeed? David was to be star in Sam Goldwyn's production of "Raffles." The goal he had worked toward for so long was his at last. And the next day it was over. The British Consul had handed him the papers from England that said, "Stand by." Whereupon Mr. Goldwyn speeded up production on "Raffles", so that David's scenes could be completed before he leaves.

What of Boyer? Charles, a member of the officers' reserve in France and now in his native country, has offered his services.

And the others? We spoke directly to British Consul Holliday in Los Angeles and this was the word he gave us: "The only man summoned to service is David Niven, reserve officer. No other Englishman in Hollywood can be summoned to service as long as he remains in a neutral country. If he wishes to enlist, he must leave American soil for Canada or England to do so."

There's Richard Greene. Twentieth Century-Fox is going right ahead with the plans for his next picture, "Little Old New York," but—

There's Alan Mowbray, president of the British United Service Club in Los Angeles and now working unofficially as aide to the British Consul. Alan says, "At the moment England seems to have all the men it needs, but I have already offered my services."

And there are Canadian-born Walter Pidgeon and British-born Basil Rathbone, both veterans of the last war. There's Basil's son, Rodion. There are Donald Crisp and Sir Cedric Hardwicke, reserve officers, not yet summoned. Ronald Colman is past the war age and Herbert Marshall is still bearing the marks of his wounds in the previous great conflict. George Brent, Victor McLaglen, Ray Milland and Claude Rains all have their final naturalization papers. The status of Errol Flynn, who has not received his final papers yet, is not clear.

But there are Cary Grant, Leslie Howard, Laurence Olivier, John Loder, bridegroom Brian Aherne, Charles Laughton, Raymond Massey, and so many others who would be sorely missed.

Hollywood, so often a little world within itself, a little world of ambition and desire and a thousand internal problems peculiar to its own profession, is face to face with grim reality. Hollywood, like all the rest of an anguished world, can only wait—and hope.

---

nic face, Frantz, who for all his name is as American as grid-r to do the great piano concer-movies ... I rushed down to ter Jeanette's party and there e plays in "Balalaika" ... he l role, but, to rantz tempera-makes up for ventional male Robert Taylor omeness helps, . Gable, Power, fine actor Cary n actor can get too, as witness ney and many r his playing at the piano te recital in the oom that lasted hours and that from Bach to z has that same his music that nna Durbin ... lity and beauty lse but in Hol-u find a person s still an "Un-

f Deanna and ad missed the Star Maker," by week end, let's ou, as a mem-ywood patrol, , in the person Paramount has another Dur-ittle girl she is, , with a good nfair to her to Durbin" label r develop along own talent, as Judy Garland t "second" her Durbin stands heartwarming st of "The Star partment can't despite Bing y smoothie, a nes, and Laura proves anew per can make ound funny, just by knowing

make it so ... but "The Star nother proof that no matter ents a picture has, you must first ... there is no story at Maker" and, therefore, it drags y, there is no story, or what es a jumbled, leaden mass, in Comes" ... and, therefore, warmth and the lovely devices nd Charles Boyer's acting are why, does Hollywood do that?

Just at the moment that you get that "down" feeling about pictures, however, a couple of delights come along ... two such varied pictures but each of them so very thrilling for very different reasons ... the first, "The Under-Pup" with Joe Pasternak's new musical discovery, Gloria Jean, and Twentieth Century-Fox's gigantic spectacle "The Rains Came" ... being deluged lately with musical child discoveries I wasn't too excited about seeing little Miss Jean but the very first glimpse of her, healthy, ebullient, smiling, and she was at once as much everybody's younger daughter or sub-deb girl friend as Mickey Rooney is everybody's son or

---

Myrna Loy and George Brent, the very finest performance of l cost a fortune ... the kind of won't be seeing for a while now over the world ... its greatne not alone in the sum of all thes as it does in th itual message I'm sure "The didn't cost a thi Rains Came" co wonderful busin ble of producir ... at such a too. ...

NATURALLY common with troubled world, the horrible ev ... but do not t the reports that has, by this con its foreign earnii be cut down, ve duced, made nothing of the happen ... have to cut it will not cut o values ... but scious of its du ... the produc the actors of Hc day that more tl produce enterta us, so luckily happy ... and tragic people o ageous by at le the release of dreams. ...

THUS in all th stantly changing wood a few thir stant ... Garb fashion show at shire ... not a went, that is by small group of who wouldn't h buttercup, but h scenes, protectec guards ... "mystery" rema when she leave pursues her, and gets a pictur usual, he is the only camerama the picture, though they all war it on Page 61) ... so the Fin nique stays unimpaired over so ... and from England comes v Shearer, quite as usual, will get man most in demand by the wc picture ... it will be Rober Donat this time ... but Norma he was first being fought over by ... that is, before he was the give the orders on the casti Tyrone Power ditto ... so s

"Really, I'm not in the mood today, Mr. Director. My Pekingese is indisposed"

"Beggin' your pardon, madame. Shall we dust Mr. Gable this morning?"

" —and when Jackie Cooper cries it just breaks me all up"

"And then again —maybe it's the kind of malt you use"

Garbo-Maniacs

[CONTINUED FROM PAGE 4]

Not long ago our Miss Lois Shirley wrote a simple, kindly story in PHOTOPLAY about Greta and her double, one Miss De Vorak. Lois' article was friendly in the extreme. She simply retailed what nearly everybody knows—namely, that the star is remote, retiring, unsocial, unfashionable in dress—and she said it all in no carping spirit.

And what happened? PHOTOPLAY was buried alive under a terrific avalanche of denunciatory mail. Not even my long nose stuck out of the mountain of missives which denounced Miss Shirley, Editor Quirk, the magazine, its hired hands and anyone who even hinted that Garbo lacked one attribute of utter and complete perfection.

I'LL quote from some. This is from a man in Oakland, Calif.:

"I like Greta Garbo for her simplicity and old-fashioned ways. . . . Keep up the good work, Miss Garbo. Lead your simple life, and remember—there will always be a critic."

From a young lady in Ruleville, Miss.:

"If Greta is cold, aloof and mysterious, this is entirely a Garbo trait. . . . I love to think of her as being mysterious. The public loves Greta Garbo with all her faults—and there can be no substitute."

From a gentleman in Berkeley, Calif.:

"You certainly slammed Greta Garbo in the August issue of PHOTOPLAY for not dressing up and going around showing off like the rest of the so-called stars. Garbo is far too clever for that. She is a genius, and does not have to dress to attract attention. . . . How happy her mother would be if she knew how good her girl was, out here all by herself. I wonder how many young girls in Hollywood are as respectable in private life as this great star, Greta Garbo?"

From a miss in Louisville, Ky., heart of the Blue Grass:

"Of all the stupid people I ever heard of, Lois Shirley takes the cake. I never had a favorite until I saw Greta Garbo. She is my ideal—she is wonderful. The thing that bores half these so-called writers is the fact that Greta Garbo minds her own business and doesn't let everyone in on her affairs. My own opinion is that Jack Gilbert married Ina Claire because he couldn't get Greta Garbo—meaning no disrespect to Miss Claire. Three cheers for Greta Garbo!"

And, most astonishing of all, this—from the wife of a druggist in Kansas City:

"I suppose all of us have a foolish wish that can never come true. Mine is to shake the hand of Garbo the Great. Have we not many Claras, Crawfords and Pages? We have one God—also one Garbo!"

WELL, there you are. Those, and a hundred like them, were stirred up by a simple little story containing nothing that hadn't been printed before a score of times about the Stockholm siren.

And what about Garbo?

The facts are just the same, but nobody cares. She can dress as she darn pleases, and does. If she wants to wear twenty yards of opaque cheese cloth to a formal gathering, it's quite all right with us. In the greatest scene Garbo ever played—the renunciation sequence in "A Woman of Affairs"—she wore a slouchy old tweed suit and a squashy felt hat. She never looked more mysterious, more alluring, and she never acted with greater authority or arrogant power.

It is probable that in the whole history of the world no artist ever grew to such great glory on utter heedlessness of what anybody thinks, says or writes.

After hours of speculation on her reactions to her life and art and the funny world around her, I have come to the conclusion that Greta Garbo simply does not care one single hoot in a Nebraska twister.

She has her job, her maid, her comfortable slippers, her windows looking out upon the sea.

She is the one great queen of the screen who not only has never courted public favor, but has actually fought to a standstill all attempts to haul her into the limelight.

Where others scrabble and squall for notice, submitting to photographers and the pawing

This eight-year-old youngster may soon be as famous as her name. She's called Mitzi and she was headlining in vaudeville when Paramount signed her for talkies. The first kid so contracted for

of the herd, Garbo crawls into a hole and pulls the hole in after her.

Whether it is a trick or whether it is the nature of the lady, it is absolute perfection. Where others leave off, she begins.

More, Garbo is the one great star who has attained unique power and public interest without one lovable screen trait.

Far from being emotionally appealing in any way, she is cinematically heedless, cold, arrogant.

I have even watched some of her magnificent scenes which seemed almost insulting to her fellow actors and to her enormous audiences.

And from her, we take it, bat an eye, gape and love it. For she is Garbo.

Garbo and her work, in addition to being tremendous rousers of men, have more women adorers than any male star of the screen. Women flock to her pictures, to wonder, admire, gasp and copy. In every hamlet of the country slink and posture a score of incipient Garbos.

For every girl child who kicks up like a Velez, a dozen whiten their faces and gaze through half-closed eyes upon a tiresome, boresome world.

And I, a calloused old picture reviewer filled with scars and aches, scuttle to her pictures

as fast as they come and sit in a daze as that astonishing figure goes about its cinematic business.

For Garbo, in her own quaint way, is an undoubted genius—one of the three or four surviving in American motion pictures. She conquers as much by what she leaves undone as by what she does, and her odd beauty has that weird, intangible quality that fascinates the beholder and makes dreamless men dream dreams.

Pardon a little personality, it adorns the tale.

I know a girl who is a calm, cool New Yorker, a trifle blasé around the edges. She meets the great and the near-great and never throws even a mild fit. Yet this Garbo girl puts her in a spasm. She snoozes through talkie after talkie, no matter how loudly the actors bellow, but she dragged me twice to see "A Woman of Affairs" and is still pursuing that Garbo opera into obscure neighborhood theaters, up blind alleys.

IN Hollywood she went Garbo-wild. Metro-Goldwyn put a huge, fire-snorting motor at her service, like a fire truck, and whenever this girl heard that Garbo was on location she jumped into the car and lit out in pursuit, cut-out open and siren screaming. The day she jimmied her way onto the Garbo set in Culver City went down in her history along with the day she got her first proposal and the day she got a bad break and met me.

She has a better collection of Garbo photographs than M-G-M, and I am under daily orders to steal more—from bent old ladies if necessary.

I drag this in to show what the Greta can do to a sophisticated New York gal who knows her Menckens and Nathans. Garbo is no respecter of persons.

The cream of the jest is, of course, that nobody knows exactly what Garbo is all about.

Reporters are poison to her, and though they chase her up hill and down canyon, they seldom get close enough to her to see more than a hank of yellow hair scooting down the cellar stairs.

Naturally, Hollywood is always alive with talk about her, but much of it is probably wild shooting from the hip.

Stories that appear about her in magazines and newspapers are, with few exceptions, pipe dreams or a dreary and sentimental rehashing of all the old tales. During the trying times of the Gilbert marriage to Claire, Garbo used excellent taste and strategy. To all the reporters who came within gunshot while she was on location at Catalina she said absolutely nothing, with her usual bland eloquence. One young sprout, it is said, broke her down momentarily—but that story has never been printed and probably never will.

GARBO, in spite of gabble and gossip, is always largely conjecture.

My hat is off to her. Not only is she a sizable artist—I have a feeling that she must be, in a sense, a great woman. She has licked the Hollywood racket to a pale frazzle. She has made almost no mistakes, personally or professionally.

She is one of the few people in the world who do exactly as they please. But—she makes millions like it.

She slouches along her own sweet way, and even her slouch is a regal gait to those who idolize her.

I smile skeptically at the odd spectacle of Greta Garbo, and yet I genuflect in admiration. As the race of queens dies out and is replaced by ordinary erring, faulty, frail men and women, she alone remains—the greatest and loneliest of a mighty line.

Exploding the Garbo Myth

[CONTINUED FROM PAGE 7]

that usually characterizes as small a community as Hollywood was uttered. Garbo came. A hush fell across the group. She completely wet blanketed the crowd. She was obviously bored and went home early. She literally said and did nothing.

I have talked to many, many people about Garbo, people who know her intimately (and there are more of them than the stories about her would lead you to believe) and I have yet to have one of them give me the slightest evidence that her silences are a mask of deep thought.

Now she does have *something* on the screen. She's not had so much since talking pictures (with the exception of "Anna Christie," a ready-made part) for the reason that the talkies require a new technique which Garbo can not easily learn. But in the silent days, and later, perhaps, too, there was something to whet the romantic appetites of all those millions of fans who go to see her, who adore her, who become maniacal over her.

As a person I can only gather that she is very sweet to her friends and both stubborn and petulant on the set, that she's done a lot of nice things for people, and that she is a shrewd business woman who keeps mysterious because she knows her limitations and because she is bored (as most of us are) when she's with people who are over her head. Oh sure, I may be wrong. I may not be mystic, nor psychic, nor attune enough to get her.

ON the screen—well, I believe that it's a trick. That something about those lack lustre eyes, that sullen mouth, that high brow, that pale, clay-like skin appeals to the imaginations of people. Rudolph Valentino had a dead nerve in one eyelid. It gave that eyelid a droop. And a nice, wholesome, Italian boy became the sinister, mysterious dream lover of a million women.

Garbo appeals in the same way. I do not want to hurt her, for she does care about the things written of her and she reads them, yet she must realize that her personality has now become public property and the facts must be met if we're to keep ourselves honest. Mind you—Garbo's a nice girl. No criticism can affect her while she makes good pictures. She's invariably lovely and kind to the new actors and actresses who work with her. She is touched by illness and sadness and expresses herself in flowers and gifts to those who are ill or sad.

But the Garbo legend is a myth—and don't let anybody tell you anything else. And her "great art" is something quite outside herself like the art of Clara Bow and Lupe Velez and other emotional machines.

Garbo vs. Dietrich

[CONTINUED FROM PAGE 15]

Dietrich may be a good actress, a beautiful woman and all that, but please understand right now that no one can be compared with Greta Garbo. Anything she does is all right with me—and fifty million others. She is the greatest and most wonderful woman of all time!" You can gather, from this tiny assortment from a great batch, the divine madness that grips the true worshipper of that amazing Swedish girl. Let us turn to the less perturbed section of the populace—the milder spirits whose judgment is settled and whose souls are more serene.

MR. J. V. K., of Cumberland, Ky., pours some oil on the roiled and stormy waters: "How could anyone get mixed up on this Garbo-Dietrich situation? Both Dietrich and Garbo can speak the same language, have the same likes and mysteries. Why not let them alone and let them become friends? Garbo is so much like Marlene Dietrich, and Dietrich so much like Greta that I am sure they would become fast friends."

A hopeful note is struck by Miss E. B., of Henderson, Tex.:

"I believe all the Garbo fans will like Miss Dietrich. She isn't trying to take Garbo's throne. She merely wants another one beside it."

And Mr. J. B., of River Forest, Ill., is a little bored with it all:

"Why this everlasting bringing-up of the 'new menace to Garbo's throne' idea? But since another 'new menace' has again come up, let's give the new girl a break. I am, of course, also a Garbo fan. But I'm not a narrow-minded maniac. Let there be (and here Mr. B. grows ironical) one God, one Caesar, one Lincoln, one Napoleon, one Mickey Mouse, *one Garbo.* But why not also *one Marlene Dietrich?*"

And Mr. J. B. strikes the keynote! He points the way to peace! Why not one Dietrich, indeed?

After all, can Marlene help it if she looks something like the Queen of Culver City?

Is Hollywood only large enough for one beautiful girl who employs restraint and whose screen personality is alive with the glamor that gives certain actresses of stage and screen their true greatness as public magnets?

I answer my own question. Certainly not.

And may I point out that the tricks, attitudes and methods of *la* Dietrich are less Garboesque than they are European? Let us, in this moment of armistice, remember that Garbo is the only European trouper to attain great Hollywood eminence since Negri's time, and that's long ago, as *tempus fugits.*

But there's no need of getting deep-dish about this war. We should get the boys and girls out of the trenches by Lincoln's birthday—nay, they should be out now, cooling off their fevered typewriters and turning to the productive arts of peace.

Miss Dietrich's "Morocco" was a hit. The country's fans and critics gave her a nice send-off. They welcomed her as a distinct personality—a fresh gift to the American screen. Great Caesar's perambulating ghost, isn't the American motion picture big enough to support two foreign ladies who drip personality, even though one is a tweedish Swedish divinity named Garbo?

As soon as Marlene had finished "Morocco," she was set at "Dishonored" by the ardent Von Sternberg, this time with big Vic McLaglen opposite. This done, she set off for Germany to see her little daughter, for whom she had been pining. She left behind her the dawn of a first-rate American reputation, born amid the thunders and alarms of a one-sided war.

God willing, she'll be back—back, I hope, in peace. She's a fine actress, this lush Teuton with the slumbrous eyes. We need her. Even the Garbo-maniacs need her, as they'll realize as soon as they cool off and discover that Marlene is no copy-cat trying to steal thrones at night. Garbo's Garbo and Dietrich's Dietrich, and thank Heaven for both. That's the attitude, and that is what will happen.

You are cordially invited to attend a big shenanigan I am promoting for the spring drinking season.

It is to be held at Madison Square Garden, New York City—a banquet seating as many as can be herded in. At one end of the table will be a throne for Greta Garbo—at the other a throne for Marlene Dietrich. Each will be exactly the same size, and contain as many diamonds, rubies, emeralds and sapphires.

A HUNDRED flappers, dressed in white and carrying olive branches and autographed photographs, will attend each monarch. In between will be Mr. and Mrs. John H. Fan and the little Fans. Each will have one eye on Marlene and one on Greta, who will both be smiling, whatever the cost.

Paramount will furnish a band to play at one end of the hall—Metro-Goldwyn-Mayer will hire one to tootle at the other.

At the proper moment, I shall rise with a glass of pop in each hand. Bowing simultaneously to both thrones (a very good trick if I can do it) I shall propose the toast, "The Queens, God bless them!" and will then drink from both tumblers at once. (Another good trick. I learned it in India from a Swami.)

And you all will drink it too—even the wildest of you Garbo-maniacs.

Hush now—nobody's trying to steal your baby's throne!

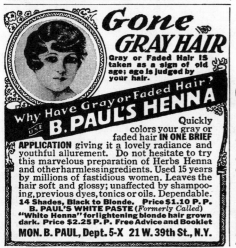

Adrian Answers 20 Questions on Garbo

[CONTINUED FROM PAGE 11]

know that a crowd will gather to look at an elephant walk up a gang plank as readily as it will to see a movie star. If you happen not to like being stared at, photographed and being talked to in front of hundreds of people, you would probably try to avoid the discomfort, if you possibly could.

Unfortunately for Garbo, she is rarely able to make an exit or an entrance into any country inconspicuously, because of passports, etc. If she were able to do so, I'm sure her goings and comings would be a joy to her instead of a horror. It isn't because she has any desire to ignore "her public." She prefers them to be interested in her on the screen, rather than in her personal life.

THIS, perhaps, is a very extraordinary quality for a celebrity to have. Most of them take to adoring crowds like a duck does to water. But because one comes along and severs herself from the crowd, is no reason why it should irritate so many people.

Q.—Since large numbers of people are bored with this mysterious propaganda of Garbo's, why does she allow it to go on, and does she approve of it?

A.—Once again it is not mysterious propaganda, any more than a person would be considered mysterious if he had a desire to travel from one city to another without reporters and a battery of cameras following him. The fact that she desires to live a private life of her own has made "mysterious propaganda." She herself is the last person in the world to approve of it or desire it.

Q.—Why does Garbo want to be alone?

A.—For the same reason, probably, that thousands of other people in the world want to be alone. It is her personal desire. You know anyone who keeps away from the tendency of group thinking is usually misunderstood, disliked, mistrusted or considered odd. Surely if she finds she cannot have the privacy and the pleasure of being unnoticed in public that the majority of us have, she has a perfect right to have that, wherever else she can find it.

Q.—What is Garbo like socially?

A.—She's shy, at times full of a great deal of fun, loves to listen to stories, but she has no curiosity about the private lives of celebrities. She prefers to judge them entirely by their performance or the thing they are giving to the world. If a man paints a great picture, she is not at all interested whether he's been married four times and why.

Q.—What does Garbo's private wardrobe consist of?

A.—Her wardrobe consists of tailored suits, various top coats of the sport variety, sweaters, slacks, berets, sport hats, stocking caps (with visors that fit over them) and sports shoes. I don't think she has an evening gown and if she has I'm sure she has never worn it. She also has several fur coats.

Q.—Why have you given her so many odd hats to wear and does she like them?

A.—Garbo isn't very fond of the fashionable hat of the moment. Nor is she fond of the fashionable hairdress. As she does not wear her hair in a way that suits the current hats and is very fond of personal-looking ones they are apt to appear rather unusual to the eyes accustomed to the prevailing mode. The combination of individualistic hat and hair arrange-

ment often gives Garbo a rather extraordinary style effect, which, in itself, is not really extraordinary.

I have noticed that these very hats usually become fashion "Fords" eventually.

Q.—As you know, there are many untrue and ridiculous stories printed about Garbo, written by people who have never seen her. Do you think she resents these stories?

A.—Naturally there are certain stories which are so far-fetched, particularly those of imaginary feuds, that any one would be upset. I don't think she pays a great deal of attention to the others.

Q.—Do you think that many of Garbo's reactions are selfish ones?

A.—I think a great many of them are. But I think they are her own business!

Q.—Does Garbo have a sense of humor?

A.—Yes, I think she has a terrific sense of humor. Most of it is of a very piquant sort that has a kind of whimsical quality. When she happens to be in the mood, she chats at great length about her observations, life and what she feels about it. I remember being particularly amused one day, after having shown her a sketch and taken a great deal of pains to explain why I had designed it for a certain scene—the colors, materials and various other reasons for its being used. During all this time she had remained completely silent but interested.

After I thought I had convinced her, she just said, "Yes." And then with a look of surprise, she said, "GARBO TALKS!" and laughed gaily.

Q.—Of all the pictures you have dressed Garbo for, which clothes interested her the most?

A.—The clothes in "Romance," "Queen Christina" and "Anna Karenina." I think the latter interested her most of all.

Q.—Several times you have been seen out shopping with Garbo. What is she like on these excursions?

A.—She's terribly interested in old brocades, old Spanish wood carvings, etc. She loves a little Spanish street in Los Angeles called Olvera Street, probably because it has some of the old world atmosphere. She adores ridiculous, silly little toys such as painted pigs and stuffed rabbits. She likes to shop but takes a long time to make up her mind about her purchases and is willing to shop a great deal for one object.

Q.—Why did Garbo allow you to photograph her in one of her "Anna Karenina" dresses when she lives in perpetual fear of the candid cameraman?

A.—She knew I was very pleased with a certain organdy dress and I had said to her jokingly, "If you weren't Garbo, I should be down on the set with my camera, making a record of this dress."

She very charmingly answered, "Get your little camera."

Q.—Is Garbo really a beautiful woman?

A.—She is a very beautiful woman, particularly in a sensitive, rather spiritual way. I think her eyes are extraordinary and her eyelashes are extremely long. And I might add—real. She has a beautiful body, slender and athletic. The myth about her large feet should be completely shattered. Probably this has arisen because of the fact that she wears a

comfortable sports shoe most of the time, because she does a great deal of walking. She is usually completely sunburned, rarely ever comes into fittings with her hair combed, never wears makeup except a dark line at the edge of each eyelid. She has lovely teeth, an easy walk, which last she probably has gotten from walking a great deal. She can jump out and into a car faster than anyone I have ever seen in my life—probably because she has done this a great deal also.

Q—In comparison with other women you have worked with, is Garbo so extraordinarily different?

Do you feel she is a person apart or is she another one of the charming women you have to dress?

A.—She is decidedly a woman apart, because she is actually so simple and has not one ounce of affectation. She is at no moment the actress and never gives me the illusion of being one until she is on the set before the lights, actually in the part. The minute that she leaves the set she's a very little girl, completely out of her atmosphere. Because she so consistently lives her life the way she wants to, regardless of criticism or the suggestions of her friends, she cannot help but be different—*because she is*. Not anything mysterious or full of hokum, but a terrific individualist, who ruthlessly defends her own code of living, by ignoring outside contact. This may or may not be good for her. That again is a matter of conjecture.

Certainly she doesn't alter from its path and goes her own way, regardless.

Q.—Do you think Garbo would act the way she does, if she were not a movie star?

A.—I think she would. Probably not quite as easily, because she has the power to do as she wishes in a much more high-handed manner than she could if she were in a less-important position in life.

But aren't there a lot of us who would live differently if we could afford to disregard outside opinion and found that we could succeed in doing it.

It's like the little boy who said, "when I grow up, I'm going to eat all the candy I want," and kept his word. Garbo, probably from a child, yearned for as much solitude as she wanted. And she has succeeded in having it against the great odds of human nature which surround her and fight her at every turn.

Q.—How much does friendship mean to Garbo?

A.—I've often wondered. Sometimes I think because she lives so remotely that she appears not to need it as much as most people do. I think, however, that she can be a great friend, provided that the friend can adjust himself or herself to Garbo's particular viewpoint on life.

Q.—Will Garbo think you have talked too much about her after you have answered these twenty questions?

A.—I have no idea whether she will or not. But I feel confident that by answering some of the many questions which are continually asked me, I can better explain that she is a human being with her own right to live her life in her own way—regardless of whether it happens to suit James Jones or Mary Smith. That's all that really matters.

273

Such a Naughty Nero

[CONTINUED FROM PAGE 53]

Be to shift his working schedule with Dick Arlen, that Dick might be free to attend a long-anticipated football game.

Char-lee straightened abruptly. He scowled ferociously at the helpless p.m.

"Rubbish!" he announced crisply. "What do you mean? Writing such confounded nonsense?"

"But, it's true!" the p.m. declared. "And, anyhow, I didn't write it. Frank did."

Snatching up the offending page, Char-lee started menacingly toward the door.

"Frank? Who's Frank? Where's Frank?" He glared at the page and flushed uncomfortably. "This silly thing makes me look like a darn sissy!"

THAT was my introduction to Charles Laughton. A modest man, he has a genuine dislike for fanfare. Is a difficult subject to interview, because he honestly hates to talk about himself.

Paramount's entire personnel, from office boy to president, adores him.

He terrorizes delighted office girls; tucks squealing stenographers under his arm and dashes the full length of the corridor with them; generally upsets the efficiency of the whole organization. And they love it.

When Charlie walks in, the staff automatically declares time out. They crowd around and listen eagerly while he relates, with exaggerated gestures, various amusing incidents of the day. They call him "Buster," and are rewarded with a terrifying scowl, then an infectious chuckle.

Laughton is an actor because he can't help it. Years ago, a chubby youngster sat in the gallery of a London theater, stifling, with difficulty, a wild desire to stop the show and shout down to the puppets on the stage that they were all wrong. Real people didn't act that way. Stomping around, and throwing themselves about. His own technique is vastly different and doubly effective. Extravagant gesturing is no part of him.

Instead, he stands quietly, fulfilling even the most difficult emotional reactions with the mere flick of an eyelash, a slight drooping of the lips. Subtle. Acting supreme.

In the short time he has been with us, Laughton has made the talkie industry sit up on its hind legs, roll over and play dead. And now, with the public clamoring to see more, he merely bows graciously and announces his intention of returning to London.

Producers toss restlessly in their downy beds, scheming frantically on bigger and better ideas to keep this new gold mine from walking out on them. Platinum-plated contracts are being held temptingly before his eyes. But Charlie continues to shake his head regretfully.

"I'm getting stale," he said simply. "They've offered me more money than I ever saw before, to stay here and carry on. But, money isn't the whole thing, if a fellow's stale. I've been working pretty consistently during the seven months I've been here, and I'm tired. Empty.

"I WANT to go back to England for a while. The change will do me good. Set me up. Then, I can come back, go to work, and feel that I'm really giving them what they're paying for. That is, if they still want me."

"They'll want you!" I hastened to assure him. He seemed rather dubious.

"I've been warned that the public will forget me in six months," he said.

Real ability is not forgotten in six months. I told him so.

Furthermore, the producers should appreciate his reluctance to give them anything but

What About Clara Bow?

[CONTINUED FROM PAGE 20]

The procession of eager young men which has marched through her girlhood has tried to leave its mark on her personality.

Clara once complained to an interviewer—

"The trouble with boy friends is that they all want to make you over into something else again. It burns me up—especially as it's me as I am that they fall for!"

Such interference with Clara Bow has done nothing to Clara Bow but make her furious.

For seven years Clara Bow has been feverishly hunting for a love that she could trust—that would stand tests and turn out to be what is hopefully known as "the real thing."

The beaux have come and gone.

THERE was Gilbert Roland. There were Gary Cooper and Victor Fleming. Bob Savage cut his wrists theatrically for "love" of her, and was quickly given his marching orders. There were momentary mentions, in the public prints, of Nino Martino, Bela Lugosi, Rex Bell. There was no printed mention at all of a handsome young Texas doctor—at least, never by name.

The Harry Richman story has been most prolonged. Harry had the glitter of Broadway night life about him.

"Ooh—I love Harry!" squealed Clara in the presence of reporters, early in the game.

And a game it's been. Engaged and not engaged—to be married, and no dice. So it's gone for a year, as thousands moaned.

A lady of the theater, Miss Flo Stanley, declared herself in. Threatening to sue Clara for alienation of Mr. Richman's boyish affections, she expressed the cynical New York view of the matter when she told the press—

"Harry's my man. He doesn't love that little kid. He's only playing with her for the publicity he can get out of it."

Poor little Clara—Clara of Page One!

Rumored attempts at suicide—hospitals for appendicitis and then adhesions—hospital for cut fingers—stepmother trouble, boy trouble, money trouble.

Grief has billowed around that tousled head.

Poor little Clara! Where could she turn? Her father seems to have had little influence. Her boy friends? Special pleaders that have come and gone. A stepmother? Almost her own age.

Her own philosophy, childish in its assumption that she can gather roses and no thorns? It hasn't worked!

At twenty-five she's still adrift. Eight years of hectic existence seem to have taught her little of self-discipline. Still with no workable scheme of life, a woman in years but the irrepressible hoyden of eighteen in her mode of living.

What is immediately before her?

After her last expedition, Clara announced in the press that she was going to be "real quiet and orderly." At the moment of trotting to press, she is.

She's busy—and therefore happy, and not harassed by her moody doubts, searchings and wonderings concerning life and love.

Her Paramount contract expires October 1.

In spite of unfortunate stories and almost tragic publicity, her pictures still make money. She has one of the truest and most wonderfully loyal fan armies in the history of pictures.

She's getting about $3,000 a week at present, and if all goes well, she'll be re-signed for another year at somewhat more.

And that's all the inscrutability of Fate allows us to know of Clara Bow's future.

What a tremendous hullabaloo the life of this big-eyed wonder-child has been, since she first broke upon us in 1922, in "Down to the Sea in Ships"!

She crashed upon the screen at the perfect, exquisite moment!

Dashing, alluring and cinematically untamed, she was flaming youth incarnate—the personification of post-war flapperhood, bewitching, alluring and running hog-wild. All the old taboos and thou-shalt-nots were knocked dead by the new freedom for adolescents.

Clara burst out just in time to be the New Youth's standard-bearer.

Point with Joy or View with Alarm, as you will, that's the truth.

Clara Bow is responsible for a whole race of second-run, imitation Bows that flood the country—a type that now seems to be giving way to the Garbo sort of thing among the infant sophisticates.

This is no "attack" on Clara Bow. It is a prayer and a boost for one of the gayest, youngest, prettiest girls who ever danced across a screen—who gave a new kind of youth to the shadow stage.

I will be a charter member of any "League for the Preservation, Care and Protection of Clara Bow."

But there's no sense in begging the issue, or playing ostrich.

CLARA faces a crisis, and we're all involved in some measure.

She's a woman in years, now, and not a schoolgirl thrust into an unfamiliar spotlight.

She can't continue to gallop off the reservation, and continue to delight us, too. She's stretched out her arms for understanding and help and trust—as have thousands of the rest of us. If she's failed to find them—as have thousands of the rest of us at times—she must develop resources within herself, a spiritual fortress that can defend her against all the varied and cruel assaults of life and destiny.

That's what men and women have to do, as best they can, when human hearts and human hands fail.

And so must Clara Bow. But first she must realize that time and her life in the world have made her a woman, and not a spoiled and wilful child!

---

the best that's in him. His decision marks him as infinitely wise and just.

Studio "red tape" amazes him. When they planned to use an extra's hands, instead of his own, in the close-up shots in "Devil and the Deep," Laughton protested. His hands are expressive, a definite part of his personality.

Why substitute other hands when his own were available?

They told him why. The picture had finished shooting, and salary complications would arise if they used him in the close-up retakes. An extra man would cost only ten dollars.

After much altercation, Charlie succeeded

in convincing them that the money was a minor issue, and the scenes were shot with his hands performing the necessary duties—gratis.

At the door of the publicity office we said goodbye. A stenographer passed us and said, with devilish intent: "Hullo, Buster!" She knew what she would get for that, and Laughton didn't disappoint her.

With a ferocious scowl, he reached out and caught her by the back of the neck.

"Char-lee!" she squealed merrily.

And, as Char-lee swung her under his arm and started down the corridor, I heard for the last time that delightfully infectious chuckle.

Close Up of the Groaner

[CONTINUED FROM PAGE 59]

This should put guest stars at ease on his programs, but a few of them have blown higher than a kite just thinking of the contrast between Crosby and themselves.

There is a belief that the day Crosby learns he is washed up in radio and pictures he will say, "Oh," and go home and eat.

His home life is a pleasant turmoil of domesticity. Fresh from his crooning, he will be confronted at the door with a report of his four sons' wrongdoings. He may spank one, put two to bed and forbid the fourth to play "Snow White" records on the phonograph. Sometimes, at the height of a feud, the boys must be fed in separate rooms. There is always noise and a visitor finds himself involuntarily ducking.

Gary, the eldest son, is almost as deep-voiced as his father and considers himself a man. If permitted, he would rule the brood with an iron hand—the same iron hand that has left its mark on furniture and walls alike without partiality. Gary has a girl but remains discreetly silent about her unless giddy with coca-cola.

During the filming of "Sing, You Sinners" the boys were brought to visit their father on location. They sat in a row, respectful and quiet, watching preparations for a scene. Then Bing started acting. Gary jumped to his feet and poked the twins. "Hey," he said derisively, "look at the old man!"

The shocked nurse elbowed Gary into a sitting position. "Don't talk like that," she admonished sharply.

"Aw," said Gary, "he knows he's no good."

Considerate to a fault sometimes, The Groaner has drastic reversals. He has let a production unit twiddle its thumbs while he watched a horse race. He has refused to work unless an unemployed property boy is hired. He would not start a picture unless a certain cameraman was used. The result was that the gratified individual lighted Bing so brilliantly in scenes that he stood out like a well-polished loving cup.

I have seen his patience tried. He is proud of his ranch home near Del Mar and the interior is spotless. There were several of us warming ourselves over a bottle after a pack trip into the mountains and finally one of the men aimed a hunting knife at the living room door. The knife glanced and knocked a large chip from the painted surface. Then somebody else picked up the knife and threw it at the door. That was the start of a contest. Bing sat watching, quietly. After a while he went outside and I

followed.

"That's a lousy trick in there," I said.

"They're just having fun," said Bing.

"It's nice of you to take it this way," I said. "If it were my house, I'd be sore."

"I am sore," said Bing.

"Then why don't you do something?"

"They're just having fun."

We went inside. The door was a mess and they were still throwing. Bing picked up the knife and held it a moment, and I was waiting. Then he threw the knife and it lodged in the door.

"That's the way to do it," he said.

Bing's Toluca Lake house is a spacious colonial affair, the second he has built in the district. Before the first house was built, he bought the available land surrounding it. Soon he sold both the land and the house and bought more property near by. If the profit from the land didn't pay for both houses, I'll eat one of his Hawaiian shirts.

He is incorporated for radio, pictures, phonograph records, race track activities and several lesser ventures. He is on the board of directors of many strange things, including an eating club. The incorporation employs two of his brothers and his father. I once worked for the outfit as a radio writer, receiving my contract from one brother, my checks from the other and an autographed picture of Bing from his pa.

"Did you ever think Bing would amount to anything?" I asked the father.

"Well," he said, "he was all right."

Bing's mother is solid American. She doesn't like to see Bing drink in a picture but she lives in her own house with the father where she won't interfere with anything. She goes to Bing's race track with her husband, and they sit in Bing's box, studying their form sheets. They look at the tips from Bing's stable and usually discard them. Then they discuss the merits of all horses. Finally the mother says she will split a two-dollar bet with the father. He talks about horses some more and goes to make the bet. It is too late.

Bing's wife, Dixie, picks her friends and sticks with them. Most of them are holdovers from the early days and Hollywood doesn't know them. That's all right with her, and it's all right with the friends.

But what I started to say is that Bing as an actor didn't interest me until I realized that off the screen, basically, he is the small-town boy who loves the full life and hates work and all its routine and will never—let him live three hundred years—amount to a row of bad peas.

It is not my fault that even God sometimes is guilty of miscasting.

Answers to cut puzzles on pages 174 and 175: Clara Bow, Janet Gaynor, Eleanor Boardman, Esther Ralston, Richard Barthelmess, Gary Cooper, Richard Dix and Richard Arlen.

Is Hepburn Killing Her Own Career?

[CONTINUED FROM PAGE 51]

Katharine Hepburn was welcomed to the screen with more genuine enthusiasm and good wishes than any actress had received for years. Hollywood—the public—believed it saw genius budding and prepared a reverent salaam to a new idol.

Hepburn replied by impudently thumbing her nose and indulging in a succession of cute caprices, made to order for a boarding school problem child rather than an artist engaged in a serious art.

At first they were amusing, even attractive, and everyone murmured "Cute!" and smiled tolerantly when she indicated that being a film star was a great big barrelhouse gag to her.

But Hepburn held her one-ring circus too long and mixed in too many acts. She was the daring young gal on the flying trapeze, she was the clown and the prima donna with a Garbo-complex—all at the same time. She was the great "What-Is-It?"

Katharine Hepburn's first great mistake has been her treatment of the press. Her idea, unmistakably conveyed, has been that La Hepburn's art was enough—its own justification and its own explanation. She was above the printed word and would have none of it—and none of its lowly minions. Ho-hum. Ho-ho-hum. Kings and potentates with armies and gold have learned better than that.

If she had any dignity or any sincerity she might have got away with it at that. Garbo has, but Garbo is sincere in her extreme desire for seclusion. Even the press realized and respected that. Even if it didn't the quiet and consistent dignity with which Garbo goes about her cloistered campaign is enough to enlist the respect of the world.

The result—what do you read, what have you read about Katharine Hepburn? Any intelligent, earnest portraits of her? Any sympathetic analyses—any presentations of the worth-while sides of her makeup?

Not often. Just the gags, the eccentricities, the scatterbrain anecdotes and stories, the pranks—the things which make readers mutter, "Why doesn't she grow up?" and pass by her blazing name on the theater marquees with a "So what?"—regardless of her personality and her talent on the screen. Reporters resented her treatment of them and sometimes wilfully, but more often, unconsciously, got back at her by making her seem silly.

And that is tragic because Katharine Hepburn *is* sincere about her work, and an earnest, democratic and fair workman on the set.

The self-laid smoke screen of her particular type of temperament (a greatly overworked word in Hollywood) erected a barrier between her and her leading men, which can't be too good for her pictures. Both John Beal and Fred MacMurray were nervous as cats when they knew they were to play with her. Both got over it when after a few days they discovered that the real Hepburn wasn't such a terror as was commonly believed.

To this day you will have a hard time convincing anyone in Hollywood that the reason Francis Lederer walked out of "Break of Hearts" wasn't a temperamental break with Hepburn. As a matter of fact, it had nothing to do with Hepburn. Lederer couldn't agree with the director about the interpretation of his rôle.

The resentment against Katharine Hepburn which has piled up behind the dam for many months and is now apparently spilling over is the same sort of resentment which piled up against Constance Bennett for several years, fed by the same tiny trickling streams.

Long before they got into print, Hollywood whispered about the petty things, the little things which did not portray the real Connie, but which taken altogether, succeeded in presenting her to those who saw her films as a pretty disagreeable person.

Connie berating a photographer, Connie ritzing a rival, Connie in a bickering quarrel with her next door neighbor over a wooden fence. Connie doing this and that bit of trivia which made those who didn't know her at all tell themselves, "She must be a hell-cat." Producers, set-workers, other actors began resenting Connie, often without knowing why, but the resentment got into the stories written for her, the pictures made with her. It seeped through to the public who buy the tickets. It cost her a lot of her glamour.

A famous and glamorous star of the silent era found herself at the peak of a popularity from which it seemed (to her) nothing could dislodge her.

She said as much, boldly, when a few of those who had helped her rise asked her reasonable favors, were refused, and accused her of "going grand."

"What if I am?" was her attitude. "I'm at the top. I can afford to. I don't need you any more."

The stories got around. From that time on she went steadily down. Desperately, when the reason finally dawned, she hired a "public relations counsel." But then it was too late.

She had committed career suicide.

Like any other form of self-destruction, this strangest of all strange Hollywood phenomena—star suicide—which is, of course, intangible, subconsious, and not always possible to explain, though it seems to work out, takes different forms.

Nancy Carroll allowed her chip-on-shoulder Irish nature to make her one of the most unpopular stars ever to step on a set.

Nancy was one of the best bets Paramount had at one time, then, for no evident reason her popularity at the box-office dimmed and practically winked out.

Nancy was notoriously hard to please—and still is. She made it hard for the people who worked with her. She had the flare-up type of temperament—and possibly that temperament irritated all who came in contact with her, and swore to get even.

It takes a great many people besides the star to make a successful picture. A great many little people seldom seen or heard about. Still photographers, hair-dressers, wardrobe women and the like. The "crew" are a close fraternity. They wouldn't lie down on their jobs even with a star they could willingly choke—but there is bound to be an undercurrent of resentment which militates against a bad-tempered star.

It can show in a picture. In a roundabout way it can kill a career.

Katharine Hepburn has a good reputation with the people who work with her on the set. Most of them like her. Most of them like Margaret Sullavan, too, another current short-sighted *enfant terrible* who has been accused of aping Hepburn's "act."

But Sullavan, like Hepburn, has been guilty of rudely treading on the toes of the people who can and would like to present her to the world which supports her salary in a favorable light. So they are forced to describe only the face she shows them—which is defiant.

She doesn't seem to know that every time she sticks out her tongue several thousands of her admirers are quite likely to stick out their tongues right back at her.

Margaret wages a continual battle with the publicity department of her studio, whose main concern is to save her skin with the public.

To snap a photograph which will further her fame they must coax and cajole her. To protect her they must plead with her. To do her a favor they must ask a favor. Even publicity men can get tired of that. Gradually an attitude, unstudied, of "Oh, nuts" results. The breaks go to those who accept them graciously.

Not long ago it was necessary for the publicity department at Universal to get in touch with Margaret to protect her from some adverse publicity. They called her home for days, were told she wasn't in. They left messages, word for her to call, sent telegrams. No response.

Finally, days later, she showed up at the studio. They told her they had been trying desperately to reach her.

"I know it," she said, "I was there all the time."

Stories such as this abound about Sullavan's and Hepburn's ring-around-the-rosy tactics, their sometime pointless and frequently exasperating jokes at the expense of those who are working in their interests. The question is —has it done either of them any good?

Sullavan's last picture, "The Good Fairy," broke no theater box-office records. And Frank Morgan drew most of the praise.

It doesn't seem at all unreasonable to wonder what can be the cause of Ann Harding's sinking spell in popularity. Possibly it is her exclusiveness.

It is only natural to suspect that Jean Arthur, now back for her third try at screen success, may bump into the fate of her first two trips unless she curbs the temper displayed on a set recently, when she angrily ripped off a costume which her director insisted on and stamped it on the floor.

By the same token, the remarkable rise of Claudette Colbert and the long sustained popularity of Marion Davies may have something to do with the fact that both are universally beloved by everyone who has anything to do with their careers. Both spurn bizarre acts, caprices, theatrical fever fits.

Good manners, sincerity, a touch of humanity—that would seem to be the diet—all else being equal—which determines a long life for a Hollywood star.

But, of course, every day there are people in perfect health who climb to the tops of high bridges, admire the view below—and jump off.

They seem to like it.

Perhaps Hepburn and the current crop of headstrong Terrible Turks rather fancy the idea, too.

One thing is certain—they'll know for sure when they land.

Isn't this a wonderful make-up job? It's Charles Laughton aging dramatically for "Rembrandt"

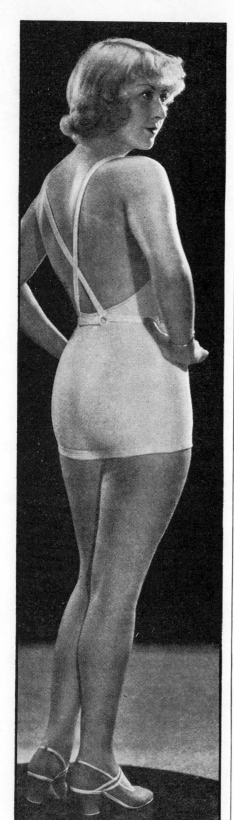

Lots of stars wear swimming suits but few stars wear them as well—or as often—as Joan Blondell. She swims for fun, swims for health, swims at every opportunity. She is wearing the new Jantzen Molded-Fit Formal. It is really three suits in one because it has three distinct back designs: the square back, the cross strap and the necklace tie for sun-bathing

Advertisement

The Girl They Tried to Forget

[CONTINUED FROM PAGE 121]

carrying the good news from Ghent to Aix, that all Hollywood was in a stew of righteous indignation in her behalf, and that she was the most talked of girl in Cinematown.

"Well, I'll be darned," she said.

Then she wanted to know—and this was much more important to her—if I didn't think the auto camp was a pretty cozy little box; and a bargain for the price; and if I could stand lamb chops for dinner; and why couldn't we all breeze up to Ham's night club afterwards; and was it true that Cavalcade had been scratched from the handicap.

Of course, you really can't expect Bette Davis to get all worked up over being a Forgotten Woman. It has happened to her too many times before in Hollywood.

I remember when the studio that first brought her to Hollywood let her languish for months without giving her an outside chance, and then dismissed her, explaining that she had "about as much sex appeal as Slim Summerville."

And I remember how the studio which now has her under contract relegated her to myriad small-time, puny rôles of no opportunity, from which "Of Human Bondage," played on a loan out to RKO, eventually rescued her.

Even after that she had to walk out on a shallow part to gain recognition.

Her rôle in "Of Human Bondage" was of a sort that no other actress of her standing would take for love or money. It was poison to what Hollywood treasures most—glamour.

I KNOW that Warners bitterly objected—at first, actually refused permission—to her playing *Mildred*.

She finally battered them into reluctant consent, but their warning rang in her ears— "You'll destroy any screen following you ever had. You'll never live it down."

She answered with a performance which made people whisper the name of another great actress—Jeanne Eagels.

And yet—at a preview of another of her pictures, I overheard a woman next to me mutter, "There's Bette Davis—that horrible girl!"

That is the sort of thing she must brave to play what she wants to play—such as her murderess in "Fog Over Frisco," and her more recent psychopathic *Lady MacBeth* wife in "Bordertown."

BUT it is her great courage which has allowed little unpretty Bette Davis, with her big rolling eyes, her turned-down mouth and her twisting, slovenly carriage, to shed her ugly duckling screen feathers and become an actress whose slighting today can cause so much concern.

Oddly enough, she once told me that she had gathered her fortitude from the same Jeanne Eagels whose genius she approaches.

Eagels had said, "Never let anyone become such a friend of yours that he can tell you whether you're right or wrong about your life or your career." Bette read it somewhere. It suited her own then nebulous convictions.

And although she has never seen Jeanne Eagels on the stage or the screen, there is a further and more striking coincidence in the fact that the same man, George Arliss, provided the turning point and the inspiration for both their careers.

Arliss, tamed, disciplined and then encouraged the tempestuous Eagels when she played with him on the stage in "Alexander Hamilton." And years later, he called in Bette Davis to give her a part in "The Man Who Played God," when her bags were already packed to leave Hollywood—the first time she was forgotten.

Wouldn't it be surprising if the parallel continued?

Wouldn't it be strange—and also disconcerting to some—if Bette Davis, the little blonde actress they tried to forget but found they couldn't—some day reached the genius of another Jeanne Eagels?

Or maybe she already has—and Hollywood just doesn't know it.

Why Women Go Crazy About Clark Gable

[CONTINUED FROM PAGE 45]

by a greater mystery than her own—a man she cannot understand.

SKILLFULLY, his producers have given him parts that make him enigmatic. He has never been all white, never been all black. Almost every rôle in which he has played holds back, until the denouement, a phase of his character that he has kept concealed. Mystery has been monopolized by women. Clark Gable has stolen one of their most potent weapons and turned it on them.

The characters which he plays today would have been repugnant a few years ago. With one exception, he has played hard-boiled guys, and his success has been based on those parts. Is it not possible that the long series of gangster pictures, making heroes of underworld characters (pardon, Mr. Hays), has led up to a tolerance, then an acceptance, then an admiration, of such men?

And, without any intent to discuss anything political or topical, may there not be an unconscious glorification of the man who, in utter disregard of all law, goes out and gets what he wants at the risk of his neck?

Women love fighting men. Clark Gable has never played the coward nor the weakling. He has been a fighter, whether outside the law as in "Free Soul" or as a Salvation Army worker in "Laughing Sinners."

BUT is Clark Gable all actor? Does he not project something of himself on the screen? He is not, and he does.

For twenty years, boy and man, I have been an observer of the screen; for these sixteen years, come next Michaelmas, as editor of PHOTOPLAY. And I can say truthfully, having had occasion to know most of the famous folks of the screen, that, all in all, no actor can hide his real personality behind greasepaint, make-up, nor art. The camera reads the mind and unmasks the individual.

LIKE AN ALL-TALKING "COVERED WAGON"!

Your Theatre will be playing "The Virginian" soon. Ask when you can see it, and other Paramount Super-Shows of The New Show World — the greatest entertainments of the greatest name in entertainment! "If it's a *Paramount Picture it's the best show in town!"*

ALL THE TENSE DRAMA OF THE BOOK PLUS

Settings of stupendous beauty — where you see and hear thousands of bellowing cattle, cowboys singing as they ride range, gunfights, campfires crackling, hair raising drama, rich humor, warm romance . . . .

"THE VIRGINIAN"

FOUR GREAT STARS: Gary Cooper in his first all-talking role, ideally cast as "The Virginian," Walter Huston, Mary Brian and Richard Arlen. Directed by Victor Fleming. By Owen Wister and Kirk La Shelle.

THE NEW SHOW WORLD IS PARAMOUNT!

"The Virginian" proves it anew! A great story, a great cast, perfect production, marvelous settings, and the most natural sound and dialogue you ever heard! In other words, *A Paramount Picture!*

Imagine a picture as big in scope and drama as "The Covered Wagon" with dialogue throughout and marvelous outdoor sound effects! That's Paramount's all-talking, all-outdoors "The Virginian" — the greatest outdoor drama ever filmed in sound and dialogue!

Paramount Pictures

TUNE IN! Paramount-Publix Radio Hour every Saturday evening, 10-11 P. M. Eastern Time over the Columbia Broadcasting System.

PARAMOUNT FAMOUS LASKY CORP., ADOLPH ZUKOR, PRES., PARAMOUNT BLDG., N. Y.

John
BARRYMORE
*Yesterday a speechless shadow—
To-day a vivid, living person—
thanks to*

VITAPHONE

Until you've heard him in "General Crack" you can but guess at the full force of the flaming personality that is the *real* John Barrymore.

Not figuratively, but literally, John Barrymore "comes to life" in "General Crack".

For here for the first time, *Vitaphone* restores the pent-up power of the thrilling voice that made him the star of stars of the speaking stage... And resplendent scenes in COLOR show you what he really looks like as he storms recklessly into the vortex of cyclonic romance and adventure, breaking heads and hearts and sweeping monarchs from their thrones to suit a gypsy whim!

This tense and virile love story from George Preedy's famous novel, has been dressed by Warner Bros. in extravagantly sumptuous trappings to celebrate this greatest of all *Vitaphone* events.

THE STAR of STARS of the SPEAKING STAGE

in "GENERAL CRACK"
HIS *first* TALKING PICTURE!

A WARNER BROS. & VITAPHONE REG'S TRADE MARK TALKING PICTURE

"*Vitaphone*" is the registered trademark of The Vitaphone Corporation. Color scenes by the Technicolor Process.

"General Crack" is another example of the treats that await you every week at theatres that feature *Vitaphone* pictures, produced exclusively by WARNER BROS. and FIRST NATIONAL

Clark Gable has never been the lady-killer in real life any more than he has on the screen.

He has been a stage actor for years. Starting out from a Pennsylvania Dutch family as a lad he has wandered all over America on his own. He has ridden the brake beams of a freight car. He has known hunger.

He has known women. He has been married twice (three times, some say), so he ought to know something of women. Six years ago, as a small part player on the same lot where he shines today above Jack Gilbert, he was unnoticed.

THEN he returned to the theater under the management of Louis MacLoon, who, two years ago, held him under contract at the lowly figure of $175 a week.

Things went bad and MacLoon was forced to release him because there was no more work in sight.

He again sought work in the movies. This time fate was kind. He got the break.

I do not want to spoil any illusions but I must tell you about the first time I ever saw Clark Gable off the screen. I was lunching in the Metro-Goldwyn-Mayer restaurant in Culver City when he came in.

A particularly effusive and beautiful blonde screen actress rushed up to him and introduced herself.

"Oh, Mr. Gable," she gushed, "I think you are the finest actor on the screen."

I have never seen a man more ill at ease. He looked around appealingly. He stood on one foot, then the other. I felt that under his rough, three-day beard (he was making retakes for "Susan Lenox") he was blushing like a school boy.

"Thanks—ah—yes—thank you," he stammered, "but I'm afraid there are a lot of them on this lot who know the tricks better than I do."

"Oh, but Mr. Gable, everyone knows you are so wonderful—"

"Yes—thanks," he said, "thanks—yes— thank you. I must be back on the set—yes— thank you."

And the big tough-looking guy in the three-day beard rushed out of the restaurant and hid in his dressing-room, lunching on a ham sandwich and a glass of milk.

November Birthdays

November 1—Laura La Plante
November 2—Dennis King
November 4—Don Alvarado, Dixie Lee, Will Rogers
November 5—Joel McCrea
November 7—Mona Maris, Alice Day, Joe Cobb
November 8—Marie Prevost
November 9—Marie Dressler, John Miljan
November 11—Raquel Torres, Roland Young
November 12—Gwen Lee, Jack Oakie
November 13—Eddie Buzzell
November 15—Lewis Stone
November 16—Lawrence Tibbett
November 17—Betty Bronson
November 18—Frances Marion
November 19—Nancy Carroll
November 20—Robert Armstrong, Reginald Denny
November 21—Jobyna Ralston
November 22—Charles Mack
November 25—Helene Chadwick, Margaret Livingston, Vera Reynolds
November 26—Frances Dee
November 29—Mildred Harris, Kay Johnson, Rod LaRocque, Genevieve Tobin
November 30—Jacqueline Logan

What's Happened to Rainer?

[CONTINUED FROM PAGE 61]

weight—I grew very thin—I began to understand things better and when I came back to Hollywood, the studio was most kind and one day we came together and they asked me what it was I wanted.

"I told them, two things. What I wanted from them and what I wanted to give them.

"First, I had to have the chains broken so I would feel freer. So my old contract was broken and they gave me a new one. You are the first to know.

"I work for my studio only six months every year from April to October. Then I return to the stage for six months to act in plays. I am happy, for it gives me back something I needed—my freedom.

"Then I told them what I wanted to give. I wanted to be a girl up there on the screen, not a glamour girl, but a girl of the people, one of the audience with the same problems as they, just as lonely perhaps or just as gay, just as human so they down there can sit forward in their seats as they watch me and say, 'There, that's me. Now let's see how she solves that problem for that is my problem, too.'

"Now since my new contract is signed and I am gaining weight (I have put on eleven pounds) I see now that all the little things I once thought inconsequential are important.

"About interviews? I tell you I am undecided. I cannot handle myself. I say things in such a way they are misquoted. I spill over. Then that is bad. Then I think, no, I won't talk any more and so columnists and writers fling back at me 'High Hat'—'Snob'—'Difficult.' One day I met a reporter who once wrote of me 'High Hat' and I ask her why. You don't know me or how I feel or think. Why do you say 'High Hat' in your column?

" 'Well, you are too hard to get to,' she replied, 'so I judge you are high hat.'

"So there is that problem, too, to work out."

WE spoke of her marriage to the brilliant young author, Clifford Odets.

"We are much alike. We both like to be alone in our work. But outside of work we are so happy to be together.

"It is a good thing we understand each other so well."

A friend who knows Miss Rainer well claims Luise made every effort to ad-

just herself to the strange and bewildering town in which she found herself. At first her loneliness took her within herself. She took long drives alone, and once found herself in Mexico unable to recross the Mexican border until the studio phoned the officials it was all right.

With her accent they were convinced Luise was a spy.

She gave up her small home and took a home in Brentwood near the mountains where she could take walks. It was during this time that she met Clifford Odets. Standing before a simple white bed sheet, on which she herself had pinned garlands of flowers from her garden, she married Odets in her own home.

Today, with hopes restored, Luise lives in a small, unpretentious apartment in Westwood. Her husband, when he can be in Hollywood, shares the simple apartment.

Apple pie for breakfast and music, good music, are her strongest likes— except, of course, children.

She'll attend every child's party into which she can possibly worm her way, and is one of those rarest of rare people who can enter into the mind and understanding of a child.

"Herself a combination of child and woman, it's easy to understand," a friend said of Luise, and went on to tell of a school play her own child had taken part in.

WHEN Luise heard of the play she instantly demanded to be taken. An important dinner date was broken so Luise could sit spellbound in a school auditorium and hungrily drink in the children as they spoke their lines.

Her extreme sensitiveness to those around her is best illustrated by a little incident that took place the night Luise won her second Academy Award.

"Aren't you thrilled?" someone asked her.

"I can only think how much work lies ahead," Luise said, "and how much more responsibility I have.

"Besides," and her eyes suddenly twinkled, "I can't be too happy about it. Over there in the corner sits a woman whose face tells me so plainly, 'Tell me, why did they give it to that one?' "

Did I say her sense of values as well as her sense of humor is restored?

The Madcap Love of the Errol Flynns

[CONTINUED FROM PAGE 63]

tricks—and of course they met, on a luxury liner America-bound!

The golden legend of the Love of Lili and Errol paints us the picture. We can see Lili in the grand saloon of the ship, surrounded by gaping males in claw-hammer coats. The big Irishman notices her and feels his collar catching fire. Elbowing through the throng, he asks her to dance.

Pulling Trick No. 1 out of her coquette bag, she says, "Come back in five minutes." Flynn didn't like this, but he did. Damita, following her plan of campaign, not new but forever good, probably said, "Oh, I'll see you around!" The old gag worked, as it always does, and Flynn said to himself, "I want that." Lili, still besieged by the hopeful horde, said the same internally. Obviously, it couldn't be long—and of course it wasn't!

ONCE in Hollywood, things began to hot up. Damita, then still raking in the blue chips from the studios, took up her film commitments, while Big Boy reported at Warners under a modest salary agreement. And all this time the terrifying type of forest fire love raged with redoubled violence.

Flynn moved helplessly toward matrimony, fighting every step of the way.

"I'm not the sort of chap who ever should marry," he told his friends—and a few days later the beautiful couple was off, helter-skelter, to Yuma, and the halter which now hitches them in the holy bonds.

It was inevitable that they should scuffle, and they did—almost from the take-off. In fact, war correspondents were regularly assigned to cover the Flynn-Damita front, and while ducking strong adjectives they wired their papers of bitter word-battles in which nothing was hurt but the feelings. During the filming of "The Green Light," Flynn packed his elegant English luggage and beat a strategic retreat, only to come back with his arms open and declarations of devotion on his lips.

His big break came when Robert Donat, the British Wonder Man, defaulted on playing the leading rôle in "Captain Blood," cut and tailored to his measure after "Monte Cristo," and the big red apple fell into the lap of Errol. He swashed and buckled through this showy part while women moaned and swooned all over the Republic, and within a week he was a big shot in pictures. Fame and adulation didn't take Big Stuff's clear eyes off the main chance. He merely told Jack Warner, with a convincing ring, that he now sported a very costly wife, and another figure or two was added to the proper end of his pay-check!

Kismet, all this time, was delivering its usual kicks in the derrière. As Flynn rode high, Damita was chuting the chutes out of the cinema picture. The time arrived when no one called her but the grocer. Hollywood experts opine that this shift of fortunes had nothing to do with the subsequent shindies, tears, rages and partings, but to this notion I significantly touch my long nose and wink sourly. Nobody can tell me that a famed and beauteous film star is going to be cut down to an occasional quickie, while her recently unknown spouse zooms to fortune, without suffering severe lacerations of her proud spirit. Within a month, Flynn was a hot shot and lovely Lili was practically nothing but his

wife. I needn't say that these things are very tough indeed to take—especially for a girl who has received the back-scratching and goose-greasing that fell to the lush lot of Damita for so many years.

But Flynn stayed strictly in character. Rich or poor, dim or famous, he was the same husky Irishman, heading in a straight line for what he wanted. He began building a house on an inaccessible mountain-top, surrounded by wild beasts and birds of the forest. The lock-step

Miriam Hopkins and Director Rouben Mamoulian are a new nightly combine about town since the fair Miriam returned from England

of married life began to grow as unbearable to him as a tight collar on a dance floor.

He hated the routine. He loathed having his days and evenings reduced to a social chart. Scheduled teas, dinners and the usual Hollywood round of free-for-all parties grew to be rank poison. He was nearly always late for dinner, simply because he hated being told that at eight he was doomed to sit down and attack the soup. If ever a man was distinctly not the marrying kind, it was this tall, handsome come-hither from Ulster.

Lili likes the hot spots, the lights, the music, the bubbles in the thin-stemmed glass, the adoring glances. Errol would probably rather be playing dominoes with Capone in Alcatraz than face a constant course of Hollywood night life. And there the poor things are!

Strictly on the record, these two spectacular people don't belong anywhere within dish-hurling distance of each other. They are oil and water. And yet, when you see them together, so glorious to look at, you can't help feeling that there is something almost miracu-

lously right about this mad, embattled teaming. They are a truly thrilling sight to see, in all their youth and beauty. As a vision of what two human beings can be when the Creator really bears down, they are nothing short of superb. As a married pair they are undoubtedly the leading example of marital madness.

Delectable Damita became what she is at present by a long course of private and semi-public worship. For years she was kept busy clambering from under mountains of costly flowers and saying yes, no and perhaps to a long and glittering line of love-struck swains. Flynn became the independent, non-conforming realist the hard way.

The son of a professor at Queen's University in Belfast, Errol didn't do much with book-learning, and in practically no time the kid was in Tasmania, at the other end of the world. He had the true stout heart and eager spirit of the adventurer. He was all jumbled up with gold and head-hunters in fabulous New Guinea, and took a good, sound rooking from high-pressure finance wolves. He was in the pearl trade in Tahiti, and appears to have been a member of the British Olympic boxing team at Amsterdam in '28. He touched all the bases, and loved it—and if, in a few weeks, he is reported as chasing the wall-eyed oophus in the Gobi Desert, hardly an eyebrow will be lifted. Flynn's like that.

He is probably the most surprised man in the world, even yet, to find himself married to a petted beauty to whom socializing and mass mauling are the very breath of life.

But there it is—the unfathomable chemical reaction commonly called love has this badly-matched, ill-mated couple in a death grip, and it shows no signs of letting go, scream and struggle though they may and do.

What can their future hold but incessant battles and passionate embraces, and perhaps a final, irreparable explosion for a grand finale? I frankly don't know—your guess, and theirs, is as good or better than mine.

IT is too much to expect that Lili, the caressed kitten, and Flynn, the clear-eyed adventurer and opportunist, will change so radically that their schemes of life will ultimately meet and blend. How can we hope for that? No—I fear they will continue to be what they are—beautiful, tigerish, proud lovers and haters tossed into each other's arms by snickering Fate. The Great Parting of Nov. 15, 1936, was followed by the Great Reconciliation of Nov. 26—and these things can go on and on, and will.

I only know that here, in the mad mismating of Lili Damita and Errol Flynn, we find a rare and perfect example of love in the grand manner. No timorous, half-hearted union based on a common liking for badminton, but a full-blooded, ardent love affair, heedless of consequences, in which anything can happen and invariably does.

I dare swear that no good will come of it, at long last. But I also say that we can be very grateful for the Flynn-Damita melange as a spectacle and as a reminder that the race is not yet dying of pernicious anemia. And we can also be thankful, perhaps, noting this weird mingling of hell and heaven, that we take our own romances with a spoonful of salt. Or are you?

Don, Alice and Ty

[CONTINUED FROM PAGE 67]

setups — sometimes Don and Alice against Ty or Ty and Alice against Don, or Alice against the two of them—and the fun never ceased. It raged during the making of "In Old Chicago" and "Alexander's Ragtime Band." It was all childish but that very factor delighted them. Alice planted garlic in Ty's dressing room but he, getting a whiff of it as he was walking that way with her, pushed Alice in the room first, locked her in and left her to nearly smother.

Another occasion was the day that Don was to die in "In Old Chicago." Alice and Ty sent him dead flowers all day long, to get him in the mood. He returned that compliment by sending Alice a necklace made of empty gin bottles when she had to do her hysterical lost-in-the-fire scene. When Ty had to do his big regeneration scene, they prepared him for it by planting a pail of garbage in his car. (You may have gathered the idea that they'd discovered Mr. Power doesn't care for unpleasant odors.) In case you think all this is pretty juvenile, remember that despite their always inventing telephones, or writing Stephen Foster's songs, or building the Suez Canal or trying to stop on screen the French Revolution, Ty and Alice are still in their twenties, and Don not long out of

them, and if your work forces you to take everything seriously all the while, you've got to relax somewhere.

Not that they always goofed around. They waited to see one another mornings with their eyes sparkling with mischief. But if they had to they could see deeper into one another's feelings. There was the day when Alice was playing in "Sally, Irene and Mary" and Don was making "Happy Landing." Don walked on her set, just to call. Alice was feeling miserable. She is a truly nervous girl and she drives herself too hard, but this day she was too pale. Don said, "Alice, you're sick."

"Oh, no, I'm not," retorted Alice. "I've just got a lousy cold and I'm tired. Don't worry about me."

Don did, however, and Don is always a man of action. He went to the telephone and told his doctor to come out and check up on Alice. The doctor took one look and ordered her to bed. She was straight on the edge of pneumonia and without such prompt action she might well have died.

Underneath all this clambake, however, they are serious about their work, so the one thing they do seriously together is discuss roles and how to play them Tyrone, the most talented, knits his handsome brows and suggests they play such and such a scene this way.

Don and Alice listen respectfully. Alice, the magical song plugger, tells Don she'd sell the tune in such a manner and he gives it a try. Then they go into the scene and all three try to steal it.

Love had its effect on them, too. Don was the old rock in that department, of course, but the other two were always bringing him the sad news about each romantic upset they would go through. The Ameche, as a matter of fact, is a rabid matchmaker, so he was forever trying to push the two of them into marriages that he was persuaded would be as happy as his own. Thus he was very much among those present, beaming like a sunset, when Alice and Tony Martin did finally, after their many quarrels, unite, and he was the joyous best man at the Power-Annabella nuptials.

But what Hollywood is waiting for is the day when the first Power or the first Faye-Martin heir arrives. For just as much as Don slaved to get his pals married, just so much double he wants them to know parenthood.

When that day comes, Twentieth Century-Fox, if it's smart, will padlock the whole studio. If they don't, Don will probably burn up the executive building for the sheer joy of it, and Alice and Ty will wreck the rest of the joint just to get even.

"Could you tell me what picture we're waiting to see?"

Behavior by Bogart

[CONTINUED FROM PAGE 70]

some picture or director or writer or producer is no good. I don't get it. If he or it isn't any good, why can't you say so? If more people would mention it, pretty soon it might have some effect. This local idea that anyone making a thousand dollars a week is sacred and beyond the realm of criticism never strikes me as particularly sound reasoning."

A COLUMNIST recently stated that Bogey "refuses to conform to Hollywood standards of behavior." Which didn't make him mad, exactly, but it did put him in a mood. A mood of cool, superior, analytical reasoning, which moved him to inquire, "Why can't you be yourself, do your job, be your rôle at the studio and yourself at home, and not have to belong to the glitter-and-glamour group?" The answer is to be found, where most Hollywood answers are found, in the box office, where fans are pouring in now to see Bogey in Warners' "Unlawful." Perhaps as many fans as the columnist has readers.

Every now and then, the Bogart gets himself into a sanctimonious frame of mind and does a little off-screen acting. He dresses up and goes out of an evening, reminding himself all the while, "Now this is a nice party and I'm going to be a little gentleman tonight. Going to remember my manners, and agree with everybody."

So he tries, but things seem to go wrong. If he pulls out the lady's chair, he forgets to light her cigarette, and when he bounds gracefully ahead to open a door, he manages to get his arm in such a position that she has to fold up and duck under it, or knock him down. The awful consciousness of being a gentleman weighs upon him.

He holds up under it for about half an hour. Then, the first thing *he* knows, he is backed against a wall and eleven people are shaking their fingers in his face and demanding to know what he "means by that."

He says people bristle at a certain set look in his face, just the way animals bristle on the backs of their necks at the sight of the enemy. He has the maddening habit of arguing things he doesn't know beans about. He makes broad statements and won't back down on them. He just can't help it.

Friends who have known Bogey for a long time are aware that he is simply the old-fashioned garden-variety tease and kidder, as his father was. But he has the most desperately accurate marksmanship toward the most irritating weakness of his victim, and can exasperate and annoy people into a choleric froth, under the fond impression that it is all just good-natured kidding in a spirit of g.c.f. I wonder the man has lived as long as he has....

HE was doing that at twenty, when I first knew him.

Our first meeting took place in Greenwich Village, longer ago than either of us cares to remember with much accuracy. Bogey was spread out like sandwich-filling all over a sidewalk. He could still talk (he can always talk), and he asked us to take him to Dr. Bogart at an uptown address. We did. Dr. Bogart, not too surprised, sewed him up. It seems Bogey was doing the Village on his own, and, when a lady in a doorway yelled for help, he responded. But the gentleman with her didn't think she needed any help....

What promised to be the battle of the century almost took place when Bogey first arrived in Hollywood. He was playing in a picture called "Body and Soul" with Charlie Farrell, and how they hated each other!

The talkies were just starting, and every little punk who ever had a line in a Broadway show had rushed out to Hollywood to displace the silent-picture actors who he was sure didn't know how to talk. This hardly applied to Bogey, who had a number of important Broadway successes back of him. But it was the general opinion of Hollywood.

The Broadway actors resented these big-shot movie stars, too, and if all the chips on all the shoulders had been stacked up, they would have made quite a fire.

To assist matters to a climax, Bogart and Farrell had two weeks of night work, during which they were packed together in the cockpit of a plane. The crew helped out the general atmosphere by throwing oil on them and firing machine guns.

It began with "Move over"; "Keep on your own side, there"; and worked up to, "If you think I'm going to take that offa *you* any more—!" from Bogey. When the scene was finished that night, Bogey extended an invitation to Farrell to take a walk in the alley.

Outside, Charlie turned and calmly asked, "Can you fight?"

"What d'you mean, can I fight? I can lick *you!*" Bogey informed him.

"Yeah, but can you *fight?*" Charlie persisted. This kept up awhile. Finally, Charlie said, "I just wanted to know, because it's only fair to tell you I was boxing champion in college, and I know how to fight."

This stopped Bogey. He knew how to *scrap.* He began to see Farrell in another light—besides having size on him, Charlie also had technique.

They decided to talk it over. Pretty soon they decided to go for a vacation on Charlie's boat, as soon as the picture was finished. They went—and right away got in a whale of an argument about who was going to sail the boat.

This was settled by the skipper, who wouldn't let either of them sail it. They are very good friends now, as long as they keep out of boats and airplanes.

EVEN Bogey's romances begin that way. Mayo Methot, who will be Mrs. Bogart in August, used to have wonderful sessions with Helen Menken, putting Bogey on the pan. The two of them fried him to a crisp, fluted the edges, garnished it all with a decoration of spirited invective, and decided unanimously that the result wasn't their dish....

At that time, Helen had just ceased being the first Mrs. Bogart. When Mayo's approaching marriage was announced, the first wire of congratulation came from—Helen Menken.

Helen is married to Bogey's favorite optometrist, to whom he introduced her. Mary Phillips, from whom he was recently divorced, will soon marry Kenneth MacKenna, who was a good friend of Bogey's in the New York days, and still is. So is Mary.

You see how it is: one has to learn to love him, and he makes it as difficult as possible. But once you're over the hurdle, he's rather a good egg who wears well, and people can't hold things against him, not even his ex-wives.

BOGEY tries to tell me some sort of fancy fiction about how there is an "old Bogart" and a "new Bogart."

This new one, he says, is a mellow lad, thoroughly seasoned and full of sweetness and light. A householder (he just bought a house, with chintz and dogs and birds and flowers all over the place), who just loves humanity and wouldn't fight with it for anything.

But don't give it a thought, children. He happens to be in love, and isn't quite himself. He'll revert to type, in time.

In fact, when I saw him, we got in a political argument before the afternoon was over, and were roaring at each other, just like old times.

Bogey says he would rather be hard to like—after looking around Hollywood and seeing the gang of sycophants and hangers-on surrounding the boys who are too easy to like. Thinks what he has is a form of protective coloration every actor could cultivate to his better advantage.

Says he is a little worse now with strangers than he used to be, if possible, because picture success makes you mistrust people. They all want something from you.

"It puts you on the defensive, times when you needn't be. But how do you know that? So you develop a certain manner of approach, and everybody immediately says you are conceited or a first-class heel.

"Well, okay. I have confidence in myself, if that's conceit. Too few people have, in this business. They think front and bluff make confidence.

"However, I need to get my ears beaten down every so often. And anyone who tells me I am a damn fool in a louder voice than I tell him, I believe him!"

So you see, Bogey's behavior may be pretty awful; but he isn't entirely hopeless. He can still be told—if you can outshout him.

286

Equally happy in each other's company are Bernarr Macfadden, publisher of PHOTOPLAY, and the captivating Shirley Temple when Mr. Macfadden visited the set at the 20th Century-Fox Studio on a recent trip to Hollywood

Tear-Stained Laughter

[CONTINUED FROM PAGE 73]

to fifteen dollars a week. While it sounded like big money to Stan, he started a nip-and-tuck race with the well-known wolf, with hotel bills and costumes to be paid for out of the insignificant sum. For almost four years Stan trouped the States in what became well-known as "A Night in an English Music Hall."

WHEN the act was disbanded, Laurel stayed in vaudeville as a single. His pantomime, though, was over the heads of the audiences in the dingy houses that gave him spasmodic bookings.

The going got tougher, but Stan refused to say quits.

Sudden cancellation of engagements was widely practiced by managers of that day, and Stan more than once was stranded far from New York, his wallet and change pocket empty. That meant riding the rods back to Gotham for a fresh start.

Oliver Hardy was convinced the world was his oyster when he was called to Jacksonville, Florida, by a film unit that agreed to remunerate him at the rate of $35 a week. Most of it went home to his mother. Then, without warning, the company went on the rocks.

Hardy was "strapped" and stranded 'way below the Mason-Dixon line. He wired his mother for the fare home.

Stan Laurel, after what to him was an extended run in Baltimore, Philadelphia and New York, felt himself a Croesus; he had saved $800. Aboard a train headed for Binghamton, N. Y., he found his coat slit and his "fortune" lifted.

"There was nobody I could ask for money," bewails Stan, "and never before or since have I seen a butcher do such a wholesale slicing as that one did on my coat."

He walked the twelve blocks to the hotel, only to find that it had no dining room—so he couldn't eat "on the cuff." He played two shows the next day before he could promote an advance for a meal.

And Oliver can tell you how, on blistered feet and an empty stomach he trudged and crawled over fifty miles of Texas railroad ties when a road show manager decamped with the receipts from a Lone Star State village. Two ham sandwiches, bought with his last dime, and raw onions and bread, donated by friendly railroad "hunkies," were his menu on his five-day struggle to the nearest city, El Paso, and hoped-for work.

Hoping union meant strength and steady bookings, Laurel teamed up with another vaudevillian and his wife, but the merger brought little improvement in his finances. Illness, "at liberty" and an insistent tummy ate up the savings of a year's work.

"An immediate engagement right there in New York was all that saved the three of us from becoming public charges," Stan admits.

WHEN Hollywood loomed as the film capital, Stan and Oliver trekked westward via different routes. And the jinx still stuck close to them. Hardy went with a "quickie" concern, but most of his pay-checks contained more rubber than paper. Some of them bounced so hard they still stick among his souvenirs—they couldn't be pried loose. Laurel stuck to producers of greater financial responsibility, but his "calls" were few and far between.

When Stan encountered his erstwhile vaudeville partners in Los Angeles, he raved incessantly about the movies' future and the enormous salaries in Hollywood.

"You're foolish to stay on the road," he told them. "Why, everybody out here is getting rich!"

"Fine!" they responded. "Let's go to supper and talk it over."

"Right-o," shot back Stan, "but you'll have to pay the check. I haven't worked in five weeks and I'm flat."

Failing to win recognition as a film actor, Stan turned to directing, first as an assistant, then in command. Hal Roach hired him to direct four comedies in which Oliver Hardy was playing fairly important parts. With three of the productions "in the can," Hardy suffered a severely burned hand, and Stan donned grease paint again to fill the gap in the cast.

ROACH saw the "rushes"—and yelled for Laurel. "Say," shouted the producer, "you're an actor and don't know it! You're wasting your time as a director!"

"I quite agree with you," answered Stan, "but I had to eat."

Roach then made three comedies using both Stan and Oliver and gradually increasing the size of their rôles. The team "clicked" so hard with audiences (exhibitors even billed them along with big features) that Roach decided to co-star them in "Hats Off." That was in 1927.

Laurel and Hardy were "made"!

While the last five years have worked a magic transformation in their surroundings, Laurel and Hardy have passed through the metamorphosis unchanged and unspoiled. True, stardom has made it possible for them to acquire fine houses in Beverly Hills, but they are homes, not show places. There are costly cars in their garages, but they still drive "flivvers."

Their wearing apparel comes from more exclusive shops, but the size of their hatbands shows no increase.

Their current cronies are the pals who "knew them when."

And Stan makes the startling claim that he has never been inside a Hollywood night club!

"Oliver and I have lived apart from the rest of the movie colony," he explains, "because the hardships of those lean years made too deep an impression on us to let us be wastrels now."

Stan is grateful for the new order mainly because it allows him to shower some of life's luxuries on Mrs. Laurel and Lois, aged five; Oliver, because Myrtle Reeves Hardy, who gave up her own film future to marry him, no longer has to pinch pennies.

Fishing and his flower garden are Laurel's only personal extravagances. A low golf score and a good tailor fully satisfy the splurging proclivities of Hardy.

The real life Laurel and Hardy stand out in sharp contrast to their celluloid characters. Theater-goers see the dumb-panned Stan as the abused victim of the dumb, yet self-satisfied Oliver.

AWAY from the cameras, though, Hardy seeks the background while Laurel takes the lead. Because he handles the team's business, originates the stories for their pictures and assists in direction, Stan draws five hundred dollars a week more than Oliver.

"And he's worth every cent of the additional money," Oliver wants you to know. "It's Stan who puts us over."

Which provides the only point on which they don't agree.

"That's unfair to Oliver," Stan protests, "without him I wouldn't have gotten anywhere in pictures."

Neither can be convinced that what they call their lucky break will continue forever.

Stan sees ahead of him a new career as a director when his acting days are over. Oliver still pores over his law books and expects to hang out his shingle when he puts away his make-up box.

Meanwhile, they're just a couple of serious-minded fellows trying to get along by supplying laughs for the rest of the world.

It's Lonely Being A Child Prodigy

[CONTINUED FROM PAGE 85]

until Deanna signed her first motion picture contract with M-G-M when she was thirteen, they lived in a modest three-room cottage near Broadway and 86th Street in Los Angeles, a district of simple homes owned or rented by wage earners. While not in want, their means were far from affluent.

As is the case with any girl who is growing up, Deanna made her circle of friends and girl-fashion, had her "special best friends"—those intimates between whom grows a strangely close and precious bond. In Deanna's case, the "specials" were Paula and Jane Rawhut, who lived close by in the same neighborhood.

All three were members of the glee club of the Manchester Avenue grammar school and later students at the Bret Harte Junior High. Deanna was taking singing lessons by that time. Her exquisite voice had begun to manifest itself when she was three. Even then she could hear a song and sing it in clear, true pitch. By the time she was eleven, her extraordinary talent was obvious. However, Mr. Durbin could not afford to give her singing lessons and, generously, her sister, Edith, paid for weekly lessons with an inexpensive teacher from her own meager earnings.

In the school glee club, Deanna sang as a member of the chorus. Not once did she admit, or even hint, that her voice qualified her for solo work.

"I was afraid the other girls might think I was getting stuck-up," Deanna told me. "I was afraid it might make a difference between us, and we were so happy as things were."

Golden, glorious days. Deanna, Paula and Janie, complete unto themselves. Sharing secrets, confiding hopes and dreams, three girls on the threshold of young womanhood, a perfect trinity. Then it happened. Separation.

It was the inevitable, of course. If her latent talent escaped notice at school, it did not in the community church. Regular members and visitors alike were startled, then thrilled with the music that poured forth from the throat of the child singing hymns and anthems. They all knew that some day some person would hear that voice who would bring it to the attention of millions.

Jack Sherrill, now Deanna's manager, ultimately became that person.

METRO-GOLDWYN-MAYER about this time was searching for a child with some semblance of a voice to play the rôle of Madame Ernestine Schumann-Heink as a girl in the proposed starring vehicle for the great diva, "Gram." Sherrill brought Deanna to Metro's attention and promptly they signed her to a term contract with the usual six months option.

Los Angeles being spread out as it is, it became imperative that the Durbins move, since Deanna must be at the studio daily for lessons and training.

Weeping, Paula, Janie and Deanna said good-by.

"But never mind," they consoled themselves. "We'll see each other all the time. Promise."

They promised, in solemn good faith. But it wasn't distance, as such, that was to keep them separated for a whole year, although that too

played its part. It was that Deanna found herself plunged into a new and strange life. Her days were spent at the studio learning the bewildering business of making movies. Even her schooling was conducted on the lot, as it still is at Universal. Replacing her former teacher of voice was Andre de Segurola, former coach of the Metropolitan Opera who today guides many of the greatest voices in the world of music.

Thus the days were filled. There was no time to see Paula and Janie. No time, really, for anything but work, work, work towards this new goal.

No new little friends were substituted for the former ones. Nor could fathers be blamed if it seemed unimportant to them, after a hard day's work, to drive Deanna or Paula across the length of the city, through heavy traffic, to visit each other.

THEN Schumann-Heink died. With her died the studio's plans for "Gram" and the brilliant opportunity for Deanna.

She made one musical "short" with Judy Garland, a none too successful affair. The six months elapsed and Deanna's contract was not renewed.

Now she had neither friends nor absorbing activity.

Sherrill's faith in her next brought her to Universal. A new contract was forthcoming. Again the Durbin faimly moved to be closer to the studio. This time the home was farther than ever from the beloved 86th Street—and Paula.

Once more Deanna was enrolled in a studio school, among strange classmates—a freckle-faced boy of seven, a chubby little girl of nine, and two sophisticated blondes of about fourteen.

Came the making of "Three Smart Girls." The original plans for "Three Smart Girls" called for an inexpensive and relatively unimportant "B" or second-class picture. In it Deanna was given a minor rôle. Her work in the first two weeks of shooting, however, proved so startling production heads called a halt.

Thereupon the studio was said to have been divided into two camps—pro and anti-Durbin. After a bitter fight, in which a number of resignations allegedly were threatened if Deanna was made the star of the picture, and *if she were not*, the showdown came. The pro-Durbins won. The budget was increased to "A" or first-class rating, the story rewritten to feature Deanna.

Box-office records everywhere proved how justified the change was.

Deanna emerged a top flight star in one picture. Immediately plans were made for her second starring picture with no less a distinguished personage than the conductor Leopold Stokowski, and ninety-nine other men playing second to this little girl's beauty, charm and ability. This picture is called "One Hundred Men and One Girl," and means just that.

It was during the making of "Three Smart Girls," and hence before her success was certain, that Deanna made her radio debut. Sherrill persuaded Eddie Cantor to give her an audition for a guest star spot on his Sunday night broadcast.

She's been the feature of the program ever since.

Thus brilliant success, fame, and growing wealth have come to Deanna. Such fame, in fact, that Al Levy, oldest restaurateur of Hollywood, remarked the other day that not since fans by the thousands came to his

restaurant to watch Charlie Chaplin eat dinner has a Hollywood star created so much interest and furor in his establishment.

BUT—that success, fame and wealth was just what was estranging and losing to Deanna the things she held most dear—her little girl friendships. Glad as she and Paula were to see each other again, cry as they did with happiness, both knew when they went to their separate homes that night that another year might very well pass before they would see each other again.

Both knew, too, that things were not, and cannot be, as they were before.

It has cost her more than Paula's friendship. It has cost her every girl's natural inheritance of carefree youth, something she did not value until she had lost it.

Her days—and nights—now are a succession of crammed schooling, fittings, make-up tests, music lessons, practice hours, film and radio rehearsals, radio appearances and actual work before the cameras.

She happened to mention to me she had celebrated her fourteenth birthday recently on her first trip to New York City.

"Did you have a party?" I asked.

"Oh yes," she answered carefully. "In fact, I had *five* parties in one day!"

The Waldorf-Astoria, biggest hotel in the world, was host at one of those parties. Universal Studios' New York offices gave a second party, Jack Sherrill the third, Eddie Cantor a fourth, and Abe Blumberg, a big dress manufacturer, the fifth.

True, they were very elaborate parties, with expensive food and such, and more expensive presents for Deanna. But—not one girl friend of her own age was there. What is happy about that kind of a birthday?

DEANNA went roller skating at a public rink in Los Angeles not long ago. She loves to skate and it had been a long time since she had had a chance, since her days were filled and you can't skate on the busy streets here at night. So what happened?

She arrived at eight p.m. At five minutes after, before she had a chance to fasten her skates, a crowd of autograph seekers had surrounded her.

Still others stood and stared. By the time the last autograph book had been signed, it was time for Deanna to go home.

Still another night loomed big in anticipation to Deanna. That night, she said she "had more fun than in a year." The event was a fudge party.

The usual preliminaries went off in fine style for Deanna. There was the buying of the extras needed for the candy, the cracking and chopping of the nuts, watching the fudge boil, testing for the soft ball in cold water that means it is time to take it from the fire. Then waiting the long, long time until the confection was cool enough to beat.

There's nothing more fun than to make fudge with the right people. It is an exciting, tantalizing adventure. But waiting with Deanna for the fudge to cool that night, patronizingly amused at her breathless impatience were her mother and father, her manager, her singing teacher and heaven knows who else. All adults living in another world, a world a girl of fourteen is not yet ready to enter or understand!

Maybe Paula and Janie made fudge in one of their homes that same night. If so, they had something Deanna did not for all her fame and money.

They had a good time.

Young in Heart

[CONTINUED FROM PAGE 78]

don't ask me why) should be withheld from the public—as follows:

He was born in London, England on November 11th.

He's fifty-one years old (isn't that awful?).

He was educated at Sherborne in Dorset, and where Alfred the Great went to school, University College, London.

He had nothing in common with Alf the G. except a 13th Century monk's cell below ground level. He's tried to keep upstairs (with many amazing results) ever since.

He was only eight when he left for school. His health seemed to demand the change. He hated and loathed every minute of it and was probably the meanest snip of a snipe ever to enter a classroom.

He earned his very first money, threepence, for singing in the school choir and sixpence for singing in the chapel choir. And was overpaid on all counts, if you ask me.

His father was a well-to-do and well-known architect, who had hopes that Roland would follow him in his profession. But when Roland kept flunking out on his examinations, his parents decided to probe the thing to the bottom and, walking into his bedroom (Roland was in bed with tonsillitis), they put it to him.

Before Roland could bring himself to murmur the dreadful word "actor" his mother, who had been regarding her progeny quizzically, exploded a bombshell.

"I think," she said, "he wants to be a cowboy."

Hi Ho, Rollo!

After that, becoming an actor was such a relief, his father sent him off to Tree Dramatic School for a try at it.

After a tour of the provinces in a stock company (how those English provinces must suffer), he landed on the London stage and has been fascinating audiences on both sides of the Atlantic ever since.

He's a naturalized American and makes a swell pot of tea.

He doesn't want to talk about his penguin collection any more. Feels it's been overdone, but has a grand assortment of canes. Get him to tell you about the one from Spain, sometime. It will kill you.

HE never intrudes his whimsicalities on other people. One has to stumble over them before they're discovered. Like his three-foot key chain. If you ask about it, he'll be only too delighted to drag from the depths of his pocket (it must be specially made) this yard-long key chain upon one end of which is fastened a tiny nest of keys. Spread along the floor it looks like an anemic rattler too relaxed to spring. Mr. Young explains he never likes to open a door while practically on top of it. The long

chain gives him plenty of room to avoid crowding. Provided he doesn't trip over it. He usually trips over it.

There's something funny about him and watches, too. He wears a watch on each wrist and one somewhere in the middle. He likes to know what time it is all over.

He carries green ink in a green fountain pen which are the only two things about him that ever match. Simply because we encountered him one day in a pearl-grey suit, a burgundy shirt, blue tie and white flower, we demanded (whatever got into us) his views on sex.

"Sex, like the poor, is always with us," he shrugged. "Besides, I was born during Queen Victoria's reign, so I'm allergic to sex."

As the radio comic says, "That ain't the way I heerd it."

He isn't a bachelor or an Elk or a Deputy Sheriff. And yet there's something faintly (oh, very faintly) reminiscent of all three about the man. I can't explain it, really.

He has twinkles in both eyes (both, mind you) that are magnified by his spectacles. He wears them off screen, both the twinkles and spectacles, with the strangest consequences.

YOU'VE heard about the upper lip? Mr. Young's, I mean? That's the feature that puts the *H* in Hades for all little writers, for you see, even if Mr. Young were inclined to be loquacious (which he isn't), it's next to impossible to understand all he says, simply because he so seldom moves his upper lip when talking. It has a mustache on it, too, but this has nothing to do with its immovability. I asked both a doctor and a barber (and once I said something about it to a brush salesman) and they all agreed that the mustache

was incidental. Probably (it's only a guess, of course) in his youth some kindly soul admonished Mr. Young to keep a stiff upper lip and he has taken the advice literally. It has paid him well, for radio comics, so called, make much of it when Mr. Young makes a guest appearance on their programs.

Its effects on writers are far reaching. "I like Gosomoso better than Dickens," he informs the interviewer.

"I beg your pardon?" says the writer, believing this to be the most eloquent form of inquiry.

"I like (this time it sounds like UncleSammadeaslam) better than Dickens," repeats Mr. Young.

The writer makes no comment. Naturally. She's left higher and dryer than two kites. Too, it hardly seems quite polite or even ladylike to suggest that one's dainty ears cannot make a gawddam bit of sense out of the remark and that, years and years hence, she may wake up in the night faced with the knowledge that undoubtedly she will enter Eternity, never knowing whom Mr. Young preferred to Dickens. That's a pretty devastating thought in any woman's life and can, as she reaches the middle years, seriously affect her whole mechanism. Throwing glands and things off balance, as it were.

On the other hand, the thought may arise that Mr. Young is merely having fun and has resorted to a sort of double talk to confuse the not-so-well-read interviewer.

Any psychiatrist will tell you this could easily result in a broody complex that could affect one's whole mental and social outlook on life. Personally, as I prefer to be glandularly rather than mentally upset, I shall attribute my inability to interpret Mr. Young's literary preference to his upper lip and let the whole thing rest with that.

High-jinks: Roland Young congratulates Dave Chasen (breaking ground for addition to his café), as Jean Rogers, Bob Benchley, David Niven, Bart Marshall and Virginia Pine kibitz

HIS design for working is the envy of every actor in the business. It's been going on for years and somewhere along the line, if it slips a cog, Mr. Young keeps right on rotating on schedule. A certain number of months each year are spent in Hollywood, making pictures. A certain period of time, usually during late spring through early summer, is spent in London, again making pictures or resting. Autumn finds him in New York, often starring in a stage play. His plays including, "Good Gracious, Annabelle," "Beggar on Horseback," "Rollo's Wild Oat," "The Last of Mrs. Cheyney" and "The Queen's Husband," all riotously successful, are results of his New York end of the program.

He seldom attends the movies and is frankly outspoken concerning his own pictures. "The Young in Heart" he thought was adult and amusing. "Yes, My Darling Daughter" offended his moral sense in that it merely implied indiscretion rather than decently asserting it. This beating behind the bush with sex on the screen Mr. Young declares "dirty" and, until one has heard Mr. Young's English inflection used on the word "dirty," one hasn't really lived. The *Topper* series he enjoys, as well he may, and he declares himself happy with "Heaven on a Shoe String," his latest. As the slimy *Uriah Heep* in "David Copperfield," the man proved himself an actor who would have warmed the heart of Dickens himself. No matter whom Mr. Young prefers.

He's in constant demand on radio programs for interpretation of an English sport's announcer which convulses American listeners. He never listens to the radio, except to good music. Never, he insists, has he heard an American call himself an "Amurrican" (as our English cousins insist we do), nor has he ever heard an Englishman say "fawncy" (as we love to think they do).

The funniest thing that ever happened to him happened in Philadelphia, which makes it all the funnier. Mr. Young was playing on the stage there, and during the run of the play was invited to a home for tea. Stepping into the living room, Mr. Young's foot came in contact with a polar bear which was quite dead, and zip went Mr. Young on the bear rug, tearing across the floor like sixty. En route he spied a tea wagon and clutching it like mad, the tea wagon joined in the disgraceful journey which terminated at the feet of the dumbfounded hostess, who stood gazing down at little Mr. Young, snug as a bug in his rug, with tea things scattered in all directions.

THE consensus of opinion among mere women and children is that Mr. Young is one of the funniest men alive. "I think," women say everywhere, "he's the cutest thing I've ever laid my eyes on. My, he must be a perfect scream to know."

In the face of all this, I must in all honesty reveal that Mr. Young is not the cutest thing *I* ever laid *my* eyes on, nor is he, to me at least, a perfect scream. For be it known, Mr. Young is probably the wisest, the richest in thought, and most tolerant of men.

He has my vote for Hollywood's greatest sophisticate, because of his knowledge of so many things and his wide circle of friends, in Hollywood, in New York, in London and Paris, among those who do things. And yet his sophistication bears roots that probe deep below the surface through great layers of wisdom and understanding to the greatest of all worth-while things: a keen knowledge of the value of simple things. He likes people who are genuine. From all walks and degrees of life they come his way to give him pleasure in thought and ideas and, likewise, they take away from him in heaped-up measure. W. C. Fields, Deems Taylor, Pat O'Brien and Rachel Field, writers, thinkers, just people, go into the construction of his inner plan for living intelligently.

He is an amazing person, not just because his work is such a delight to behold, but that he goes inward and deep in even greater proportion to his tremendous outward cleverness.

Of course, he brings the "perfect scream thing" on himself and can blame no one but himself. Not that he would have it otherwise, we believe. For example, the last time we saw Mr. Young, our interview over, heaven help us both, he was sitting quietly with pad and pencil.

"We will ignore it," we said to ourselves. "We'll pay no attention. We'll just slip away without looking."

We couldn't quite make it. We had to take one peep over his shoulder. As heaven is my judge, Mr. Young was drawing a polka-dotted elephant resting ecstatically on its neck, its four feet extending upward in the breeze.

We got away from there in a hurry. As far as we know, he is still sitting there quietly drawing pictures of bees and elephants in the weirdest kind of poses.

Or at least we wouldn't put it past him.

Roundup of Characters

[CONTINUED FROM PAGE 91]

show world believes in faithfulness in marriage, honesty in relationship between husband and wife. She abides by her beliefs.

Her favorite expression at all times is, "Well, I'm on the Lord's side."

Arthur Treacher:

The old bromide of when is a butler not a butler can be answered in only one way—when he's Arthur Treacher ("Pip" Treacher to his friends).

Actually he began in movies playing a gentleman. But the six-foot-four Englishman in full evening regalia promptly bumped his head on the overhanging microphone and couldn't read his lines for the goose egg on his brow. So they demoted him to adenoidy, arch-nosed butlers. Which he doesn't mind playing at all.

A bachelor, he lives in an English-type annex to a rabbit warren in the country; plays a very tired game of tennis but simply goes to town on squash which he plays with Buck, the colored locker attendant at the Athletic Club.

The combination of Buck and Pip, waist-deep in a game of squash, is just one of those things, that's all.

After four years of service in the War, he gave way to those old choir boy's urges and became, of all outrageous things for Treacher, a chorus boy. But the trouble was if he kicked straight up he knocked over the props. If he kicked out, the little blonde in the row ahead landed flat on her face.

It was a dog's life really. So he became a stock player all over England and then on to New York and the stage —at long, in-between intervals. Tried out once for radio, reading a love scene. The sound man had to be carried from his box screaming with hysterics.

Pip's feelings were hurt.

Tested out for movies, too, but the director took one look and snarled, "Where did you get that Adam's apple?"

Pip's feelings were crushed.

And for weeks he practically strangled himself trying to swallow his Big Apple.

Landed in Hollywood and went into a co-operative theater project where everyone shared the profits, only there were seldom any profits. All six feet four of him seemed caved in at once. It was a fine how-do-you-do, indeed, until casting directors began noticing him (as if they could miss him) and business picked up.

He's considered Hollywood's A-1 gourmet. According to local restaurateurs, the lad knows how to order the perfect dinner. But he's definitely against veal loaf and gravy. Especially with gravy.

Had to sleep catty-corner in beds all his life until he built a house with beds long enough to lie in, with doors tall enough to get through without stooping and chairs high enough to sit in.

Pip once complained to a friend at a party that strange ladies were always loitering about, ". . . if you know what I mean." It was explained that, because of his height, ladies in crowded rooms would always say to their husbands, "Look—I'll meet you near Treacher."

He and Shirley Temple are that way. (Remember them in "Curly Top?") She admires every inch of him from the ground up. She comes to his knees.

But she isn't his only admirer. Ask the fans who saw him (or will see him soon) in "Mad About Music."

Oh, certainly, practically everyone says, "Well pip, pip," when they leave him.

RICHARD BARTHELMESS

"IN THE DAWN PATROL"

GREATEST AIR EPIC EVER!

Five thousand feet up! . . . Forty whirring, purring propellers singing a song of death. Forty roaring, streak-fast war-eagles making a shambles of the sky. Forty youngsters sporting with fate—for they must live greatly, or not at all! . . .

Forty famous stunt flyers helped Dick Barthelmess crowd "The Dawn Patrol" with more thrills than you'd get in a dozen actual flights. And the author of "Wings" has packed the story with heart-throbs such as only heroes know! "Take off" to "The Dawn Patrol" the minute it comes to town.

With
Douglas Fairbanks, Jr.
Neil Hamilton
and 4 other stars. Directed by Howard Hawks. From the story "The Flight Commander" by John Monk Saunders. Adaptation and dialogue by Howard Hawks, Dan Totheroh, and Seton Miller. "Vitaphone" is the registered trade-mark of The Vitaphone Corporation.

A FIRST NATIONAL & VITAPHONE PICTURE

Ridin' in on a thrilly furore
and a roarin' riot comes

"The BAD MAN"

"*I make ze love to you myself—personal . . .
What? Because you are marry you do not
wish to spik of love! Leesen Lady — eef
Pancho Lopez want woman, he take her,
dam queek!*"

* * *

Listen to him! The perfect lover with a
broken accent to mend broken hearts! —
L'il old Cupid with a six shooter—the Robin
Hood of the deserts—The greatest character
ever brought to the talking screen by

Walter
HUSTON

Assisted by Dorothy Revier, Sidney Blackmer,
James Rennie
DIRECTED BY CLARENCE BADGER from
Porter Emerson Browne's melodramatic uproar.

"Vitaphone" is the registered trade-mark of The Vitaphone Corporation.

First
National
Pictures

VITAPHONE Picture
REG. TRADE MARK

A FIRST NATIONAL &
VITAPHONE PICTURE

C. Aubrey Smith:

High on a California hill, where the sky bounces off a mountain top into the sea, lives one of Hollywood's best-beloved actors, C. Aubrey Smith. Beloved not only by friends who know him intimately, but by fans everywhere who look forward to glimpsing the six feet one of him holding his own on a motion-picture screen. At seventy-four, he's young and vital and alive. And, to the envy of his less-feathered friends, he has all his hair. Down to the last iron-gray strand. He leaves the toupee wearing to the youngsters of thirty. C. Aubrey (he of "Little Lord Fauntleroy" and more recently "The Hurricane" fame) sports his own.

On a clear day, Catalina can see the wide-striped blazer worn by the actor as a morning coat. Catalina can even spot it through a dash of fog. It's just that loud. The trousers are always tweed and his pipes are constantly arriving at that enviable state known as ripe.

English as Yorkshire pudding, his house is his castle. Only it's really a dream come true. Passing by a certain mountain spot on his daily travels from M-G-M studios (where he was lost in the two-year vastness of the Weissmuller "Tarzan" epic), he grew to love that mountain. To look forward each morning and each evening to seeing it. To note how the sun dipped over its humped crest or rose over one peculiar edge that looked for all the world like Sitting Bull in profile.

So he bought it. And scooped off the top, scalping Sitting Bull for a fare-thee-well.

To his home he brought his wife, three dogs, two canaries, two parakeets, one alley cat—all in the best of health and pleased as Punch.

On a plateau above the house he built his cricket field. Most any day, a group of English friends may be seen whooping it up on the Smiths' bit of green.

Confidentially, his wife declares he's plain batty over sports. Whooping and fandangoing around on the sidelines, "like a spoilt boy or like a plain madman," she says. "And as far as that goes," his wife says, "he's a lunatic about animals too, especially dogs."

Birdhouses he's mad for. And builds them all over creation. Even the birds are dumbfounded at the sudden building boom. High up on a mountain top like that.

In 1890, when young Smith decided to leave his work on the London Stock Exchange to try the stage, his father was outraged. "Think of your sisters," the old gentleman shouted, "how outraged they would feel to have their brother an actor."

Tours with Ethel Terry brought him to America. In 1915, he made his first movie, and, off and on, has been making them ever since.

His eyebrows are thick and bushy like the shrubbery stubbornly clinging to his mountain side. His voice, he thinks, is his best asset. Like all actors he wears suède shoes and a ring on his little finger. Slightly deaf, he cups his right hand gently over his ear.

His capacity for an overwhelming enjoyment of life and the living of it is his secret of perpetual youth. He has one daughter, married to a British Navy officer in the West Indies. His eyes make constant voyaging to her picture on his desk.

Oh, yes, the C. is for Charles. With Smith such a plain name, he felt Aubrey a trifle more hottish. For an actor, he says. And along with the striped blazer, I think he's got something there.

Herman Bing:

Crosby, a Barnum and Bailey elephant, and Herman, the only Bings on the movie horizon, are each unique in his own way. But somehow Herman seems slightly "uniquer" than the others. There's the matter of accents for instance. Herman has three.

1. His sauerkraut accent.
2. His gefülte-fish accent.
3. His blum-budding accent with the adenoid touch.

All are in constant demand by the movies that first brought Herman from Germany as assistant to Director Murnau.

His handling of English became the talk of the town. "Well, Bing asked the prop men for empty horses today," the story would go. Or, "Bing assured George O'Brien not to worry. If he drowned in a scene they'd asphyxiate him."

The team work between Bing and Murnau also became food for meaty story telling.

Murnau would shout, "Bing, where are you?"

"Bang, here I am," Bing would answer, thinking himself quite a card.

His mother in Germany didn't raise her boy to be a comic. An opera singer herself, she hoped her son would sing "Pagliacci" for dear life one day. Instead, he gravitated to German movies. And after Murnau's sudden death in America, he left the mechanical end for the comical end, rolling his "r's" and zooping his "snoodle zoup" all over the screen.

He's proud as Punch of his harem, consisting of his mama, his daughter Ellen, a senior in Hollywood High School, two sisters, two nieces, one cook and one woman manager, all living in the same house.

The wife, who died several years ago, he misses deeply. His one hobby, etymology, grew from his habit of tormenting the king's English. While other stars are off to Palm Springs or tennis matches or night clubs, Bing is home with his verbs tracing the rascals right down to their very roots. Actor Herman actually knows more verbs, their customs, habits and ancestors, than a casting director does actors.

Between pictures (his latest is "Bluebeard's Eighth Wife") he makes personal appearances, playing the piano, singing his German songs and going to town with his sauerkraut story telling. At home he spends his time away from

the harem end of things—listening to music or fondling a dictionary.

Potato pancakes and dumplings (the dough not the blonde kind) he adores. And Gott in himmel, wiener schnitzel—iss dot someting?

Capitalizing on an impediment of speech, he has turned a liability into an asset. Exactly as he capitalizes by his satirical exaggeration on the screen. The ridiculous antics of pompous individuals who dramatize their job—the big blustering bluffer, the little executive with the Napoleonic complex, the dictator executive with the fearful soul, the meek hero and the arrogant coward,—all these are objects of Bing's curiosity, his scorn and his amusement.

And, oh, yes—he's even less pretty off the screen than on.

Alan Mowbray:

Butler, orchestra leader, opera singer, magician, and plain ham actor—how are you, Mr. Mowbray?

No matter the rôle played by Alan Mowbray (including all of the above), his friends always exclaim, "My dear, how perfectly you were cast!"

Sophistication—an overused, miscast word in Hollywood—fits him like a glove. A soft suède glove with a platinum horseshoe tucked inside. His remarks are gems of wit, lined and interlined with barbed steel shafts that find their mark in the most devastating and deflating portions of the anatomy.

There, now, is Alan Mowbray.

An Englishman who is nuts over the idea of becoming a papa to two American children.

Married to an American, he has two children, both born in California. A situation that intrigues the actor's English fancy no end. He calls them P.M. and A.M for short. Patricia is five. Alan, Jr., or "Butch" Mowbray in polite circles, is three.

For four years and three months, Mr. Mowbray shivered through the paroxysm of a world war and now, just think, he says, "There's actually a powder puff man in his life." Driving to the studio he'll think, "Down there at the studio there's a man with a powder puff waiting just for me—to powder my face. What a world," and he'll lean out and bow stiffly but pleasantly to men, women and children on the march.

It was while he was acting his rôle in George Bernard Shaw's "The Apple Cart" that movies grabbed him. He began by playing George Washington with a teddibly British twang and Valley Forge viewpoint. He was slightly terrific.

After twenty-nine pictures (the current one being Hal Roach's "Merrily We Live"), he's agreed, for the first time, to sign a contract. And only, as he warned Hal Roach, did he sign it because he learned do-nuts and coffee were served free on the Roach sets every day.

The do-nuts and coffee got him.

He reads widely and currently with a purpose other than enjoyment. One day he hopes to become a producer, either of pictures or stage plays, and so must know stories.

He's a playwright of some success. "Dinner is Served," his own play, was produced on Broadway. He has just completed another called "In the Spirit" which he hopes to have produced.

Englishmen whose accents grow more and more British the longer they remain in America bore him terrifically. Always prefers amiability to confusion. Figures life is too short for fussing.

Solidly educated, he's well informed. And his one luxury is cigarettes costing eight cents apiece.

"Have one?" he'll insist with a light of satisfaction in his eye, while his very own powder puff man lingering near makes it a bit of an all right world for Mr. Mowbray.

He's happy about the whole thing.

Eric Blore:

"He rambled, yes he rambled—he rambled all around—in and out of the town."

Remember the old college tune with freshmen in tiny caps hollering like mad?

Eric Blore says that song was written about him. Eric says back in the beginning he wasn't so much an actor as a rambler—not the rose variety. All over every stick and stone in every way station and hamlet in England, his native country, he rambled.

You should know what he did to Australia, Eric says. Why, they even played to the Bushmen; and once (of course, Eric says this, remember, not me) they even played to a bunch of overcurious kangaroos.

The play was "The Merry Makers." The kangaroos died off like fleas, Eric says.

A brilliant mind, a funny face with a funnier mouth that does a Susy Q. all of its own, Eric is another comic gone the way of all butlers.

His first great Hollywood success, however, was as a waiter in "The Gay Divorcee."

His mind is quick and alert. His perceptions keen. His head slightly bald on top. And positively anemic around the edges. His remarks, witty, intelligent, are usually satirical.

His father, Harry Blore, was an honor student at Trinity College, Dublin.

Eric wasn't.

His father is today a member of the Board of Education in London.

Eric isn't. Eric never will be.

But he *is* one of the finest comedians in all Hollywood.

"America has never appreciated the capabilities or artistry of Blore," English critics cry.

But Eric doesn't cry. He thinks he is doing all right. Thinks Hollywood a divine place to live. Calls it "a man's town." Claims he's Anglo-American by absorption. Eric absorbs like a sponge.

"Such a cozy unlonely feeling—having all my old friends around me here," he says. "Just think, I can telephone Bart Marshall any time I want to. He's right here. In the town with me. Before this I'd maybe see Bart fifteen minutes every four years between jumps at Chicago.

"Hollywood is like an excursion boat and all my friends are on it."

Blow the whistle, Captain. Here comes Blore around the bend.

There's something about treacle pudding that gets him. And something about Black Velvet, a combination of stout and champagne, that also gets him. Oh, definitely gets him.

English foods are still his favorite but he's learned to enjoy hot dogs and has discovered a secret concerning the over-heated canines. They must be eaten at the beach to be enjoyed. Away from the salt air they lose their "ummph." No sea air—no ummph in hot dogs.

He wears a cute bow tie and high-waisted pants that almost meet the bow tie head on.

He's completely frustrated over the fact no one ever gives him a birthday present because his birthday comes on December 23. His friends wait till Christmas. It's done something to Blore's soul—this putting off like that.

During his early struggles he decided to become a singer. His first appearance was in a tough English music hall. He followed directly after Harry Lauder.

The audience encored Lauder all through Eric's song and finally grew to feel this interloper was somehow hindering Lauder's return to the stage.

Still Eric sang on, until one husky leaned over the balcony and cried, "Are you going to get out of there or shall I have to come down and throw you out?"

Eric took the hint.

About that time Herbert Marshall came along in a review and gathered up Eric. He's been hitting on high ever since.

Has been married twice. Is the amazed papa of an eight-year-old boy, Eric Blore, Jr.

He golfs. Reads Robert Benchley and Charles Dickens. His favorite of all actors is the late G. P. Huntley.

His latest picture is "The Joy of Living."

Edward Everett Horton:

Squire of Belly-acres, gentleman farmer extraordinary, scene stealer de luxe, bachelor and how, are just a few of the titles bestowed by Hollywood upon the perspiring brow of one Edward Everett Horton.

Perspiring because Eddie is generally in a first-class dither over one of his several projects.

Either Eddie's cow is having a calf just at dinner time, or one of his innumerable outhouses is burning its way to the ground, or, worse yet, one of his ranch buildings is reaching a state of completion. Each proving a major catastrophe all its own. Especially the one about the completed building.

You see, Horton has a theory about that ranch of his. A theory that pretty well characterizes the man himself.

He began with an acre and a house that has expanded (and how, is beyond him) into sixteen acres with sixteen buildings. A building for every acre. And now he feels if he stops building some dire thing will descend upon him.

He figures the constant building gives employment to the twenty men whom he can't bear to throw into sudden unemployment. Heaven wouldn't forgive him, Eddie feels. Besides, the financial outlay (with no help from the government) is so terrific it keeps him working fifty-two weeks of the year, which is a good thing all the way round. Keeps him on the screen and working like mad, at any rate.

When the barn received the last finishing touches, he was panicky for all of an hour. And then he had an idea. He merely turned the barn, hayloft and all, into a little theater and began a new barn all over again.

You can't beat him. Except at tennis. Just six months ago he took up the game. He was wearing a suit of red flannels at the time, as sort of a reducing means. Everything, Horton claims, shrunk but him. The underwear, the tennis court, his partners—all, all diminished. Eddie put on weight.

He has all the crotchety, set-in-his-way characteristics of the bachelor. And has a fixed idea in his mind every writer in town at some time has written a cooking story about him.

"I didn't like that cooking story you wrote about me," he greets each scribe accusingly. "I really can't boil an egg, you know." (Business of dirty looks at confused writers who never in their entire existence wrote a cooking story on Horton.)

He'll leave a writer stranded in the middle of a sentence to take his place before a camera without so much as a "pardon me." "Now quote me accurately," he'll scold. "Quote me accurately."

He's been four times to Europe making pictures in England, and each time returns with crates of furniture that require four new buildings as storage. He moves furniture around on off days.

Somewhere he picked up the idea everybody else's hats look better on him than any he can buy.

It has him constantly eying other men's hats. And brooding secretly.

Once in the swing of a gay, bantering conversation, he's tops, revealing a ripe sense of the ridiculous.

Secretly, he's always yearned to be a Beau Brummell. A knock-out on wheels. But he never quite makes it. Either his coat does nip-ups in the back or his vest button pops during a love scene.

Snobs are his favorite people. They're so pathetic, he states.

He'll grab up a pair of hair brushes on the set between scenes and really go to town. Brushing his plentiful head of hair with strong sweeping backward motions.

Florida water lets loose the ragamuffin in him. Horton refreshing himself with Florida water on the set is a sight not to be missed.

A graduate of Columbia University, he began play-acting in school theatricals. And came on to California where he became the reigning matinee idol of the day.

He's never played on Broadway. Several times he's almost done it and then backed out. He'd rather be tops in Hollywood than flops in New York.

He wears reading glasses, and walks about the set talking his lines to himself—which is confusing, in a way, to visitors, who think Horton has suddenly gone bats.

He's up on modern things. Well read, well informed, well versed. He's a better listener than a story teller only, he adds, with that notorious twist of his head, he gets off a good one now and then.

He likes best of all his rôle with George Burns and Gracie Allen in their new film, "College Swing," because, in this one, he really gets the girl.

He gets the itch, too.

But the girl's worth the torture he feels.

It seems they gave all the comedians in town to "Bluebeard's Eighth Wife"—Horton's in it, too!

Love Life of a Villain

[CONTINUED FROM PAGE 94]

before I met her . . ." And thus began this inspirational love story in which the screen's prime villain plays a major rôle.

It was in the winter of 1921. Basil Rathbone was playing in "The Czarina" on Broadway. In one matinee audience sat two women. As the tall, dark, attractive English actor strode on the stage, one of the women turned to the other and said, "There is the man I'd like to be my husband." Two years later they met at a party. They fell in love at once and were married.

"What Ouida saw in me then, I don't know," confessed Basil. "But looking back, I can tell you what I see in myself. I was a man living from day to day and perfectly content in doing it. I had no plans, few ambitions. I had come back from the war, where life had been like a long, terrible dream. At the front I had never thought about what would happen or why. There was no past and no future. Nights were either wet nights or dry nights. The important things to me then were whether my billet was warm or cold, the food good or rotten.

"I suppose when you meet death daily for a long time you give up trying to order things. I came out of the war comparatively untouched. That is, I wasn't shell-shocked or scarred up. But I had lost all sense of life's realities.

"I found I was still a good enough actor. I got some good parts in London. Whatever they offered me, I took. Money meant nothing to me. I never thought of getting ahead. I never cared about it.

"Somehow I expected to be taken care of—as I had been in the army. I shrank from decisions. I never went after things I wanted. I hated any sort of battle or argument. I just wanted to be let alone—to vegetate. I was completely negative."

IT was hard to believe the words I heard. Basil Rathbone, one of the most positive personalities in Hollywood, branding himself as a negative, shrinking soul!

"I remember how shocked I was," he continued, "at something that happened in London. Perhaps it prepared me a little for Ouida's influence, later to bear fruit. I had had a bit of London success in a series of plays that John Barrymore did in New York, notably 'Peter Ibbetson.' When Barrymore's latest Broadway hit, 'The Jest,' came to London, I naturally expected to play it. In fact, I counted on it heavily. But I made no effort to get the part. It never occurred to me they wouldn't offer it to me. Such a thing seemed out of the question. Well—it wasn't. Someone else did it, and I was stunned. But still the lesson didn't sink in.

"I was still in this semi-helpless, negative state when I married Ouida. She made me positive.

Last year the Rathbones gave a memorable "Bride and Groom" party. This year the real thing took place in the garden of the Rathbone home when Rodion, son of Basil, married attractive Caroline Blake Fisher, dramatic student. The wedding party, left to right: Mrs. Rathbone, Mrs. Cedric Frances, Constance Collier, the bride and bridegroom, Walter Wurdeman, Cedric Frances and Basil Rathbone

"I'll never forget her as I first saw her. Everything about her was definite. The way she looked, the way she talked. She was completely opposite to me. I was indefinite. I fell in love with her on the spot. I have never fallen out of love.

"Ouida taught me some very important things at once: that you are as important as you make yourself; that you must have respect for yourself or no one will respect you; that an actor, particularly, must be aggressive; that it's all very well to expect and accept breaks and good fortune, but it's not enough. You must back yourself up.

"My wife was Ouida Bergere before we were married. She was a successful screen writer. Paramount was pay-

ing her a thousand dollars a week, so I think you might say she was well along on her career. The day she married me she quit writing, abandoned her career. Or rather changed it. For twelve years, Ouida's career has been—me.

"She was a practical woman then, as she is now. She knew first that there should be only one pay check in a family. Two pay checks mean two separate lives. If she continued her work she would have to be in Hollywood, while my interests were still on the stage in New York. She said, 'If you are very much in love with something, you must be with it. I can't write in Hollywood when you are in New York. So I won't write!'

"But I think she knew, too, that the

Among the wedding guests were Ruth Waterbury, Norma Shearer and Merle Oberon

"MOROCCO"

with
GARY COOPER ° MARLENE DIETRICH ° ADOLPHE MENJOU

Reckless soldier of fortune, Gary Cooper. Adolphe Menjou, sophisticate, man of the world. A flaming cafe beauty, Marlene Dietrich...mysterious, alluring, dangerous as the Sahara. "Morocco," the turbulent story of these three.

Directed by
JOSEF VON STERNBERG
Adapted by Jules Furthman. From the play "Amy Jolly" by Benno Vigny.

In "Morocco" Paramount presents the continental star, Marlene Dietrich, whose ravishing beauty and exotic personality will electrify all who come under her spell. A not-to-be-missed Paramount Picture, "best show in town."

Paramount 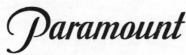 Pictures

PARAMOUNT PUBLIX CORPORATION, ADOLPH ZUKOR, PRES., PARAMOUNT BLDG., NEW YORK

After Breaking All Records in
HELL'S
Opens in London Receiving Greatest

THE LONDON MORNING POST
acclaims "Hell's Angels" "The finest achievement yet shown on any screen."

LONDON DAILY EXPRESS
says, "Greatest masterpiece the screen has ever known."

An Interior View of the Giant Zeppelin Used in "Hell's Angels"

"THE TALKIES' FIRST

BOSTON EVENING TRANSCRIPT:

"The most spectacular sky saga yet filmed, far above such aerial circuses as 'Wings' and 'The Dawn Patrol.'"

ZIT'S THEATRICAL WEEKLY:

" 'Hell's Angels' can follow all the others and still make them look like the preliminary bouts."

THEATRE MAGAZINE:

"No theatregoer who is decently grateful for the divine gift of eyesight should fail to see 'Hell's Angels.' Beside the sheer significance of 'Hell's Angels' all stage spectacles and colossal circuses become puny. Deserves to be witnessed and applauded in every picture-house in the world."

Los Angeles, New York and Boston

ANGELS

Praise Ever Accorded a Motion Picture

LONDON TIMES:

"Has no equal on the screen."

LONDON DAILY SKETCH:

"London was thrilled by 'Hell's Angels' as never before. Unbelievable excitement after excitement flashes upon the screen."

Actual Scene from "Hell's Angels" Showing Authentic German Dirigible Flown in the Picture

GREAT SPECTACLE"—*Motion Picture Magazine*

HARRISON'S REPORTS:

"The best spectacle that has ever been produced in motion pictures."

NEW YORK GRAPHIC:

"Most beautiful shots and thrilling action the movies have yet built."

LOS ANGELES HERALD:

" 'Hell's Angels' will never be surpassed for sheer thrills and spectacle."

SEATTLE STAR:

"Stands alone as greatest of air pictures. A production which will never be duplicated."

EXHIBITORS' HERALD-WORLD:

"Undoubtedly one of the world's greatest motion pictures. Presents spectacles such as never have been seen before, and does so without interrupting the thread of the story."

THE KNOCKOUT PICTURE OF THE YEAR!

Don't fail to get a ringside seat at your favorite movie theatre to see Wallace Beery as "the Champ" fight for his boy, Dink (Jackie Cooper). You will be thrilled beyond words by this story of a battered, broken down pugilist trying to stage a comeback because his boy believes him to be the greatest fighter in the world. You will not be ashamed to brush away a tear as the Champ makes his last great sacrifice for his boy. And you will say, with millions of other movie fans, "Beery is great — Jackie Cooper is marvelous — The Champ is truly the knockout picture of the year!"

He loved this boy of his more than anything else in the world—but knew that the best thing he could do for him was to go out of his life forever . . . a world of pathos and cheer in a picture you will never forget!

WALLACE JACKIE

BEERY · COOPER
The CHAMP

with Irene RICH — Roscoe ATES

A KING VIDOR PRODUCTION

Story by Frances Marion   Dialogue Continuity by Leonard Praskins

A METRO - GOLDWYN - MAYER *Picture*

job of making me over would take all of her time and energy. I was a pretty hopeless case."

Basil Rathbone laughed. "Frankly, I suffered from the worst inferiority complex Dr. Freud ever imagined. I had no assurance whatsoever. Conversations with people terrified me. I was a social flop *par excellence*—you know, the kind of chap who sits by himself at parties and says 'Yes' and 'No' or perhaps 'Really?' when he's spoken to. I didn't let myself express my thoughts. I was too afraid. In spite of my years and all I had gone through, I was actually timid with people.

"It must have been bad, because it was so obvious. Every fortuneteller I ever went to spotted it at once. They invariably told me I was dangerously lacking in the 'civic side,' as they sometimes called it, or the 'social side.' They always said my social outlets were dammed up by fear. That was before 'complexes' were popular.

"Developing that 'social side' of me has been one of the hardest jobs my wife or anyone ever faced, I'm sure. I am naturally a shy person, but she knew how important such a side is to everyone—not only an actor, but a doctor, lawyer, writer, businessman. So she set about it.

"She did it very cleverly. She did not demand much of me in the way of social activity. But Ouida made me enjoy the times we did go out or entertain. She brought me in contact with interesting people. She drew me out and turned the conversation to me. I can hear her now saying, 'What do *you* think about it, Basil?' I'd have to speak up then, and, with a little encouragement, I soon found myself talking and liking it."

I had to smile. In Hollywood today the Rathbones are celebrated as hosts. They move mostly in the circle of picture people interested in the arts. The Max Reinhardts, the Edward G. Robinsons, the Henry Blankes, the Charles Boyers are among their intimate friends. When Basil and his wife entertain, it's very much of an event, too. Hollywood has seldom seen a party to match the costume affair they gave celebrating their eleventh wedding anniversary last year. It was a brilliant event, and I said so.

"I'm glad you mentioned that," said Basil. "I think it was a grand party, too, and I can say so because I come to my own parties as a guest. Ouida does it all and when Ouida does anything she does it right.

"But she never overdoes it. It is only because what she attempts is done so well that it's remembered. She still demands little of me in the way of social activity. We are at home three hundred nights in the year, easily. That is because the home that Ouida has woven about me is so attractive to us both that neither of us wishes to be anywhere else.

"I do not like to play the often quite despicable characters I do. To be convincing, I have to summon up such unpleasant thoughts and feelings. I am frequently worn out and discouraged after a day with them at the studio.

"But when I come home in the evening it is to a home that has been created about me and in which I feel at once happy. My wife has a quality of relaxation and assurance about her which immediately restores me. She is small but colorful, dainty but strong. She always reminds me of a Goya painting. I draw new life from her."

IT was getting dark. Basil Rathbone reached up and snapped on the light.

"No," he protested, "don't go yet. Let me tell you of Ouida's latest gift to me. I think it is the finest thing I have ever known. She has brought me back my son, Rodion. He is the son of my first wife. We have been separated since 1919. He is here now, living with us, working in the technical department at Warner Brothers, and loving it. Ouida did it alone. Unknown to me, she made friends with Marian, my former wife. She wrote my boy in England and made friends with him, too. She brought us together again, and now my happiness is complete. And I owe this, as I owe everything, to her."

We were shaking hands. The glow of the lamp revealed the strong, good features in Basil Rathbone's sensitive face.

"You can see," he said, "that for a thousand reasons I owe my wife a debt of gratitude I can never repay. The least I can do is give her the credit. Because of Ouida, life to me is intensely enjoyable. She has helped me live in an age of super-realities and at the same time to hold onto my dreams— which she loves as dearly as I do—and as I love her."

He looked away into the dusk. "I think," he said, "a great many Hollywood husbands might say the same thing—if they would."

"Or if they could," I suggested. Then I left, thinking what a really bitter travesty on Hollywood it is that a man of Basil Rathbone's warm and sentimental soul should be known all over as a cruel, black-hearted villain.

Jackie Coogan visited the "Peck's Bad Boy" set to see Jackie Cooper in the rôle Coogan played more than ten years ago. Director Edward F. Cline stopped work long enough for a "bad boy" reunion

Ever meet Mickey Mouse's daddy? The little cartoon comic, who seems to be about the most popular star in the world, is created by Walt Disney, the smiling gentleman here. And as you see, he has his star well trained in yessing, an old Hollywood custom

Hollywood At Play

[CONTINUED FROM PAGE 107]

THE STARS IN COCOANUT GROVE

in the photograph on pages 106 and 107

THE extreme left-hand couple on the floor is Maureen O'Sullivan and Johnny Farrow. Next, Viola Dana and Sidney Lanfield, and third from the left, Hoot Gibson smiles at his partner. Behind Hoot, Dick and Mrs. Arlen, and in the lower right hand corner of the page, Marie Prevost and Buster Collier.

On the right-hand page in the foreground are (left) Helen Vinson with Al Hall, and (right) Skeets and Mrs. Gallagher. Behind these couples we see, left to right, Zeppo and Mrs. Marx, Kay Francis and Kenneth MacKenna, Clive and Mrs. Brook, Carole Lombard and Bill Powell.

On the steps at the left, Ruth, Tom and Mrs. Mix are being shown in, while to the right on the stairs a similar service is being performed for Adolphe and Mrs. Menjou (Kathryn Carver).

---

and Day'?" she asked Phil several weeks before it was heard in Hollywood. "Get it." And he got it. Somehow, Joan's prophecies concerning song hits always come true.

And then there's Joan dancing around rather dreamily with Ricardo Cortez or Gary Cooper or Clark Gable, often to the strains of "Waltzing In a Dream," and *holding a creamy white gardenia between her teeth.*

You should have seen Mr. Sight-See-er Tourist the first night he beheld that. And a visiting Elk leaned out of the balcony so far he lost his balance, clutched a palm tree and swung on the same limb with a petrified monkey until help came.

But, by gosh, he was goin' to make sure he saw what he thought he saw, and tell the folks back home the latest way to sport a corsage.

DIGNIFIED little Joan Bennett moves gracefully about the floor with hubby, Gene Markey. Joan has a very stately way of holding her aristocratic head and she carries herself straight as an arrow when gliding around. She looks up and sees sister Constance with the Marquis coming down the stairway. Joan smiles . . . then she sees Gilbert Roland just behind Connie and knows that it is to be *his* tango instead of Hank's.

Doug Fairbanks, Jr., moves from table to table for a little chat with friends. His quick eye takes in the panorama and stops for a brief moment on a table across the floor. It is Joan, smiling dreamily into the handsome face of Franchot Tone.

Doug moves on. The next moment he is gliding beautifully across the dance floor with—Katharine Hepburn. Glamorous, interesting, unusual Katharine who keeps Hollywood puzzled as much as Doug does. There should be something in common, at least, between these two personalities when they begin chatting. It's Harris, night after night, behind the waving baton, who instantly senses the stars' moods. Knows, almost, what these world-famous people are thinking.

There was something about the way little Alice White smiled, something big and hurt about her eyes, as she sat at her table near the dance floor, which told Phil the story of what was to come. The parting of the ways with her fiancé, Cy Bartlett. The baton waved a bit slower that night, the music beat and throbbed in sympathy.

It happened the next day, that break. And it was Phil who knew again instantly when Cy and Alice made up. That evening he played "Say It Isn't So," and Alice smiled.

Above the softly lighted floor are balconies. It's interesting to watch the progress of a shy

and blooming new romance. They sit at their balcony table, far in the background. At a glance, Phil takes it in, and knows. Gradually, with carefully selected music, he brings them out. A waltz, a tango or a love song and, sure enough, they're smiling over the rail for all the world to see.

THE romance of Dick Powell and Mary Brian bloomed in the Cocoanut Grove. A balcony bloom. Cary Grant first saw the lovely Virginia Cherrill from behind a palm tree in the Grove.

There was the night a few years back when the lovely Jean Harlow sat at a ringside table and Howard Hughes sat directly across. Howard and Jean hadn't known each other. But that waving, fluttering baton, that steady smile and, finally, the music to "Can't We Be Friends," did the trick. Jean and Howard were dancing. This was long before tragedy stalked into Jean's life—before her first break in Hughes' picture, "Hell's Angels."

The red carnation, the very dark, crimson flower in the button hole of Phil's dinner jacket, had all the up and coming movie boys on the jump. Hollywood florists were almost hysterical trying to find the same flower. But the nearest they could come to it was an anemic light red. While Doug Jr., who knew the secret, smiled and said nothing. As a matter of fact, the flower is especially dyed each day for the orchestra leader. And, is that an idea?

It's to the strains of the Argentine tango that Charlie Chaplin and Paulette Goddard do their fanciest stepping. The dips, the glides, the twirls of Charlie and Paulette, are something to write long letters home about.

It was in the midst of the dreamiest waltz, one Tuesday, that a commotion was heard at one end of the orchestra platform. The door to "The Little Club," just adjoining, had opened and, in a body, out stepped the Four Marx Brothers. Phil immediately sensed danger, took a firmer hold on the baton and "Take Me In Your Arms" floated out over the Grove.

Without a word or a minute's planning, the four Marxes stepped to the front of the platform and immediately began singing "Dinah." Which had absolutely no connection with the music being played.

"Dinah, is there anything finer," they yelped, while the waltz went on. "In the state of Carolina," they quartetted while the drummer hesitated and missed two beats and a bang. The saxophonist was playing half "Dinah" and half waltz. The piano player was feebly wiping his brow. "Dinah" kept right on going. The dancers, after trying to "Dinah" and waltz at the same time, stopped in utter astonishment.

With a bing-bang of the baton, the orchestra immediately swung into "Dinah" just as the Marx Brothers decided that "Take Me In Your Arms" was a better tune anyway, and, heaven help us, here was the orchestra on "Dinah" and the Marx Brothers on "Take Me In Your Arms," and half the audience rolling on the floor and the other half up the palm trees with the coconuts.

At the sad, very sad, conclusion, the Marxes took a bow and announced that, really, all they were looking for anyhow, was the check room.

And twenty-seven gentlemen, including Joel McCrea, Richard Arlen and Gene Raymond, rushed them to the check room, while "Take Me In Your Arms" got off to another start.

FROM Harris' bandstand, it's interesting to note how the different stars dance. He can give you the low-down on them all. Gloria Stuart and her husband, both beautiful dancers, glide quickly and swiftly across the floor. Gloria with her eyes closed. Joan Crawford and her partner are rather slow, dreamy dancers. Joan always with her head thrown back, as if listening to far off music, and the everlasting gardenia between her teeth or resting fragrantly in the palm of her hand.

Dorothy Mackaill, the jolliest dancer on the floor, calling to this one, or chatting with that one. Mae Murray, once a professional, is a smooth, perfect tangoer.

Carole Lombard is in perfect rhythm with Bill Powell. Joan Blondell and Georgie Barnes step lively.

When a certain player wishes to publicly announce that all, alas, is over, he attends the Grove with a new heart interest. And the world accepts it as a public announcement. Los Angeles newspapers recently carried the

"As artist to artist" in the Ambassador's gay Cocoanut Grove. When Thelma Todd and husband Pasquale De Cicco were still good friends, shown in a momentary aside with Phil Harris, who waves the baton for his famous orchestra. Phil has a prominent rôle also in "Melody Cruise"

announcement that a certain actor and his wife had parted. "Couldn't be," Hollywood shrugged. But when the star appeared at the Grove the very next Tuesday night with another lady, Hollywood knew that he wanted to tell them it was true. The same thing happened to Lowell Sherman and Helene Costello. To Eleanor Boardman and King Vidor. "The Declaration of Independence," the Grove has been dubbed.

Here, among the palms and lights, come motion picture executives and officials. Searching for talent. More casting is done in the Cocoanut Grove than is really done at the studios.

For instance, there were those two RKO-Radio scouts who sat night after night, at a table near the orchestra. With one eye cocked downward, Phil went through his program. Wondering. Glancing over the floor to see who might be spotted for what was, evidently, a big rôle. Thinking perhaps that by certain selections he might bring out their good points. And then, at the end of two weeks' watching, the men arose and walked over to Phil. "Like to see you," they said. So, behind sheltering palms, they told him. Carefully they'd been watching him, that grin, that red, oh so red, carnation, and would he make a picture for them?

For once, the baton wouldn't wave. It merely fluttered. And so Phil Harris came to the movies in that grand three reeler, "So This Is Harris." With more pictures to come.

In fact, they wanted only a two reel short, but the thing turned out so well, the powers that be decided not an inch of those three reels could be cut.

No wonder the boy friends of those lady stars watch with a jealous eye when Phil steps up to the edge of the platform and begins his song. And Phil, standing there with the lights pouring down upon him, knows what's going on.

"When It's Darkness on the Delta" he sings, while all the time to himself he thinks, "Look at that bozo. Trying to edge that blonde cutie away. Doesn't want her to listen, eh? Well, she'll listen and he'll like it." And on the song goes, and she listens and the boy friend does like it. Never dreaming, of course, that behind those twinkling blue eyes of Phil's and those deep, full teasing notes, a comedy all his own is going on.

There are always certain people of the movie colony who make spectacular entrances. With the music swelling a little louder or growing a little softer.

Mary Pickford, for instance, always draws a grand sweep from the orchestra, and Mary usually has more than one escort.

Claudette Colbert, with her own husband, Norman Foster, also draws a special serenade. Here *is* an occasion.

But it's Maurice Chevalier, zat gay Maurice, with the lovely Lilian Harvey, who makes ze one grand splash. Zowie.

Down the steps they come, the Frenchman and the English star. Every eye fastened upon them. The trumpets trump, the flute flutters, the drums roll and Phil's grin grows wider.

While right behind them, always, comes the tall, French secretary of Maurice's. It's always a threesome, never a twosome, for Chevalier.

And can he dance? *Mon Dieu* and a hot cha-cha. Ask Phil.

Occasionally, an erring husband comes tripping blithely in with a cutie on his arm. Immediately, Phil seizes the large, ebony baton and makes a sweeping no-no-no across instead of the usual up and down gesture. The gentleman knows to take to his heels. Wifie is probably present.

But the climax of climaxes was reached recently. The beauteous Peggy Hopkins Joyce had arrived in town. The Grove was abuzz with excitement. Everyone knew the lovely Peggy would certainly be at the Grove

HER TRAINING TABLE IS AT THE "RITZ" . . . YET SHE HAS 'ATHLETE'S FOOT'

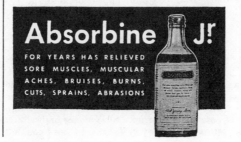

in a blazing mass of diamonds that would have even the stuffed monkeys throwing coconuts at the customers.

And then, Tuesday night arrived. Ten o'clock came. No Peggy. No diamonds. No handsome prince of an escort. Eleven o'clock came. Twelve o'clock. And then, suddenly, even the orchestra let out a sour, surprised note.

There, at the top of the stairs, stood Peggy.

Without a single piece of jewelry and clutching the arm of Jack Oakie in a white sweat shirt. Only Phil's quick action in snapping the orchestra into "Only a Shanty in Old Shanty Town," saved the day.

Oh, it's a place of comedy. Of tragedy. Of heartaches. Of heart throbs. Of romance. This Cocoanut Grove of Hollywood. While above it all stands Phil Harris, looking down. Waving a gay baton. Seeing. Understanding.

Robbing the Cradle for Stars

[CONTINUED FROM PAGE 81]

voice, "It's a sign of fame. Great fame."

Today, Shirley Temple's name is on every lip. I dare say without any exaggeration whatsoever, Shirley Temple is the most popular actress in Hollywood today.

And she is just five years old.

Naturally this invasion of child talent has had its effect upon the motion picture industry. The change is felt in every department from the casting office right up through the wardrobe and writing departments.

IN almost every wardrobe department the frocks of mature stars lie neglected while groups of sewers gather about little frocks of fluff to "Ah" and to "Oh."

Writers who could write child dialogue had to be brought in. "But would a child say that?" is now the favorite wail that floats through the windows of every conference room in town. What a blonde siren would say to her heavy sweetie on the screen is no longer important.

Oh, it's left its mark all over town. Behind it all is plenty of thought and effort, grief and woe, headache and gray hairs.

The nervous director, once furious at the least delay, is now off in some corner with The Child (they speak of him with reverence) perched on his knee. Together, they are going over the scene. If it takes an hour, or days even, what of it? The Child must understand. Let the adult stars stand around and get corns if they want to. The Child is the one who will draw in the shekels at the box-office these days.

Directors who once kicked over chairs and gave the movies back to the Indians when more than five takes were necessary, now go on with one take after another. The baby star must get it right.

After the seventeenth take in "You Belong to Me," in which Helen Mack, Lee Tracy and little, six-year-old David Holt took part, Helen nervously approached Director Al Werker.

"Was I all right in that scene, Mr. Werker?" she asked.

He stared at her open-mouthed. "Why, Helen, I—I—guess so," he said. "You see, I forgot you were in it. I was watching David."

It's no wonder, however. Two days after shooting had begun on that picture, they knew it was no use. The picture was David's. "Give it to him," Lee Tracy graciously said. "The kid's got everything." So, changes were made and Lee and Helen Mack played second fiddle to an unknown boy.

When the picture was previewed, hard-boiled critics sat up and howled themselves silly. Little David Holt had pulled a Shirley Temple and the town isn't over it yet.

A little brown-eyed lad, no bigger than a minute, David came all the way from Florida with his mother and baby sister to break into movies. At three David was trouping all over the State of Florida with a group of kiddies. Singing, dancing and one-night-standing it like an old timer.

But, once in Hollywood, it wasn't so easy until David's neighbor, a veteran actor, brought David to the notice of a casting director. It was all over then but the shouting, with Paramount grabbing up his option, co-starring him with Max Baer, and even testing his baby sister, aged three.

It's the same story in every studio in town. Out at Universal they go into long raptures over their little Baby Jane Quigley, just three. And is she a sugar-plum!

We watched her make a scene with Claudette Colbert in "Imitation of Life." The camera was going and all was ready. Claudette read her line first. The baby looked up strangely, but went right on to the end of the scene. The minute the director called "Cut," that tiny little mite of a baby cried out, "It's wrong, it's wrong, she said it wrong."

Claudette actually grew scarlet beneath her make-up. "She's right," she shrugged. "I did change a word. I'll be more careful the next time," she promised Jane with a smile.

Mickey Rooney, the little Irisher, is the clown of the bunch. Soon after he was signed by Metro-Goldwyn-Mayer, we went over to the studio to look over the Rooney individual, aged eleven. A ripe old age, that practically makes him the grandpappy of the bunch. (Unless you include Frankie Thomas, now twelve, on the stage since he was nine months old.)

As we passed the darkened prop department, the sound of jazz, sizzling hot, floated out the door. There, at a prop department piano, pounding out red hot melody and doing an imitation of Cab Calloway at the same time, sat little Mickey.

He keeps his entire set in a constant state of hysterics and in "Hide-Out" stole practically all the laughs from the chagrined Bob Montgomery.

He played the part of Clark Gable as a child in "Manhattan Melodrama," and did all right with the rôle.

"Yep, I got myself a contract all right," Mickey said. "Don't think it was easy, though. It took years of hard work."

AMONG the army of baby free lance players, little Cora Sue Collins is the busiest on the lot. And feels a bit uppish because she was chosen among dozens of others to play Garbo herself, as a child, in "Queen Christina."

You must believe me when I tell you this little brown-eyed miss, who tore out our hearts in "The Strange Case of Clara Deane," owes her success in Hollywood largely to herself. Her mother was anxious to bring Cora Sue to Hollywood and pictures from their home in West Virginia, but lacked the money. "I suppose I could borrow a little money and sell silk stockings on the way," she said, "but I couldn't

possibly subject you and your sister to such chance."

"Oh, but Mother, we want to," Cora Sue cried. "We shan't mind if things get bad."

"Not even when it means sitting up in a day coach all the way?" her mother asked.

"Shucks, no. I love sitting up," Cora Sue said. And so it was decided. The going was pretty bad. Long after they arrived in Hollywood. But Cora Sue was true to her word. She never complained. And the break finally did come.

No, it isn't all chance when these "babes in the Hollywoods" let forth a stream of tears that wrecks the heart of every fan in the audience. Babes that they are, they've known a bit of strife and work and grief themselves. They aren't just children. They're troupers.

OVER at RKO Studios they scream loudly to all who will listen about their little three-year-old Jane Preston, who made her début in "Anne of Green Gables."

"Wait till you see our Jane," they boast. "You'll forget all the others." And on they go, bragging about their Jane like any fond and adoring parent.

Then there's Richard Ralston Arlen, sturdy son of Richard Arlen and Jobyna Ralston. Look at the job of work Ricky did in "She Made Her Bed." A comer? Certainly.

There are two other little girls the studios are keeping their eyes on. Virginia Weidler and Carmencita Johnson. They caught on in "Mrs. Wiggs of the Cabbage Patch."

And more young—very young—men:

Ronnie Cosby, nearly seven now, who can make a lion sit up and take notice. He did that, with the loss of some of his own hide, in "King of the Jungle," some time ago. He was nearly five then. Since that time he's been in eight pictures, and going strong. Another comer is Scotty Beckett, who wowed 'em in "Whom the Gods Destroy." And Billy Lee, who has just started his screen career with Paramount. And Buster Phelps, who has been in twelve pictures. And has two more signed for. Then the inimitable Spanky MacFarland of the Hal Roach comedies, who has made a hit in feature pictures, too. A grand actor and trouper. A natural!

Those are all in Hollywood. But the East is beginning to brag. It has Jackie Borene, recently on location with Ben Hecht and Charles MacArthur. Jackie first came into notice because of his voice. His sister, Sally (a song-and-dance miss herself), found the kid brother so good she gave up her job in order to manage him. He's a Paramount discovery, so he'll probably land on the Coast in short order.

And, of course, Dickie Moore can't be passed up. He's proven his worth, and keeps right on proving it.

A RARE picture it is that goes out of Hollywood without its child prodigy today. A friend tells of meeting Director Mickey Neilan hurrying to the front office with a script of his latest picture, "The Lemon Drop Kid," under his arm.

"What's the matter, Mickey?" the friend asked.

"Matter? Why, listen, they've given me a picture to direct with no child in it. What do they think I am? I want a child like everybody else."

And he got it. Baby LeRoy was written in.

Yes, it's a new era in pictures. If it keeps up, and it has every appearance of doing so, it wouldn't surprise me to see some of the old timers take to rompers and safety-pins. For it's the day of the new youth in Hollywood.

MOTHERED BY AN APE—HE KNEW ONLY THE LAW OF THE JUNGLE

—to seize what he wanted!

TARZAN THE APE MAN

with
Johnny **WEISSMULLER**
Neil **HAMILTON**
C. Aubrey **SMITH**
Maureen **O'SULLIVAN**

Based upon the characters created by EDGAR RICE BURROUGHS

Adaptation by CYRIL HUME
Dialogue by IVOR NOVELLO

ANOTHER MIRACLE PICTURE

directed by W. S. VAN DYKE
Creator of "TRADER HORN"

METRO-GOLDWYN-MAYER

THE MOST DANGEROUS SPY OF ALL TIME, men worshipped her like a goddess, only to be betrayed by a kiss!

For her exotic love men sold their souls, betrayed their country, gave up their lives! Here is one of the truly great dramas that has come out of the war—based on the incredible adventures of Mata Hari—called the most dangerous woman who ever lived. Who but the supreme Greta Garbo could bring to the screen this strange, exciting personality! Who but Ramon Novarro could play so well the part of the lover who is willing to sell his honor for a kiss! See these two great stars in a picture you will never forget.

It was beyond the powers of mortal man to withstand the lure of this siren.

The lives of a million men—the destinies of nations—these were the stakes she played for.

Greta **GARBO** *in* **MATA HARI**

Ramon **NOVARRO**

with
LIONEL BARRYMORE
and
LEWIS STONE

Directed by
George **FITZMAURICE**

A METRO-GOLDWYN-MAYER PICTURE

George Bernard Shaw, greatest living man of letters, gives in at last to the talkies! Here the whiskered Irish playwright is shown on the set at the British International Studios, near London. About him are some of the players who are filming his comedy, "How He Lied to Her Husband"

Mad, Merry Malibu

[CONTINUED FROM PAGE 113]

purchased. A year later came fire number two and, while the fire engine snorted in all its red painted glory up and down Malibu's back road, seven houses burned down. *There was no water.*

Fire number three, one year later, and the hose wouldn't reach. A dampish drizzle played lightly about the flames. And more homes bit the dust.

Malibu, we salute you.

And while fire raged, smoke belched and timbers crashed, a real estate agent stood midst flame and smoke, like the boy on the burning deck, and sold the lot next door to an eager customer. While cinders fell under his coat collar.

He bought it, I tell you, he bought it.

Malibu—well, I can't go on.

And Leila Hyams found two collies, four scotties, a police dog, four children and one rabbit, slightly scorched, piled into her front bedroom by frantic owners. Two days later all was safely disposed of but the rabbit. No one ever came to claim it.

Week nights are comparatively quiet, except for Bert Wheeler's visitors and assorted sizes of Marx Brothers. But come Saturday night and tired out picture stars race home from the studios to get "away from it all" and find themselves attending a beach version of the Mayfair. Swanky parties. Swanky food. Satin slippers full of sand. Crashing one another's parties. Behaving as they never dreamed of in Beverly Hills.

Breakfast along the gray white way is usually at eleven. Sandwiches in the patio (what, you didn't know about the patios?) at two, and buffet dinner from seven Friday night until ten Tuesday morning.

CLIQUES are formed. There's the handball, tennis-playing clique who haven't seen the ocean for years and years. They have a vague idea that it's there. When it grows dark, they merely turn on one of the many searchlights that adorn the front of many homes and the game continues.

Then there's the fishing clique. Buster Collier, Arline Judge, Wesley Ruggles, Leila Hyams and others who hire boats to go far out on the briny deep.

While the wives and husbands who didn't go fishing stay home and form the bridge-playing clique. Is that a laugh or not?

Then there's the "simply ravishing, my deah" clique that comprise all visiting celebrities and visit weekly with Lil Tashman. Such delightful parties, my dear.

And the yacht-cruising clique, who anchor offshore and wave madly to those on shore who wave madly back to those offshore—I mean.

How'd I get on this yacht anyhow? The yacht-wavers comprise the Richard Arlens, the Charlie Farrells, the Richard Barthelmess' and others.

THEN there are people who actually go in the water. I mean beyond the first wave. They get wet. And love it. Betty Brent is the champion get-wetter.

Why, even the servants clique. The Spanish fronts won't associate with the frame huts and the Swiss chaleters don't even see the mere cottagers. Nix.

There are those who have cliqued themselves clear out of Malibu. Just as Mary and Doug pioneered themselves out of Hollywood into Beverly Hills, so have some gotten too ultra for Malibu.

There are just two places for them to go. Above or below the potteries. My yes, there's a pottery. Must have our little local industry, you know.

So we have above-the-potteries-Malibuites and below-the-potteries-Malibuites. Both are nice.

A star's career may be watched in this fashion. From Malibu to above the potteries. Promising. To below the potteries. He's arrived.

Casting for pictures has been known to take place on the sands in a very large way. For instance, Estelle Taylor was having a snooze on the beach when she was awakened by a click-click-click. She opened her eyes to see Wesley Ruggles, the director, snapping pictures of her luscious form. The next day the test was shown at the studio and won for Estelle her grand part in "Cimarron." Where she wore long panties, seven petticoats and a satin basque.

Too, a man never knows from year to year whether the interior of his home will be Queen Anne or Louis the Fourteenth. It depends on the wife. One wife may like Anne but next year the new wife favors Louis. Or Chinese Buddhas. With plenty of incense. The third year his even newer wife may prefer early Harper's Bazaar and think she's on the Mediterranean.

And nothing will prevent her from going Riviera. Nothing.

Some go in for interior decorations with inferior decorators. Where every little doodad has a meaning all its own. Others get a great kick out of furnishing their own. It's not unusual to have a famous head suddenly thrust itself out of an upstairs window and scream, "Quick, I've just finished my bathroom curtains. Come quickly."

And the Keystone cops fade completely out of memory's picture as an entire colony race wildly to see the simply adorable accordion pleated, crepe chiffon, hand-embroidered bathroom curtains. That cute, they are.

BUT Connie Bennett combines interior decoration with common sense. William Haines, who has a terrific flair for knowing what's right in a home, has done Connie's beach home. Smart simplicity is the keynote with *red buckram* lampshades.

Just plan red buckram. While Fay Wray's are plan white silk.

Louise Fazenda claims her new house is a late Fazenda model. The bed may not be a gem of art but the mattress is swell. The curtains may not be anything to write to Congress about, but they're sunfast.

There is also the comical situation of waking up one morning and smelling the bacon frying for one's bitterest enemy, next door. Who has moved in overnight.

And that has been known to happen in the land of fueds and fever.

And there's the store. The good old general store across the highway. That might, from a bird's-eye view of the outside, be the general store of Si Perkins' over at Pumpkin Center, by gosh. And at that, it might be on the inside, too, with its queer little vegetable stalls and painted blue shelves. But on those shelves, brother and sister, on those shelves. It would pop the eyes of Mrs. Van Astor herself. What a store this has turned out to be. Gleaming jars of stuffed mangoes, in vinegar. Little blue snails with a Chevalier accent all over the bottle. Artichoke hearts in sherry. Walnut catsup. And try that on your baked beans sometime. Stuffed oranges and pineapple in grenadine. Bottles of crème de menthe.

And on those rickety vegetable stands. Well, name anything out of season and Mr. Bills, the owner will have it. You'll find raspberries at the Malibu general store when the only other raspberries in the state of California will be a loud, hissing noise.

It's the prize general store of the world. The symbol of Hollywood. Moved a bit to the north. Where famous stars gather to gossip, shop, and take turns at the telephone.

MALIBU. For eight years more it will carry on the glamorous traditions of a motion picture colony. Then the leases will be up.

Where Jack Gilbert races out of his house every morning, bosom bared to the sweeping winds, head flung back, to the water's edge, glancing quickly up and down and if no one's looking, wetting one large toe on the right foot and rushing back.

Where parties get bigger and waves dash higher. Where in eight more years a lady will step down from a stone mansion on an overlooking hill and say, "Amscray." And the great conflagration of 1940 begins.

When the gay, mad spirit, that will never die as long as pictures are made, will go right on and take itself somewhere else.

From Hollywood to Malibu.

From Malibu to Somewhere Else.

The stars cannot stand still in their courses.

Why Constance Is Unpopular in Hollywood

[CONTINUED FROM PAGE 115]

ran toward her; tumbled; fell. Connie helped the child up. Then she dashed through the crowd, paying them as little attention as possible. "High-hatting" them.

The publicity which resulted said Connie knocked down the child in her effort to avoid those who had come to pay her a courtesy, "while passing through in her private car."

OF course, Connie might have been more gracious. No question about that. But she wasn't in a private car and she is, honestly, afraid of crowds. No question about that. Shy, too. Always self-conscious about meeting people. She once said, "I must be spoken to first. I cannot get courage to speak to those I do not know well!" Anything Connie does is honest. Honest to the point of being rude. She told me, "I don't like the stage. I couldn't stand it. I couldn't bear the people looking at me. That's why I prefer pictures."

Directors usually like her. Intelligent ones. She helps them make good pictures. The productions are as much hers directorially as theirs. She will not do what seems silly or inconsequential even for a picture.

When Paul Stein was doing "Born to Love," he issued a call for Connie for nine o'clock in the morning. Connie was on time. She is rarely late. She sat until four in the afternoon without working. She told him:

"I am not going to come any more unless you are certain you are ready for me. I'm not going to sit around on a set from nine until four. It is absolutely unnecessary and it isn't fair. You might as well resign yourself for I simply will not do it. When you need me, really need me, I will be here." She left. She was never called again unless she was needed.

Her friends are limited. She will not mix with people simply because they are "other celebrities." In spite of the fact that she is one of the wealthiest women in the city, she does not entertain except at little, intimate parties.

When Joel McCrea was friends with Constance, he told me: "I have never known a woman as pretty who was as intelligent." Today, he speaks in the same way of her.

She is also the most argumentative. I went down to her to talk about this story. Told her frankly what I was going to do. She admires frankness above all other qualities. She refused to be quoted. Said she would put up no defense! It was beneath her dignity.

But she talked—not for quotation. How she talked. To be perfectly frank, I couldn't get a word in edgewise. She told me her side of all these stories I have printed and many more that there is not room to print.

AND again and again she said, "I lost my temper. I couldn't be blamed for what I said in a fit of temper, could I?"

It's never entered Constance Bennett's head to control her temper. It's never entered her head to play politics as Hollywood plays them. If she's square and honest and does what she's supposed to do to help make good pictures—that's enough. She's earned her money and her fame and her right to the inheritance which her father, Dick Bennett, handed down to her.

When the three Bennett girls were fifteen, father Dick told them to live life as they desired. "Go out and get what you want!" he warned them. "You're only in life a short time; make the most of it." We understand he also instilled the idea that a man who isn't worth chasing isn't worth having.

Well, they've lived up to those instructions. There's something else, too. Constance Bennett was born with a platinum spoon in her mouth. She has never known want. She's never had to hunt a job today so she could eat

tomorrow. She was educated in the best private schools in this country and Europe. Her broad A is as natural to her as Gloria Swanson's Middle Western twang was once to her.

The rest of Hollywood isn't like that. It has fought and suffered and struggled. It has starved yesterday and eaten caviar today. Connie has had only the caviar. Hollywood resents that. It feels that it belongs to those who have *climbed* rather than to those who have *inherited*.

Connie thinks she is tolerant. She says she is. There she is wrong. She doesn't know the meaning of the word tolerance. How could she? People have to suffer to comprehend what others may suffer; they have to *starve* to understand hunger. It isn't her fault, but tolerance is as foreign to her nature as intolerance is to Marion Davies! Marion is generous because she knows from experience what it is to be without money. Connie has no conception.

CONNIE is truthful but her penchant for argument, her high order of intelligence which makes her feel the right to be *victor*, makes her shape things to her own convenience. Her friends will admit that, if you press them on the matter. For example: A writer told her she would not quote her. She didn't. She merely used the information which Connie had given—in the writer's own language. A writer's prerogative, surely. But Connie swore the writer had promised not to use the information. Connie twisted the situation to suit her convenience when she didn't like the results of what she, herself, had said.

Connie's father gave some facts about her youthful days to another writer. Connie was furious; lost her temper. She and her father barely spoke. When the fight got into print, Connie was again much disappointed. Connie had told it herself. When reminded of the fact, she assailed the people who heard her for not having intelligence enough to refrain from repeating it.

She may have blamed herself for talking of it in the first place—but I doubt it.

There are few to whom she will listen. Only to those who have stood their ground and insisted with sane arguments which her intelligence has been forced to accept—after they have mustered the courage and perseverance to say them! When convinced, she is sincerely fair. "I was wrong; I am sorry." But only those with courage know that. Most of Hollywood is too intuitively resentful to try the experiment.

I revert to this matter of truthfulness. An example from her youth. Her father, Dick Bennett, is a splendid poet. When Connie was a débutante attracting beaus as a honeysuckle does bees, she liked to appear perfect in all things. Father would write the poetry; Connie would memorize it and recite it as though she had written it.

She never *said* she wrote it.

She wouldn't lie. But she left the impression which pleased her.

A CLEVER woman. Too clever for Hollywood! Too beautiful; too rich; too attractive to men; too highly paid; too gold-bespooned; too outspoken; too intolerant of stupidity (of which there is much in any city!); too indifferent to what is said about her; too dominant; too sincerely afraid of other people; too much talked about. Hollywood could not be expected to like her.

You could. I do. Plain, every-day people like exaggerations. And Connie is an exaggeration!

They Don't Want to Be Stars!

[CONTINUED FROM PAGE 161]

I hated it and wouldn't return to it for anything!"

Paramount has a good looking lad, Johnny Engstead, who is of the same opinion. Johnny works in the publicity department, but he has all the qualifications of a Gary Cooper. There is a genuineness about him that has endeared him to fellow workers. It is generally felt at Paramount that Johnny has loads of stuff to offer on the screen.

But Johnny can't be bothered. "I'm in the best of all departments now," says Johnny, "and I happen to know it. Maybe I'd make more money in front of the camera, but what about ten years from now? I'm learning something where I am. I've seen several quit their good jobs in the studios to act, but in the end they all want their jobs back. I'm plenty satisfied!"

OUT at M-G-M you will find stunning Margery Prevost, sister of the famous Marie, busily working in the modern settings department. Margery is another one who could (did, in fact) but won't. Fresh from Ziegfeld's "Follies," Margery arrived in Hollywood a few years ago all ready to get famous in a movie way.

Her sister backed her and the parts began rolling in. But Margery's interest waned. Acting lost its appeal and in its place came an intense interest in interior decorating and set dressing. Against the advice of all those interested in her film career, she quit the studio cold and got a job in the interior decorating department of a large Los Angeles store. Her ingenuity at the work became known and soon the studio called her back as an authority on interior decorating. Now she is assistant to the chief, Cedric Gibbons, and is through forever with the make-up box.

"We all knock around a bit before we find what we want," Margery told me, "and that's what I was doing when I was in front of the camera. But why anyone should want to be in the movies when they could have such fascinating work as I now have is beyond me. Let 'em have their big salaries and fame and let me go right on learning to be the best decorator in the world. No more movies for me!"

Radio has a youth in Kenny Wesson whom any casting director would welcome. Kenny works in the sound department, but strictly of his own choice. He could as easily be working in front of the mikes, because the boy has all the earmarks of a born actor.

Clever he is, and easy to look at, with a sure-fire personality and an irresistible boyishness. He sings, too.

And does things with his feet!

BUT Kenny, in his own words, "would rather go to work any day than act! Working where I do," he continued, "I see how they make it. I've watched actors come and go (mostly go) for nearly ten years now, and it just makes me like my job more. And now, if you'll excuse me, I'll get back to it."

I hope reformers read this article—the kind of reformers who say American youth is jazz-mad.

It was my impression, in talking with these young men and women, that they are anything but that.

On the contrary, they are almost too serious for their years.

More power to 'em for keeping their heads in this land of make-believe and phony glory. More power to 'em for upsetting the ancient Hollywood theory of: "Scratch a milkman and find a movie actor."

The Girl Who Played Greta Garbo

[CONTINUED FROM PAGE 133]

that assistant directors stand up when she passes by. And Geraldine has so reconstructed her mind that she fancies they stand up when she walks on the set. In reality they do not even find her a comfortable chair

GERALDINE sits close by the star all day long on the set. She watches her every move. When interviewers arrive and Garbo refuses to see them, Geraldine fancies that they have sought her and she imagines what she would have said to them. What magnificent interviews she could give. Would that she were Garbo!

In her simple room with its meagre furnishings at the Studio Club, her life is really lived. The little, plain bed becomes a canopied couch, with solid gold cupids to hold back the silken drapes. Her ordinary white bathtub becomes a sunken pool of black marble and gold. The ivory comb and brush set is genuine Lalique studded in diamonds. She wears the figurative crown of the queen, while Garbo, herself, chooses the staid, quiet atmosphere of the Beverly Hills Hotel.

It is Geraldine's delight to be mistaken for the star and it is a common enough mistake for Garbo's awkward slouch and dowdy clothes to allow her to pass unnoticed in the crowd. Geraldine has the grace and is to the manner of stardom born. An out-of-town visitor told a friend of his great news.

"Where does anyone get the idea that Garbo never goes out?" he said. "Why, I saw her at Plantation the other night with a bunch of people. She was the gayest of the gay. She was dressed in a gorgeous gown and was the center of an admiring group. And she was sweet enough to smile graciously at everybody."

Upon that particular evening Greta Garbo, the actress, was in her room at the hotel reading a script.

Her private life had been at Plantation.

The rumor spread in Hollywood that Garbo had come back from Europe several weeks before scheduled time. One of the newspaper reporters had a friend who said that Garbo was seen in a smart shop buying a pair of grey suede gloves. Her double had needed gloves.

In order to supplement her meagre income Geraldine is one of the regular models at Montmartre on Wednesday. As she arrives and leaves the sight-seers mistake her for Garbo.

Geraldine De Vorak was born to Hollywood stardom, as Garbo was not. Garbo acts for the camera. Geraldine pleases the public.

The other extra girls complain that the double is haughty. What woman who wears the royal raiment would not be? It is her right to live up to what she has made herself.

There is little in common between star and double. Garbo sits in wide-eyed wonder at the striking likeness between herself and her stand-in girl. Geraldine dismisses Garbo with a gesture. *She* is Garbo.

BUT the Frankenstein that she has built within herself has become her undoing. She copied the master too closely. She made herself too nearly in the image of Garbo.

Garbo arrives on the set at her own leisure. Geraldine arrives on the set at her own leisure.

Garbo, the great actress, may conduct herself thus.

Geraldine, an extra girl acting as double to a star, may not.

Geraldine's slight contract was broken. She returned to the extra ranks.

Garbo's new double does not look so much like her, but her hair is more nearly the same color. It is better for the lights.

Will the new double play the Garbo rôle?

Or has Geraldine floated so long upon the Lethean waters of stardom that her life will always be colored by the amazing interlude when she played at being Garbo? Has she so definitely become a star that the long discouraging hours of extra work will be only a cross that every star must bear? Surely her imagination will override time and place and discomfort!

The Man All Hollywood Fears

[CONTINUED FROM PAGE 119]

commission, Inspector Barnett arrived backstage, to inform Mae that unless she cut out some of the lines he was going to close the show.

Mae was willing to coöperate.

"What do you want me to take out?" she asked.

"Take out the whole play," suggested Vince, "and burn it—then take a train out of town."

Bobby Jones bit hard when he made his movie début. Vince was enlisted as his caddy in an exhibition match. He proceeded to give unsolicited advice to the king of the links. Leo Diegel, who had been Barnett-baptized before, was in cahoots. Diegel asked Bobby what to use on a particular shot.

"A three iron," said Jones.

"Too long," scoffed Vince. "Use a five."

Jones frowned. "You carry the clubs, son," he cautioned.

"Say, smart guy, I've been caddying for a long time, and I ought to know."

Jones controlled himself. But Diegel purposely over-played the shot, and added coals to the fire by musing that the caddy must have been right.

From then on Vince sneezed when Bobby putted, asked for autographs at trying moments, and swished Jones' clubs in practice swings as he drove.

"Those are imported clubs," warned Bobby, turning red.

"I don't know why you import them," argued Vince. "You can't even use domestic clubs."

On the eighteenth hole, Bobby blasted a phenomenally long shot (he afterwards told Vince, he was imagining the ball was his head when he hit it!). The crowd gasped with astonishment as the great drive rolled to the edge of the green.

In the silence, Barnett sniffed.

"Sarazen would have gotten on," he observed.

FEW stars have escaped uninsulted from a meeting with this unparalleled menace to composure.

Helen Hayes started when she heard Vince remark that he "sympathized with the poor wife of Charles MacArthur, who is a no good bum."

He pretended to be oblivious to the fact that she was the "poor wife."

Wera Engels, who prides herself on her trim figure, couldn't believe her ears when she heard him, posing as a compatriot, berate her for "letting herself go" in Paris and getting fat and sloppy.

Kay Francis, Gary Cooper, Jack Gilbert, Marion Davies, Spencer Tracy, George Raft, Buddy Rogers, Jean Harlow, Wallace Beery, Eddie Cantor, Al Jolson, Lew Cody, Norma Talmadge—all have "burned" with flaming faces in uncomfortable moments with an insulting stranger afterwards identified as Vince Barnett. For every "rib" takes place in the presence of many others. Somebody has a good time.

Dick Barthelmess heard "Dr. Hoffman," a "foreign sound expert," advise him to retire or else take voice lessons from Texas Guinan!

Jack Dempsey discovered his blood-pressure rising when one of his "waiters," at his own Barbara Hotel opening, snatched a cigar from between his teeth and ground it on the floor, angrily shouting "no smoking!"

Dolores Del Rio learned from a "big German producer" that she was a "flop in Europe, where audiences demand acting."

As a matter of fact, every star in Hollywood has at one time or another suffered or been in on a Barnett "rib-roast."

Even Garbo freezes as she floats by a grinning individual who has the audacity to greet her with "Good morning, Miss Hepburn!"

VINCE BARNETT has a sort of ethics to his insulting. He never picks on weaknesses, because weaknesses exposed or derided result in hurts—and he has found that you can get a "goat" just as readily by attacking strengths or points of pride.

If his victims get mad, he is delighted—but if they get hurt, he is sad, and hurries to apologize. Really "ribbing" with him is an inherited talent. His father did it for thirty years in Pittsburgh!

So far he has only one rival in Hollywood—George Bernard Shaw—and it's the regret of his life that he wasn't on hand to match insults with the peppery Irish sage who left a trail of tears and ruffled feelings after his visit last spring.

Just the mere mention of it makes him sad.

"What a chance," he murmurs wistfully. "What a grand chance!"

Hedy Lamarr Vs. Joan Bennett— and Other Dangerous Hollywood Feuds

[CONTINUED FROM PAGE 123]

wife," but that Gene and Hedy, too, were most welcome to come to Joan's home at any time to call upon Melinda, her attitude, even if it is a little over-cautious, becomes perfectly understandable. But it is also quite understandable that this caution should annoy the beauteous Hedy, just as it must annoy her that Gene's very yacht is named "The Melinda." And it is, obviously, sheer bedevilment that makes Joan dance with Reggie Gardiner at parties and hang on his every word with the most flattering attention.

Of course, Hedy may very well come to understand the great honesty that is Joan's and that quality of intellectual charm and great humor she possesses which makes Gene Markey still her friend, even though they were divorced a good two years before he even met Hedy. It is a safe prophecy that the visits of Melinda will get worked out amicably, for Joan and Gene and Hedy are all charming, civilized people. As it is, Gene does see Melinda every day, either at the studio or at Joan's house. Father and daughter lunch together several times a week and each Saturday they go on a shopping spree with each other. But the same peaceful ending can scarcely be expected of the feud between two of M-G-M's leading ladies—Joan Crawford and Norma Shearer. That is a truly bitter one.

To some extent there has always been antagonism between Joan and Norma, for no two people could be more opposite in temperament—Joan, all passion, impulse, warmth and boundless generosity, and Norma, all intelligence, calm, reserve and cool poise. Theirs is that eternal conflict between the mind and the emotions.

Joan has always smarted under the fact that despite her enormous box-office strength she has never had the glittering million-dollar pictures of the type that have been wrapped around Norma. A "Mannequin" is all very well but no comparison, certainly, to a "Marie Antoinette" from the point of view of prestige, investment or actual production value. But "The Women" was the first time that, star next to star, they played together and almost at once the friction between them began to manifest itself.

It began with hair—or, more exactly, a hairdresser, M-G-M's Sydney Guilaroff. Norma had first claim on his services, but Norma, like scores of Hollywood girls, has no sense of time whatsoever, whereas Joan is amazingly punctual. This meant that while Norma might call for Guilaroff at six o'clock, she often wouldn't keep the appointment until ten or even later, and meanwhile Joan would have to wait, quite naturally burning up the while.

The girls skirmished about clothes, lines, positions and everything else during the actual shooting of "The Women," but it wasn't until nearly the final day that the war broke out in earnest. Joan wasn't in the scene. It was Norma's scene, done in close-up, which is always nerve-wracking. Joan had to be present, to stand in, outside of camera range, but where Norma could see her, so that when the scene was timed Norma would be looking at the right height to be seeing Joan. Also, Joan had to answer Norma's speeches. Joan was called to be present at nine o'clock. She came at nine but Norma didn't arrive until one. Joan kept her temper and all might have passed satisfactorily but Joan was knitting when she got up to rehearse the scene. That made it Norma's turn to burn. She said Joan was being deliberately distracting. Joan put the knitting behind her back. That didn't help either. The two girls faced each other, both elaborately pretending they didn't quite know who was bothering whom. It took all of Director George Cukor's wily diplomacy to get the scene recorded at all, and then not until Joan had fled to her dressing room and cried and Norma had expressed in graphic words her general opinion of other women stars. When, upon completion of the picture, Norma gave a party for the whole cast, Joan (and Paulette Goddard) pointedly stayed away.

The feud that is going on between Dorothy Lamour and Patricia Morison is neither so worldly and humorous as the one between Lamarr and Joan Bennett, nor so bitter as that between Crawford and Shearer, but it is right there, nonetheless. This is not so much a battle of wits as it is one of figures and crowning glories. For up until La Belle Morison came along, Sarong Lamour was Paramount's leading glamour girl. Her hair was always longer than any costume she wore. Her sultry personality and crooning voice were regarded as most unique and very negotiable.

But then just as everything for Dorothy was glowing like your fourth cocktail before dinner, Patricia was discovered—Pat who has a husky voice, too, and a dark cloud of long hair (thirty-nine inches in length as compared to Dotty's thirty-six-inch tresses), and a chassis such as would make all women hope she would trip and break a leg. What's more, Miss Morison could really act. Miss Lamour, looking at her, was, like Queen Victoria—not amused. Here, a la Crawford, was a girl, who is all quick emotion and spontaneity, being confronted by a new and rival beauty, who not only knew what she wanted but showed every promise of getting it. It was enough to bring out the most

Fred R. Archer

Shed no tears for poor Rin-Tin-Tin. He died after having lived fourteen useful years, rich in service, and now goes to the best of dog heavens, we are sure. He earned, during his lifetime on the screen, $300,000, and his name is to be carried on, for his son, Rin-Tin-Tin, Jr., has been carefully trained in all his father's tricks and will carry on in his father's rôles

feminine in Dorothy—and so far it definitely has.

When it comes to the Davis-Hopkins battle, the trail is dark and hidden (mostly by the Warner publicity department). By way of throwing everybody off the scent, Betty and Miriam actually posed in boxing gloves, glaring their hate. That was supposed to be so funny, you would never think it was real. It was funny and it wasn't real. The set battles were, however, but they were subtle ones, and the net result of them was that two brilliant performances grace "The Old Maid," so perhaps it was all to the good.

For the Hollywood girls know how to fight for their place in the camera by means of daggers, harpoons or merely dirty looks. And, considering all they have at stake, they'd be stupid if they acted otherwise. Survival of the fittest is the first law of Hollywood human nature. It has to be, and since one touch of Hollywood human nature is about the only thing left in this darkening world that makes us all grin, let's be thankful for it. Almost anyone can go along sedately, being Nice Nellie all over the place, but it takes girls with dash and fire and wilyness to meet competition at fifty paces—and knock it dead.

Charlie Chan's Chance

WARNER OLAND in another amazing adventure of Earl
Derr Biggers' master sleuth! With eyes that see all, lips that tell
nothing, Charlie Chan unmasks the most sinister crime of his career.
Directed by John G. Blystone, with Alexander Kirkland, H. B. Warner,
Marian Nixon, Linda Watkins . . . . A mighty murder mystery!

FOX

311

BACK STREET

Fannie Hurst's

POWERFUL HUMAN STORY IMMORTALIZED ON THE SCREEN

◆

Waiting—always waiting —in the shadows of the back streets . . . longing for the man she loves . . . asking nothing, receiving nothing—yet content to sacrifice all for him.

WHY?

IRENE DUNNE
LEADING WOMAN OF "CIMARRON"
•
with
JOHN BOLES
LEADING MAN OF "SEED"
Directed by JOHN STAHL

Universal Pictures

UNIVERSAL CITY, CALIFORNIA   *Carl Laemmle*
President   730 FIFTH AVENUE, NEW YORK

312

Hollywood's Soldiers of Fortune

[CONTINUED FROM PAGE 127]

happily married, with a seventeen-year-old son as strapping as he is, and a beautiful daughter of fifteen. Reconciled to a settled and luxurious life, he stays put. But his nostalgia for action and adventures expresses itself in the much publicized "McLaglen Light Horse." Actually, this is as well-drilled, trained and equipped a cavalry troop as you could find anywhere. McLaglen often longs for an excuse to lead it into real action. His only hope at present is for a scrap with the Communists.

ONE of the most colorful figures in the mysterious regions behind the scenes in the studios is Howard Hill, noted athlete and hunter. With bow and arrow he has traveled the wilds of Mexico, the U.S. and Canada, and his adventurous wanderings attracted such hunting companions as the late Glenn Curtiss, the aeroplane magnate, the late Arthur Brisbane, and the late Harvey Firestone. Hill killed the only true big horn sheep ever shot with bow and arrow by a white man, and later spent two years producing a wild animal picture, "The Lost Wilderness," featuring hunting with this primitive weapon.

But strange things can happen, even to champions! During the shooting of "Robin Hood" (on which picture he was technical director), the company was sent on location to the back country near Hollywood. It was a stretch of country noted for wild boars, so Hill and actor Basil Rathbone and a native decided to go on a bow and arrow wild boar hunt. The native brought his rifle along—just in case.

They sighted the boar in a manzanita thicket. Hill's first arrow merely wounded the boar, which thereupon immediately charged the little party.

Rathbone managed to climb to safety in a small tree—but not before the boar had ripped his trouser leg. Then the boar charged Hill.

The archer realized that he wouldn't have time to use his bow, so he made a flying leap into (or onto) the top of a manzanita bush. There he lay, less than two feet under the boar's belly, spread-eagled, while the boar ran around looking for him.

The native finally saved the day by shooting the boar with his rifle. Modern weapons do have their uses, even to a man who holds the national archery field championship and has been California field archery champion since 1934.

IN one of the writer's cells at one of the largest studios is a quiet studious-looking fellow, usually occupied as a scenarist. You probably know him as Major Herbert O. Yardley, author of many fascinating magazine articles about secret service work, and of a book, "The American Black Chamber." (Incidentally, the book revealed so much that the Japanese War Department protested.)

Yardley won his rank—and certainly earned it—not in action on the field, but at his desk. His skill at decoding documents is spoken of with awe at all gatherings of cryptogram fans. While he was in command of the American Black Chamber (for the decoding of enemy documents during the War), he was forced to take elaborate precautions to keep foreign governments from finding out about his work. Every few weeks he would move his office; he received all his mail through a cover-up address.

Despite all these precautions, Yardley began to have the feeling that he was being followed and watched. He hired a private detective to follow him and discover if he were being shadowed. The detective was unable to learn anything.

Finally, one day, while Yardley was in a bar in New York, a stranger struck up a conversation with him and introduced him to a beautiful girl. A few days later, in the same bar, the same girl approached him and asked him to buy her a drink. He quickly realized that the idea was to get him drunk—so he decided to turn the tables on her.

He began ordering drinks with ginger ale on the side. Then he would take a drink, and pretend to sip the ginger ale as a chaser. Actually, he was not swallowing the liquor, but secretly spitting it into the ginger ale each time he pretended to sip from it.

Naturally, the girl had to drink every time Yardley apparently did, so soon the girl was drunk and Yardley wasn't. Then, he opened the girl's purse, found out where she lived, took her home, put her to bed, then searched her room. Before he left her room, he found a note which proved she was an enemy agent.

The girl disappeared the next day, and Yardley was never bothered again.

After the War, Yardley established a new record. He broke down the Japanese diplomatic code, the first time such a thing had ever been done. So doing, he changed the course of the Washington Disarmament Conference. It was due to Yardley that the naval ratio was fixed at 5-5-3 instead of 10-10-7 as Japan had proposed.

Some gentlemen in Congress, a few years ago, decided that it was unsportsmanlike for Uncle Sam to have a cryptoanalysis bureau! So the American Black Chamber was broken up, and Yardley was thrown upon a cold, cold world. He wrote another book which told a lot of startling facts. Pre-publications rumors were so violent that Congress passed a special act to prevent its being published. Whereupon Yardley went to Hollywood!

IF you look over the Who's Who of Hollywood adventurers, you will find a polyglot, cosmopolitan lot. One of them is dark and romantic Ivan Lebedeff, writer and actor. In the pomp and circumstance, the alarums and excursions incident to Napoleon's Russian victories

and later the retreat from Moscow in "Conquest," there was nothing strange to one black-eyed actor down in the cast list as a "Cossack Captain." Lebedeff had seen practically the same things in his own life.

Born in Lithuania, Ivan was the son of a father who was high in the confidence of the Czar. Ivan graduated from the University of St. Petersburg, was trained for the diplomatic service in the Imperial Lyceum. When the War broke out, he enlisted as a volunteer in the Third Regiment of Dragoons, and, after being wounded, was decorated by Nicholas II, the last sad remnant of the Romanoffs. For capturing a high-ranking German general at Nevel, Lebedeff was made aide-de-camp to the Czar. After being wounded again and gassed, he was transferred to the Roumanian front. Whereupon the Revolution broke out and he found himself an officer without any men — very disconcerting for a soldier—so he joined the Air Service on the Roumanian front.

When the Allies took over Odessa on the Black Sea, Lebedeff was made Food Administrator. When the Allied troops withdrew, he was arrested by the Bolsheviks, along with other civil officials. The Reds tossed him into jail—a foul, smelly jail.

One afternoon, a few days later, the jail guard was changed, and Lebedeff was surprised to discover that the new sergeant of the guard was a former servant of his family. The old retainer recognized Lebedeff and did him several favors — finally agreed to help him escape.

Late one night the sergeant came and unlocked the door and escorted Lebedeff to the outskirts of Odessa. Here the old fellow turned to leave his former master, insisting it was his duty to go back and be shot for his treachery to the Red cause.

But Lebedeff couldn't see any sense in that idea, so he hit the old man over the head with a club, stole a horse and wagon, tossed the guard in, and managed to drive to safety behind the White lines.

Shortly afterwards, Lebedeff organized a White Troop to attack Odessa and offered the old servant a job as a soldier. But the old boy refused to fight his Red comrades, and finally deserted, going back to the Bolsheviks.

Lebedeff never saw him again.

But even Lebedeff and the other brave adventurers among the White Russians were unable to prevent the inevitable, and he finally took refuge in Constantinople. More resourceful than other luxuriously trained and aristocratic refugees, he overcame even dire poverty, made his way to Vienna and Paris. There he met, by chance, D. W. Griffith, who saw in him the man he wanted to play a part in "The Sorrows of Satan." Thus, the former officer of the Imperial Dragoons, with the scars and memories of so many hard-fought battles, came to Hollywood, where he lives successfully today.

EVEN on the distaff side (what the Victorians used to call the distaff side) you will find people with fascinatingly adventurous backgrounds. For the last few years, working in the research department at M-G-M, there had been a handsome, vivacious lady who is known as the Number One Girl of Hollywood's Bookworm Corps. Nathalie Bucknall has memories almost as colorful and spine-tingling as those of her countryman, Ivan Lebedeff. Like him, she was born of the Russian nobility. In fact, she was educated with the daughters of the Czar, her father being Ivan de Fedenko, Counsellor of State. After the November Revolution in 1917 her life wasn't worth a kopek. Literally hunted from house to house, she had many narrow escapes from capture by the blood-hungry Bolsheviks. She finally took refuge in the British Embassy in Moscow and was actually there when the Reds raided it. As a matter of fact, a British officer died in her arms. After that, she became a member of the Second Women's Battalion of Death. How she finally made her escape from the land of the Soviet Terror is almost a book in itself. Incidentally, she was awarded the order of the British Empire for Red Cross work.

During Miss Bucknall's research work on "Marie Antoinette," the soul-stirring scenes of the French Revolution must have brought back many bitter memories to this amazing woman. She knew it could happen again—and did.

Then, too, there is Cherie May. This pretty woman gambled her life at least once a week for the past twelve years. She has doubled for practically every woman star in the game. Once upon a time she was a housewife. She married young, had two children, divorced. Disguised as a man, she rode the rods across the continent, and for a while worked as a ranch hand in Northern California. Of course she couldn't keep her sex secret indefinitely. She was discovered and promptly fired. Lacking an occupation, she was put to desperate straits to support her children whom the courts were about to take away from her and put into an institution. At the eleventh hour, by dint of copious lying, she got a job as a parachute jumper from an understanding director. She had had no experience whatsoever. Now, she's the number one stunt woman of Hollywood.

PROBABLY the best known of that famous gang of Hollywood stunters is Dick Grace. His story is so typical that he could well represent the whole company, living and dead, of "Hollywood's Suicide Legion," composed of Frank Clark, Art Goebel, Leo Nomis, Ira Reed and others.

Most of these men were World War flyers. Like Dick, they've all cracked up many times, intentionally and otherwise. At this writing, Dick's record is thirty-two deliberate crack-ups. He's the only man who ever fell out of a plane at 1000 feet and lived to tell the tale. (He fell into the ocean and escaped with a mere broken neck.)

Grace has always insisted that the nearest he ever came to death was when he was asked by a meticulous director to dive a land plane into the ocean.

A motor boat was stationed near by to pick up Grace after the crash, but the crack-up left such a pile of floating wreckage that the men in the boat were unable to find Grace. For nearly a half hour, he floated, unconscious, under the debris, until he finally came to and managed to attract their attention.

The men in the boat said afterwards that if Grace had been unconscious for five minutes longer, they would have left him to drown. They thought no one could possibly live after the terrific impact of that fateful crack when the plane hit the water.

Whenever a military story is to be filmed, one of the first men wanted around the lot is Captain Louis Vandenecker, Hollywood's ace technical director. His latest work was done for "The Life of Emile Zola" and "The Adventures of Robin Hood."

From his earliest days, fighting and adventure were in this man's blood. To satisfy him his parents, Belgians, sent him to a military school as soon as he was eleven years old. But that was too slow. He ran away at sixteen, and, being mature for his age, enlisted in the French Foreign Legion at Marseilles. He was shipped overseas at once and won his corporal's stripes in the campaigns against the fierce, veiled Tauregs of the desert.

During the World War, one of his decorations was earned when, under a withering machine-gun fire from the Germans, he managed to rescue several wounded comrades. At Hartmannsweilerkopf he was carrying an important message when a piece of shrapnel hit him in the leg. Wound and all, he delivered the message on which the existence of an entire division depended. Later, he went through twenty-three different operations before finally overcoming the consequences of that wound.

After the Armistice, Vandenecker went to Poland to help fight the Reds. During a battle with the Russians, he became isolated in advance of the Polish troops. Coming to a small village he started to enter it when he suddenly realized it was occupied by Russian soldiers.

Discovering a Russian overcoat lying by the road, he hastily put it on and made a run for the nearest house. His plan was to hide inside until his own troops arrived.

But as he stepped inside the doorway, he was horrified to discover there three Russian officers. Throwing off his coat, he drew his pistol and ordered the Russians to surrender.

He was so excited that the gun dropped from his hand to the floor. For a few seconds he thought the Russians were going to draw their guns—but they meekly put their hands up. They said later they thought the Poles had taken the whole town.

For nearly an hour Vandenecker held the Russians at the point of his gun while he waited for the Polish

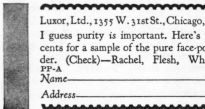

troops to catch up with him. Just as the Russians were restlessly beginning to behave as though they were planning a concerted rush upon him, the Poles arrived.

No tale of Hollywood's soldiers of fortune is complete without mention of two of the best known stars in the business—Errol Flynn and George Brent.

There is almost no hazardous occupation at which Flynn has not tried his hand. He has certainly gone far "For to admire and for to see, For to be'old this world so wide." Hollywood, considered a rather exciting place in itself, Flynn considers dull. Nothing ever happens there. When he can't find any excitement, he keeps his hand in by riding radio cars with the cops all night. His life is filled with amazing exploits.

Born in Ireland, son of a biology professor, his first wanderings were at the age of four, when his parents took him to Tasmania. His first enthusiasm was for boxing; he was good enough to become the amateur middleweight of Ireland and represented his country in the Olympics of 1928. He then decided that the bourgeois life was not for him. Working his way before the mast to Tahiti, he was successfully pearl fisher and gold prospector, until a British film company, hearing he was a collateral descendant of Fletcher Christian (yes, the Mutiny-on-the-Bounty Christian), drafted him to play the rôle of his ancestor in a picture. Flynn turned out to be a natural-born actor. "By gad, he said, "if I can make money at this game, I'm for it!"

Off he set for Hollywood and fame. But despite two profitable occupations, writing and acting, he is restless. Only a short time ago one heard of him in Spain.

When his friends begged him to stay home—"Why go to Spain, Errol. You'll be killed"—he replied. "So what? Maybe I'll be killed. Maybe I'll be run over by a car when I leave the studio. That's a chance you take. When my number is up—it's just up! That's the way I figure it!"

Another Irishman with a spectacular background is George Brent. Before he was out of his teens he had seen and practiced more varied kinds of life than most grown men. He has herded sheep in Ireland, sailed aboard a freighter, worked in the gold fields of South Africa (a recent rôle in "Gold Is Where You Find It" was just duck soup for Brent).

After finding time to get an education at the University of Dublin, he became a dispatch runner for Michael Collins, the famed young chief of the rebel Sinn Fein. The Irish Rebellion, settled finally, perhaps, the other day by De Valera and Chamberlain, was coming to a climax. No hot-blooded youth could resist that, and it was a proud day for George when the dread Black and Tan set a price on his head.

During this period he "covered up" in the daytime by attending rehearsals of the Abbey Theater Players. But, because he was usually up all night on the business of the Rebellion, he practically always fell asleep during rehearsals.

Naturally this aroused suspicion and, finally, the British sent a squad of soldiers to arrest Brent. The soldiers were given orders to get to the Players and "arrest the man who is sleeping there."

By a quirk of fortune worthy of Hollywood itself, another member of the cast happened to be asleep that day—while Brent was awake enough to

escape attention. So, as soon as Brent saw the soldiers arresting the sleeping actor, he realized that the Tommies were really after him—and made a prompt escape. By the time the soldiers had discovered their mistake, Brent was safely in hiding.

Osa Johnson, widow of my late and old friend Martin, now also makes her headquarters in Hollywood. The life of fascinating adventure that she lived with Martin is too well-known to need retelling here.

I find I've mentioned only a few of Hollywood's adventurers. You never can tell in what rôle you will find them. At Warners there is a property man named Clarence Eurist. In the background of his life are an international swimming championship, a Nicaraguan campaign, a Navy Cross for bravery under fire.

Frederick Cavens, head of the largest fencing school in Hollywood, was once instructor at the Belgian Royal Military Academy, and later fencing champion of all Europe.

One of Hollywood's principal men of mystery is Abdsolem Ben Mohammed Kombarick. He was first brought to Hollywood by Herbert Brenon. He now commutes between Hollywood and North Africa almost regularly. When he's asked personal questions about his career, he replies with few words and a sardonic smile. This has given rise to the rumor that he has been mixed up with all sorts of strange things, including gun running to foreign countries, and that he is closely involved in the Spanish Civil War. Maybe he is— nothing about these Hollywood adventurers would surprise me!

Paul Muni's superb acting and its heart-rending frankness bring "I Am a Fugitive From a Chain Gang" most applause from readers. Added to strong cinema red meat, audiences find the picture to be a powerful sermon against crime and a spotlight on an appalling penal problem of today

Now It's Horses

[CONTINUED FROM PAGE 129]

Bing optimistically calls it a business. He hopes to cash in later on.

Six of his thoroughbreds are yearlings, but a week after Santa Anita has opened, they'll be eligible to race. All horses celebrate their birthdays on the first of the year. Sadly remembering Zombie's ill-fated monicker, Bing has christened his string with less macabre surnames.

Friend Andy has Bing's close pal, Andy Devine, to thank for his title. Aunt Kitty was named after Kitty Lang, the widow of Bing's former guitar player. The fussy habits of the Crosby legal adviser inspired Madame Attorney. Bing's favorite golf course was honored in Lady Lakeside, and the famous twins are responsible for Double Trouble. Bing had his heart set on calling a new racer Jacqueline Oakie which he knew would burn Jack to a nice crisp, but the racing commission turned it down. They said it was too long, but they probably wanted to keep harmony in Hollywood.

BING keeps his prancing pets down on his ranch at Rancho Santa Fe where they sniff their oats in brand new stables under the expert care of trainer Albert Johnson, who rode three Kentucky Derby winners to victory. Johnson and Bing hope that Khayam, a brand new yearling and son of the famous Omar Khayam, will lead them home at Churchill Downs in a year or so.

But so far the Crosby colors have yet to adorn an important purse. Hopes don't keep red off the ledger—and the ink continues to flow freely—not only for Bing but for Clark Gable who still has his Beverly Hills and three new yearlings too young to race this season, for Spencer Tracy and Director J. Walter Ruben, also nursing along some infant prodigies, for David Butler and Leo McCarey of the B and M stables, for William LeBaron, Louis Lighton, Raoul Walsh, Leon Gordon and other big film shots who are building up racing strings, and especially for Director Al Green who has a hungry horde of thirty racing thoroughbreds.

Joe E. Brown, in fact, is the only movie owner who has padded his bank balance substantially from flying hoofbeats. Joe E. risked a few hundred on a selling plater called Straitjacket last year at Santa Anita. But Straitjacket tied up in the back stretch and Joe E. couldn't find a Houdini to ride him.

So he dug deeper to claim Captain Argo, a sprinter with a reputation, at Narragansett Park. The Captain dented the Brown bankroll for $4500, but the first time he heard Joe E. yelp he sprinted home to win a $5000 purse, the second time Joe hollered he galloped for $2500 and the third time it was worth $3500. That's making money. Argo couldn't stand prosperity, however. He died before Joe E. could

flash him at Santa Anita, so the Brown hopes will be carried by a brand new substitute, Captain Barnsley, who is said to have ears attuned to his master's raucous railside voice.

If the horse fever stopped with the stable owners, Hollywood would be comparatively normal, but that of course is far from the case. The sad truth is that the germ is more virulent when it attacks those with loose money to back their judgment of other people's horseflesh There is where the wailing wall begins.

Most neophyte movie owners have learned enough about the galloping colts to shun the bookies unless their horse has a more than even chance. Bing Crosby seldom backs his entries with large bets. Joe E. plays them heavily, but Joe doesn't have many horses, and he doesn't race often. When he does, he means business.

Last year most Hollywood bets were chump bets. Starting with a caution becoming greenhorns, the Hollywood wageroos became bolder and bolder until they bet on anything Only a few seasoned old railbirds like Al Jolson—who once bet $75,000 on one horse in one race (and lost)—really had any idea what they were doing when they laid it on the line.

The average Hollywood bet was placed on whispered hunches, tips, the nice sound of a nag's name, the color of his coat or the haircut of his jockey. A large percentage of wagers were inspired by sentiment. The old wheeze, "When in doubt bet Bradley" was changed for a while to "When in doubt bet Crosby," until Bing had to ask his friends please *not* to back his nags. The money they were dropping embarrassed him.

Clark Gable's Beverly Hills went to the post in his maiden race at Agua Caliente backed to the withers with Hollywood gold. All of Clark's pals tagged him purely out of sentiment. Beverly came in a winner and paid eight dollars for two. So everybody backed him from then on, without even glancing at the competition.

THE winnings soon vanished and more, too, when Beverly got out of his class. And then, as if to point an object lesson, the bangtail, sent to Tanforan, the San Francisco racetrack, by Clark and forgotten, romped home in three successive starts to pay forty for two, thirty for two and twelve for two bucks!

Neither Clark nor any of his friends had a dime on him!

Actors and actresses have always been good sports. And, of course, a horse race without bets is like poker without chips, or bridge without arguments.

There will be, however, two definite classes of movie gamboleers.

One will wear the impassive mask of wagering experience. He will possibly have placed his bets before he came to the track, through

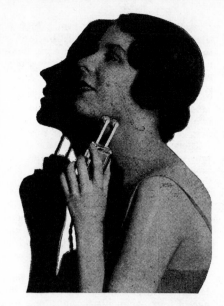

Velvetize your skin with the
Velvetskin Patter

JACK BENNY ("Road Show," M-G-M) came from vaudeville to Metro to act as master of ceremonies in "The Hollywood Revue," where his drolleries won public acclaim everywhere. Jack is a veteran comic and M-C of the two-a-day, his rambling monologue, with the aid of a property fiddle, having been known and liked for years. Jack's always good.

MARLENE DIETRICH

as the "Blonde Venus"

Dietrich the glamorous — Exotic beauty of "Morocco" — Tragic heroine of "Dishonored" — Lovely derelict of "Shanghai Express" — Now more entrancing — more gloriously luscious — as a girl who played with love. Only Dietrich can give such beauty, such dignity, such allure to the scarlet letter!

MARLENE DIETRICH
in "BLONDE VENUS"

with HERBERT MARSHALL
CARY GRANT · DICKIE MOORE
Directed by JOSEPH VON STERNBERG

Paramount *Pictures*

PARAMOUNT PUBLIX CORPORATION, ADOLPH ZUKOR PRES., PARAMOUNT BLDG., NEW YORK

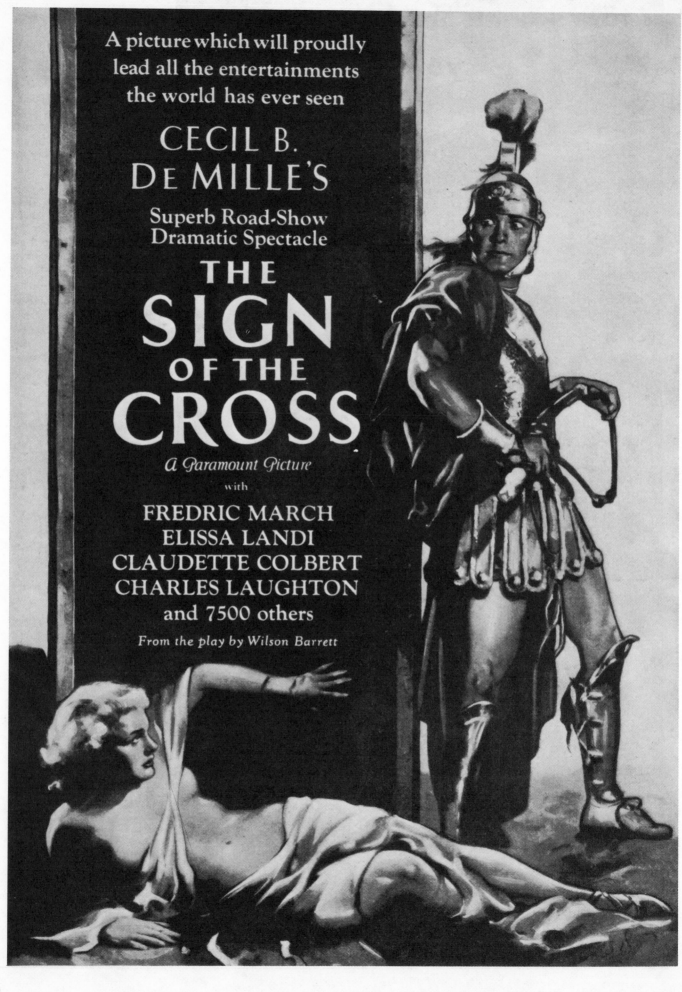

A picture which will proudly
lead all the entertainments
the world has ever seen

CECIL B.
DE MILLE'S

Superb Road-Show
Dramatic Spectacle

THE
SIGN
OF THE
CROSS

A Paramount Picture

with

FREDRIC MARCH
ELISSA LANDI
CLAUDETTE COLBERT
CHARLES LAUGHTON
and 7500 others

From the play by Wilson Barrett

his legally outlawed but irrepressible book-maker, as he has been doing all year, while they ran at Saratoga, Narragansett Park, Hialeah or Havre de New Grace. He is the dyed-in-the-saddle-soap pony addict. A frayed tip of the latest Racing Form peeps from his pocket.

The other's excited flush will betray the unaccustomed boot the whole business hands him (or her, of course. Every day is ladies' day at Santa Anita. Kay Francis, Joan Bennett, Marion Davies were star boarders at Santa Anita last year.) He will slide his wager under the parimutuel wicket, even as you and I, carefully avoiding, as a rule, the No Limit window in the exclusive Clubhouse, where he will, of course, be holding forth. Very possibly he will be clutching a sucker dope sheet, promising a sure winner in every race. He has just bought it for fifty cents to help him lose fifty to fifteen hundred cocoa nuts.

The cool and calloused type may emit a soft "Damn!" when his nag wilts in the challenge stretch and then hurry to cover his system on the next race. He is used to the breaks. Pat O'Brien and Director Howard Hawks belong in this class. They kept a direct wire humming from the set to the tracks all during the filming of "Ceiling Zero." In between scenes they telephoned their bets. A steady five hundred "across the board" was Hawks' system. He is supposed to have cleaned up a cool $22,000 in the last few months.

But the more excitable movie railbird may put on a bit of fireworks at the finish. Such as Jimmie Durante's nip-ups last year when he saw five hundred of the best come home on the nose of a long shot, and rushed to the pay off window only to discover the horse had been disqualified!

OR like Bing Crosby who (before he had acquired his betting poise) relieved his emotions after losing a close one by tossing odd pieces of furniture across the Clubhouse lobby.

Bing, incidentally, has had plenty of luck backing his racing judgment—but it's all been bad. Nevertheless, the tremendous publicity he has received from his race-horse activities causes him to be popularly tagged a turf authority, and this brings him loads of grief in the form of collect telegrams.

Self appointed touts and handicappers flood him with unwelcome tips on races and track information via pay-and-you-can-read messages. Since they might be wires important on other matters, Bing pays the toll. It has been

costing him around the sum of $200 a month.

But the real proof that "horses break more hearts than women" in Hollywood as well as in the Bluegrass Belt comes from the sad story of Virginia Mack, a likely mare, who represented the racing resources of Claude Binyon, Bob Ives and Howard Green, three studio scenario scribblers of note.

All Hollywood's Playing This Game

Gather 'round, all you parlor game hounds—for that's what you do to play Hollywood's current time-frittering favorite. It's called "Words and Endings."

Here's what you do.

Take a letter—any letter. One of you starts by naming the letter. Say it's "d." The next one supplies another letter—any letter—say it's "u." "Du" isn't any word—in English—so you go on around, the object being to keep from spelling a word

Because the player who puts a letter on and ends a word has to toss a chip in the center.

Either a chip or a match or a beer cap, or whatever you are using for money.

Continuing the example we picked—say the next letter picked is "c." Well—"Duc" also is no word in English, so here we go again. Now the next player has to be careful. If he names the letter "k," for instance, he pays—because "Duck" is a word. However, if he's smart he'll name, let's say, "h." That passes him safely. "Duch" doesn't spell much—but it leads to "Duchy," "Duchess" and a lot of things.

The problem of the rest of the charming circle is to keep away from letting the letter they give end the word—get it?

When you end one word, you start another.

Sometimes there's a smarty in the crowd who knows a word no one else does.

If he claims the word ended on his predecessor and proves he's right (better have a dictionary handy) that unlucky gent has to forfeit two chips.

But if he's found to be bluffing or mistaken, it costs the caller two chips.

Everybody starts with the same pile of counters, and the first one who finds his all gone, automatically brings up the pay-off. The player with the biggest pile left wins the chips in the center.

It's a great game—and don't regard it as too lowly. You'll find, after a few sessions, that it's something like chess, you have to ponder and think ahead, and you can take all the time you want in supplying your letter.

If you're real clever at it, you can even arrange to stick the heavy winner for a loss.

Virginia entered a county fair race at Pomona, near Hollywood, which dangled a sizeable purse. She won in a walk but when owners Binyon, Ives and Green extended their palms, the officials stated with regret that Virginia Mack was officially dead! It seems her former owner, wishing to assure her of an old age in deep clover had declared her deceased to keep her off racetracks the rest of her days. Protests were of no avail. The judges couldn't pay for

a dead horse. Nobody likes to do that.

So the owners went into a huddle, registered the dead-alive Virginia Mack under the name of Reborn and entered her again. But reincarnation didn't pan out. She hasn't won a race since!

Smart money circulated freely in Hollywood last year, and does again this year—mainly because the innate ego of an actor makes him doubly sure he knows a good thing when he sees it.

But thinking yourself clever isn't always being so clever, where racehorses are concerned—as Spencer Tracy found out only a few weeks ago.

Spencer's groom for his hopefuls, April Folly and Wait For Me (Jean Harlow thought that one up while they were making "Riff-Raff" together), had a horse of his own that looked good. Spencer himself had clocked the animal in amazing time on the training track. The horse was absolutely unknown. So Spencer conceived a fast one. They would enter the nag as a sleeper in a county fair race with a bunch of dogs who had never won more than a dollar watch in their lives. They would back him with the bankroll and clean up It was all very simple, and very sure. He was to waltz in at long odds without even breathing hard.

The plan went through and the day arrived. The Tracys were on hand, en famille. The groom in his first striped suit, cane and spats. Spencer with all his spare cash on the line. Mrs. Tracy with the family silver practically in hock for a fistful of betting tickets.

The wire lifted and twelve horses tore out. A little later eleven horses—cripples, old soldiers, lame ducks and dogs—pounded by the finish line. But the Tracy surprise sleeper—the wonder horse — was still running. He came in sometime the next morning.

AND if it seems strange to you that Mrs. Tracy wept and Spencer raved and the groom disappeared for a week, then you don't realize yet just how seriously Hollywood is taking this horse racing season.

Furthermore it may seem slightly silly to you for a whole community of super sophisticates to get all hot and bothered over a lot of ponies running around in a circle.

But if that's your opinion, all I can say is you don't agree with Hollywood at the present writing. No, sir, not exactly.

And, after all, that's what makes a horse race a horse race, isn't it?

A difference of opinion?

Will "The Grapes of Wrath" Be Shelved?

[CONTINUED FROM PAGE 261]

ing of Steinbeck's story on the screen in any way.

In writing the screen play, I failed to find any important matter that seemed to me to call for much trouble in the form of censorship. It goes without saying that neither profanity nor obscenity is possible on the screen of today. It may be that the loss of this saltiness would have made "The Grapes of Wrath" a lesser book than it is. That's a matter of opinion. But I do not feel that censorship can possibly lessen the great drama and emotion of the picture. Steinbeck wrought too greatly for such a minor modification to damage his American epic.

What pressure and how much was actually brought to bear on Zanuck, I know only vaguely, for none of it was passed on to me. My guess is that he wheedled and mollified a lot of people who were on the point of busying themselves with trouble. All I do know is that not once during the writing of the script, or before it, did he offer me any directions as to my treatment of the story in the book. His one suggestion, in the event I was planning otherwise, was that I start the script with *Tom Joad*

thumbing a ride in the truck. That was the way the book started and that was the way he wanted to see the picture start. Beyond that, his instructions were simply that I get as much of the book as I could into a screen play.

Three or four times during the two months I needed to write the screen play, he called me in to see if certain scenes from the book which clung in his mind were being included in the script. That was all.

For the second draft we made only one revision of any importance. We held *Uncle John* down. His moody melancholy over the long-ago death of his wife seemed to hamper the drama of the family's flight and fight for life. It was this second draft that was given to Steinbeck, who made a courteous effort to conceal his relief that the story had not been converted into a backstage melodrama, and okayed it with a promptness that was all the reward that I could wish as the adaptor. This is the script from which John Ford will direct the picture.

How well it will satisfy Steinbeckians I can't say. I don't know. I should say that nine-tenths of the dramatic action

of the book is in the screen play, and, to the best of my purpose and ability, the same sociological emphasis. Ninety-five per cent of the dialogue is from the book and the remainder, obligatory in instances of transition of sequences, is as shy and unpretentious as it should be. The ending, which is from the book but not as that, is one that Steinbeck himself suggested in New York, before any word of the script had been set down on paper.

I like to hope that the chief difference between the book and the picture will be the difference in the two mediums. Admittedly, the screen, as long as it is governed by its present rules and conditions, would be inadequate for all that Steinbeck had to say.

For that, a book was the natural and incomparable medium. But there may be a measure of compensatory satisfaction in the opportunity, in a picture, to see the country he described and the people he created; the dust country, Highway 66, the camps, the Hoovervilles, and the long roads of California; and, above all, the members of that tough and magnificent American family, the *Joads*.

Hollywood's Unmarried Husbands and Wives

[CONTINUED FROM PAGE 131]

—merged after they slipped into the unique Hollywood h a b i t. Marriage couldn't have worked more of a change.

Bob bought the acres next to Barbara's ranch. He started putting up a ranch house within a good stone's throw of hers. He bought horses. He spent every minute of his spare time working on the place. Overnight, he turned into a country squire. When, in the middle of it all, he was called to England, the work never stopped. Barbara supervised it. While Bob was away she ordered the things she knew he wanted. She oversaw the decoration and furnishing of the place. It was all ready when Bob came home.

Bob's house and Barbara's house stand now on adjoining knolls. The occupants ride together and work together and play there together in their time off. Bob trained and worked out for "The Crowd Roars" on Barbara's ranch. Almost every evening, after work at the studio or on the ranch, he runs over for a plunge in her pool.

If it isn't fight night—they've long had permanent seats together at the Hollywood Legion Stadium—or if they're not asked to a party—they're always invited together, just like man and wife—they spend a quiet evening together at either one or the other's place.

Or if Bob has a preview of his picture, Barbara goes with him to tell him what

she thinks of it, and vice versa. Bob saw "Stella Dallas" four times. Once he caught it in London and bawled so copiously that when he came out and a kid asked him for his autograph he couldn't see to sign it! But he was a long way away from Barbara then.

When he's home, he's a little more critical. But never of Barbara's ice cream. Bob has never forgotten his Nebraska boyhood ecstasy licking the dasher of an ice cream freezer. That's why Barbara whips him up a bucketful every week, before they roll off to see the folks.

All in all, it's an almost perfect domestic picture. But no wedding rings in sight!

Even gifts and expressions of sentiment take on the practical, utilitarian aspect of old married folks' remembrances when these Hollywood single couples come across. Just as Dad gives Mother an electric icebox for Christmas and she retaliates with a radio, Bob Taylor presents Barbara Stanwyck with a tennis court on her birthday, with Barbara giving Bob a two-horse auto trailer for his!

THE gifts Carole Lombard and Clark Gable have exchanged are even more unorthodox. Whoever heard of a woman in love with a man giving him a gun for Christmas! Or a man, crazy about

one of the most glamorous, sophisticated and clever women in the land, hanging a gasoline scooter on her Christmas tree!

For Clark, Carole stopped, almost overnight, being a Hollywood playgirl. People are expected to change when they get married. The necessary adaptation to a new life and another personality shows up in every bride and groom. All Clark and Carole did was strike up a Hollywood twosome. Nobody said "I do!"

Clark Gable doesn't like night spots, or parties, social chit-chat, or the frothy pretensions of society. He has endured plenty of it, but it makes him fidget.

Carole, quite frankly, used to eat it up. She hosted the most charming and clever parties in town. She knew everybody, went everywhere. When the ultra exclusive and late lamented Mayfair Club held its annual ball, Carole was picked to run things. It was Carole who decreed the now famous "White Mayfair" that Norma Shearer crossed up so wickedly by coming in flaming scarlet—an idea you later saw dramatized by Bette Davis in "Jezebel."

These things were the caviar and cocktails of Carole Lombard's life—before she started going with Gable. But look what happened—

Clark didn't like it, Carole found out —quickly. What did he like? Well, outside of hunting in wild country white men seldom entered, and white women never, he like to shoot skeet. Shooting skeet, of course, is an intricate scoring game worked out on the principle of trapshooting. It involves banging away at crazily projected clay pigeons with a shotgun.

Carole learned to shoot skeet—not only learned it but, with the intense proficiency with which she attacks anything, rapidly became one of the best women skeet shooters in the country!

Gable liked to ride, so Carole got herself a horse and unpacked her riding things.

He liked tennis, so she resurrected her always good court game, taking lessons from Alice Marble, her good friend and the present national women's champion. Playing with a man, Carole had to get good and she did—so good that now Clark can't win a set!

It goes on like that. Clark, tiring of hotel life, moved out to a ranch in the San Fernando Valley. What did Lombard do? She bought a Valley ranch!

Carole has practically abandoned all her Hollywood social contacts. She doesn't keep up with the girls in gossip as she used to. She doesn't throw parties that hit the headlines and the picture magazines. She and Clark are all wrapped up in each other's interests. While Gable did all the night work in "Too Hot To Handle," Carole, though working, too, was on his set every night. She caught the sneak preview with him and told him with all the candor of the little woman, "It's hokum, Pappy—but the *most excellent* hokum!"

Like any good spouse might do, Carole has ways and means of chastening Clark, too. When she's mad at him she wears a hat he particularly despises. Carole calls it her "hate hat."

Their fun now, around town, is almost entirely trips, football games, fights and shows. Their stepping-out nights usually end up at the home of Director Walter Lang and his new wife, Madalynne Fields, "Fieldsie," Carole's bosom pal and long-time secretary. They sit and play games!

Yes, Carole Lombard is a changed woman since she tied up with Clark Gable.

But her name is still Carole Lombard.

THE altar record, in fact, among Holly-wood's popular twosomes is suprisingly slim.

Usually something formidable stands in the way of a marriage certificate when Hollywood stars pair up minus a preacher.

In Clark and Carole's case, of course, there is a very sound legal barrier. Clark is still officially a married man. Every now and then negotiations for a divorce are started, but, until something happens in court, Ria Gable is still the only wife the law of this land allows Clark Gable.

George Raft can't marry Virginia Pine for the very same good reason; he has a wife. Every effort he has made for his freedom has failed.

Some of them, like Constance Bennett and Gilbert Roland, go in a perfect design for living, apparently headed for perpetual fun with each other. Connie maintains one of the most luxurious setups of them all, with a titled husband in Europe and Gilbert Roland her devoted slave in Hollywood. Years have passed and the arrangement seems to please everybody as much now as it did at the start. Why should it ever break up?

On the other hand, the unmarried partners sometimes get a divorce—or at least a separation, a recess, a moratorium—whatever you care to call it. Calling the case of Charlie Chaplin and Paulette Goddard requires more than a bunch of handy nouns.

No one has ever been able yet to say definitely whether or not the gray-haired Charlie and his young, vivacious Paulette were ever married. Such things as public records exist for just such purposes, of course, but in spite of the fact that none can be unearthed, a strong belief hovers around Hollywood that Charlie and Paulette did actually take the vows, some say on his yacht out at sea.

But when, a few months back, Charlie was seen more and more in the company of other young ladies and Paulette began stepping out with other men, an unusually awkward contretemps was brewed. What was it? The breaking up of a love affair? Or the separation of a marriage? If a divorce was to be had, there had to have been a marriage. But was there? Charlie wouldn't talk; neither would Paulette. Hollywood relapsed into a quandary. It's still there

as concerns the Chaplin-Goddard unmarried marriage. Meanwhile, both Charlie and Paulette seem to be having a good time with whomever they fancy. But the interesting thing is that Paulette still entertains her guests, when she wishes, on Charlie Chaplin's yacht. So maybe she has an interest in it that a mere separation couldn't efface.

THE most tragic, as well as perhaps the most tender match of them all gave way to an irresistible rival wooer, Death. At the time of Jean Harlow's untimely passing, she and William Powell had reached an understanding that excluded any one else from either's thoughts. Both had fought for happiness in Hollywood without finding it, until they found each other. Then Death stole Jean away and Bill has never recovered from the effect of that stunning blow.

There was only Jean Harlow's family, her doctor and William Powell in her hospital room the night she lost her fight for life. Jean died in Bill's arms.

In every way since, he has acted as a son-in-law to Jean's mother. He bought the crypt where Jean lies today and arranged for perpetual flowers. This year, on the anniversary of her passing, Bill Powell and Mrs. Bello, Jean's mother, went alone to visit Jean's resting place. He sent Mrs. Bello on a trip to Bermuda last winter to recover from the severe grief she has suffered since Jean's death. She visited Bill regularly during his recent spell in the hospital. Both have one regret—that Bill and Jean never got to be man and wife.

And that, it seems, would point a lesson to the unique coterie of Hollywood's unwed couples—Bob Taylor and Barbara Stanwyck, who could get married if they really wanted to; George Raft and Virginia Pine, Carole Lombard and Clark Gable and the other steady company couples who might swing it if they tried a little harder. You can't take your happiness with you.

For nobody, not even Hollywood's miracle men, has ever improved on the good old-fashioned, satisfying institution of holy matrimony. And, until something better comes along, the best way to hunt happiness when you're in love in Hollywood or anywhere else— is with a preacher, a marriage license and a bagful of rice.

Fashions in Passions

[CONTINUED FROM PAGE 251]

in "Nothing Sacred" and with Fred MacMurray ducking you to the drowning point in "True Confession." From both those scenes you emerged looking like a leftover Christmas tree on February first. Honest, you did, Carole, for all the beauty God and Wally Westmore gave you.

But your men kept right on loving you, just the same, which is, of course, all any female cares about.

Of course, I know if Freddie and Fred hadn't responded, you could always go home after your day's work and call up Clark Gable, which is certainly my idea of the perfect end of any day. But, if following your example, I let my boy friend duck me in a lake or use me as a flying tackle, as an expression of his deep passion for me, can I go home and call up Clark Gable? Well, all right, I could call

him. I've got his telephone number. But what would it get me? It would get me his butler saying, "We're so sorry, Madame, but Mr. Gable is indefinitely out of town!" That's all it would net me—and I'd still have to go to the hairdresser's and sit under the dryer for two hours.

Carole, I ask you, you with that lovely face, and your Pekineses, and your star sapphires, and Clark Gable right on tap, do you think it is fair to ask the rest of us to try to keep up with you, *to try to keep up with you*, to try to be burlesque but bewitching?

NOW you Irene Dunne. That Lombard had a wicked gleam in her eye always. But you, after all, you were called a lady. You acted like a lady. You are a lady. You showed us sincerity in "Cimarron" and "Back Street."

But now you, too, have gone wacky. In "The Awful Truth" Cary Grant thought it was a scream when you, pretending to be his sister, invaded his fiancee's house, and made a general fool of yourself. You were funny, too, but dear Miss Dunne, don't you understand that if the rest of us went around invading houses like that our boy friend would not only think it wasn't funny but have us run out of town for displaying such awful manners?

And another thing I'd like to ask you is this. Why have cold, wet toes suddenly come into the fascinating game? Rosemary Lane gave out with ten of them in "Hollywood Hotel" when she wandered around calf deep in a fountain with Dick Powell. She looked about as enticing as a bill collector to me in that scene, but Dick Powell ate it up. Is this a trend? Must a girl risk pneumonia these days to prove her sex appeal?

WITH you, Miss Hepburn, I'll be brief. (I never shall forget that flight from Los Angeles all the way to Newark with you shouting above the noise of the motors just what you thought of the press, only you never looked at me and I never looked at you. Remember, Honey? Just like one family we all were, a family of boa constrictors.)

Your pictures ran thick and thin after your first success in "A Bill of Divorcement": your delightful *Jo* in "Little Women" and that perfect "Alice Adams" balanced against trash like "Spitfire" and your perfectly ghastly performance as "Mary of Scotland."

Still, and for all that, you continued to be one of the most original, most interesting figures in the whole movie industry. And then you did "Bringing Up Baby" and down you clunked. You acted so demented that Cary Grant couldn't have really had enough brains to pick up leaves, let alone be the paleontologist the plot called him, to fall for you. You fell plunk in a stream of water, and then just sat there, with your hair hanging and your knees at *the* most grotesque angle. You walked across a ballroom with the back of your dress gone and your white drawers showing and what I'd like to know is, where on earth did you get drawers like that? Who makes them that way any more? Who wears such things in this day of horseless carriages?

However, that scene relaxed us women, anyway, because we knew we'd never have to copy those. We couldn't, unless we invaded a theatrical costumer's or an antique warehouse.

NOW as for you, Claudette, it isn't as if I didn't know you pretty thoroughly

CLIMAXING WARNER BROS.' GLITTERING PARADE OF MUSICALS!

Glorious "42nd Street"—magnificent "Gold Diggers"—actually surpassed by the master makers of musical films!
... In this new show packed with surprising novelties! ... Jimmy Cagney singing and dancing for the first time
on the screen! Stupendous dance spectacles with hundreds of glorified beauties, staged UNDER WATER! New
laughs and song-hits from Gold Diggers' famous stars ... All directed and staged by the internationally famous
creators of "42nd Street", Lloyd Bacon and Busby Berkeley. CAN YOU EVEN *THINK* OF MISSING IT?

"FOOTLIGHT PARADE"

JAMES CAGNEY • RUBY KEELER • DICK POWELL • JOAN BLONDELL

GUY KIBBEE • RUTH DONNELLY • FRANK McHUGH • HUGH HERBERT

and when you started going in for idiocy like sliding down that ski slide in "I Met Him In Paris" with nothing between you and the ice except your following—well, it wasn't as if I couldn't do that, too. As a matter of fact, I could do it better than you could because there is a lot more to me than there is to you in that locale. But listen, snooks, when you go into "Bluebeard's Eighth Wife" and get Gary Cooper (which is one of the things I wouldn't mind getting, either), how on earth do you expect me to follow your methods?

You remember that gray suit that Travis Banton designed for you at a cost to Paramount of about five hundred dollars, and which you had made at Eddie Schmidt's at another cost to Paramount of $175, and on which you yourself spent three fittings?

What slayed me was that, when they finally filmed the scene, only your hat showed and heaven alone knows what that cost. Now if I had on $675 worth of suit, I'd not only have to show all of me that was socially permitted, but I'd have to keep on showing that same costume daily for the rest of the fiscal year to break even.

Then when you and Travis were planning the negligee for you to wear when Gary spanks you, you two figured it ought to make a man a lot madder if he had to fumble around through a lot of ruffles. So ruffled from hem to toe you were, which is a mighty cute idea, I'll admit. But you are a smart girl, and a business girl, and do you think that's any example to set the rest of your public?

Has American womanhood got to figure its lure down to the hemline now, and, before planning a date, must we calculate how to be enticing though spanked?

Finally, to all of you girls, I do wish you wouldn't be quite so rich. That was all right, too, when you were glamorous. The boy friend and I could watch you, as we watched the Duke of Windsor or Mrs. Harrison Williams or someone way beyond us. It was a pipe dream, that lovely mood you find at the bottom of your third cocktail. We took you—we took your glamour pictures—just like that third cocktail, as an occasional little spree into another world.

But now that you girls are being socked on the jaw and dropped in mud puddles (ah, there, Loretta) it brings you down, in action anyhow, to our level. And if what you are trying to imply is that even the rich get tacky-looking, with their hair uncombed, and all that—well, what can we dream about then? To take up my initial plea, how can we copy you? Mentors, it is up to you to help us. Otherwise we will be encouraging the heavy date to stay home with us and listen to the radio. Because those heroines in the radio stories are still in the old-fashioned lure business. They are still using the skin you love to touch, and the come-hither of perfume, and the charm of good grooming to get their men. So we feel comfortable with them. Not but what we like you better, really. You are naturally much more alluring and beautiful and charming and all the things we do want to be.

So what do we do? I ask you.

Yours, in worried devotion,

RUTH WATERBURY.

Why We Roosevelts Are Movie Fans

[CONTINUED FROM PAGE 255]

the public demand.

I think, however, that movies themselves are doing an educational job along these lines better than most of us realize and that we are gradually going to see a change in the taste of the people, brought about by higher standards lived up to by the producers themselves.

In the classroom the possibilities for the educational use of films are, I think, very great and have not as yet been used to the fullest extent. In fact, it is only the wealthier, better equipped schools that are able to use the movies at all. It seems a great pity not to use a form of teaching which, for both children and adults, is so easy to understand and remember afterwards. Adult education is carried on all over the country today and should be greatly aided by the use of the right kind of movie.

I remember hearing a learned gentleman who was much interested in education advance the theory that with the development of television, the small country school would be able to bring great teachers and famous foreign visitors into their classrooms as easily as if they were actually there in person.

If properly used, it seems to me that the movies may accomplish much the same thing as this gentleman had in mind. A course given by some brilliant professor might be given through the medium of the movies in every little school throughout the country. Any great foreign teacher or speaker coming to this country might, through this medium, become a familiar figure to children everywhere.

There is great opportunity also to teach our children English and voice culture through the movies, for they can have the best teachers in the country teaching diction, recitation and expression through the medium of the talking film. This can be done in the smaller rural schools as well as in the bigger schools of the cities, for, once the school is equipped with the proper apparatus, the cost is small. The individual teachers who are qualified for this work are few, and they command high salaries. Adult education classes, in which foreign men and women are

learning our language and its correct pronunciation, would find this method very helpful.

The reading of good books will be increased greatly by having the masterpieces of literature dramatized and given in the movies. It is never possible to film an e n t i r e book, but if you awaken a real interest it often happens that young and old will read the book to know the whole story, whereas, in all probability, many people would never have known that the story was interesting had they not seen it on a movie screen. "Tom Sawyer," which is one of our favorites, is an excellent example of this.

Of course, if you know a book very well and are very fond of it, you may not agree with the way it has been dramatized, and it may give you an unhappy evening. I h a v e carefully avoided seeing "Peter Ibbetson" because I happen to be very fond of it as a novel and I was told that in the movie it is essentially changed in a way that I feel sure would spoil it for me.

Perhaps it is necessary to do this to bring it up to date as a play, but I really question if this amount of latitude should be permitted to the dramatist. If you are writing an original play, you have every right to make your characters do what you wish or what you feel they must do, but, if certain characters have been created by an author I doubt if you have a right to change them into different people.

FINALLY, we come to the possibility of using the motion picture as a character-building instrument. We must make information about films which are being shown in every theater available to parents so that they may know what is suitable and what is unsuitable for their children. While this information is at present available to anyone interested enough to obtain it, through the Women's Clubs' services, it may require a statement on the part of the producers and the theater managers in the local newspapers as well. This is just a step towards making pictures a help in building character, but it does not mean that children will not often be taken to see pictures which are not suitable for them. It puts the burden of responsibility on the parents, however, for all that the producers can do will have been done to protect the children from seeing films not suited to their age.

Plays could be written for very little children with the object of teaching ethics and morals. I remember well the type of book which was given to my generation to improve our understanding of the proper "guiding principles," but I doubt very much if the children of today would read these books and take them seriously.

It is possible, however, without actually preaching a sermon, to glorify some of the fundamental good traits of human nature. Kindness, gentleness, honesty, generosity and love may be shown in plays about animals so that little children can understand these virtues; also, in the dramatization of some

of the old fairy tales and in stories of everyday life the world over.

Our children should not be allowed to believe, however, that there are not other qualities in human nature: hate, greed, fear, dishonesty, malice and cruelty, these should all walk across the stage with the consequences which they may bring in daily life. Facing the realities is good even for the very young.

Love of country may be inculcated through the movies as well as in many other ways. Children actually seeing fine episodes in their history and in contemporary happenings which illustrate the qualities of character which we wish them to acquire will get a point of view without listening to a sermon.

Children should realize what a government in any country may do that is wrong and that patriotism consists in holding to the highest standards in public questions as one would in private life. Countries, like people, deteriorate under indifference and lack of attention from their citizens, and this can be well shown in the movies.

IF THE movies undertake to be a factor along the above lines, they will become a strong educational and character-building force, but primarily they will always remain, I hope, a form of enter-

tainment, and, as such, they fill an important place.

I hope they will not take the place of the real theater, for anyone who appreciates and understands what the dramatic art really means will always feel the greater power and force of a personality as projected by a great actor or actress across the footlights. The movies, however, will bring knowledge and pleasure daily into the lives of many hundreds of thousands who can rarely see a finished professional dramatic production.

As a purveyor of entertainment alone, the responsibility of the movie producer is heavy because his audience is vast, and so I want to say my last word on the question of creating good taste. The highly cultured people of the world are those who have good taste.

There is, of course, a certain kind of robust fun, even vulgarity, which is not contrary to good taste, but some things in literature and the arts have always presaged decadence. Those things must be kept from the drama if we are to promote good taste. Here is the great challenge to the movie producer of the future—will movies be an instrument in the development of good taste and are we growing up to be a nation with artistic knowledge and appreciation?

Payboy of the Western World

[CONTINUED FROM PAGE 256]

hair and an ear-yanking grin came in to file his daily piece for the papers. Will Rogers liked to kick around with the folks in Claremore whenever Hollywood and the busy world let him run away. Gene Autry tapped out the dispatch, accepted a stick of gum and got acquainted. The next night he played a few of his tunes and talked, learned about the show world and the big towns and Hollywood and stuff. Gene wasn't much good at railroading from then on. When he'd saved up fifty bucks he ordered a pass to New York. When he got there he quit his telegraphing job. For keeps.

The screen was wide open and hungry for a Gene Autry when he finally drifted from small-time radio to Hollywood. Only nobody knew it.

He came to Hollywood in a low, lean Western year. He didn't come to buck the cowboy star racket. He came to Hollywood because the boss of Republic studios, then Mascot, had once peddled Gene's records and knew the sure-fire pull of his voice. With misgivings—because he showed his screen greenness at once—they cast him in a serial called "The Phantom Empire." Nobody noticed him—in Hollywood. He was no Barrymore. From an acting standpoint he was as stiff and awkward as a muddy boot.

But in the hay belt, and in the cheap admission city picture shows, where serials bloom, something different went

on. Gene Autry was like manna to a starving section of forgotten — Hollywood forgotten—movie fans. He had what they liked—and they said so, out loud. The studio starred him in a Western feature.

Since then they can't shoot Gene Autry's pictures fast enough. Today he carries along the whole Republic studio. Autry Westerns sell the entire program. Today Gene's the most popular Hollywood star in the world. Two to one over Taylor, three to one over Gable. Believe it or not.

JUST recently Hollywood succumbed to this realization with a high fever. For the resulting delirium—have a look:

Fifty to seventy-five Westerns are on studio programs for this year. Seven separate studios have lined up anywhere from six to twenty-six rough-riding reelers aimed at the nabes and the sticks. Why? Well, I'll tell you later.

There is only one retirement on record. Dick Foran, a Princeton boy, who never smelled branded beef in his life, has discarded his phoney chapparajos. It wasn't because his pictures flopped, nor because Dick flopped, nor because he married a Los Angeles society girl and went high hat. It was just because Warner's needed him for bigger stuff. They're hunting another cowboy now.

George O'Brien is getting back in the

saddle at RKO, and Colonel Tim Mc-Coy is creaking leather once more. Buck Jones merely moved from Universal to Columbia. Ken Maynard forsakes his circus for Hollywood this winter, old Hooter Gibson is looking around for the right deal and even Tom Mix is talking comeback. Bill Boyd, at Paramount, is so solidly set in the *Hopalong Cassidy* series that nothing, not even Cecil B. De Mille, could shake him loose.

AND you can blame all this on Gene Autry. Or, as I said, if you live in the sticks, you can thank him.

But why? How? What did Gene have? What has he got now?

Well, I'll tell you—if you must know. The boy's got sex appeal. He's the first cowboy star that ever had it in a sizable dose. Ninety per cent of his terrific flood of mail comes from the sweet pretty things. Old women want to mother him. Young ones want to marry him. Girls want him to be their sweetheart. You should read his mail. Or maybe you shouldn't. Some of it's pretty warm.

And the paradox is this: he's about as much of a ladies' man as Hitler. He's shy, he blushes, he tightens up inside a mile of a skirt. His director has to coax him into a final fade-out peck with his leading lady. He's safely married and thoroughly domesticated. He goes to bed early. Doesn't smoke, doesn't drink. Even on the screen he's about as sinister as a bottle of milk, and just as fresh and clean. That's one reason Gene got off to a head start.

If you remember, about four years back a hot wind of sex and sophistication swept over Hollywood—and the chill gust of a resentful public answered it. There was the clean-up campaign, the Will Hays "clamp downs," the Purity League. There were also a lot of people who were neither sophisticated, nor clever, nor smart, nor risqué, and didn't want to be. They were country people. In them Gene plainly struck a responsive chord.

But he could sing, too, and play. And so, for the first time in the long, rough-and-tumble record of Western pictures, Gene brought something entertaining for women as well as men. And women, as everyone knows, rule the world. Women and the autocrats they serve—kids.

That's what Gene Autry means to the millions in the South and the West and the small towns in every section of this country, Canada, South America, England and the Orient. But what about Hollywood?

To Hollywood, producing Hollywood, Gene and his quiet staggering success is both a lesson and a promise. The lesson is never again to forget the down-to-earth people upon whom the movies have always depended. The promise is the unlimited rewards to come from pictures prepared to please them.

GENE AUTRY'S pictures cost around $50,000, which is very small potatoes as moving-picture budgets go. They gross between $200,000 and $250,000 as regularly as clockwork. But most strictly stick screen fare is cheaper than that. Feature-length movies, costing as low as $12,000, go out to get what they can where they can. Exhibitors play them because they're desperate for something to give the kids on Friday and Saturday, because the small-town family trade must have plain movies for plain people at a plain price. But they hurt in the long run.

Straight Westerns and their stars will probably never return to the glorious days when Tom Mix drew $17,500 a week at Fox. They have to be dressed up expensively into pictures like "The Plainsman" to stand that. Gene Autry gets $7500 a picture, but only a few months ago he drew $250 a week. Smaller, independent studios make Westerns because most big majors with a weighty overhead can't afford to. At least, that was the general idea, until Darryl Zanuck made his bid for Gene.

But more eyes are wide open now and Mr. Zanuck does not loom any more demented than a fox. A Gene Autry can sell many stars far more famous than himself in more territories than you ever imagined. He can swell the returns from their pictures and build their names, too, in that now very respectable orphans' home of the movies—the once lowly sticks.

ON the social side, however, I am afraid Gene Autry will never slice much ice or press the tempo of Hollywood up or down a beat. For his twenty-eight years and Gallic ancestry, he is about as lively and spectacular as an oyster. He and his quiet, Missouri-bred wife, married long before fame snatched him by the shirttail, live in a modest house in the San Fernando Valley, and he's just bought a few more acres over near Burbank for his horses. The Autrys never go out stepping; in fact, Gene doesn't own even an ordinary business suit or a pair of lace oxfords. He had one pair some time ago but he says he lost them and his wife has to believe him.

They wanted Gene to show up as a guest star when Rudy Vallee opened at the Cocoanut Grove the other night but someone said "tuxedo," and Gene fled. He's never had one on in his life. He travels around in a subdued show cowboy garb, nothing to compare with the resplendent sartorial sunbursts of Tom Mix in his salad days. His idea of a good time is to load his white-stockinged black mount, "Champ," in a specially built trailer and go out on the road for personal appearances. Folks like him and he likes folks. Incidentally, he breaks house records wherever he goes, and he pads his picture income past the $100,000 a year bracket thereby. Radio is after him this fall, and he has just turned down $5000 a week for a circus jaunt. But up until this year he didn't even keep a record of his checks.

HE talks with a sparing drawl, but his quiet Dutch-blue eyes show that still water runs deep. He's always amiable and nice to get along with, but he knows what he has and what to do about it. People don't impress him. His wife lured him to the Troc, cowboy rig and all, just once—a few days ago. Walter Winchell spotted him, and Gene will always remember Winchell's crack, "You've got a swell press agent—whoever he is,"—because he doesn't even have a press agent!

Gene left before twelve o'clock that night. But latest reports have it that he's coming back for more. He's been seen a lot recently at the night spots, in full regalia, and—annoyed that more of the celebrities don't recognize him!

There's a striking something about him that recalls Will Rogers, another cowboy who did all right in Hollywood. It couldn't have come from the casual contact back in Claremore; it's just that Gene and Will were the same breed of man underneath. Gene Autry has what Will Rogers had—the common touch. And like Will, he can't forget his home town.

The proudest moment of his life took place a short time ago. That was when Tioga talked about changing its name to Autry Springs, Texas!

So the battle raged! And the focal point of that not-very-private war was "Freaks." Boohs and hisses and shocked surprise accompanied lots of letters, while some of the writers felt it made blessing counting easier to see those poor unfortunates. At the left is one of the controversial scenes with Baclanova and midget Harry Earles

The New "Shady Dames" of the Screen

[CONTINUED FROM PAGE 219]

blossom complexion and a rather high pitched voice. Tut, tut, Elissa, it simply won't do.

At the moment M-G-M is concentrating upon Jean Harlow. Funny thing about Jean. She made her screen début as the old-fashioned vampire of the Theda Bara tradition in "Hell's Angels." But she's being made over now, into the modern version—hair pushed back (it's red now instead of platinum—see p. 332), eyebrows a mere wispy line and eyes half hidden beneath put-'em-on-with-glue lashes.

EVEN Norma Shearer attempted glamour in "The Divorcee," "Strangers May Kiss," "A Free Soul" and others. She went after it with such vigor that even Adrian, the head gown designer at M-G-M, demurred at her suggestions for clothes.

Norma bought that revealing costume that brought amazed gasps from the audience when she appeared in it in "A Free Soul."

And then Norma did a right-about-face. The public was annoyed with her for substituting glamour for romance. Letters poured in to her begging, "Please, Norma, stick to romance."

The public had enough shady dames without little Mrs. Thalberg.

Several mothers, who always allowed their children to see Norma Shearer's films, wrote to her begging her to return to straight dramatic rôles and good clean pictures that children could see.

Norma is a smart girl. Having finished "Strange Interlude," she's rushing into "Smilin' Through," as sweet a little story as you'll **see.**

Maybe you remember when Jane Cowl played it on the stage and Norma Talmadge did it in pictures.

"Possessed" began Joan Crawford's glamour cycle. "Letty Lynton" carried through. In that picture Joan did as good a piece of dramatic acting as she has ever done, and all her admirers knew it, but even so, hundreds of them wrote to PHOTOPLAY to protest about her screen morals and to beg her to return to the gay type of "Our Dancing Daughters" film in which she became famous.

Strangely enough, although Garbo started the vogue by packing them into the theaters, the public was grateful to her for those scenes in "As You Desire Me" when she was a sweet, charming, young girl. And they expressed the wish that she would play such scenes again in other films.

THE public will not allow Janet Gaynor to follow the new vogue. Poor Janet—she's more than anxious to try her hand at something a trifle daring, yet when it was announced she had cut her long bob short, dyed her hair redder and insisted upon being sophisticated, hundreds of letters begged her to let her curls grow back and remain just sweet. Incidentally, one of the gallery pictures in this month's magazine is of Janet with her hair done in the fashion you'll never see on the screen —the way she wants it but the way the public doesn't. She is now letting her hair grow again.

This caricature of Garbo, by Joe Grant, empha-sizes the facial characteristics of the star—the heavy lips, half-closed eyes, high forehead and snaky eyebrows, which have apparently been taken as a model for the new school of shady dames

This change in the women stars has brought about a change in the men. The pretty boys, the matinée idols, the gallant, protecting heroes have been replaced by the Clark Gables, James Cagneys, George Rafts and Johnny Weissmullers.

Each studio is hunting for second Clark Gables—men who knock women down, kick 'em around and make 'em like it.

The shady dame has become the heroine instead of the vamp; the rough guy is the hero, instead of the villain. A few years ago had Johnny Weissmuller presented himself to any self-respecting casting director, he would have been listed immediately as a heavy—one of those big, strong guys whom the handsome hero could overcome single-handed. But not now— no sir, Johnny was cast as the hero in "Tarzan, the Ape Man."

Even that big, burly Wallace Beery is a hero in many pictures.

And as the style in heroes and heroines has changed, so have movie plots. Marriage is not a necessity on the screen these days and, in spite of the censors, illicit love is sometimes glorified.

THE wave has swept even farther. Second leads, juveniles, ingénues have all been touched by the new vogue, for on the screen the sweet young girl is left in the lurch while the shady dame walks off with her man. So Hollywood girls, trying to get a break in pictures, have realized that in glamour lies their fortune.

At a recent Hollywood luncheon I noticed a number of the newer players, girls like Frances Dean, who is making her first picture for Educational. With very few exceptions, these young girls had rouged their mouths until they looked like nothing so much as members of a minstrel show just about to ask Mr. Bones a leading question.

Now remember, make-up cleverly and subtly applied is necessary to the charm of every woman. I'm only speaking of the exaggerations.

Even Colleen Moore has gone glamorous, with a new hair style, new make-up and false eyelashes.

As a novelty, this new sex is interesting. Garbo was and is fascinating.

BUT her imitators—not only among the actresses of the screen, but among the thousands of women throughout the world—what of them?

For the screen stars are imitated—of that there is no doubt— and if this new type of woman becomes the standard, will there be a place for the sweet, simple, natural, thoroughly feminine type which has inspired the world for ages and ages?—the secret ideal of most men?

Fortunately, even caviar becomes tasteless when you have had too much of it.

This new sex was daring and therefore attractive as long as it was unique, but when everyone from all the screen stars to your next-door-neighbor attempts glamour, it becomes just a bore.

Norma Shearer has already turned her steps toward screen

Marlene Dietrich
in
"THE SCARLET EMPRESS"
(Based on a private diary of Catherine the Great)
directed by JOSEF VON STERNBERG
A PARAMOUNT PICTURE

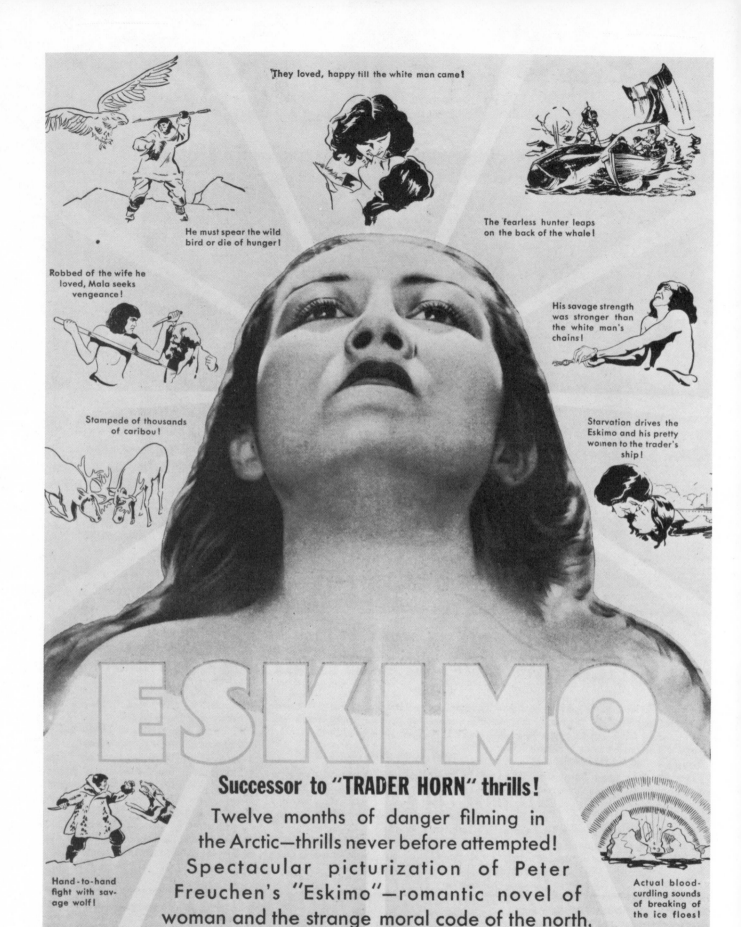

They loved, happy till the white man came!

He must spear the wild bird or die of hunger!

The fearless hunter leaps on the back of the whale!

Robbed of the wife he loved, Mala seeks vengeance!

His savage strength was stronger than the white man's chains!

Stampede of thousands of caribou!

Starvation drives the Eskimo and his pretty women to the trader's ship!

ESKIMO

Successor to "TRADER HORN" thrills!

Twelve months of danger filming in the Arctic—thrills never before attempted! Spectacular picturization of Peter Freuchen's "Eskimo"—romantic novel of woman and the strange moral code of the north.

Hand-to-hand fight with savage wolf!

Actual blood-curdling sounds of breaking of the ice floes!

Directed by W. S. Van Dyke who made "Trader Horn"... Associate Producer: Hunt Stromberg

A METRO-GOLDWYN-MAYER Picture

simplicity. And so has Constance Bennett.

Before long, Joan Crawford may discover that good, honest stories concerning the problems which face the majority of girls today are better than highly colored yarns about shady ladies.

When she does, she will change her make-up and her mannerisms and come back to us as the normal, lovable, girl whom we have adored from the beginning of her stardom.

PERHAPS even Garbo will change when she realizes how much approval she rated for the sweet scenes in "As You Desire Me." Or perhaps Garbo and Dietrich are the two women who are able to keep on being shady ladies, thereby giving us the spice for our cinema sauce.

And we'll find in Garbo and Dietrich women to watch but not to copy, women who are exceptions rather than rules, and we'll discover ourselves looking for new Marguerite Clarks, May Allisons, Lillian Gishes and Janet Gaynors to adore.

The Tragedy of 15,000 Extras

[CONTINUED FROM PAGE 137]

These people saw no glitter, no romance, no bright mirage of stardom. To them, it was hard work and serious work. To it they gave all their thought, time and strength, exactly as any man or woman who loves his job. All the money they could possibly spare went into the replenishing of their wardrobes, so necessary to the ten and fifteen dollar pay checks. They gave time and money to maintaining their appearance. Hair must be waved, clothes pressed, hands manicured. But less and less money came in as the mob of unqualified drifters increased. And the amount of work had to be distributed over thousands of pleading, starving people.

Furthermore, the type of picture being made cut down the demand for extras. The gorgeous spectacles, with the exception of an occasional De Mille picture, gave way to homey little dramas demanding few supers.

Now the professional extra was fortunate if he worked one day out of three or even four months. When the hue and cry of these people grew louder and louder, the NRA Code Committee took the matter in hand. A committee composed of men and women entirely outside the motion picture industry was formed. Its job was to whittle down the extra list so that, instead of thousands of extras eking out less than a bare existence from motion picture work, hundreds might earn a livable wage.

The committee asked each casting director from every studio to send in a list of recommended extras. These lists were gone over carefully. If Mary Smith was recommended by three casting directors, Mary was put down as having three votes, and it looked pretty good for Mary.

If Jack Jones was recommended by one director, he in turn was given one vote. Naturally, the extras receiving the most votes, or, in other words, the extras considered capable by the most studios, remain on the list.

Hollywood is waiting now, fearfully, anxiously, to see what this great army of discarded extras will do. There are no factories, no sweat-shops, no mills in Hollywood to swallow them up. And among these hanger-on extras there exists a strong bond of friendship and co-operation not found in the professional extras. They were ever-eager to help each other in work. What will they do in unemployment?

ONCE I saw an extra come dejectedly out of the casting office at M-G-M and join the group that lingered about the gate.

"No luck?" someone asked him.

"I could have the job if I had a pair of glasses. It means five dollars—God knows I need it."

Without a word, an old man removed his glasses and handed them to the young chap.

"Here, Buddy," he said, "I can't see much without them, but I'll sit right here and wait."

The young fellow reached eagerly for the glasses, then stopped suddenly. "But look—I can't do that! You know how this business is. I might be in there till late tonight."

"That's all right. You're hungry, aren't you? I'll wait in the alleyway."

All day the old man sat there, unable to move because, without the glasses, the world was a foggy blur. After sundown, a chill wind came up.

It was past eight o'clock when the young fellow came out with the spectacles, and found the old man shivering but uncomplaining in the alleyway.

"It's tough on you, my being so late," the boy apologized. "But at least, we can eat now! I'll bet you've been hungry as long as I have!"

IT is quite usual, among these extras, for five or six of them to live together in one room. When a call from the studio comes for one, there begins the hectic business of assembling a decent outfit. This fellow's suit, that one's shoes, another's best tie, and so on. Until the lucky one is sent off looking quite well-dressed. And the others sit around pantless, coatless, shoeless, till their pal returns with their clothes and a few dollars. Then they eat again.

Two extra girls have been driven to the extremity of living in a tent. Other forlorn souls have retreated to a shantytown near Universal City, where they manage to exist in huts crudely fashioned from scraps of tin, iron and lumber from the junkpiles.

Some extras who hang about the M-G-M studio have banded together, into a sort of little club. They take turns, sitting in a broken-down automobile in a vacant lot across the alley, while another member is stationed near the telephone in a nearby pool hall, in case a message for one of them should be relayed there by Central Casting. No such message has ever come, but who knows? That's the sort of hope the extra feeds on—pathetic, futile.

"No work—nothing today—no work—no work—I'm sorry—nothing today." Hour after hour the monotonous drone goes on in the Central Casting Office.

Occasionally it is broken by a frantic voice.

"YOU'VE got to help me! Anything!" And the next second the drone begins again, "No work—I'm sorry—nothing. No work."

And yet they still pour in, demanding jobs, demanding to register, demanding to know why they haven't been called.

"You can see that some adjustment had to be made," Miss Mell, of the Central Casting Bureau, said to me. "It isn't so much the young ones I'm worried about. It's the older ones—the old men and women."

The telephone rang, and Miss Mell answered. I could hear the frantic hysteria in a girl's voice as it carried over the wires. Miss Mell talked to her patiently, calmly. But the girl's wild accusations, pleadings, oaths and denouncings, grew louder.

"Please, please," Miss Mell tried to talk to her.

Finally the girl broke into tired sobbing. There was a click of the receiver, and the room was quiet again.

"You see, it isn't really I whom she hates," Miss Mell said. "It's the thing I represent to her—security. Someone who possesses a job."

THESE scenes will be eliminated when the fifteen thousand names are struck off the list. But what scenes will take their place?

It's Hollywood's burden, certainly. And yet, Hollywood is not to blame. For years it has done everything in its power to discourage the influx of movie-struck people drifting in. For years warnings and pleadings have been sent out that there are no jobs in the motion picture industry.

And still they came, thousands upon thousands.

What will become of them now?

Hollywood doesn't know the answer. The extras certainly don't know the answer.

"Charity—it will help out some," an old man said in a shaking voice.

"We don't want any of that Russian stuff, is all I know," said another, discussing their fate.

"You mean Communism?" I asked him.

"Yea. We don't want that. We'll get along—somehow."

Those Who Wish They Hadn't Posed for the pictures on pages 92 and 93 are, from left to right: Carole Lombard, Myrna Loy, Joan Crawford, Ginger Rogers and Mae West.

"GINGER" ROGERS ("Young Man of Manhattan," Paramount) is an Independence, Mo., girl who was discovered by Paul Ash, and was a sensation singing in Publix presentations. Then she went into "Top Speed," a Broadway musical show, and scored again. Paramount, who found Helen Kane the same way, lost no time in getting "Ginger" on the dotted line.

The Star-Maker Whose Dreams Turned to Dust

[CONTINUED FROM PAGE 139]

The only picture he ever "cleaned up on" was "Way Down East." It made money, not because it had been cheap to produce, but because it was phenomenally popular. He put tremendous sums of money into the making of it, went heavily into debt. He paid $175,000 for the story, in the first place. Then, with customary care, he insisted on filming it in New England, and waiting for each of the four seasons to roll around so that none of the scenery would need to be faked. The company started to work in the fall. Production continued during the bitter cold New England winter, through spring, and into the summer.

GRIFFITH was rewarded by seeing his picture run for over a year in a Broadway theater at a five dollar top!

In part, his screen glory was due to his canny ability to spot talent.

Two girls came knocking at the door of the old Biograph studio one day to see Gladys Smith—Mary Pickford, of course. Griffith answered the door. The girls were Lillian and Dorothy Gish.

Griffith approached a young man in a theater lobby one night and urged him to go into pictures. The man was Doug Fairbanks.

Once a freckle-faced youngster sneaked into the studio to watch her sister play an extra bit. Griffith saw the girl—plain, unattractively dressed. Her name was Mae Marsh.

Griffith gave Wallace Reid his first chance in **"The Birth of a Nation." He launched Constance Talmadge on her movie career in "Intolerance."**

He noticed an electrician on the set one day, took him off the job and gave him a featured rôle in a movie. The man was Charles Emmett Mack.

Henry B. Walthall, Miriam Cooper, Carol Dempster, Ralph Graves, Blanche Sweet, Seena Owen, Eric Von Stroheim, Richard Barthlemess, Robert Harron, Mildred Harris, Gladys Brockwell—all were Griffith-made stars. But Griffith never grew rich on these "finds." And the stars, incidentally, rarely found happiness in the success that Griffith gave them. Tragic deaths cut short the careers of four of them—Wallace Reid, Mack, Gladys Brockwell and Bobby Harron. And sorrows and misfortunes accompanied the others.

TODAY, a number of the famous people once associated with Griffith have slipped into oblivion or, like the director himself, are living in comparative obscurity, hoping they may still be given a chance to "come back." The exceptional Richard Barthlemess alone among the erstwhile protégés of Griffith has enjoyed uninterrupted movie stardom. The Gish sisters are much better known to the New York stage than to pictures now. Fairbanks and Pickford still are prominent names, of course, but they have been in retirement for lengthy periods in recent years.

For himself, Griffith says he doesn't want to "come back."

"I am tired of movies! To suggest my making another film is like asking a pensioned bricklayer to build another wall."

But his dreams belie his words.

And, finally, he admits that he does think of yet another movie—another picture of the South. It would be a story of the great Southwest, with romantic, adventurous Sam Houston as the central character.

A pioneer in introducing startling ideas, new developments in picture making, Griffith now has only one plan for improving pictures. And that, strangely enough, has nothing to do with the producing of movies, but rather with

exhibiting them. He wants, by some means, to make sure that everyone who sees a picture, observes it from the very beginning. He feels that good feature pictures are carefully built, and that the artistic and dramatic effect is lost when the latter part of the picture is seen first.

In large theaters, Griffith would have a second auditorium where shorts and news reels would be shown to late-comers, while they waited for the next feature showing to begin. The plan is expensive, but Griffith, as usual, is thinking of the artistic effect—not of the money bags!

GRIFFITH is not bitter because others reaped the fortunes that his pictures made. He laughs when he tells you that he worked at Biograph for only fifty dollars a week, because he thought his pictures weren't making money, and afterward discovered that a few men there were cleaning up on his productions. For him the weeks of toil without salary on "The Birth of a Nation" were filled with adventure. And the debt he plunged into to make "Intolerance" was well worth while, because the picture was an outstanding example of cinematic technique.

So now a columnist has written that David Wark Griffith is broke, in need. Certainly, many of the brilliant names, once associated with his, are forgotten. And his old movie masterpieces, when run off on the new and faster modern projectors, jump and flicker foolishly.

His glory is in the past.

Griffith knows that. He wishes they wouldn't revive his pictures. He wishes editors wouldn't speak grandly of his past productions as "works of art."

"They aren't!" he says. And adds, dramatically, "When motion pictures have created something to compare with the plays of Euripides, or the work of Homer or Shakespeare or Ibsen, or the music of Handel or Bach, then let us call motion picture entertainment an art—but not before then."

Here's the Jean Harlow you used to know —aloof, mysterious, icy. On the screen she was a siren, but a cold, calculating one

Now look at the new, red-headed Jean—a gay, youthful hoyden

The Star Creators of Hollywood

[CONTINUED FROM PAGE 167]

Having arrived with the firm intention of becoming a producer at once, he became a prop boy—and liked it. That was twenty-two years ago. Twenty-one years ago he became his brother's assistant director. And twenty years ago he was given a camp chair of his own.

Universal kept him on for several years, during which he turned out the tidy sum of fifty pictures, and then he went to Fox. Nineteen-nineteen was the beginning of the industry's adolescent period, and Ford was one of the greatest influences of maturity.

Only a true son of Erin could so perfectly depict Irish woes and glories. Ford is now directing Barbara Stanwyck in "The Plough and The Stars"

He made "The Three Godfathers," which was pretty grown-up for that period, and helped introduce the art of light and shadow on the screen; he broke the collective hearts of American audiences with "Four Sons," a four handkerchief picture, and then made the same hearts pound wildly with excitement at "The Iron Horse."

He made "Three Bad Men," and "The Black Watch," and "Arrowsmith." He made "Men Without Women," which contrary to all expectations really didn't have any women in it, and he made "The Brat" and "The Lost Patrol."

When a grateful committee, finally, gave him the Academy Award for his superlative "The Informer," he put the gold statue on some shelf or other and began "Mary of Scotland."

"How?" I asked him. "How do you do these things? I want to know how you get your effects, what your technique is, all your methods, whether you work more with camera than with sound, what you do about casting, what you do with a bad script, how you direct a picture—everything."

He didn't even flinch. Sitting there, strik-

ing match after match, his hair rumpled by thoughtful fingers, he started, surprisingly, at the beginning.

The routine of his first efforts on any picture is of course dependent on the circumstances, the type of story, the particular stars who are scheduled to work in it.

"When they gave me 'Mary of Scotland' to do, my first thought was of Hepburn," Ford said, with only a trace of brogue in his voice. "She was already set for the rôle, and it wasn't as if she were just any talented pretty young actress who could be dressed in anything and photographed casually. In that case the primary problem was the star and we had to solve it before we could start on story or script.

"I asked the studio for a print of every picture Katharine had ever made—'Bill of Divorcement,' 'Morning Glory,' 'Little Women,' 'Alice Adams,' all of them—and then I called in the wardrobe department and set men and the story adaptors; together we looked up portraits and old woodcuts of the period costumes Mary Queen of Scots wore, and photographs of the rooms in her castle. We sketched gowns and ruffs, we planned backgrounds and settings in rough outline.

"When we had some sort of working basis for departure, we locked ourselves in a projection room and, one each night so long as they lasted, ran the Hepburn pictures. We studied every angle of her strange, sharp face— the chiseled nose, the mouth, the long neck— and then adjusted the sketches to fit her personality. We planned photographic effects, decided how best to light her features and what make-up to use in order to achieve for her a genuine majesty."

He paused to relight the inevitable Ford pipe. "After that was time enough to worry about the story."

With "The Informer" the approach was entirely different. It was a picture, in the first place, which the studio was not enthusiastic about making—Ford had met the author in Ireland, liked his masterpiece, and had come back to Hollywood aflame with the desire to put it on celluloid. Producers read the book with indulgence, muttered that it was too realistic and too gloomy for popular appeal, and turned away. Ford persisted for four years, and during that time studied every detail of the story, planned every scene of the picture in his mind.

So that when RKO gave in finally (he offered to make his little film portrait for $300,000 in a corner of an unused sound stage) the director was ready. He invited Dudley Nichols, who did the adaptation, for a week's cruise aboard his boat, and in seven days together they wrote the script.

A few extras, Victor McLaglen, and three weeks of shooting, were all the necessary requisites. Ford sent his picture to the cutting room with $40,000 left from the budget.

BUT his approach to "The Informer" and to "Mary of Scotland" were admittedly exceptions. "Usually I take the story," he told me, "and get every line of printed material I can find on the subject. And then I take the boat and simply cruise until I've read it all.

"I eat, sleep and drink whatever picture I'm working on—read nothing else, think of nothing else; which is probably the reason the continuity and mood of my products stay at an exact level."

He works directly with each department during the long preparations for any of the motion pictures he directs. His hand draws the design for a set fireplace. His own suggestions are the inspiration for certain gowns and coiffures and uniforms—and most important of all, much of the dialogue (especially in his Irish portraits) comes from the Ford typewriter. His is the quality of versatility, coupled with good ability and complete knowledge of whatever trade he puts his hand to; so that you are inevitably aware of his special genius when his pictures live their sixty minute lives on your favorite theater's screen.

For the sake of simplicity, the various basic secrets of John Ford's great success must be classified into four or five distinct divisions. Seated across the stained, round table in the prop Dublin pub—with the tangible mood of fog enclosing the windows and the smell of onions and old beer heavy in the air, he analyzed, in a detached good-natured voice, the elements that make him 1936's ace of directors.

Casting was first, and of supreme importance. "After all," Ford said sitting back, "you've got to tell your story through the people who portray it. You can have a weak, utterly bad script—and a good cast will turn it into a good picture. I've thwarted more than one handicap of that kind with the aid of two or three really fine actors.

"With the exception of the stars who are signed for parts by the studio in advance, I insist on choosing names for myself. And I spend more time on that task than on any other."

He's enough of an egoist to resent really big stars on one count alone; they have their own styles of acting, their own very vivid personalities, their own settled methods. So that instead of molding them into the picture he has visualized (an impossibility on the face of it and in any case) Ford has to rebuild his story and his mood around their concrete, unplastic entities—which is gall to his palate and hellish torment to his peace of mind.

Wherefore, when the choice is his, he selects lesser but capable lights, and through sheer labor builds the performances he wants—with the mood and the aura and the detail of the story he is telling inexorably intact.

McLaglen is the classic example of this premise. "The studio spent weeks trying to foist better known heavies on me," Ford went on, "but I knew Vic could do the job, and I knew I could handle him exactly as I wanted to. I won in the end—and you saw the performance he gave."

But the strongest forte of Ford is his selection of bit players. You may have noticed in his pictures the constantly recurring faces of ex-celebrities, men and women who once rode the crest of the Hollywood wave and who have, through various adversities, but mostly because of changing public opinion, been relegated to the motion picture backwash. These people he hires for two reasons: one based on objective intelligence, one on mere subjective sentiment.

"FROM my chair as a director," he said seriously, "I'm able to see that these ex-stars will, after all, give a better performance even in the smallest part than any casual extra would; and it's my contention that the bits in any picture are just as important as the starring rôle, since they round out the story—complete the atmosphere—make the whole plausible. You've seen, certainly, a good many really fine scenes spoiled suddenly by a background player who is obviously reciting his lines, or blundering awkwardly through his action. I won't have that. A woman walking down a street, while people like Barbara Stanwyck and Preston Foster create a love scene, must walk as well and as naturally as a star would do it, or the effect is lost."

He paused for a moment, and then grinned. "The other, and just as important reason, is that when I was starting in this town those people were kind to me. I want to repay a little of that if it's in my power."

On Ford's private lists are one hundred names—not all of the once great—from which he picks his cast for every picture he directs. Always the same people, always the same results; they know his techniques and his wishes, they are capable and hard-working. To my knowledge it's the only list of its kind in the movie colony.

They help, too, these people, in the building of story. "A good many of the most outstanding incidents I have filmed have been things that members of the company have actually seen or actually done during their lives. For these pictures that deal with the Irish uprising I've looked up former black-and-tan soldiers, former rebels, former onlookers, and given them parts; it adds to the sincerity because in the mass demonstration scenes they remember their own experiences and have real tears in their eyes—and every now and then some extra will offer a suggestion that lends to the authenticity of the production.

"Some of them—George Shields for instance—were really in the Dublin post office when it fell. They were in this pub we've reproduced when the call came to mobilize. I

talk with them all informally, and get their opinions, and listen to their anecdotes, and as a result get a better picture."

Which explains, in a measure, some of the superlative effects that have startled you in the multiple John Ford productions you have seen. You remember, of course, the unforgettable scene in "The Informer" where the boy is shot and drops lifeless from a window, while in the agonizing silence his fingernails scratch loose down the wooden sill: one of the extras in the "Informer" company had watched (and heard) that happen at some lost time in his life, and had carried the memory of it through the years until the day came for Ford to use it.

"That particular sequence almost caused me a lot of trouble." The pipe quivered with Ford's laughter. "There was a convention of producers being held at the time, so the rushes were sent up for them to see one afternoon; I asked them what they thought of the scene—and they told me it was all right, not to worry because the sound department could cut out the unfortunate sound of the scratching nails! I'm really afraid I insulted them a little during the next five minutes."

But not all of the touches of realism are garnered from the well-stocked memories of carefully chosen extras; more than a few are transplanted to the scene direct from the storage vaults of Ford's own subconscious. In "Plough and the Stars" you will see a little comic interpolation which to many will seem an improbable bit—merely because the banalism about truth and fiction is still true.

Ford was in Shanghai during the Sino-Japanese war (he recounted this to me as if he were discussing a bridge game) and found time during a particularly cluttered afternoon to see and store away this amusing slice of experience. Shells, as he remembers it, were bursting like exaggerated fireworks over the narrow streets of the old city, and he stood sheltered in a doorway while bits of metal whizzed down at comet speed. Suddenly, around a corner, a plump Chinese nobleman came running—retarded by his heavy silks and splendid trappings, tripping and terrified. His attendants lay dead beside his overturned sedan chair in the street behind;

the sky was bursting; and there was no place of refuge.

Then, as an exceptionally huge shell boomed overhead, he stopped short, looked up, and with a quick motion opened his painted umbrella.

He lifted it above his head, took a long breath of relief.

In his new safety he waddled sedately down the sidewalk and out of sight.

Ford shot that scene, translated of course to the mood and circumstance of the Dublin neighborhood, on the afternoon I was there. Sometimes accidents have happened too—it's the luck of the Irish—which have brought him more credit for certain gorgeous shots than his genius really deserves.

"The Iron Horse," as an entire picture, was great through the sheerest luck and the grace of God, he admits. They had planned it, you see, with the intention of making a class B picture. George O'Brien, the star, wasn't so much then, and all they wanted was a little story about the building of a railroad. The script

When he directed "Mary of Scotland" the temperamental Katie Hepburn met her match in this quiet, unpretentious man who thinks the picture is more important than a star, and has proved it. "Mary" is another hit

was written to fit California weather, of course, and the company was dressed for sunshine.

But when they detrained at Reno there was a blizzard that blinded the entire town, snow lay in five-foot drifts, and the shrieking wind was penetratingly painful. They'd spent too much money to go back.

So they filmed their picture in the snow, while each man's breath made frosted plumes like fantastic comic-strip balloons and each man's clothes were glued to his body with frozen perspiration. They shot the Indian raid scenes during a storm, remembering that such hardy savages as these did not, probably, wait for the summer months for massacre. And when spring finally came they utilized it naturally, in the course of things.

The result was a masterpiece of movie making.

JOHN FORD is great, then (secondly) simply because he visualizes a motion picture as a whole, and in terms of the complete production, rather than as a grouping of scenes; "I very seldom play a sequence to its full effect," he told me with careful emphasis, "and so my stuff is usually confusing to both cast and pro-

Wallace BEERY

The screen which has waited ten years for a picture to equal the thrill, the epic humanity of "The Big Parade" now welcomes "VIVA VILLA." Because in its 1001 nights of amazing, romantic adventure...in its story of riotous revolution and revelry...in its blood-tingling heroism is entertainment that will pack the theatres of the nation!

"Viva Villa"

An all-star cast with thousands of others
in METRO-GOLDWYN-MAYER'S Giant of Screen Triumphs!
Directed by JACK CONWAY
Produced by DAVID O. SELZNICK

● Coming events cast their shadows before

You will soon be seeing MAE WEST in her new picture, "BELLE OF THE NINETIES," with ROGER PRYOR, John Mack Brown, John Miljan, Katherine DeMille and Duke Ellington's Orchestra. Directed by Leo McCarey. A Paramount Picture.

ducers in its uncut form. Before I make a single set-call I outline the story, as it will appear on the screen, in my mind, and separate details are subordinated to the final complete effect."

Third, this unpretentious Irishman works with a camera as a 1936 *Aladdin* would work with his lamp; he carries under contract—year after year—one super-cameraman named Joe August, and since the two of them work upon the same basic premise, and since both follow mentally the same artistic groove so far as motion pictures are concerned, between them they manage to achieve a special end that no other director, and no other technician, has managed to reach in all the years Hollywood has been a movie center. Joe is allowed to dream as much as he likes, and insofar as common sense will allow, photograph as he likes—a system which, according to Ford, helps Joe to feel that he really has something to work toward and a responsibility of his own; not deliberate psychology, perhaps, but good.

Sound is of secondary importance to Ford, but nevertheless of great consequence. Forty per cent of the time (and this will amaze you) he uses a silent camera without even a mike for moral persuasion on the set.

"In the first place I can talk to my people while a scene is shooting," he explained, "and give them suggestions about expression or movement; as a result I don't have to make so many takes. I've discovered that if you rehearse a scene too much it looks artificial and —well, *rehearsed*.

"Lighting, as a matter of fact, is my strong point. I can take a thoroughly mediocre bit of acting, and build points of shadow around a ray of strong light centered on the principals, and finish with something plausible—anyway that's my one boast. If you'll watch in any of my pictures you'll see the trick I use for special effect: while the stars are running through their lines a diffused glow settles over the background assemblage, which at the same time begins to murmur and then to talk intelligibly. And the louder the voices, the stronger the glow, until the main actors are merely part of a group and the general realism is achieved. It always works. Good technique is to let a spot follow a bit player with an important line or two of dialogue across a shadowed set until his part of the scene is finished, too."

SO far as the industry—as an industry—is concerned, he has pretty definite opinions. "Just now we're in a commercial *cul de sac*," he complains mildly. "We have time schedules, we are ordered to direct a certain story in a certain way because that's what the middle-west wants and after all the middle-west has all the money. But the profession on the whole is progressing steadily. Actors are getting to be better actors, technicians are learning more about their trade every day, and the success of such simple deathless portraits as 'The Informer' is making it easier for those who have ideals about pictures, to make blasting demands in the interests of their convictions.

"Eventually motion pictures will all be in color, because it's a success and because it's a natural medium. And we'll go out to a Maine fishing port or to an Iowa hill and employ ordinary American citizens we find living and working there, and we'll plan a little story, and we'll photograph the scene and the people. That's all pictures should do anyway, and it'll be enough."

Agree with him, or not; but in his very definite statement you must discover the essence of his personality, both as a man and as a director. Simplicity, real sincerity, hatred of ostentation: greatness.

They, Too, Were Stars

[CONTINUED FROM PAGE 142]

Grace Cunard, Francis Ford, Flora Finch (John Bunny's leading lady), Alice Lake and King Baggot are among the many who make a living this way.

But there are others who continue to force Hollywood to yield them success by applying their experience and contacts, tempered with more than a dash of wit and ingenuity, to the business of making a living, although without the glamour and fame of yesteryear.

Helen Ferguson and Eileen Percy have heeded the call of printer's ink. Helen, left a comfortable fortune by her late husband, William Russell, lost every penny in a crash of a Beverly Hills bank, and started a publicity business.

Today Helen ranks among the most active press-agents of Hollywood, with a long list of clients, including Fay Wray, Gene Raymond, Johnny Mack Brown, Patsy Ruth Miller and Sidney Blackmer.

EILEEN PERCY, still as beautiful as she was when counted among the leading serial queens of the screen, writes Hollywood news in a column which is syndicated.

Seena Owen recently initiated a literary career by joining the scenario staff of Paramount studios, a route followed before by Raymond Griffith and Ralph Graves with more than ordinary success. Ray, whose lack of an audible voice sent him from a top-ranking star's berth to retirement overnight when the talkies came in, is Darryl Zanuck's right hand writer and producer at 20th Century, and Ralph occupies a similar spot at M-G-M. Douglas MacLean is at Paramount as an associate producer.

Movie stars confronted with the problem of raising their boys to be soldiers have enabled Earle Foxe, who was starred for years in two-reelers and who was featured in many early releases, to make quite a good thing out of the Black-Foxe Military Academy, one of Southern California's most pretentious institutes.

Max Asher, the old Century Comedy star, clings to Hollywood with his magic shop; George K. Arthur, the English comic, produces his own stage plays at the Hollywood Playhouse; Gardner James improves cinema minds at his Boulevard book shop; Ann Little manages the Chateau Marmont, fashionable Hollywood apartment, and Hank Mann, still doing sporadic screen rôles, keeps the grocer paid with his new beer parlor—a Repeal idea emulated by Francis X. Bushman, the first male beauty of the screen and heart beat of the nation's matrons.

BUSHMAN, it was, who, not over two years ago—boasting that he had spent a million dollars in his life and was accustomed to luxury—offered to marry any woman who could keep him in the style to which he was accustomed! (No one took him up.) He opened a liquor store in Chicago, where he had made his unusual offer, when the country reclaimed John Barleycorn.

But reclamation is exactly what ruined the once immensely wealthy director-producer, Edwin Carewe, famed as the discoverer and developer of Dolores Del Rio.

Carewe, who always had the propensity for spreading his interests, taking turns at "angeling" stage shows and magazines, went into the garbage reclaiming business on a big scale not long ago.

The company, known as the Biltmore Conservation Company, operated in Dallas, Texas, and Petaluma, California. Ambitious city contracts were obtained and the garbage turned into chicken feed and fertilizer. Carewe

dropped thousands in the venture and today is in bad financial straits.

If you don't mind jumping from garbage to marriage, it's easy to account for many former big stars who have found the answer in Hollywood marriages and screen retirement.

Theda Bara, as the wife of Charles Brabin, the director, is a prominent social leader in the colony. Jobyna Ralston is satisfied with being just Mrs. Richard Arlen. Enid Bennett is Mrs. Fred Niblo; Marjorie Daw, Mrs. Myron Selznick; Mildred Davis, Mrs. Harold Lloyd; Laura LaPlante, Mrs. William Seiter; Bessie Love, Mrs. William Hawks; Gertrude Olmstead, Mrs. Robert Leonard; Cleo Ridgley, Mrs. James Horne; Constance Talmadge, Mrs. Townsend Netcher; Rosemary Theby, Mrs. Harry Meyers; Virginia Valli, Mrs. Charles Farrell, and Jewel Carmen, Mrs. Roland West.

Marriage also has called away many stars from the town which made them famous. Irene Castle became a Chicago McLaughlin; Dorothy Dalton is the wife of Arthur Hammerstein, the stage producer, and lives in retirement on Long Island; Rex Ingram took Alice Terry to live with him abroad, where he recently adopted the Moslem faith; Carol Dempster married Edwin Larsen, a New York banker.

PHYLLIS HAVER, the Sennett beauty, is the wife of the wealthy William Seeman of New York; Madeline Hurlock boils the morning eggs in Manhattan for Marc Connelly, playwright of "Green Pastures" and Pulitzer prize winner; and Gladys Walton is the wife of a Universal film exchange manager in Chicago.

The list of forgotten stars winds on endlessly, with every year that passes adding new names to the scroll.

Hollywood is too busy to keep track of its alumni, failures or successes. Like the rest of the world, it must ever look to the future instead of to the past.

But it is dangerous as well to speculate too much on the future, so in Hollywood the stars take the fruits of today while they hang, rich and ripe with wealth, fame and adulation, hoping against hope that the harvest will always be bountiful, that never will *they* have to stand in the crowd by the wayside to watch the dazzling parade pass by with only this wistful claim to distinction—

"Once I, too, was a star!"

Do you remember this advertisement —one of the most familiar of ten years ago? And do you know who that cute little girl with the demure curls and the bunch of violets is? Madge Evans posed for this ad when she was a child star in pictures. And users of Fairy Soap didn't know that some day they'd be seeing the lovely grown-up Madge on the screen

"All Women Are Sirens At Heart"

[CONTINUED FROM PAGE 164]

because I try to avoid the obvious in type. I never cast a typical vampire for a vampire rôle. There is no great excitement in seeing that sort of woman preparing her net for a man. One anticipates every move before she makes it. But there is a thrill in seeing a lady of refined background and culture lose herself in the game of love.

"Perhaps also I get good results from my players because I do not start a picture until I know every character in the story as intimately as if they had been friends of mine in the flesh. Consequently, there is no indecision in characterization after we get going."

"I want to know your purely personal impressions of the lovely ladies you've directed," I pleaded. "There come to mind Pola Negri, Mary Pickford, Florence Vidor, Jeanette MacDonald and Miriam Hopkins."

"Thoughts of Pola are saddening," he mused. "She should be at the summit of her career today. She is not old, some years under forty, which is young for an emotional actress. And Pola has almost limitless emotional depths.

"At the beginning of her career, her work was her passion. Everything and everybody were subservient to it. I have never known anyone so tireless and conscientious about her work as Pola was in those early days. Her ambition consumed her.

"But when success and world adulation were hers, Pola could not control herself. She could not hold her own emotions in check. She allowed that great caldron of suppressed desire to overflow, spread itself, and be wasted in a dozen different directions.

"POLA should never have married. She is one person whose nature is absolutely true to her physical type. She is brunette all through. There is something of the savage in her. Perhaps primitive would be a better word. Refined, of course, through education and associations, but dangerous when not under leash.

"Of course, one can never say when a great actress' career is over. There's no time limit for those things if the will is strong enough.

"If Pola can conquer herself, she might again conquer the public."

"And Mary?" I queried.

He shifted his cigar and was thoughtful for a moment.

"Mary Pickford is something more than a great actress. She is a great person. My first American picture, 'Rosita,' was made with her. That was eleven years ago. My English was very poor then. Her kindness and coöperation made working with her a joy.

"Mary is trembling before what someone has called, the altar of time. Yet she is not old. It is only because the world insists that Mary shall always be a child. It seems to me that the public has always expected more of Mary Pickford than any other screen actress. It's because she represents an idealism never to be associated with any of the newer actresses.

"She is a great comédienne. She has what Marie Dressler has as an older woman—comedy touched with pathos. Mary possesses indomitable courage and pluck.

"FINANCIAL insecurity gave her a great driving force in earlier life. Perhaps a hunger for further artistic development at this period of her life may carry her to greater things.

"But in any event, somewhere in the corridors of time, Mary Pickford's flame will still flare on."

"What do you consider a woman's greatest asset?" I suddenly asked him.

"Charm," he answered without waiting a split second. "Charm is the most important thing in the world to a woman. It is a composite quality, impossible to analyze. It takes a little part of so many things to produce charm.

"Florence Vidor has it to a large degree. She is the essence of refinement. Under the right circumstances, her type might defy the rules of chastity, but never the rules of decorum.

"She has a very sensitive, intelligent mind. There is constant conflict between thought and emotion with her. At times, it may have retarded her professional career, but it produced an intensely fascinating woman.

"Florence is what I call a brunette with a blonde soul. Marriage and motherhood have been good for her. Should she ever return to the screen, you would see a deeper, more highly versatile actress, with fire and emotional intensity."

"You know, of course," I reminded him, "that the public gives you full credit for having developed both Jeanette MacDonald and Miriam Hopkins?"

"It has been fun working with them," he answered. "They are both very interesting personalities, and totally different.

"When Jeanette first worked for me in 'The Love Parade' she was still an ingénue. I mean by that, an ingénue at heart, within her own soul. She was very, very pretty and knew it. Her beauty and voice had given her some success on the stage, but she was undeveloped within.

"She did not make you feel.

"In sophisticated comedy today, she has few equals. And Jeanette is still improving herself. She will go on. How far, depends on how long her ambition remains at the pitch it is today.

"There is a very level head underneath that red gold hair, and a sense of humor not often found in beautiful women."

The Maestro got up to take a turn around the room. He's a restless fellow. The big cigar was being replaced by a fresh one. I bolted headlong into the subject of "Design for Living" and the fact that Miriam Hopkins was to play the lead in it. As the Noel Coward play stands now, she seems unsuited to the part.

He grinned at me again. "Are you rabid on the subject of the Coward play? I find nearly everyone goes to extremes about it. They either think it is the very best, or the very worst play, they've seen. I hope your heart will not be broken to know that we are completely re-writing it. Had to, of course, for the screen. Miriam Hopkins will be ideal for the girl who loves two men very, very much as we are developing it.

"MIRIAM is a very complex personality, and fascinating because of it. She is that most unusual combination, a blonde with an earthly quality not suggested by her physical make-up.

"Her type is an irresistible siren. Her almost baby face gives no hint of the tigerish possibilities of her emotions. If she cared enough, she could be all things to a man, a wife, companion and mistress, but Miriam will seldom care enough.

"She is a self-sufficient person in many ways, loving her books, loving her solitude. There's nothing spurious about any part that she plays. She's capable of feeling every scene she does.

"Well, here's to them, and the many other lovely ladies I've directed," he said.

We drained glasses of *Herr* Lubitsch's favorite Pilsner. Life, love and lager! Great combination—

Just look at the crowds that tried to get in to see "Grand Hotel" on Broadway, the most blasé street in the world. And it seems that every other person in this photograph wrote us a letter to praise or criticize Garbo, Joan or Beery

Hollywood's New Miracle Man

[CONTINUED FROM PAGE 165]

ing teeth and black, curly hair reveal his Italian origin. That origin was in Palermo, Sicily.

His sixth birthday was spent in the steerage of the ship which brought him with his family to the Land of Promise—a land which Frank made keep its promise.

The family settled in Los Angeles and Frank was sent to grammar school. He and a younger brother used to race out after the last bell and grab up a bundle of newspapers and establish themselves on a down-town street corner.

IT was then his flair for the dramatic and his understanding of the human side of things began to show. When the newspapers didn't go fast enough, Frank and his brother, Tony, put on an act. Frank's idea, of course. Frank would grab his young brother and belabor him, or so it looked to startled passersby, and yell imprecations at him for not selling the papers. The kid brother would yell his lungs out and weep heart-brokenly. Sympathetic clucks came from the kind-hearted public. The poor kid, the tough older brother. The pennies began to fall. In a matter of minutes, Frank and the brother, hand in hand, would dash for home, the pennies in Frank's pocket jingling sweet applause to their act.

But Frank was soon out of that. He ran a paper route of his own, he played a guitar at social affairs, he became a "pipe crawler" for a steel company, he entered California Institute of Technology, with a burning ambition to become an engineer. To do this, he waited on tables, did other odd jobs, the while he edited the school paper. As for his scholastic standing, the end of his freshman year saw him with a five hundred dollar scholarship in his pocket and a round-trip ticket to the leading universities of the country. Included was the magic city of New York.

What he did in New York clearly mirrors his character even then, and his intense zeal to see, learn and know a vital background for the humanness that is in his pictures. In the metropolis, Frank slept on park benches—and with the expense money thus saved, took in symphony concerts, theaters and museums.

With graduation from college came the war, a lieutenancy in the Coast Artillery, and then the restlessness of the slack water period of early post-war days. He found a job tutoring the scion of the wealthy Baldwin family at the famous Baldwin Rancho near Los Angeles. The Baldwin Rancho housed one of the most extensive libraries in California. There Frank Capra spent every leisure hour.

There first crystallized his longing to himself create and tell stories to the world, stories that the world would like to hear—and see.

HOLLYWOOD was the natural step. And to a hostile Hollywood Frank went—a Hollywood which forced him to sing for his supper in cafés and to prune trees in the sun-baked orchards of San Fernando Valley at twenty cents a tree—in order to live during the frequent stretches of empty studio promise.

But Frank Capra learned about making movies from the ground up—as a technical worker, a co-director of screen novelties, a Hal Roach gag man, and finally a comedy director at Mack Sennett's—with varying up-and-down fortunes. Mostly down. When he made a suc-

cess of Harry Langdon's comedy features, Langdon decided a director wasn't important. (Langdon probably has changed his mind by now.)

It wasn't until Capra had a talk with Harry Cohn, the youthful, vigorous Columbia boss, that he really started going places. Cohn assigned him to an unimportant program picture, titled "That Certain Thing," with Ralph Graves and Viola Dana.

So promising and unusual was the result that Columbia released it with some fanfare—and signed Capra to a long term contract.

He has been there ever since. He directed the most significant picture Columbia had yet made in "Submarine." To him were entrusted the first audible films the studio undertook. He accounted for the success of the Barbara Stanwyck pictures. His "Flight" and "Dirigible" focused even reluctant eyes on Columbia pictures. "American Madness" revealed the dramatic power he could summon, ranking among the best of its year. "The Bitter Tea of General Yen" turned out to be a popular production.

At last came "Lady For a Day," which just missed the Academy Award by a hair—and "It Happened One Night" certainly one of the most popular pictures of this year.

All these at Columbia—which is home, and will be home for a long time to Frank Capra.

Oh, the other studios would like him—how they'd like him—and to Hollywood, which often views success in terms of "bigger and better and more super-colossal," it is sometimes a little puzzling why Frank Capra stays on contentedly at his present headquarters.

As Capra himself explains, his position at Columbia, with its privilege of complete freedom of thought and action, is a tremendous factor in his chances for turning out the kind of pictures he wants to turn out.

Which brings us to how Frank Capra works his magic. Frank Capra's pictures ("It Happened One Night" is the best and freshest example) stand out particularly for three things:

A WEALTH of delightful, human incidents. Surprising twists to the story. Natural, easy characters. He couldn't inject these incidents without what Capra calls "a mind that is allowed to function flexibly."

For instance:

"It Happened One Night" was crammed with incidents that made audiences squirm delightedly in their chairs, sent them out into the lobby chuckling to each other about Clark Gable's hitch-hiking thumb-jerk, "The Walls of Jericho," and "The Man on the Flying Trapeze."

That very human bus sequence grew right on the set.

He recalled his rule:

"A dull scene is just so much footage—"

So, Capra explains: "I had heard a record of 'The Man on the Flying Trapeze.' I thought, maybe some hill-billies would be fun—playing it on their guitars! Well, when they started singing, the tune and the words were so catchy that everyone on the set began singing it, too. Another idea. Why not let the whole bus join in? And that's what finally evolved."

Here is the point Frank Capra made:

"If I had been working at a larger studio, limiting my actions, I would have had to leave

the set and run get an okay to hire the hill-billies; run get another okay to hire each extra hill-billy, each extra singer, until I probably would have given up the idea rather than tangle myself up in a maze of red tape.

"At Columbia, I can follow up any inspiration of the moment while the picture is being made without asking anyone except myself—and the opinions of the people who are working with me."

A MAJOR surprise in "It Happened One Night," he considers the appearance of Clark Gable in the type of whimsical, good-natured rôle he had. The part was originally written for Bob Montgomery. Audiences would have expected Bob to be such a fellow, but when they saw Clark doing it, they were surprised—and delighted.

But the surprising story twists—they weren't there at all. "You just thought they were," says Frank.

"Actually, the stories of 'Lady For a Day' and 'It Happened One Night' were pretty obvious, and full of holes. The plots weren't even new.

"So the story developments were disguised by the incidents which took place. Any audience can guess ahead of flat plot scenes. But by entertaining them, making them forget the plot and stick with the characters through a wealth of incident, you bring them to a surprise turn in the story—a pleasing surprise."

Trickery—that's what—but how the public loves to be tricked in the Capra manner!

As for his characters—his actors—how does he get them to turn in, consistently believable performances?

First of all, on a Capra set—the actor—not the play, is the thing. Anything which might detract from the interest in the natural action of the characters is taboo. Trick shots and spectacular photography is eyed askance by this director.

"Will the audience look at the trick business or the actors?" Capra asks himself before he allows mechanical innovation.

He ushered Barbara Stanwyck, Walter Connolly and Jean Parker into the limelight. He restored Gable, Claudette Colbert, May Robson and Nils Asther to high favor. He even tries to keep himself out of it as much as he can. He wants no directorial "style" to show.

"I try to remain just an appreciative audience," he says.

NO wonder actors love to work with him—no commotion, no temperament, no theatricals—but every break in the world. They don't have to press, they can relax. They're never "on the spot."

But Frank Capra, the most valuable, the most widely acclaimed director in Hollywood, strangely enough, is on the spot every time he goes on the set. He's on it right now, making "Broadway Bill."

"I *have* to make them a picture every time I start," he grins.

What he means is that his actors, his crew, his bosses, Columbia's salesmen, a thousand movie theater owners, and a million movie-goers—all Hollywood and all the world—expect every picture bearing the legend, "A Frank Capra Production," to be a world beater.

Don't Go Platinum Yet!

[CONTINUED FROM PAGE 184]

shops from $2 to $6, not counting the shampoo and wave. Bleached hair should have an oil shampoo at least once a week or oftener, which adds another $1.50 or $2. All dyed or bleached hair needs constant attention to brushing, oiling and shampooing to retain a glossy appearance, without which no head of hair is attractive. And platinum is one shade that cannot be neglected.

Remember also, *excessively* bleached hair can not be permanently waved. No reputable shop would take a chance with it. The possibilities are that it would become a gelatinous mass after the permanent, and every vestige of it break off at the roots, leaving the customer in need of a wig rather than a wave.

Are you feeling terrible now? Well, bear with me a while longer. I have more sad news.

You can't have platinum hair and dress like ordinary folks. You must have expensive clothes to live up to that hair. It is theatrical and spectacular. You must have theatrical and spectacular clothes. You must always look your best. No simple clothes with that hair. No ma'am! Furs and velvets and laces and brocades are an absolute necessity. Platinum hair, like the metal for which it is named, is the most expensive of all.

If you're still deadly determined to go platinum, then be sure of a few things about yourself first.

You must be young—not more than twenty-five. You must have a transparent skin. You must consider the color of your teeth, for teeth that are at all inclined to be yellow seem even more so with platinum hair.

You must be sophisticated, or at least highly modern. You simply must not consider it if you're the old-fashioned type. You must have sparkling eyes and should have a tip-tilted nose.

Your make-up will need careful attention, for platinum hair lightens the entire color tone of the face.

Now don't let all this discourage you about making the most of whatever share of beauty you have. That is every woman's right and duty to herself. Moderate bleaching and tinting of the hair is an accepted method of enhancing the attractiveness of women, and with the new style in hats which displays the hair so generously, blonde hair will probably have a greater vogue than ever before.

It's one thing to have a light bleach to bring out the high lights in one's hair, but something else again to go platinum.

Here is the consensus of opinion among the best hairdressers in New York, Chicago and Hollywood:

"It is absolutely ruinous to the hair of the average person. If you go platinum you can expect to have nice hair for a period of six months only. Then it will break off and the life will be gone." (John, at R. Louis, New York, who has treated Jean Harlow's hair.)

"When naturally dark hair is bleached to the *average* blonde shade it loses ninety per cent of its life. The platinum rinse makes it even lighter; therefore, you can judge its effect upon the hair." (Semon, of the Dorothy Gray salon, New York.)

"IT will cost you, dependent upon the original color of your hair, from $14 to $40 a month for the bleaching alone and this does not include waves, which must be had at least twice a week, because platinum hair does not hold the wave. And, not including time spent on waves, it will take from twelve to twenty hours a month of your time." (Emile, New York.)

"If you become a platinum blonde you must change your entire makeup, using completely different color of rouge, powder, lipstick, etc. Your hair must be washed and waved at least twice a week and dyed once a week." (Reno, of Charles of the Ritz, New York.)

"It is the most expensive of all hair dyes

and requires only the most expert handling." (Mary Elizabeth Johnston, head of Hudnut Salon, New York.)

"The coating left by the rinse makes the hair very difficult to manage for soft effects, as it stretches the wave in both permanents and naturally curly hair. It sometimes even takes out a natural wave." (Kathleen Mary Quinlan, New York.)

"Truly elegant women will consider it no more than a fad of the moment and will not

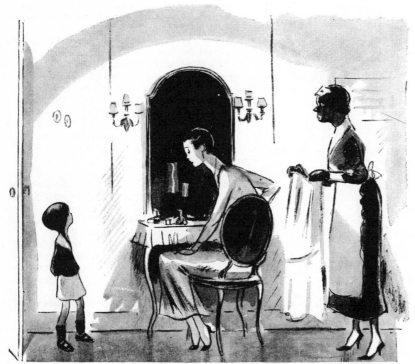

Two men spent two hours daily making up Boris Karloff as the *Monster* in Universal's "Frankenstein"

subject their hair to it." (Madame Helena Rubenstein, New York.)

"Platinum bleaching is injurious to the hair, even when expertly done." (Dimitri—from Antoine of Paris—at Saks Fifth Ave., New York.)

Paul, of Fifth Ave., New York, refuses to do the job at all, for he says it ruins his permanent wave business, because the hair breaks off and leaves nothing for him to wave.

"Normal bleaching is not particularly injurious to the hair, if given care with oil shampoos and brushing, but bleaching necessary for a platinum color kills the hair and the results will be disastrous unless one is naturally very blonde to start with." (Anna, of Anna Louise, Hollywood.)

"The strenuous bleaching necessary to a platinum color is not approved by Elizabeth Arden. The patron is informed of this and we only give the treatment if she insists upon it, or has already had it elsewhere." (Eugene Fleugel, of Elizabeth Arden, Chicago.)

Summing the platinum question up it seems to be this:

IT is a *fad*, and as such is all right for the movie stars and stage folks. They have enough money and time to do it, and not only can they afford the very best hairdressers, but they have the privilege of going back to natural when the hair begins to break and it's all in the service of Art. It looks great on the screen but it simply isn't for the likes of you and me—the average girls who do the average things.

Jean Harlow herself, fighting against the continuance of the ultra-sexy rôles in her screen career, decries the "platinum" craze more than anyone else. She has expressed herself on the question to PHOTOPLAY representatives who have aided in the collection of the information contained in this article.

Copyright 1931, LIFE Publishing Company

"Do you mind if I dye my hair blonde, Mummy—I'm not getting any-where with the men"

Another GARY COOPER, JEAN ARTHUR Triumph
CECIL B. DeMILLE'S
"The PLAINSMAN"

Cecil B. DeMille brings you Gary and Jean in their grandest picture . . . the story of Wild Bill Hickok and Calamity Jane, the hardest boiled pair of lovers who ever rode the plains . . . a glorious romance set against the whole flaming pageant of the Old West . . .

"You've got courage enough to kill a dozen Indians...why haven't you courage enough to admit you love me?"

"Save your fire, boys, 'til they come close and then blast the varmints. There's got to be room for white men on these plains."

"Gentlemen, my name is Wild Bill Hickok and I think we can settle everything very...very peacefully...unless somebody wants to deal out of turn."

"Go ahead. Do your worst. We'll still be laughing at you. Laughing at a great chief so small he'd kill two helpless persons for spite."

ONE OF THE GREAT PICTURES OF ALL TIME!

Freddie BARTHOLOMEW
as Harvey—pampered by luxury ... the sea made him a man

Spencer TRACY
as Manuel—hardy sailor who taught Harvey the ropes . . .

Captains Courageous

THE MOST EXCITING PICTURE SINCE "MUTINY ON THE BOUNTY"

Again—as in the stirring "Mutiny"— you *live* the roaring drama of men against the sea. You share the struggles, the heartaches, the laughter of courageous souls who leave the women they love to dare the wrath of the angry waves ... men in conflict with their destiny enacting the most thrilling story the screen could offer. A brilliant triumph that takes rank with the greatest pictures M-G-M has given you!

Lionel BARRYMORE
as Captain Disko, whose life was lived where men are fearless . . .

A Metro-Goldwyn-Mayer Picture Directed by VICTOR FLEMING

Captains Courageous
RUDYARD KIPLING'S greatest story of struggle, adventure and life!

Melvyn DOUGLAS
as Harvey's father whose wealth couldn't buy his boy's love.

342

"Give us more pictures with George Raft," the fans implore.
And no wonder! George brought a fascinating new type of villain
to the screen in "Dancers in the Dark," with Miriam Hopkins

Charm? No! No! You Must Have Glamour

[CONTINUED FROM PAGE 187]

seduction? Would the fans stand it? Would they ever go to see her pictures again? Look at Norma today. One small seduction! Shades of the purity league! Look what she did in "The Divorcee," in "Strangers May Kiss," in "A Free Soul."

Certainly a little peccadillo is now one of the minor vices. Nowadays the heroine goes right out and gets her man and does with him as she wills.

Nobody minds, and the fans seem to like it. Money, box-office money, speaks.

IT'S all because now Norma has glamour. A self-made glamour, it is true, but glamour nevertheless. Her clothes (that loose evening gown she wore in "A Free Soul"), her spritely, gay manner, her rippling laugh—which, if you ask me, ripples over our screen a little too fluently—her madcap method of living—all these things have surrounded her upon the screen. Shearer, with that sixth sense that has made her what she now is, realized long before the rest of us that this was the new mood.

She even, upon occasions, surrounds her personal life with an aura of glamour.

If you were to see Dietrich in "Three Loves," a German film made before Joseph Von Sternberg found those black silk stockings and garters, you would not believe her the same old poker face who met the firing squad in "Dishonored."

She is, in "Three Loves," rather plump, rather bouncing and she skips through her scenes with a lightsomeness that the glamorous ladies never allow themselves.

And if "Gosta Berling's Saga," Garbo's first important Swedish epic, happened to cross your line of vision, you will remember Garbo then as a rather cow-eyed, heavy heroine who hadn't any notion what it was all about. A far cry—a far cry, indeed!—from these two early European ladies to the women we know upon the screen.

And who would ever have thought that the plump Joan Crawford of "Sally, Irene and Mary" could be the same vivid, exciting girl of "Our Blushing Brides"? "Sally, Irene and Mary" recalls the fact that Constance Bennett played the lead in that film. She didn't make much of a hit.

She had glamour then when nobody could use it.

So instead of going on and sinking into slow obscurity she married a young millionaire, led a gay Parisian life, got a divorce and returned to enroll, as best pupil, in the glamour school.

I hate to keep harping on it, but it seems to me that one of the great screen tragedies is the case of Aileen Pringle—a woman much before her time. She lived, upon the screen, in that sharply defined black and white era when a woman was very, very good or very, very bad. Those nice gray heroines were unknown.

Aileen has glamour—the playmate of the intelligentsia, the smart sophisticate—all the things that are required.

But when she was a star, nobody knew what that was all about.

Maybe she'll make a come-back, like Shearer. She deserves it.

Lilyan Tashman, of course, set about to make herself smart, sophisticated, glamorous. It was a definite campaign on Lil's part and she's succeeded.

And being glamorous is the only hope of movie survival.

Where are the ingénues?

I've already mentioned three. But there are others—Betty Bronson, Madge Bellamy, Mary Philbin, Colleen Moore, Marceline and Alice Day, Jeanette Loff and many, many more. All nice girls.

Gone—all gone.

BUT even before this group, even before the day of the vamps already mentioned there was an ingénue era. It runs like this—sweet girls, vamps, sweet girls again and now glamour.

There was Mary Pickford, Mary Miles Minter (who imitated her none too successfully), Blanche Sweet, Edith Storey, Lila Lee (the "Cuddles" Lila and not the girl who blossomed into sophisticated rôles later), Lillian Gish, May Allison, Mae Marsh. Remember those glorified close-ups?

A girl could not be a star without a halo of golden hair.

The halo was supposedly made by pure sunlight but in reality it was an electrician's trick.

If you will glance with me through the contract lists of the various studios, you'll find the truth of all this.

We now want something to tickle the imagination, something to whet the sophisticated appetite.

Something to lift us out of ourselves away from the people who behave like human beings—the people we know.

Among the feminine players at Paramount, you'll find the most outstanding are Dietrich, Lilyan Tashman, Eleanor Boardman (no longer

the ingénue, but a woman with a woman's mind), Claudette Colbert, Juliette Compton, Carole Lombard, Kay Francis. The only real ingénue is Frances Dee. But she's been taken up by Director Von Sternberg, so who knows what might happen.

AT M-G-M you'll find the Garbo, the Crawford, the Shearer. Marion Davies is a light comedienne. Certainly Leila Hyams is far from being ingénuish. And there's also Hedda Hopper.

Anita Page is still there, but she has not made good her promise of stardom. No glamour, you see.

Dorothy Jordan is an exception, and yet she does seem to put more into her rôles than mere sweetness.

Pathe is knee deep in glamour—Pola Negri, Ann Harding, Constance Bennett. There is also Helen Twelvetrees, who began by being Gish-y and ended by being "Millie."

The same condition exists at most of the other studios. But there's one amazing exception. Janet Gaynor is Sweetness and Sunshine in its most advanced stages and yet you love her. "Daddy Long Legs," a sweet, sweet picture, upset everything by insisting upon breaking records at the box-office. This is, it seems, some strange phenomenon, fo. which there is no accounting. Of course, the public taste is as ephemeral as a penny balloon and maybe by the time this gets in print you'll be bored with glamour and wanting something else.

But at the moment, glamour has it, and if the lovelorn column conductors want to keep abreast of the times they'd better start doling out advice about how to achieve it. You simply won't be able to get a date for the junior prom without it.

It is difficult. Charm and sweetness are more easily managed because they're more understandable.

Glamour is as elusive as Garbo being interviewed.

Looking at it purely objectively it seems to be something that one gets by sitting quietly in a corner and letting not a flicker of intelligence, interest or even just a faint suggestion that you're really living, cross the face. It seems to be, also, something about never smiling—except in a slow, bitter way. And it seems to be mentally counting ten between every word of every sentence. But it's more than that. That is the Dietrich-Garbo glamour.

Shearer glamour is being sparkling but not meaning a single word or gesture.

It all seems to center about unrest and wanting something or other which never seems to happen.

We're getting pretty doggone neurotic, we are.

I PERSONALLY haven't been able to get the straight of the thing. Dull little girls suddenly burst out as glamorous, gorgeous ladies. I ought to be able to give you advice about how to do it, but since I've not been able to go glamorous, I always think I'd feel a little silly if I tried it and I know my friends—the mugs—would laugh. I'm not much of a one to tell you how.

The best way, I believe, if you insist upon bringing all this into your personal life, is to sit alone with your soul in your favorite darkened theater and watch the screen antics —or rather the total lack of antics—of Garbo, Dietrich, Elissa Landi, Pola Negri, Constance Bennett, Lilyan Tashman, Tallulah Bankhead and like ilk. Then go out and try to be glamorous. You must do it for social success these days.

Cut off the curls, slick down the hair, get lithe, go blonde, very blonde, and try glamour on your friends.

You'll probably get laughed at—but better luck next time!

At least, you simply must stop being charming.

Beauty and Personality are Inseparable

[CONTINUED FROM PAGE 189]

wrong way it pulls the cords in the neck exaggerates them and also shows up your Adam's apple. So many girls have written asking me what to do about correcting such a neck that I'm glad I have a chance this month to tell you about it, Bette.

IT all comes from faulty head posture. To keep your head in a correct line you have to strengthen the vertebrae which control the neck and head. So, every day I want you to sit in a relaxed position and, with three fingers of each hand, jab deep under the first three vertebrae of your spine. Work on these vertebrae, giving a deep massage to the muscles around them until you can feel your chin drawing down.

Now practice correct head posture. Let your chin relax naturally. Don't roll your eyes up. Keep them straight ahead. Concentrate every minute so that you will remember to pull your chin and jaw in.

Habits are hard to break. You need all your intelligence and courage and, perhaps, a little help from your friends. Let your pals know that you won't be sore at them if they yell at you every time they see you with that jaw stuck out, "Hi, Bette, pull your chin in!"

For, when you stick your jaw out, it hardens your face, brings out ugly muscles and cords in your neck. Also, remember that you'll have a much softer appearance if you refrain from pushing your hair back in such a hard line. Keep it fluffed about your face. And for heaven's sake, Bette, lay off making your mouth up in that extreme fashion. Remember when Joan Crawford did it? Remember how all her admirers got up on their hind feet and told her they didn't like it? She changed it at once.

She used her head, realized she had made a mistake and set about to rectify it.

And now about your nose. I changed Ruth Chatterton's nose, but you can change yours,

yourself, by covering your fingers with cold cream and gently, gently pinching it, as if your nose were soft clay. Slowly and gently shape your nose into a beautiful mould with your own two hands and squeeze off a bit of the end of it. You must be very careful not to bruise the nose. So don't press too hard. It will take a little time but it will be so worth while when results are accomplished.

SOFTEN the lines of your face, Bette, first by the practical physical methods I've given you and then by training yourself actually to feel an inner warmth for people. Give a lot of yourself. Don't draw inside yourself. Get out of the physical habit of wrong head posture and beware of the mental habit of cynicism off-screen. Play up to your own charming type. Begin today. I tell you this in all sincerity and

Love,

SYLVIA

Answers by Sylvia

Dear Sylvia:

I notice that in many of your diets you include raw red or white cabbage. I wonder if the whole leaf should be eaten or if it should be chopped up. What is the best way to prepare it? M. H., Eau Claire, Wis.

You can eat it any way you like as long as it isn't cooked, but I think the most appetizing way to prepare it is to shred it or chop it up fine and then squeeze a generous supply of lemon juice over it. It makes a delicious salad, contains many valuable minerals and should be included in your regular diet once a day.

My dear Sylvia:

I have very large wrists and, although I've read all of your articles (I think), I don't remember that you have ever given an exercise for reducing the wrists. Would you be good enough to tell me how to reduce my wrists? Mrs. M. R. L., Olympia, Wash.

You can shave off your wrists in the same way that I've told you how to take down other parts of the body that are lumpy—by my squeezing and slapping method. With the fingers and the palm of one hand, work on the opposite wrist, digging into the excess muscles. If you've read my articles you know how this is done. Then put a Turkish towel over the wrists and slap them good and hard. In this way you can reduce the muscles and squeeze off the fat cells. I want every woman and girl to remember that her body is like sculptor's clay and she can model it exactly as she wants it modeled.

Dear Sylvia:

Is it okay if I substitute an extra glass of orange juice for the mid-morning tomato juice you give in your wonderful diet? I like orange juice and don't like tomato juice. M. H. D., Boston, Mass.

Orange juice and tomato juice do *almost* the same thing, but not quite. The tomato juice

DON'T deny yourselves the joy of good health, girls, when Aunt Sylvia offers you the chance to get it by asking her a few questions!

Health means happiness, and you must have both of these in order to look your best. I have helped many of the stars of Hollywood, and countless girls who, like yourselves, read about the stars and envy their charms. Seeking my advice puts you under no obligation, of course. Just write to Sylvia, care PHOTOPLAY Magazine, 221 West 57th Street, New York City. Enclose a stamped, self-addressed envelope.

SYLVIA

is so swell for your complexion that if I were you I wouldn't give it up entirely unless I had a skin like rose-leaves. I believe you can learn to like it. Drink it ice-cold and squeeze a few drops of lemon juice in it. Why, baby, it's delicious. Come on, now, try it just one more week and remember how much it will improve your complexion.

Dear Sylvia:

Kindly give me an exercise for reducing the ankles.

Mrs. R. D., Washington, D. C.

Well, I'll certainly say you're brief and to the point. Okay, I'll try to be as much to the point. This is the way to make your ankles small. Lie on the floor on your back with your toes pointed straight in front and your arms above your head, as if you were a straight line from the tips of your fingers to the tips of your toes. Now, without moving the position of the toes, spring to a sitting position and try—with your hands—to touch the tips of your toes. Of course, this is impossible since the toes are still pointed, but *never* move the position of the toes all the time you're trying to touch them with your hands. You'll feel a sharp pain in

your ankles as you do this exercise. Then you'll know you're doing it right. Do that five times in the morning and five times at night. You'll notice a big improvement in a very short time.

Dear Sylvia:

To settle an argument please answer this question. Which do you consider most important, a beautiful face or a beautiful figure? T. S. B., Jeffersonville, Ind.

A beautiful figure—and I'll tell you why. If you have worked hard for a beautiful figure— if you're thin and lithe, you'll have radiant good health. That will show in your face, make your eyes bright and sparkling and give you the illusion of beauty of face, no matter what the bone formation of the features is. You can't camouflage your figure. You can look beautiful—even if you aren't—by being sparkling and vivacious and animated. I've seen some great, big, fat women with faces that were actually beautiful. I've seen these women sitting in a room when a girl with a grand figure—and a face not so pretty—entered. What happened? The girl with the neat figure got the attention of all the men at once, and the fat girls were left out in the cold.

Dear Sylvia:

My shoulders are so broad that I'm all out of proportion. I'm really quite skinny. I wish you would tell me something to do. D. W., Lynchburg, Va.

Telling people what to do is my easiest job. What you need is to put on weight, to build up until the rest of your body is in proportion to your shoulders. Wide shoulders are fine and very fashionable. But if you're skinny the answer is—don't stay that way. Send me a self-addressed, stamped envelope and I'll send you my general building-up diet and exercises. It's a very long diet so I haven't space enough to give it here.

Ginger Rogers' Rules for Slaying
the Stag Line

[CONTINUED FROM PAGE 195]

"Off the dance floor: it's awfully important,
especially if you don't go out dancing frequently, to practice as much as you can in between times. You can enlist the aid of your
brothers or cousins or the boy across the street
or anyone you know to help you. Being a good
dancer is just like being good at anything else;
if you were a tennis player and you only played
in a match once a month you certainly wouldn't
expect to win unless you kept in practice between matches.

"When you can't find a partner to lead you
at home, roll up the living room rug two or
three times a week, turn on your radio and
dance by yourself. It's good for you. I do it
myself nearly every day. Try out any movements or steps that pop into your head. Relax, and express your personality through your
feet. If you've got a big mirror watch yourself in it while you dance, taking notes on your
posture and grace. You can't imagine how
limbered and in what a grand dancing mood
it'll keep you. It's not only beneficial but a
lot of fun besides.

"**O**N the dance floor: never be nervous! Being nervous is just about the worst thing
that can happen to your dancing. Even the
most experienced dancers sometimes become
selfconscious when they find themselves with a
partner who is difficult to follow; and self-
consciousness, I know only too well, can make
lead of dancing feet. The fear that you are not
dancing well, the fear that you may not be
able to execute a certain step, can actually
produce a physical reflex that will so tighten
your muscles you're just sure to fumble.

"So there's only one thing to do when a man
is hard as the dickens to follow—keep relaxed,
don't worry about the mistakes you've made or
are making, and go ahead and *dance* as though
you hadn't a care in the world for your feet!

"And while we're on the subject of partners
who are hard to follow, there's a secret you
might remember. At every dance, no matter
how large or small it is, there are always the
inevitable stags who are such poor dancers that
no girl could follow them well. You know how
it is, some men just never learn to lead effi-
ciently and they're naturally sensitive about it.
They realize too that the girls who are getting
the big rushes don't particularly want to be
bothered with them.

"So if you can dance with the poor dancers
and do your darnedest to stay away from their
unruly toes, and bear up under the strain to the
extent that you can make them feel you're
really enjoying dancing with them—let me tell
you they'll appreciate it. They'll rush you to
death. And that's a grand way to secure right
there the beginning of a stag line all your own.

"Rhythm is born in all of us. To be a desirable dancing partner you don't have to be
able to do all the intricate fancy steps that
happen to be in vogue; the stag line doesn't
expect it because few of them themselves can
do them. All you have to do is be a good
average dancer and anybody who spends the
time and effort can accomplish that. The girl
who makes a good dancer of herself has a lot
of her ballroom popularity already assured.
The rest depends on—well, lots of things."

At that point Ginger, completely out of
breath, stopped to order, wait for and drink a
glass of cream to help her gain back some of the
pounds she lost during her intensive practice
with Fred Astaire for the dance routines in
"Follow the Fleet." Then she got back to our
subject again.

"There are really so many things besides
dancing ability that can influence a girl's
popularity at a ball. First and foremost, of
course, you want to look your loveliest from
your gown right down to the smallest detail
about you. I don't know of any place (unless
it's before the camera) that every item of a
girl's physical attractiveness is subject to
closer scrutiny than at a dance. I think you
ought to allow yourself at least two hours
dressing time and be sure that you're groomed
to complete perfection.

"And what's just as important—try to stay
that way! The exercise of dancing can make
you wilt so quickly. Many girls, I've noticed,
carry a small compact on the floor with them
and are constantly splashing powder on their
noses between dances. I think the smart
thing to do is to leave your compact, lipstick,
comb and everything with your wrap and do
your primping in private. I do. Every dozen
or so dances I dash into the dressing room and
take a thorough look at myself in a full-length
mirror. Instead of just a nose-powdering I
usually find a twisted seam, a loose earring, a
wave out of place, smudged mascara, all sorts
of things that should be fixed. I repair them
then go back on the floor and forget all about
my appearance until I feel it may be needing
another check-up.

"I'd like to add a word against sensational
gowns. I'm sure you've noticed at nearly
every dance you've attended the inevitable
two or three girls who have selected extremely
daringly-cut, attention-attracting dresses to
help to put them on the map, so to speak, with
the stag line. Frankly I don't think it really
gets them anywhere. A girl who has to be
sensational to appeal to the stag line is putting
her worst foot forward.

"**T**HE same thing goes for sensational dancing. You know—there's always the girl who
insists on doing a razmataz Yazoo-Shakedown
or something right up in front of the orchestra
Hotcha. Suggestive. Showoffish. She may
attract the curiosity of everybody in the room,
but I bet her poor embarrassed escort slinks
outside for a smoke until the dust settles under
her heels. It's so much smarter, really, to
dance tastefully and gracefully. No girl ever
got to be a belle-of-the-ball because she staged
a spectacle."

Ginger took time out to show me her wardrobe of off-screen evening things. They're the
loveliest, most glamorous gowns you can
imagine, mostly pastels because she's fond of
soft colors, with a sprinkling of all-white.

"Well, now we're getting somewhere,"
Ginger continued. "If you're a good dancer
and you're attractively groomed and your poise
is perfect, then the chances are you're doing
okay. But to get a *huge* rush instead of just a
big one here are some of my pet secrets.

"If it's a big dance and a crowded one, pick
a corner or an end of the room and try to
dance around it all evening. The poor stags
who are bewildered in a sea of girls will know
where to find you when they want to cut **in**,

345

without having to go looking the entire length of the floor and getting bumped on all sides. If you're danced out of your corner or 'headquarters,' just say to your next partner, 'Dance me back over that way, will you?' and he will. This is really an awfully good scheme; the stags will appreciate it and you're certain to be cut in on more frequently.

"However, if it's a big dance and you don't know enough stags to assure you a successful evening, it's better not to stay in one place.

"Another little trick that's a good way to increase cut-ins is to wear or carry something individual by which the stags who want to find you can spot you at a distance. I know a college girl who does an awful lot of prom-trotting and does it darned successfully. She carries to every hop she attends a bright red chiffon handkerchief which trails from her left hand over her partner's back. On a crowded floor that girl can be seen for miles. Bright flowers in your hair or an unusual bow or something on the back of your dress can effect the same thing.

"**H**ERE'S another point, too—if you want to keep your stag line, don't sit out too many dances. When you want to rest sit on the sidelines somewhere and talk; you can still be seen there and the tempo of your rush won't be lessened the way it will if you just disappear outside for three or four dances.

"People have often asked me if I talk while I'm dancing. In pictures, no. But I must confess that when I'm just dancing for the fun of it at a party I usually talk a blue streak. I always have. Somehow dancing and bright,

charming conversation go together and I think the girl who can entertain a man, who can dazzle him with delightful patter while she's dancing with him, stands much more chance of attracting him than the girl who's just a good dancer alone.

"Now and then, though," Ginger added, "you do run into a partner who takes his dancing seriously and doesn't like chit-chat. Just go ahead and dance your best with him and save your bright speeches for the stag who will appreciate them.

"**L**ASTLY—and oh! this is such a big point—I think it's *terribly* important at a dance for a girl to *look* like she's having a good time! If she's smiling and vivacious and wears an air of confidence about herself she's sure to attract partners all over someone who looks a little bored or scared or too sophisticated. There used to be a girl in my class at school who wasn't pretty nor was she such an expert dancer, but she always radiated such fun at our school parties, she always seemed to be having such a grand time, that the stag line just couldn't resist her. She got lots more cut-ins than the best-looking girls in the class just on the strength of her contagious manner. I think I first learned that lesson from watching her. And I don't think it can be emphasized too much.

"It's really awfully simple. If you can just be on the dance floor what you are in your own living room—charming, and confident of yourself—well, whether it's a dance or a party or a picnic or a twosome, you're sure to slay the stags."

LILLIAN ROTH ("The Vagabond King," Paramount) has been before the eyes of the amusement world a comparatively brief time. She came to New York's attention in the summer of 1928 as leading singing and dancing soubrette in Earl Carroll's "Vanities," the famous revue. A short term in vaudeville, and she went West to catch on nicely in pictures.

Would You Quit Work for $250,000?

[CONTINUED FROM PAGE 215]

It was George Jessel, the Broadway ha-ha boy, who pulled the wise-crack about contract buy-ups that's become famous. It was Fox who signed Jessel when the talkie craze first drove the producers nutty. George's stuff, grand on the stage, just didn't go over in talkies. The same old parley followed, and when George walked out a free agent, he boasted:

"Me! I'm the only man who was ever paid $75,000 not to appear on the screen."

A funny angle is that Jessel had taken a $5,000 lease on a Hollywood house. Fox paid that off, too.

Billie Dove, the voluptuous, is another beauty, besides Ina Claire, who is headed for a comeback despite the fact that her contract was bought off. Billie was big money in silents, for First National, but as in other cases, she wasn't so good under the microphone. She made four talkies. They were fairly popular pictures, but not popular enough in ratio to her $5,000-a-week salary to make her profitable. When the thing was straightened out, she and First National had settled on about a fifty-fifty split for the rest of her contract—about six months—and Billie was free.

Did Billie sit back and wail? No. She had her divorce from Irving Willat, the director, and Millionaire Howard Hughes, who had

just completed "Hell's Angels," was sending her dozens of American Beauty Roses, and denying nothing.

So Billie will go to work for Mr. Hughes' Caddo Pictures Company, and is studying elocution and voice so she can give Howard's microphones a worthy battle.

Monte Blue's contract was bought up, long ago, by Warner Brothers, for about $50,000 cash, it's reported. Monte is young and rich. He should worry. Another case is that of Norma Terris. Norma played the lead in "Show Boat" on the stage, and sounded swell. That was when talkies were singies, and the producers were signing up musical comedy stars by the dozen.

Fox signed her. She came to Hollywood and made one picture—opposite J. Harold Murray in "Married in Hollywood."

Everybody thought it was just a publicity gag when her fiancé came to Hollywood just as the picture was released, and they were "married in Hollywood." Soon afterward, Norma's contract was bought up by the Fox people, and she'll probably never make another picture. How much? "Plenty," is all anybody will tell you.

Lenore Ulric's contract was bought up, too. Lenore is another stage star who hit bad luck with stories and direction in pictures. She just didn't get over with the fans in

"Frozen Justice" and "South Sea Rose." Anyway, Lenore is back on the speaking stage, and glad of it. So are the New York theatrical audiences.

With her is her husband, Sidney Blackmer, who is still under contract to First National. Blackmer, whose contract still has about six months to run with First National, was offered about twenty-five per cent of his salary-to-come for his contract, it is rumored. But Blackmer didn't want to sell out, and so, come first of the year, he will end his stage engagements and go back to Hollywood to finish his talkie job.

IN some cases, studios don't buy up contracts. There is substituted a process called "Letting 'em die on the vine." This is usually the procedure when an actor declines to be bought out, and insists on sticking to his contract. The producers shrug their shoulders and pocket their loss. They go on paying the actor his full salary—but they don't give him or her a single part to play. In other words, the actor simply disappears from the screen for the term of his contract—and that's bad business for actors. Because by the time they're free agents, they're no longer in demand, and it's tough picking for them to find work.

Carlotta King had it happen to her. Louis B. Mayer heard her in "The Desert Song" when the musical film craze was on, decided she was great, and signed her. Tests weren't so good; the cameras weren't kind to Carlotta. She has never made a picture for M-G-M, but drew her salary—somewhere between $750 and $1,000 a week—until her one-year contract expired.

At Radio Pictures, Arthur Lake signed a long-term contract. They thought they had a big bet in Arthur for those adolescent rôles. He did "She's My Weakness" and didn't get over so well. Exhibitors said he wasn't good box-office. So overtures were made to young Lake to sell his contract. Hurt and indignant, Arthur said no. "All right," said Radio Pictures.

And since then, Arthur, though he draws his salary, has not been on the screen.

Lottice Howell, who came from the New York stage and made "In Gay Madrid" with Ramon Novarro, is another who is drawing pay but making no pictures. So is Marcia Manners, the Paramount player who was signed for musicals.

She is an American girl with a lovely Europe-trained voice, who hasn't made a picture yet, although she's drawing her salary on a one-year contract.

VIVIENNE SEGAL, who was signed by Warner Brothers for musicals, hasn't been making pictures during the most recent period of her contract. Warners, by the way, learned a lesson. They're not signing stage stars for any half-year or one-year terms any more. They're signing them for one picture, with an option to renew if they click. That's saving the Messrs. Warner some cash.

Jack Gilbert snapped his finger at the contract-buying gag. As stated long ago herein, he made "His Glorious Night" and the fans were disappointed in his voice.

M-G-M, under contract to pay him $250,000 per picture for four pictures, were terror-stricken.

If Jack's voice was as bad as that, the million-dollar outlay would be sheer loss.

They offered him a half million, it is reported, to tear up the contract and release them.

Jack, magnificently brave and confident, insisted on making pictures. "I'll show them!" he said, and held M-G-M to the contract.

He was in a pretty spot, because the contract made it imperative that pictures actually be produced.

M-G-M couldn't just pay him and let him stay idle.

So Jack went ahead. Well, he overcame

his voice handicap as you all know by now. And he's glad, and so is M-G-M.

There are other cases—most of them not so big-named as these you've been reading about. There are dozens of playwrights, song-writers, directors, technicians and others who were signed on long-term contracts, who went to Hollywood, who didn't click for one reason or another, and who were finally bought off.

It cost the producers thousands—for nothing. Thousands that might have been spent in making fine movies, instead.

And they holler about putt-putt golf courses ruining business!

ARE YOU POPULAR?
THE SECRET OF CHARM

A healthy, vivacious girl with a clear skin and bright eyes is sure to win admiration and be popular.

If your complexion is bad, if you have ugly blotches and pimples, if you have a fetid breath, people will avoid you.

Dr. Pierce's Golden Medical Discovery will help to clear your skin, brighten your eyes, sweeten your breath, and make you more "peppy."

Send ten cents for an acquaintance package of the tablets to Dr. Pierce's Invalids Hotel, Buffalo, N. Y. There is no charge for confidential medical advice by mail.

Hollywood Snubs Paris

[CONTINUED FROM PAGE 193]

with a leading modiste shop, where he had opportunity to outfit many prominent actresses of the stage. This awakened his interest in theatrical costuming, and he worked with Florenz Ziegfeld on the gorgeous "Follies" for a while.

Nine years ago, Walter Wanger asked Banton to go to Hollywood and put his ideas into a picture called "The Dressmaker from Paris." Banton intended to stay on the Coast six weeks. He has been there ever since, except for his trips in search of inspiration. Eight of these took him to Paris—but Paris, last year, he says, was too "shabby" for him to want to go back soon.

BANTON was born in Waco, Texas—Tex Guinan's old home town—thirty-eight years ago. When he was five, his family brought him to New York. His academic schooling ended when he "flunked out" of Columbia University.

Then he entered the Art Students' League, and eventually turned to dress design.

He isn't the traditional type of designer— no monocle, French mustachios, elaborate gestures and cream-puff language. He looks like a good many men who attend Chamber of Commerce meetings.

But Banton is, today, one of the few men who exert any large influence on women's styles of the world.

Who Is Your Husband's Favorite Actress?

[CONTINUED FROM PAGE 197]

throaty voice. The stride, slowed down to the Garbo tempo, would be stunning. But this girl always tears through a room like a squirt of seltzer. She wouldn't have to sink her voice way down to the plumbing—it's there already—but the way she uses it will never make papa close his eyes and imagine Greta has him enfolded in her sensuous embrace. The girl I mention sounds off like a fog-horn and is about as mysterious as a black eye. She's really a very swell girl, and popular.

She has a lot of pride. Naturally, every woman wants to be loved for herself and not because she reminds a man of somebody else. This one has apparently decided she would rather let her husband go off now and then on a harmless emotional binge with Garbo and his imagination, than make any effort to be a little Garbo in the home. She is confident he will always come back, good as new. (One nice thing about these picture affairs—they're harmless, and quite inexpensive.)

A CERTAIN local automobile dealer has been married only a year to a dear, little plump blonde, and he is obviously crazy about her. So how can you account for the fact that he torments the poor dear with his tremendous enthusiasm for tall, dark Kay Francis?

Perhaps he does it for the fun of seeing her sputter. Perhaps he likes a change in type when he goes to the theater. But it proves a man can be sincerely in love with his wife and still enjoy looking at another woman who isn't the least bit like her. (It's the double nature of the brutes.)

It is extraordinary the number of quiet mousy little males who seem to get a bang out of Mae West. Look around you, next time you see one of her pictures. All the henpecked husbands in town will be there. "Here is a woman who really understands men," their rapt concentrations seem to say. "She would never be a nag or a chatter-box or take away our rights. We could tell her anything and she would comprehend it." Mae is an out for a flock of frustrations.

Many girls resent their suitor's interest in his favorite actress because they feel the picture queen has more money to look beautiful, the facilities for it are available, and she is always presented to the best advantage.

It is good keen competition, all right. But regard it as a standard to live up to, and above all things, don't do your resenting out loud. This gives any man the edge.

It is always a mistake to carry your desire to please to the extent of too-obvious imitation. You can never *be* another person—and you don't want to be another person. Men hate copy-cats. You can adapt your voice, your clothes, your coiffure, your attitude. But it is silly to strive to please to the extent of bleaching your hair or gluing on eyelashes that wave languidly down to your chin, if the rest of you doesn't belong.

The other night I listened in brazenly on a little scene between husband and wife leaving the theater. "Boy, how that Lombard girl can wear clothes!" exclaimed the man.

I looked to see if the missis reacted. She did. She looked as if she yearned to push him off a cliff. "Oh, clothes! clothes!" she disdained. "Anybody can put on a lot of clothes and look pretty."

My unspoken answer to that was "well, why don't you?"

An attractive woman, but the fact was almost concealed. An old beret was jammed down over her hair, a pair of loose slacks whipped around her legs. She wore sandals meant for the beach, from which raw toes stuck out to the cruel world. Her face was entirely innocent of make-up. There is about one man out of ten who approves this sort of sloppy-comfortable get-up. This husband was one of the other nine. He didn't go for it. "You don't have to be clothes-crazy" was his Parthian shot, "neither do you have to look as if you dressed to paint a house!"

Often it is a bother to get dressed just to go up the street to a picture show—but it is also a bother to lose your man.

In the smaller communities and the suburbs, you frequently see some quaint costumes going into the theater. The idea is to be comfortable —a perfectly laudable idea—what with the lights out most of the time anyway, you figure. But man is a strange creature. Even in this emancipated age, he would rather wait half an hour for a girl to get ready who shows results, than wait five minutes for one who slips on the top stair and comes down. (The joke has a beard—but you get the idea.)

If your husband is an inarticulate sort of a guy who would be embarrassed to admit his favorite actress—or even hint that he has one —you will have to do a little probing. There is always *one* whose picture he goes to see without fail. If she happens to be Jean Harlow, and you are an anxious housewife, maybe a little frivolity on your part would be a good idea. Or maybe you should take off a few pounds. Have you ever noticed how these lads who claim to be crazy about you plump take a new lease on life when you get the bulges off your hips?

A SURPRISING number of men suffer with Claudette Colbert trouble, and an equally surprising number of wives either dismiss it as a joke or wonder what they can do about it.

I suspect one wife of taking the hint. She has had her black hair cut in a most becoming bang, and trimmed her figure down to perfection. Then suddenly, she began to dress for dinner every night. Now don't snicker and accuse her of being affected. She has to get the dinner herself, just as many wives do, but you can get a much better dinner with your arms bare. Maybe it was her own idea, maybe she decided that was what the *soignee* Claudette would do. Anyway, she slips into a snug little black dress, does something miraculous to her hair—and you would be surprised how frequently papa shows up with flowers these winter evenings.

Of course, girls, if you're going to continue being hot and bothered over Clark Gable and John Boles, you may as well expect the other side of the house to retaliate in the only possible way.

After all, remember *you* are the girl he selected. His movie crush is an indirect way of informing you about a few details—how he likes to see clothes worn, and hair and figures, whether he likes his answers snappy or meek and mild . . .

Find out his favorite actress—and take the hint.

Every kind of question is coming in about Harpo of "Duck Soup." Tell us the secret of your charm, Mr. Marx. The ladies certainly seem to love you

The Truth About Voice Doubling

[CONTINUED FROM PAGE 209]

for Paul Lukas. Mr. Lukas, an exceptionally fine actor, is handicapped for American pictures by a foreign accent. For that reason, therefore, it is necessary for someone else to speak his lines. And Davidson is said to receive five hundred dollars a week for this service.

Many individuals in Hollywood are wondering why Davidson has seen fit to submerge his own personality for this sort of work, for he is regarded as fully as gifted an actor in his own right as Paul Lukas. He is listed in all casting offices as a five-hundred-dollar-a-week man. It may be, of course, that he has an arrangement to appear in other pictures, too.

There are a number of ways of doubling the voice on the screen. Usually it is done through a method known as "dubbing." This means

that it is done after the picture is shot. "Dubbing" is a term handed down to the movies by the makers of phonograph records. When portions were taken off several phonograph records to make one record, the process was referred to as "dubbing." So "dubbing" it is these days in pictures.

Most of the doubling that Margaret Livingston did for Louise Brooks in "The Canary Murder Case" was accomplished by "dubbing." Miss Livingston took up a position before the "mike" and watched the picture being run on the screen. If Miss Brooks came in a door and said, "Hello, everybody, how are you this evening?" Miss Livingston watched her lips and spoke Miss Brooks' words into the microphone.

Thus a sound-track was made and inserted

in the film. And that operation is called "dubbing."

All synchronizations are dubbed in after the picture is finished. The production is edited and cut to exact running length, then the orchestra is assembled in the monitor room (a room usually the size of the average theater) and the score is played as the picture is run. The sound-track thus obtained is "dubbed" into the sound film or on to the record, depending upon which system is used.

If foreign sounds stray into the film, such as scratches and pin-pricks, they are "bloped" out. Some call it "blooping." This means that they are eliminated with a paintbrush and India ink. The method is not unlike that applied to the retouching of photographic negatives.

Voice doubling is sometimes forced upon the producers as an emergency measure. Such was the case with Paramount in connection with "The Canary Murder Case."

THEY called Miss Livingston to the studio one day and said, "Miss Livingston, we are up against it and we think you can help us out. We want to turn 'The Canary Murder Case' into a talkie and Miss Brooks is not available. We think you can double for her. Will you do it?"

She thought it over. Well, why not? It meant experience in the talkies, *and double her usual salary*. So she wore clothes that duplicated Miss Brooks', "dubbed" some of the stuff and played some of it straight, her profile always to the camera.

A few times she missed the timing, and as a result her words did not come out even with Miss Brooks' lip movements.

After it was all over a very amusing incident occurred. Miss Livingston was sitting in a restaurant in New York and the friend with whom she was having dinner remarked, "So you have been talking for Louise Brooks, have you?"

From a nearby table came a strange voice. "Yes," quoth the voice, "and it had better be good!"

They looked around in astonishment and there sat Louise Brooks!

Of course, they all laughed and immediately went into a huddle about Hollywood.

A surprisingly large number of players in the film capital are now training their voices, in diction as well as singing, for the express purpose of avoiding the necessity of voice doubling. Vilma Banky, for instance, spends two hours a day perfecting her English. And James Burroughs, Bessie Love, Carmel Myers, Billie Dove, Gwen Lee, Jacqueline Logan, Frances Lee, Leatrice Joy, Armand Kaliz and innumerable others are all taking vocal lessons. Most of these have sung professionally at some time in their career.

In that worthy picture, "Alibi," Virginia Flohri, a widely-known radio singer, doubled for Irma Harrison who, you remember, sang a song in the cafe as *Toots*, the chorus girl. Miss Harrison simulated singing while Miss Flohri actually sang into the microphone off stage. In this instance their timing was not perfect.

MISS FLOHRI also sang for Jeanne Morgan in the Romeo and Juliet vaudeville number, if you remember it, and Edward Jordan sang for Robert Cauterio.

Obtaining suitable voice doubles is often a difficult task. The voice must not only fit the player, it must suit the characterization as well. And good singing voices are not always easily found. One reason for this is that persons of marked vocal accomplishments are frequently reluctant to double. They are afraid their voices will be recognized, that it will cheapen them. A notable case in point was that of Marion Harris, the vaudeville headliner, who turned down an offer of $10,000 from Universal, according to one of her representatives, to substitute her voice for a film player, presumably in "Broadway."

No end of problems develop, of course, in connection with registering the voice. When

You thought Irma Harrison sang as the cabaret darling of "Alibi," didn't you? She didn't. The voice you heard belonged to Virginia Flohri, a well-known radio singer

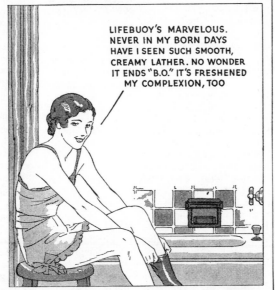

Douglas Fairbanks did his bit of talking for "The Iron Mask" his stentorian tones all but wrecked the recording apparatus.

BEFORE beginning, he was cautioned by the sound engineers to speak softly. However, for Doug this was impossible. He could not get dramatic effect with his conversation thus cramped. As a result the first uproarious line of his speech brought the sound men pouring out of the mixing chamber like a swarm of mad hornets. Much argument ensued. Finally Earle Browne, director of dialogue, hit upon the bright idea of moving the microphone thirty feet away and turning it so that it faced *away* from Fairbanks.

Laura La Plante's problem in "Show Boat" was quite the opposite of Doug's. The most difficult thing she had to learn in working with a double was, not to sing silently, but to finger a banjo perfectly. She realized, naturally, that the eyes of countless trained musicians would be upon her in audiences the world over. In consequence, she could not fake. She had to be convincing. So she spent several weeks learning the correct fingering of a banjo.

Some of the stars, of course, actually play musical instruments, though few have done so professionally. There's Bessie Love and her ukulele, and a few others. In "Mother Knows Best," Barry Norton actually played the piano while Sherry Hall sang his song. Sherry stood before the "mike" just outside the camera lines and Barry played his accompaniment and at the same time spoke the words of the song inaudibly, putting into them the proper timing, a thing possible to him because of his knowledge of music.

Of course, every effort is made on the part of producers to guard the secret of doubling. Picture-makers feel that it spoils the illusion, that it hurts a production's box office appeal. In this respect, however, they are wrong. I know this from my own personal experience in exploitation work. In nearly twelve years of steering the box office destinies of photoplays— especially film roadshows, some of the largest of which I have handled personally—I have yet to encounter a single set-back or loss because the public had knowledge of a double's work. On the other hand, I found that it often stimulated business to let the public in on a secret or two.

Eva Olivotti, one of Hollywood's most promising voices, assured a friend that, if it became known that she doubled for Laura La Plante in the singing numbers of "Show Boat," she would never be able to obtain another job. That is an example of the fear instilled into the hearts of the doubles by the companies for which they work. They are afraid even to breathe the nature of their employment.

THE fact remains, however, that Miss Olivotti *did* sing Miss La Plante's songs, and sang them very well, indeed.

Songs for "The Divine Lady" were "dubbed" in after Miss Griffith completed the picture. An odd complication developed when it came to doubling the harp. It had been arranged for Zhay Clark to play this instrument for Miss Griffith, but when that portion of the picture was viewed it was discovered that Miss Griffith's fingernails were longer than Miss Clark's, and that her hands, therefore, could not substitute effectively for Miss Griffith's.

So Miss Clark spent two days teaching Miss Griffith the fingering of the harp, and how to come in with the orchestra. Then the star did the scene herself. The music and songs, according to those acquainted with the facts, were "dubbed" in the East—a feat easily accomplished merely by watching the picture on the screen and getting from doubles a sound-track that would fit properly.

Voice doubling is often done in the monitor room after the production is complete, the double playing the designated instrument or reading the lips of the player and timing his words to fit these lip movements.

But voice doubling seems to be on the wane. As time goes on, there will be less need for it.

In rare instances, of course, it will be done where stars can't sing or play the instruments called for in the script. But stars are rapidly learning to sing and play. It won't be long now until a majority of players can boast of these accomplishments.

Then, too, microphone miracles are becoming more prevalent every day. This is due primarily to rapid improvement in equipment. Josef Cherniavsky, the musical director for one company, says: "Give me a person who is not tone deaf and I will make him ninety-five percent perfect in talking pictures." Perhaps Mr. Cherniavsky is a wee bit enthusiastic, but at least his outlook indicates the present Hollywood trend.

Bearing out his statement, it is interesting to note that if a voice has tone quality, but lacks volume, the fault can be easily corrected by the amplifier. Take Alice White. Alice sang her own songs (unless I have been terribly fooled, and I suspect I have!) in "Broadway Babies," sang them sweetly, but in a piping little voice that couldn't be heard off the set. Yet when the "play-back" gave evidence of surprising volume in her tones, loud cheers went up from company officials. The "play-back," by the way, is a device which plays back the voices of the cast from a wax record shortly after the scene is filmed. It's an invaluable check-up.

The problem of the foreign player is, of course, difficult to solve. At first it was regarded as an insurmountable obstacle. It is being discovered by producers, however, that what they thought a hopeless liability in the beginning has actually become an asset. In the case of feminine players in particular, accent is a decided charm. Such foreign players as Baclanova, Goudal, *et al*, are giving up the thought of perfecting their English. Nils Asther is studying English religiously. Care will always have to be exercised, nevertheless, in casting these players.

Another instance of piano doubling occurred in "Speakeasy," that splendid underworld picture about the prize-fighter and the girl reporter. Fred Warren, an exceptionally capable pianist, doubled at the piano for Henry B. Walthall. This was accomplished by tying down the keyboard of the real piano at which Walthall sat, so that when he struck the keys, nothing happened. You will remember, of course, that he sat facing the audience in such a position as to conceal his hands. Warren sat off stage at a real piano, about fifteen or twenty feet away, in a spot where he and Walthall could see each other. The recording "mike" was near Warren. As he played, Walthall imitated his motions. They had rehearsed the thing to perfection.

Although voice doubling is to the public the most interesting phase of sound work—because it is hidden from public view, no doubt—it is one of the comparatively simple things which confront producers. Problems much more subtle really vex them. For instance: New caste has grown up with the advent of conversing pictures; sound engineers are competing with directors for prestige and dominance; there is often open warfare between directors and monitor men; the new terminology of the business—"dubbing," "bloping," the invention of "split sets"; the mere fact that light travels faster than sound—a circumstance frequently baffling to engineers, and one that gives them grey hairs.

Just recently sound engineers found out that perfect synchronization in a big theater is virtually impossible—all because light travels faster than sound. If you are sitting comparatively close to the screen, all is well. If you are sitting in the back of the house, or in the balcony, it's another matter. Sound vibrations reach you after you have seen the image speak. The speed with which light vibrations exceed sound vibrations will depend of course upon where you sit. And this is a problem that sound engineers are trying to solve.

So you see producers have other troubles than doubles!

350

"Gone With the Wind" Indeed!

[CONTINUED FROM PAGE 265]

ment that brought Ronald Colman in. Was tested by Selznick twice, once in Hollywood while on the stage in "Reflected Glory." It was a simple color test but it gave the newshawks ideas. Tested again in New York by Director George Cukor. Is a professional choice, being considered the best actress of all the candidates. Would satisfy Dixie, hailing originally from Alabama. Her pappy represents that state as Speaker of the House of Representatives in Washington. Talu could probably recapture a sugar-lipped drawl, all right, but the years and an aura of sophistication are against her. The part would be like long delayed manna from Heaven for her, bestowing the great screen break her rooters have long wailed has been denied a great artiste. Only a luke-warm choice in the popular response. But vigorously opposed by an opinionated minority.

Miriam Hopkins is the red hot choice of Atlanta and the South. Leads other actresses by a nice margin in the letter deluge. One reason, she hails from Bainbridge, Georgia, right close to home. Is a good subject for color, if it is used, except that she'll have to wear a wig. Played *Becky Sharp*, the character generally compared with *Scarlett O'Hara*, but that might work against her.

BETTE DAVIS is the number one Hollywood selection. Just missed cinching the part by a matter of minutes. On her way to England, Bette was told by Warner's New York story board they were buying a great story for her, "Gone With the Wind." But by the time they wired Hollywood for an okay, the hammer had dropped. The day His Majesty's courts decided that Bette was a "naughty girl" and "must go back to jail" her low spirits were lifted by a columnist's clipping calling her the ideal *Miss O'Hara*. Answers to *Scarlett* now around the Warner lot. Bette is the only Yankee girl to score below that well-known Line. Ranks third in the Cotton Belt. Is considered to be just the right age to handle the assignment and blessed with the right amount of—er—nastiness. No complaints from the home folks on her southern accent in "Cabin in the Cotton" or as *Alabama Follansbee* in "The Solid South" (stage).

But—Bette is in the doghouse, chained and collared, and one of the main issues of her legal whipping was her loan out demand. Warners can—probably would keep her in the cooler. Selznick, in fact, is supposed to have said, "Bette Davis? Great—but could we get her?"

Margaret Sullavan holds second spot in returns from down yonder. Is a Virginia girl, and knows what to do when a lady meets a gentleman down South. Handled brilliantly the lead in "So Red the Rose," another Civil War picture. Fractious and fiery enough to make *Scarlett* a vivid character. Tagged next to Bette Davis in Hollywood.

And the *Field*—Katharine Hepburn, Claudette Colbert and Jean Harlow.

Now as if puzzling about all this were not enough to set a body weaving baskets in the clink, Messrs. Selznick and Company announce that they want for *Scarlett* and *Rhett* not Hollywood stars at all. No—instead they have arranged to canvass all the finishing schools of Dixie, and ogle Junior Leaguers at very lovely teas and discover an "unknown" *Scarlett*. A similar search, minus the tea, is hoped to dig up an indigenous *Rhett*.

Thus, they say, everything will not only be peaches and cream for professional Southerners, but what is much more important, two brand new stars will be born. Why take other studio's stars and build 'em? Isn't this going to be the greatest picture of all time?

Well—as to the first idea—it's great if it works, is the opinion of the Hollywood wise ones. But it won't work, they say. Whom are you going to find in the sticks to handle parts like those? Whom could you dare gamble on?

And that "greatest picture of all time" stuff. It smacks strongly, I grant you, of the old mahoskus. It's press agent oil of the most ready viscosity and has flowed freely around every epic from "The Great Train Robbery" to Shirley Temple's latest cutrick. But this time the answer that snaps right back out of your own skeptic brain is, "Why not?"

These gentlemen—Whitney and Selznick—have, and they know they have, the greatest screen story of our day. If you don't think so, here's the cold cash proof: The day after they laid $50,000 on the line for the picture rights, another studio offered them $100,000. The next offer was boosted to $250,000. The last bid, not long ago, was $1,500,000 and an interest in the picture besides! Tie that.

They said "No" and they are still saying the same. Mr. Whitney and Mr. Selznick are not ribbon clerks. They shot $2,200,00 on "The Garden of Allah." They will pinch no pennies on "Gone With the Wind." If color will help it (and it probably will) they'll shoot an extra million. Sidney Howard is writing the script. George Cukor will direct. Walter Plunkett is designing costumes. These men are all top flight.

SO you can be reasonably sure of this—when finally you see "Gone With the Wind" you'll see a picture dressed in the best trappings of modern production, primed with meticulous preparation, artistic thoroughness and as many millions as it can comfortably stand.

But as for who will be *Scarlett* and who will be *Rhett*—well, the riot squads are doing a nice business, thank you. And good citizens of Hollywood scowl across Cahuenga Pass at North Hollywood muttering "Dam' Yanks!" While out in Beverly Hills the South Side of the Tracks is threatening to secede if somebody will only fire on the Brown Derby.

It looks as if we'll fight it out on this line if it takes all summer. Everybody's welcome, and usually it doesn't require a second invitation. Just casually mention the subject. You'll see. Matter of fact, the only person I can think of offhand who doesn't seem to be at all upset about the matter is the lady who wrote the book.

Early in the fray, Margaret Mitchell allowed it would be nice if a Southern girl could play *Scarlett*. But the reaction was so violent that it must have surprised her. At any rate she announced the other day it was her one desire to remain only as the humble author, and to a close friend she confided:

"I don't care what they do to 'Gone With the Wind' in Hollywood. Just so they don't make General Lee win the war for a happy ending!"

CHARLES RUGGLES ("The Lady Lies," Paramount) is one of Broadway's sure-fire character comedians. He has appeared in innumerable musical shows, most recently in the short-lived but beautiful "Rainbow," and in "Spring Is Here." Charlie is a brother of Wesley Ruggles, the film director, and is noted as a delineator of comical stage drunks.

Is Jack Gilbert Through?

[CONTINUED FROM PAGE 212]

none on the lot. His manager was included with a nice job and the right to handle Gilbert's affairs as well. An iron-bound document, without options!

But as the great financial powers of the studios battled for Gilbert's signature, another force was working.

Warner Brothers had used a trick device whereby the shadows of the screen stepped up and spoke words.

The device was crude and the wise guys shook their heads and said, "Oh, it can't last. It's just a novelty. There will always be silent pictures."

GILBERT returned to Hollywood with his contract in his pocket. He watched his bungalow grow on the lot. He was anxious to rid himself of the old agreement and start on the new. He was happier than he had been for some time.

Fox bought the controlling interest in M-G-M. All was saved. But the little talking device had been perfected.

The films had learned to speak and all the stars must speak, too.

Gilbert's voice!

What about Gilbert's voice?

What about the voice of the man who is virile as a steel mill, lusty as Walt Whitman, romantic as a June moon?

Gilbert's voice! You heard it in "His Glorious Night." It is high-pitched, tense, almost piping at times.

His friends have known for years that it was completely unsuited to the strength and fire of the man.

Jack's great art is pantomime. Remember those remarkable closeups of intense eyes? Gilbert is always keyed up to the highest pitch of excitement.

It is the thing that made him the great actor he is. It was tremendous on the silent screen. He spoke through his eyes.

But any singer will tell you that the voice is right only when the body is relaxed. The voice, to be convincing, must flow calmly.

Gilbert was caught unprepared for the talkies.

While other stars were trotting to elocution teachers and voice specialists, Gilbert was flying to an obscure town in Nevada and getting married to Ina Claire.

HE had one more picture to make under the old contract, and he threw in another for good measure because he was happy and because he was a boy with a new wife, a new contract and the anticipation of a honeymoon in Europe.

"Redemption" was his first talking picture. It was a great mistake. He tried too hard. He was nervous in the new medium. He had been so sure of himself in the old.

All during this time, sitting across from Jack at the breakfast table, was a woman who could have taught him every *nuance* of line delivery. Ina Claire could have taught him to speak.

If you have ever tried to learn any-

thing from your wife, anything that she knows better than you, you will understand.

"Redemption" was a sorry affair. It was temporarily shelved. But in the meantime Gilbert had to make a talking début. He promised to do a picture before he went to Europe if it could be rushed through in four weeks. It was rushed. The result was "His Glorious Night." It was released while he was in Europe.

Almost before he stepped off the boat, upon his return, he asked:

"How's my picture? What do the critics think of my picture?" For Gilbert's career has dominated his life.

His friends had to tell him that his first talkie was not good. He could see the criticisms for himself.

He suffered anger, then shame, and then anger again.

WHAT went on in his mind was masked by a forced gaiety.

And the studio officials, bound to him irrevocably under the contract which had cinched a financial deal, heard bitterly the echoes that Gilbert's picture inspired. Gilbert's voice had failed in his first talking release. The fans were shocked when he spoke.

He rides into the driveway of his studio bungalow in the morning. The studio is bound to him under a contract that cannot be broken. He gives every outward appearance of a successful man, but his voice has failed, he has lost heavily on the stock market and he is separated from his wife.

They call it a temporary separation, but I cannot help but believe that it is the beginning of the end.

Gilbert has no talent for domesticity and Ina is a positive woman.

His career has gotten on his nerves and Gilbert must fight his battles alone. Garrulous as he is, he remains at heart a lonely soul, as all creative artists are.

Well, what is there left for him to do? No matter what happens he will earn a million dollars in the next two years. But it isn't money that counts with him. Gilbert could not retire. His art means more to him than wealth and fame. He would go insane if he were idle.

What then? He *must* learn to talk. But how?

If he could go away and have six months in a small stock company it would make him over. But John Gilbert could not do this for professional as well as personal reasons. Well, then, a teacher.

The actor, himself, takes first one side and then the other. One minute he is angry and considers himself the victim of a huge plot, the next minute he is sad for what he considers a failure, but dominating it all is this spirit:

"DAMN it! I'll show 'em. I'll show 'em I can talk. I'll get a human story. I'll play a real rôle and not that of a puppet. I'll make a come-back. I'll show 'em. They can't down me. They can't ruin me with one bad talking picture!"

He was caught unprepared. Hollywood said that Corinne Griffith couldn't talk, but she learned. Hollywood said that Gloria Swanson was through, but she isn't. Some folks in Hollywood persist that Gilbert is finished. You hear it from his enemies, of course, not from his friends.

Personally, I don't believe it. Or maybe it's because I won't. But I cannot believe that a man who has battled life single-handed, who has taken all the hard knocks right on the chin, will let a little thing like a talkie device down him.

I believe that Gilbert will come back strong, that he will wake up, start in earnest, make some vital gesture, hurl some new defiance and really equip himself for the microphone, the terror of Hollywood.

Gilbert is not through!

He'll learn. He'll equip himself. He'll show 'em. And more power to him!

Bruno

Ina Claire's own Hollywood home, after leaving the hilltop manor of Husband John Gilbert. Located in Beverly Hills, Ina's little home is stucco, glass and tile, in the best nouveau-Hollywood tradition. It isn't the House That Jack Built!

INDEX

Only names of persons and titles of films have been indexed. Film titles appear in *italics*. References to illustrations appear in *italics* at the end of each entry. A vertical rule separates references to text from references to illustrations.